A NEW IMPERIAL HISTORY

Culture, Identity, and Modernity in Britain

This pioneering collection of essays charts, for the first time, the emergent terrain of an exciting new field in British studies, the "new imperial history." Leading scholars from history, literature, and cultural studies take on the problems of identity, modernity, and difference in eighteenth-century Britain and the empire. They examine, from interdisciplinary perspectives, the reciprocal influences of empire and culture, the movements of peoples, practices, and ideas effected by slavery, diaspora and British dominance, and ways in which subaltern, non-western, and non-elite people shaped British power and knowledge. Creating a colorful and original colonial landscape, the essays move through Britain, America, India, Africa, and the South Pacific in testament to the networks of people, commodities, and entangled pasts forged by Britain's imperial adventures.

Highly readable and based on ground-breaking research, the analyses of the imperial dimensions of British culture and identities in global contexts will challenge the notion that empire was something that happened "out there" and demonstrate its far-reaching implications for British identity and everyday life in the eighteenth century, and perhaps even today. This cutting-edge collection displays the pleasures and potential enabled by thinking a new imperial history that investigates new kinds of evidence and subjects, and is not always written by imperial historians, or even by historians.

KATHLEEN WILSON is Professor of History at the State University of New York, Stony Brook. Her first book, *The Sense of the People: Politics, Culture and Imperialism in Britain, 1715–1785* (Cambridge, 1995), won the Royal Historical Society's Whitbread Prize and the Jon Ben Snow Prize from the North American Conference on British Studies. Her most recent book, *An Island Race: Englishness, Empire and Gender in the Eighteenth Century*, was published in 2003.

A NEW IMPERIAL HISTORY

*Culture, Identity, and Modernity in Britain and
the Empire, 1660–1840*

EDITED BY

KATHLEEN WILSON

CAMBRIDGE
UNIVERSITY PRESS

PUBLISHED BY THE PRESS SYNDICATE OF THE UNIVERSITY OF CAMBRIDGE
The Pitt Building, Trumpington Street, Cambridge, United Kingdom

CAMBRIDGE UNIVERSITY PRESS
The Edinburgh Building, Cambridge, CB2 2RU, UK
40 West 20th Street, New York, NY 10011–4211, USA
477 Williamstown Road, Port Melbourne, VIC 3207, Australia
Ruiz de Alarcón 13, 28014 Madrid, Spain
Dock House, The Waterfront, Cape Town 8001, South Africa

http://www.cambridge.org

First published 2004

Printed in the United Kingdom at the University Press, Cambridge

Typeface Adobe Garamond 11/12.5 pt.   *System* LaTeX 2ε   [TB]

A catalogue record for this book is available from the British Library

Library of Congress Cataloguing in Publication data
A new imperial history: culture, identity, and modernity in Britain and the Empire,
1660–1840 / edited by Kathleen Wilson.
p.   cm.
Includes bibliographical references and index.
ISBN 0 521 81027 2 – ISBN 0 521 00796 8 (pbk.)
1. Great Britain – Colonies – History – 18th century.   2. Great Britain – Colonies – History – 17th
century.   3. Great Britain – Colonies – History – 19th century.   4. National characteristics,
British – History.   5. Great Britain – Colonies – Civilization.   6. Great Britain – Civilization.
7. Imperialism – History.   I. Wilson, Kathleen.
DA16.N49   2004   909′.0917241 – dc22   2003049545

ISBN 0 521 81027 2 hardback
ISBN 0 521 00796 8 paperback

For Nick and Hannah

Contents

Illustrations

Contributors

EITAN BAR-YOSEF is a Lecturer in the Department of Foreign Literatures and Linguistics, Ben-Gurion University of the Negev, Israel. Exploring the effects of empire on metropolitan literature and culture, his work has appeared in *Journal of Contemporary History*, *Dickens Quarterly* and *English Literature in Transition, 1880–1920*. His book *Images of the Holy Land in English Culture, 1799–1917* is forthcoming with Oxford University Press.

MICHAEL H. FISHER is Danforth Professor of History at Oberlin College and has published widely on relations between Indians and Britons, both in India and Britain, during the early colonial period. He focuses his research on the circulation of people and ideas within the expanding arena of the British empire. His most recent books include *The First Indian Author in English: Dean Mahomet in India, Ireland and England* (2000) and *Counterflows to Colonialism: Indians in Britain, c. 1600–1857* (2003).

DURBA GHOSH is Assistant Professor of History at Mount Holyoke College, and a former Mellon postdoctoral fellow in Women Studies at Wellesley College. She is working on a manuscript entitled *Colonial Companions: Sexual Transgressions, Racial Mixing and Gendered Order in Early Colonial India*, which examines conjugal relationships between native women and European men *c.* 1760–1840.

HARRIET GUEST is Professor of English and Director of the Centre for Eighteenth Century Studies at the University of York. Her most recent book is *Small Change: Women, Learning and Patriotism 1750–1810* (2000). Her next book will be a study of William Hodges and Captain James Cook.

MARGARET HUNT, Professor of History at Amherst College, is attached to the University of Massachusetts-Five College Ph.D. program in History. Her book *The Middling Sort: Commerce, Gender and the Family in England 1680–1780* (1996) won the Morris D. Forkusch Award from the American Historical Association for the best book in British, British Imperial, and British Commonwealth History. She has written articles or book chapters on violence, women and the law, sexuality, marriage, and the military in the early modern period.

WALTER JOHNSON is Associate Professor of History and American Studies at New York University. The author of *Soul by Soul: Life inside the Antebellum Slave Market* (1999) and editor of a forthcoming collection entitled *The Chattel Principle: Internal Slave Trades in the Americas, 1808–1888*, he is at work on a book about capitalism and slavery in the Mississippi Valley.

COLIN KIDD is Professor of History at the University of Glasgow. He is the author of *Subverting Scotland's Past: Scottish Whig Historians and the Creation of an Anglo-British Identity, 1689–c. 1830* (Cambridge, 1993) and *British Identities before Nationalism: Ethnicity and Nationhood in the Atlantic World, 1600–1800* (Cambridge, 1999). Since 1999 he has co-edited the *Scottish Historical Review*. His current interests include the interactions of race and theology in the Protestant Atlantic world and the political theories of the Scots Presbyterian Covenanting tradition.

FELICITY A. NUSSBAUM is Professor of English at UCLA and the author most recently of *The Limits of the Human: Anomaly, Race and Gender in the Long Eighteenth Century* (2003) and editor of *The Global Eighteenth Century* (2003). Among her other publications are *Torrid Zones: Maternity, Sexuality and Empire in Eighteenth-Century English Narrative* (1995) and *The Autobiographical Subject: Gender and Ideology in Eighteenth-Century England* (1989), which won the Louis Gottschalk Prize from the American Society of Eighteenth-Century Studies. Her current work is on the material world of the eighteenth-century theatre.

NICHOLAS ROGERS is Professor of History at York University, Toronto, and co-editor, with James Epstein, of the *Journal of British Studies*. He is the author of two books on popular politics in the eighteenth century and of a textbook entitled *Eighteenth-Century English Society* (1999), co-authored by Douglas Hay. His most recent publication is *Halloween: From Pagan Ritual to Party Night* (2002). He is currently completing a book on naval impressment in the long eighteenth century.

GILLIAN RUSSELL is Senior Lecturer in English, School of Humanities, Australian National University, Canberra, Australia and author of *The Theatres of War: Politics, Performance and Society, 1793–1815* (1995) and co-editor, with Clara Tuite, of *Romantic Sensibility: Social Networks and Literary Culture in Britain, 1770–1840* (2003). She is currently working on a project on sociability, women, and the theatre in London, 1760–80.

SUDIPTA SEN is Associate Professor of History at Syracuse University. He publishes on British–Indian encounters on the subcontinent. He is the author of two books, *Empire of Free Trade: The English East India Company and the Making of the Colonial Marketplace* (1998) and *Distant Sovereignty: National Imperialism and the Origins of British India* (2002).

PHILIP STERN is a Ph.D. candidate in the Department of History at Columbia University and a graduate fellow in history at the Columbia University Institute for Social and Economic Research and Policy. His current project, "One Body Corporate and Politick: The English East India Company-State in the Later Seventeenth Century," concerns the foundations and impact of Company state-building and claims to sovereignty in Asia and Europe. He is also developing a study of the African Association and British exploration in Africa in the eighteenth and nineteenth centuries.

KATE TELTSCHER is Senior Lecturer in the School of English and Modern Languages at the University of Surrey Roehampton. She writes on travel writing and colonial discourse on India, and is author of *India Inscribed: European and British Writing on India, 1600–1800* (1995), as well as numerous articles. She is currently working on a biography of George Bogle, the first British envoy to Bhutan and Tibet.

HANS TURLEY is Associate Professor of English at the University of Connecticut and editor of *Eighteenth Century: Theory and Interpretation*. He is author of *Rum, Sodomy and the Lash: Piracy, Sexuality and Masculine Identity* (1999), as well as many articles about the eighteenth-century novel. He is currently working on a biography of Rochester.

KEVIN WHELAN is Professor of History and inaugural Michael J. Smurfit Director of the University of Notre Dame's Keough Centre in Dublin. He has published fifteen books and almost a hundred articles on Irish history, and has lectured on Irish topics in a dozen countries. His most recent book is *Fellowship of Freedom: The United Irishmen and the 1798 Rebellion* (1998).

KATHLEEN WILSON is Professor of History at Stony Brook University. She publishes on culture, empire, and Englishness in global settings in the eighteenth century. Her book *The Sense of the People: Politics, Culture and Imperialism in England, 1715–1785* (Cambridge, 1995) won prizes from the Royal Historical Society and the North American Conference on British Studies. Her most recent book is *The Island Race: Englishness, Empire and Gender in the Eighteenth Century* (2003). She is currently at work on a study of British theatre and empire, 1720–1840, in sites that range across the Atlantic and Pacific worlds.

Acknowledgments

The editor would like to thank the following people for offering advice, ideas, and encouragement for this project: Nicholas Mirzoeff (massively), John Brewer, Antoinette Burton, Linda Colley, Harriet Guest, Young-Sun Hong, Lawrence Klein, Ned Landsman, Philippa Levine, Iona Man-Cheong, Gary Marker, Felicity Nussbaum, Mrinalini Sinha, Dror Wahrman, anonymous readers for Cambridge University Press, and all of the contributors. I was given the usual warnings from various well-intentioned colleagues about the travails of editing collections, but it has to be said in this case the warnings were needless: the contributors have been prompt, enthusiastic, and patient, and the editor alone responsible for any delay and recalcitrance. Special thanks go to Roy Ritchie at the Henry E. Huntington Library, for inviting me to organize a conference on the "new imperial history," and to the conference participants for sharpening my ideas and allowing me to survey the path-breaking grounds of a new field; to Iain McCalman and the Humanities Research Centre at the Australian National University, for support and examples of cross-cultural scholarship at its most exciting; to Paul Armstrong, former Dean of the College of Arts and Sciences, and Gary Marker, former Chair of the History Department, at Stony Brook University (formerly the State University of New York at Stony Brook, back in the days when public education was esteemed) for research leave; and to William Davis at Cambridge University Press, for taking a risk. I am equally grateful to the National Endowment for the Humanities and the John Simon Guggenheim Memorial Foundation for funding that gave me the time off to pursue this and other projects. Warm thanks to Carol Fellingham Webb for careful copyediting, and to Jenise De Pinto and Alex Tolin-Schulz for help with the index. For health, happiness, and domestic felicity I am indebted, as always, to Nick and Hannah: *sans les quelles, je ne puis pas être.*

Introduction: histories, empires, modernities

Kathleen Wilson

The single Dress of a Woman of Quality is often the Product of an hundred Climates . . . Trade, without enlarging the British Territories, has given us a kind of additional Empire.

The Spectator (1712, I: 295–6)

Settlement [in the Darien] would be agreeable to the Laws of Nations, the Principles of Christianity, and the Constant Maxims of the British Nation, whose Possessions are founded in Reason and Justice, not Chimerical Grants, Butchery of Millions of Innocent Peoples, and other unjustifiable Means.

James Knight to the Duke of Newcastle, November 20, 1739[1]

History [is one of] the blessings of a more exalted civilization and education, which give us in every respect so great a superiority over these nations, and assign to us so high a rank in the scale of rational beings.

Johann Reinhold Forster, *Observations Made During a Voyage Round the World* (1778), 608

Can there be a "new imperial history"? In the past two decades scholars from a range of disciplinary and geographical locations have raised serious questions about the capacity of conventional historical narratives to account for non-elite and non-western pasts. Rather, History, shaped by the political and epistemological models of Enlightenment and modernist Europe, continues to universalize Eurocentric historical experience to the rest of the world, assessing the "emergence" and "development" of nationalism, capitalism, and modernity through the stagist paradigms central to historical knowledge. As a result, whether focused on particularities or general trends, individuals or *mentalités*, History as a discipline and craft invariably measures or assumes a cultural distance between "us" and

---

[1] BL, Add MS 22, 677, f. 27, Letters Relating to Jamaica.

"them" while also taking on "an ontological power in providing assumptions about how the real social and natural worlds are constituted."[2] The very notion of an "imperial history," whether new or old, may be but an artifact of European dominance and metropolitan perspective, that assumes as fact the paradigms and locations forged by and within western imperial modernity. To quote the famous argument of Dipesh Chakrabarty, "insofar as the academic discourse of history is concerned, 'Europe' remains the sovereign, theoretical subject of all histories, including the ones we call 'Indian,' 'Chinese,' 'Kenyan,' and so on."[3] To found a "new imperial history" on such an edifice, if not impossible, would only be a means of "adding to" established narratives, rather than replacing or even reconfiguring them.

None the less, energized by the political and imaginative wakes of post-colonial and cross-disciplinary scholarship, many of the same writers have pursued historical analyses that are geared to doing precisely what they themselves acknowledge simultaneously to be impossible: namely, to recognize alternative modes and sources for understanding the past, to probe at the limits of historical knowledge, and to make the "subaltern" – from indigenes to women, and all others rendered silent or invisible by the historical archive – "speak." In British studies, most of this exciting new work has been influenced by a rather remarkable re-discovery of the importance of empire in the British past, and a simultaneous interest in the methodologies of social and cultural history and criticism to address questions about identity and difference in imperial settings. In eighteenth-century studies (the concern of the present volume), after decades of comparative neglect, the imperial dimensions of British domestic culture, politics, and social relations are starting to come into focus, significantly revising our conceptualization of Englishness and Britishness and the categories through which "colonizers" and "colonized" are understood.[4] Certainly the importance of empire was a cardinal assumption to generations of historians, and the rise

---

[2] That is, from anthropology, literature, art history, geography, and feminist and postcolonial studies as well as history, and Atlantic, Pacific, and Indian Ocean societies. See the works by Antonio Benítez-Rojo, J. M. Blaut, Partha Chatterjee, Frederick Cooper and Ann Laura Stoler, eds., Nicholas Dirks, Greg Dening, Johannes Fabian, Reinhart Kosselleck, Uday Singh Mehta, V. Y. Mudimbe, Gananath Obeyesekere, Gyan Prakash, Naoki Sakai, Gayatri Chakravorty Spivak, and Robert Young in "Further Reading" at the end of this volume. Quotation from Bernard Cohn, *Colonialism and its Forms of Knowledge* (Princeton University Press, 1996), 5. Feminist theorists, of course, have long made the same point about the exclusion of women from the historical archive.

[3] Dipesh Chakrabarty, *Provincializing Europe: Postcolonial Thought and Historical Difference* (Princeton University Press, 2000), 27. Chakrabarty's fine book has proved invaluable in sharpening and extending the argument presented here.

[4] See the works by Srinivas Aravamudan, David Armitage and Michael Braddick, eds., Laura Brown, Linda Colley, Martin Daunton and Rick Halpern, eds., David Eltis, Elijah Gould, Matthew Edney, Michael Fisher, Durba Ghosh, Richard Grove, Jonathan Lamb, Peter Linebaugh and Marcus Rediker,

and fall of its importance in British historical studies can be related to specific political moments. J. R. Seeley, writing on the verge of High Victorian imperial take-off, recognized how intimately connected were the history of nation and the history of empire; as he famously remarked in 1883, surveying the scale of English expansion in the long eighteenth century, "the history of England is not in England but in America and Asia."[5] Many scholars today would add that the history of America and Asia was in part also in England, in a material and imaginative testimony to the entangled nature of early modern – and late modern – pasts. The eighteenth-century British empire presents us with interconnected and interdependent sites of historical importance, territorial and imaginative, that can disrupt oppositions between metropole and colony and allow us to rethink the genealogies and historiographies of national belonging and exclusion.

Within this framework, the present volume attempts to investigate the potentialities and limits of a "new imperial history." However, such a slogan seems to invite a stereotyping that the analyses presented here eschew. Certainly, the resounding clarion call of "the new," in history as in other aspects of social and intellectual practice, seems to invite us to shake off the shackles of the hidebound in favor of the innovative, the exploratory, and the controversial as it simultaneously relegates traditional approaches to the proverbial dustbin. Yet this book begins by proclaiming that it is *not* out to substitute a new orthodoxy for an established one; neither is it calling for the evacuation of established political, social, or intellectual histories. For the kind of "new imperial history" at work here has at its heart the importance of *difference* – in historical settings and forms of consciousness as well as in historiographic and critical practice – that supports and extends the pluralities of historical interpretation. "New ways of theorizing difference are central to the task of writing new imperial histories," Catherine Hall has argued,[6] and questions of difference, its ascription and maintenance among colonizers as well as colonized, were also central to colonial projects and imperial visions. Between 1660 and 1840, the chronological parameters of this volume, the taxonomic projects of ethnography, natural history, and global knowledge, as well as the ideals of "civilization's" diffusion, began both to fuel and to reflect British economic, political, and territorial expansion. In this rapidly changing world, notions of national belonging were

---

Paul Lovejoy, ed., Clare Midgley, Felicity Nussbaum, Joseph Roach, Nicholas Rogers, Sudipta Sen, Charlotte Sussman, Kate Teltscher, Beth Fowkes Tobin, James Walvin, Roxanne Wheeler, and Kathleen Wilson in "Further Reading" at the end of this volume.

[5] J. R. Seely, *The Expansion of England* (London: Macmillan, 1883), 10.
[6] Catherine Hall, "Introduction," in Catherine Hall, ed., *Cultures of Empire* (Manchester University Press, 2000), 16.

formulated and altered to suit new international and imperial circumstances and the question of national identity itself became particularly unsettling. The assumption of imperial power and colonial territories not only generated conflicts, ambiguities, and desires, in other words, but also produced a more "precarious sense of self."[7] Within the complex encounters and societies generated by the British empire's increasingly global reach, "difference" was a political strategy rather than a verifiable descriptive category, a highly mobile signifier for power relations, often "ascribed in the context of domination" as Himani Bannerji has remarked,[8] while also thereby becoming a source of identification and social practice.

Exploring questions of difference within and between societies where radically dissimilar social and political conditions and forms of consciousness were at play remains a formidable and perhaps even quixotic undertaking; the essays collected here make no pretense of proffering easy solutions. What they do offer are examples of the difference that "difference" can make in the crafting of historical and critical narratives of empire and its impact. Centering questions of difference requires alertness to the past's inaccessibility, an openness to alternative modes of historical being, and a capacity for humility and uncertainty in our engagements with historical archives and issues. It also forces upon the historian and critic a recognition of the radical insufficiency of dichotomous notions of difference inherited, in part, from the eighteenth century itself, when the interplay of alterity and similitude propelled by British expansion made possible notions of essentializing "national" characters and the claims to historical distance. These categories of difference and filiation were paramount in imperial policy; indeed, the maintenance of European national identities and ties were as crucial as settlement to the legitimatization of claims to legal and political "dominium," or territorial possession and rights to govern.[9] Historical claims of difference also present to scholars the problem of translation – that is, the "practice producing difference [and similarity] out of incommensurability"[10] – that speaks to the fragility and materiality of social identities

---

[7] Kate Teltscher, *India Inscribed: European and British Writing on India, 1600–1800* (Oxford University Press, 1995), 7.

[8] Himani Bannerji, "Politics and the Writing of History," in Ruth Roach Pierson and Nupur Chaudhuri, eds., *Nation, Empire, Colony: Historicizing Gender and Race* (Bloomington: Indiana University Press, 1998), 287–90.

[9] Elizabeth Mancke, "Negotiating an Empire: Britain and its Overseas Peripheries, *c.* 1550–1780," in Christine Daniels and Michael V. Kennedy, eds., *Negotiated Empires: Centers and Peripheries in the Americas, 1500–1820* (London: Routledge, 2002), 237–8, 260n. Mancke distinguishes "dominium" from "imperium," or the extent of a ruler's sole jurisdiction: 236.

[10] Meaghan Morris, "Forward," in Naoki Sakai, *Translation and Subjectivity* (Minneapolis: Univeristy of Minnesota Press, 1997), xiii, quoted in Chakrabarty, *Provincializing Europe*, 263n.

in historical settings. The analysis of difference accordingly requires that the irreducible relationships between the imaginative and the material be acknowledged and analyzed from a range of disciplinary and theoretical perspectives. The chapters in this volume hint at the pleasures, potential, and dangers enabled by thinking a new imperial history that is grounded on difference: that investigates new kinds of "evidence" and subjects; moves across as well as within disciplines and locations; interrogates the shifting historical grounds of cultural and national production; and is not always written by imperial historians, or even by historians.

MODERNITIES

To address questions of difference is to address questions of identity. Yet the concept of identity in history-writing has become a topic of debate. Scholars have criticized its overzealous use, arguing that "identity" is too subjective a category to be analytically useful, that it is anachronistic, a product of late twentieth-century politicization of the term (as in "identity politics"), or that, as a psychological construct, it has no purchase within early modern societies as a mode of self- and collective location. Yet arguably these critiques depend upon a subjective reading of identity as a voluntary act, a way of constituting the subject through individual agency that is willed rather than imposed.[11] Such a reading seriously misrepresents the ontology of identity as a coercive process. Indeed, in societies where slavery was a fact of life and crucial to the economic viability of the imperial system dominated by Britain and its cultural networks, identity was structured in part by the epistemic violence attached to the notion of human property. As David Eltis has rather drily remarked, "On board a slave ship with the slaves always black and the crew largely white, skin colour tended to define ethnicity."[12] The unique, predatory, and ubiquitous presence of slavery in British societies in this period is crucial to recognize, making "slave" and

[11] See, e.g., Rogers Brubaker and Frederick Cooper, "Beyond 'identity,'" *Theory and Society*, 29 (2000), 1–47; Colin Kidd, *British identities before Nationalism: Ethnicity and Nationhood in the Atlantic World, 1600–1800* (Cambridge University Press, 1999); for a more optimistic account, see Dror Wahrman, "The Problem of English Identity in the American Revolution," *American Historical Review* (hereafter *AHR*), 106 (2001), 1236–62; and Wahrman, "On Queen Bees and Being Queens: A Late-Eighteenth-Century 'cultural revolution'?" in Colin Jones and Dror Wahrman, eds., *The Age of Cultural Revolutions* (Berkeley and Los Angeles: University of California Press, 2002), 251–79.

[12] For cogent statements about the importance of chattel and indigenous forms of slavery to British imperial power, see Robin Blackburn, *The Making of New World Slavery* (London: Verso, 1998); David Eltis, *The Rise of African Slavery in the Americas* (Cambridge University Press, 2000), 226; Indrani Chatterjee, *Gender, Slavery and the Law in Colonial India* (Oxford University Press, 1999).

"free" crucial markers of identity, and the social performances of nationality, freedom, gender, and rank – by men and women, slave and free – acts of resounding political importance. Categories of identity in the long eighteenth century were, in other words, shaped by the political, economic, and cultural conditions of the period, and thus differed from those which came before or after. Within forts, factories, and plantation colonies, as well as in Britain itself, social location and value were ascribed to people on the basis of factors that included not only legal status (e.g., "slave" and "free," head of household or dependent), but also national origin, gender, skin color, religion, family connection, reputation, and geography. At the same time, however, these social relations, or identities, were multiple and contingent, bound to a historical social order and both concretized and challenged through the practices of everyday life. Identity was a historical process, rather than an outcome, a negotiation between individual conceptions of self and collectivity and their social valence.[13]

Given that much of the philosophy and conjectural history of Enlightenment thinkers focused on the ethics and technologies of self and collectivity – of the ways, for example, that an individual's "sensibility" marked the most advanced point on the continuum of human progress, that "identity" itself was constituted, or that attributes such as "national manners," "race," or gender were natural or acquired – the historical dimensions of the philosophical problem of identity have to be recognized in our own histories of the period.[14] Although the contributors stand at various points in the debate on identity as a historical analytic, the volume nevertheless advances the argument for the importance of engaging with problems of identity in eighteenth-century historical settings, the changing role of the body as a marker in the process of ascribed human value, and the importance of performance as a means of disrupting as well as confirming such ascription. Tracking the relations between empire and identity may require a revision of the model of metropole-to-colony diffusion traditionally used by historians, for such attention makes clear that the most decisive breaks with established practices and attitudes occurred in the novel and

---

[13] For an elaboration of this definition of identity see Kathleen Wilson, *The Island Race: Englishness, Empire and Gender in the Eighteenth Century* (London: Routledge, 2003), 1–28.

[14] For Enlightenment debates, see Karen O'Brien, *Narratives of Enlightenment* (Cambridge University Press, 1998); J. G. A. Pocock, *Barbarism and Religion* (2 vols., Cambridge University Press, 2000); David Armitage, "The New World and British Historical Thought," in Karen Kupperman, ed., *America in European Consciousness, 1493–1750* (Chapel Hill: University of North Carolina Press, 1995), 60–75. Adam Smith's *A Theory of Moral Sentiments*, 2nd edn. (London, 1761) is crucial to this conceptualization of identity and its historical moorings.

culturally hybrid environments of empire, correspondingly reshaping the understanding of difference at the supposed center.

"Modernity" was a crucial relation of many eighteenth-century British people's notion of identity, and this book seeks to underline the importance of their understanding of modernity to our own. Britons' own self-conceptualization as "modern" hinged on the emergent historical consciousness, expressed in the opening quotation by J. R. Forster, that was produced by contact and exchange with and narratives about a widening world and Britain's place in it: History, in other words, was a "sign of the modern."[15] The practices of empire and nation-state building and their various constituencies also made possible the invention and representation of categories of collective identity that would continue to shape group and individual consciousness for a century or more to come. These foundational relations of modernity deserve sustained attention. Indeed, the patterns of British imperial power in the period from 1763 to 1840 have recently been recognized as providing the framework for imperial dominance in the late Victorian period.[16] Yet Britain's eighteenth-century empire has too often been neglected by scholars of other centuries as a "transitional" phase sandwiched between the verities of "early modern" and the cataclysms of "modern" transformations. Moreover, the consolidation and extension of parliamentary and colonial authority in the Hanoverian decades, uneven and sporadically ineffective as it may have been, also adumbrated localized versions of an emergent governmentality that sought to intervene directly in the internal lives and social, sexual, and gender practices of its subjects.[17] The histories of the interpenetration of British imperial strategies of rule and technologies of gender, racial, and national differentiation within the nation and empire demonstrate that new narratives of modernity need to be written – ones which take sufficient account of the impact of developments "out there" on the priorities, visions, and imaginations of those "in

---

[15] Nicholas Dirks, "History as a Sign of the Modern," *Public Culture*, 2 (1990), 25–32. See also Patrick Joyce, "The End of Social History?" *Social History*, 20 (1995), 73–91; Wilson, *Island Race*, 7–15, 84–89; Sudipta Sen, *Distant Sovereignty: National Imperialism and the Origins of British India* (London: Routledge, 2002), 27–56.

[16] C. A. Bayly, "The British and Indigenous Peoples, 1760–1860: Power, Perception, Identity," in Martin Daunton and Rick Halpern, eds., *Empire and Others: British Encounters with Indigenious Peoples, 1600–1850* (London: UCL Press, 1999), 22; and Bayly, "The First Age of Global Imperialism, 1760–1830," *Journal of Imperial and Commonwealth History* (hereafter *JICH*), 26 (1998). 28–48.

[17] See Michel Foucault, "Governmentality," in G. Burchell, C. Gordon, and P. Miller, eds., *The Foucault Effect: Studies in Governmentality* (London: Continuum, 1991), 87–104. This emerging colonial governmentality, ignored until recently, is evinced in the lineage regulations of colonial assemblies in America and the West Indies and the power of the East India Company in the East.

here," and which recognize that crucial features of "modernity" may have been forged in and through colonial frontiers long before the nineteenth century.

For our purposes, modernity signifies the unfolding set of relationships – cognitive, social, and intellectual as well as economic and political – which, however valued or construed, produced among their contemporaneous witnesses the conviction of historical *difference*.[18] As James Knight's hubris in the opening quotations indicates, and many of the following chapters confirm, Georgian Britons fretted over or boasted about the distinctiveness, superiority, and modernity of Britishness, and British imperial endeavors played a large role in sustaining or challenging that perception and self-image. At the same time, modes of British and English cultural production and consumption were constituted in part by bodies, practices, and exchanges of people across the globe, trends which writers like those at *The Spectator* delighted in pointing out. These influences of empire were not uniformly felt, and were uneven in their impact, but they were still powerful: the layout and specimens within botanical gardens, horticultural practices on landed estates, architectural styles, clothing, fabric, and food fads, tea, coffee, sugar, and chocolate and the rituals and institutions they generated, scientific societies, the national museum, religious missions: all were predicated upon colonial goods, imperial trading connections, and knowledge and artifacts culled from exploration, colonization, and colonial emissaries abroad.[19] Political jeremiads on the corrupting impact of luxuries on the polity and the "stadial" or stages theory of Enlightenment thinkers were equally propelled by the commodities, information, and practices brought home by explorers, voyagers, colonial settlers, and natural historians. The dramatic expansion of print culture itself over the century was owed in no small measure to the public's appetite for travel and colonization accounts, which rivaled sermons in their popularity in circulating libraries and were cannibalized and excerpted in periodicals and newspapers. And graphic and performance media, such as paintings, prints, drama, statuary, and pottery

---

[18] Wilson, *Island Race*, ch. 1; Miles Ogborn, *Spaces of Modernity: London's Geographies 1680–1780* (New York: Guildford Press, 1998).

[19] Richard Drayton, *Nature's Government: Science, Imperial Britain and the "Improvement" of the World* (New Haven: Yale University Press, 2000); Sidney Mintz, *Sweetness and Power* (New York: Viking, 1985); Susanne Seymour, Stephen Daniels, and Charles Watkins, "Estate and Empire: Sir George Cornewall's Management of Moccas, Herefordshire and La Taste, Grenada, 1771–1819," *Journal of Historical Geography*, 24 (1998), 313–51; James Walvin, *Fruits of Empire: Exotic Produce and British Taste, 1660–1800* (New York University Press, and Basingstoke: Macmillan, 1997); Kathleen Wilson, "The Good, the Bad and the Impotent: Imperialism and the Politics of Identity in Georgian England," in Ann Bermingham and John Brewer, eds., *The Consumption of Culture: Image, Object, Text* (London: Routledge, 1995), 229–52.

documented, idealized, or memorialized Britain's colonial achievements, military victories, and national aspirations.[20]

Even the project of state-building in the Hanoverian decades – a process that few historians would any longer dispute, although its long-term success is still debated – was a cultural as well as political project that was closely linked with Britain's emergence as an imperial power.[21] In this respect, the changes in the meanings of the word "culture" in the eighteenth century are illuminating. For most of the period, "culture" meant to cultivate or improve, but by the 1770s it had also taken on the meaning "to civilize."[22] Enlightenment epistemology, exploration, and imperial expansion had wrought this change in meaning, as in other "keywords" of the period, ranging from "race," which went from denoting a breed or stock to one of the broad differences among humankind, to "nation," which added to its older juridical and biblical concepts of a "people" the idea of political-territorial particularity.[23] "Modern" constructions of sex and gender, too, were forged through the practices and ideologies of colonization and slavery and bequeathed to the metropolis.[24] As Eric Hinderaker has noted, "Empire is a cultural artifact as well as a geopolitical entity; it belongs to a geography of the mind as well as a geography of power."[25] As such, both empire and culture were increasingly seen to have redemptive and progressive possibilities.

[20] Wilson, *Island Race*, 8–11; Felicity Nussbaum, *Torrid Zones: Maternity, Sexuality and Empire in Eighteenth Century English Narrative* (Baltimore: The Johns Hopkins University Press, 1995); Roxann Wheeler, *The Complexion of Race: Categories of Difference in Eighteenth-Century British Culture* (Philadelphia: University of Pennsylvania Press, 2000); Michael Heffernan, "'A Dream as Frail as Those of Ancient Time': The In-credible Geographies of Timbuctoo," *Environment and Planning D: Society and Space*, 19 (2001), 203–25; Margaret Hunt, "Racism, Imperialism and the Traveler's Gaze in Eighteenth Century England," *Journal of British Studies* (hereafter *JBS*), 32 (1993), 333–57; Kathleen Wilson, *The Sense of the People: Politics, Culture and Imperialism in England 1715–1785* (Cambridge University Press, 1995), chs. 1 and 3; Beth Fowkes Tobin, *Picturing Imperial Power* (Durham: Duke University Press, 1999); Peter Hulme and William Sherman, *The Tempest and its Travels* (Philadelphia: University of Pennysylvania Press, 2000); Ania Loomba, *Shakespeare, Race and Colonialism* (Oxford University Press, 2002).
[21] John Brewer, *The Sinews of Power: War, Money and the English State, 1688–1783* (London: Hutchinson, 1989); for a critique, see J. A. C. Cookson, *The British Armed Nation 1793–1815* (Oxford: Clarendon Press, 1997). For the mutual complicity of state and colonial expansion in this period, see Philip Corrigan and Derek Sayer, *The Great Arch: English State Formation as Cultural Revolution* (Oxford: Blackwell, 1985).
[22] Samuel Johnson, *A Dictionary of the English Language*, 4th edn (London, 1773).
[23] Wilson, *Island Race*, 6–15; Nicholas Hudson, "From 'Nation' to 'Race': The Origin of Racial Classification in Eighteenth Century Thought," *Eighteenth Century Studies*, 29 (1996), 247–60.
[24] Kathleen Wilson, "Empire, Gender and Modernity in the Eighteenth Century," in Philippa Levine, ed., *Gender and Empire* (Oxford University Press, 2004). Cf. Thomas Laqueur, *Making Sex: Body and Gender from the Greeks to Freud* (Cambridge, MA: Harvard University Press, 1990).
[25] Eric Hinderaker, "The 'Four Indian Kings' and the Imaginative Construction of the British Empire," *William and Mary Quarterly* (hereafter *WMQ*), 3rd ser., 53 (1996), 486.

Through state policy as well as social relations and cultural practice, the shifting geopolitics and chronopolitics of empire created some of the critical *conditions of possibility* for an eighteenth-century modernity. These conditions of possibility were consolidated and extended over the period studied here, from the 1660s to the abolition of slavery in 1833 and its aftermath, and so may trouble the traditional distinctions between the "first" and "second" empires that are common in current histories.[26] They included defensive and aggressive wars; a fiscal-military state that encouraged investment, accumulation, and innovation as well as coercive forms of trade; the growth and dissemination of cultural and imaginative media through which British people came to recognize their own historical and religious difference and distinctiveness; and the far-reaching networks that allowed these ideas, people, and commodities to travel and be transformed. Certainly transoceanic flows of peoples, goods, and ideas were millennia old.[27] But what changes in this period are both the scale and nature of the movements, the technologies of production and exchange that reinvented older notions of insiders, outsiders, and the mobility between them, and the conflation of geographic distance with temporality in ways that secured "the peripheral relation of the colony in metropolitan thinking." It was precisely through such processes that the nation-state strove to claim a new relationship to its subjects, and its subjects struggled to claim a stake in the nation. "Forging the nation" was thus inextricably bound to transnational and colonial developments.[28] The chapters that follow suggest that attention to the ideologies and representations of difference, including History itself, can significantly illumine the practices and perceptions of these developments, and help us better grasp the implications of an eighteenth-century imperial modernity, the legacies and categories of which have refused to fade.

[26] The "first" empire was enabled by English political domination of Ireland and Union with Scotland, and centered on British overseas settlements in North America and the West Indies and the establishment of British supremacy in the slave trade. The "second" empire (1763–1840) was defined by a turn towards the East (especially in the wake of the revolt of the American colonies), a more regulatory and rationalized imperial apparatus, and the extension of British power over a proliferating range of peoples and territories, such as India, New South Wales (1788), and Gambia and the Cape of Good Hope (1795). The phrase "conditions of possibility" is taken from Fernando Coronil, "Introduction," in Fernando Ortiz, *Cuban Counterpoint* (Durham: Duke University Press, 1994), xiii–xiv.
[27] Janet Abu-Lughod, *Before European Hegemony: The World System, AD 1250–1350* (Oxford University Press, 1989); Amitav Ghosh, *In an Antique Land* (New York: Knopf, 1993); Sanjay Subrahmanyam, *Merchant Networks in the Early Modern World* (Aldershot: Variorum, 1996); Kenneth McPherson, *The Indian Ocean: A History of People and the Sea* (Oxford University Press, 1998).
[28] Parama Roy, "At Home in the World? The Gendered Cartographies of Globality," *Feminist Studies*, 27, 3 (2001), 709–10; Edward Said, "Always on Top," *London Review of Books*, 20 March 2003; Linda Colley, *Britons: Forging the Nation 1707–1837* (New Haven: Yale University Press, 1992); Wilson, *The Sense of the People*.

EMPIRES

There was not one but many imperial projects in the Georgian period, engaged with by planters, reformers, merchants, explorers, missionaries, settlers, adventurers, indigenes, and the enslaved. The legacies and specificities of power and its failures need to be analyzed, not assumed: there is no universal colonial condition or imperial experience, but discrete practices of power and ways of imagining it in specific historical periods. Hence it is vital to take stock of the ways in which eighteenth-century peoples' own understandings of empire and overseas expansion changed through the century. Although there was unquestionably a more widespread apprehension within Britain after the Seven Years War that the "empire of the seas" had been conjoined with an "empire of conquest,"[29] such an assessment is by itself inadequate, based on a metropolitan perspective that conflates official glosses on colonial intentions with concrete practices and consequences. Native Americans, at war with the British at intervals throughout the long eighteenth century and demographically decimated by European and African diseases even in times of peace, would surely have disputed the argument that Britain did not possess a "territorial" empire before the 1760s, as would the millions of displaced Africans and impoverished Celts who had similarly lost land, culture, and people since the 1600s through the expansionist initiatives of British traders, colonists, and military leaders alike.[30]

Further, throughout the century people wrote and spoke about more than one empire – the "empire of the east," the "New World dominions," the "empire of the seas" – or even denied, like Adam Smith, that the British had an empire at all, only "the project of an empire."[31] Contending interpretations of empire's benefits and dangers continued to be recurrent themes in

[29] P. J. Marshall, "Empire and Authority in Later Eighteenth Century Britain," *JICH*, 15 (1987), 110–15.
[30] Bayly, "British and Indigenous Peoples," 19–41; Francis Jennings, *The Invasion of America: Indians, Colonialism and the Cant of Conquest* (Chapel Hill: University of North Carolina Press, 1975); James Axtell, *Beyond 1492: Encounters in Colonial North America* (New York: Columbia University Press, 1992); Daniel Richter, *The Ordeal of the Longhouse: The Peoples of the Iroquois League in the Era of European Colonization* (Chapel Hill: University of North Carolina Press, 1992); Colin G. Calloway, *The American Revolution in Indian Country* (Cambridge University Press, 1995); Blackburn, *Making of New World Slavery*; Philip D. Curtain, *The Rise and Fall of the Plantation Complex*, 2nd edn (Cambridge University Press, 1998); Nicholas Canny and Anthony Pagden, eds., *Colonial Identity in the Atlantic World 1500–1800* (Princeton University Press, 1987); and Canny, *Making Ireland British 1580–1650* (Oxford University Press, 2001).
[31] H. V. Bowen, "British Conceptions of Global Empire, 1756–63," *JICH*, 26 (1998), 1–27; Wilson, *Sense of the People*, Introduction; David Hancock, *Citizens of the World: London Merchants and the Integration of the British Atlantic Community, 1735–1785* (Cambridge University Press, 1995); P. J. Cain and A. G. Hopkins, *British Imperialism: Innovation and Expansion 1688–1914* (London: Longman, 1993).

cultural production and political argument over the period. Perhaps most importantly, the declining relative commercial value of Europe to British economic strength and the corresponding importance of the Atlantic trade in all its manifestations, the interpenetration of private trading initiatives and official colonial governmental and imperial structures, and the involvement of a range of ordinary people as well as "gentlemanly capitalists" in overseas ventures ensured that the eighteenth-century British empire continued to be maritime and commercial as well as territorial and conquering into the nineteenth century, *and* that British people throughout the world clung to the image of the empire as maritime, Protestant, and free long after its actual character had changed.[32] Within the competitive international contexts and increasing economic complexities of eighteenth-century empire, commercial and territorial peripheries penetrated each other, as trade fostered increased governmental regulation of the transoceanic economy, and settlement both conferred British dominium and created commercial entrepôts which enhanced the reach and profitability of the empire of trade.[33] Similarly, on the subcontinent, mercantilist goals and the exercise and extension of military, political, and national power were not antithetical even in the early phase of East India Company rule, as parliamentary proceses in Britain and administrative priorites in India mutually impacted each other.[34]

And the often tenuous and incomplete nature of metropolitan authority in this period – as Bernard Bailyn has put it for the American colonies, "the almost paralytic division of authority among the secretary of state, the board of trade, the army, the navy, and the treasury" along with "the constitutional fault line in the structure of imperial government" running from king in Parliament through the colonial councils and assemblies[35] – was just one aspect of the eighteenth-century British empire's instability; as such, this empire was always in the making, changing, and in process. As war-weary Britons from London to Calcutta recognized, British power abroad was a precarious entity, and Britishness a symbol and a commodity, that was constantly threatened, as well as redefined, by the predatory wars of the period as well as the cultural *mélange* of English, Scots, Irish, European, Native American, Indian, and African that jostled, often violently, for authority,

[32] H. V. Bowen, *Elites, Enterprise, and the Making of the British Overseas Empire, 1688–1775* (Basingstoke and New York: Macmillan and St. Martin's Press, 1996); David Armitage, *The Ideological Origins of the British Empire* (Cambridge University Press, 2000).
[33] Mancke, "Negotiating an Empire," 235–66.
[34] Sen, *Distant Sovereignty*, 2–26, and his chapter in this volume.
[35] Bernard Bailyn, "The First British Empire: From Cambridge to Oxford," *WMQ,* 57 (2000), 647–60.

wealth, and freedom. Yet the transformation of the English into the British
state after 1707 had conjoined the fiscal-military state with private big and
small investors to produce far-flung networks of power and kinship, so that
Scots, North Americans, and Irish, men and women, white, black, Asian,
and Amerindian, began to identify with a culture that was both "distinctly
British and distinctly imperial."[36]

Vigorously expansionist and precariously vulnerable, as a historical production, the eighteenth-century "empire of the seas" was neither unitary
nor static, and metropolitan Britain could not be insulated from or immune
to its infiltration, either imaginatively or materially. The insistence upon
a connection between what went on "out there" and what goes on "in
here" is one of the main distinguishing features of this volume of essays:
the interrelations between empire and British society are always to the
fore. The empire of the seas and the empire of conquest interpenetrated
each other over the period, generating social, cultural, and epistemological
networks as well as political and economic ones. Our attention to these
networks through the lenses of cultural history and criticism underscores
the vital place of everyday life in forging the many links that connected
men, women, and children living across the oceans, registering degrees of
both consanguinity and difference.

HISTORIES

In the present moment, when globalization, diasporas, and new forms of
political terror have propelled a battening down of disciplinary as well as
national hatches, new and old imperial histories have become disputatious
undertakings.[37] The publication and reception of the five-volume *Oxford
History of the British Empire* is a case in point. An impressive project covering the sixteenth through the twentieth centuries, it marks a watershed
in the study of the British empire, not least because it is produced in a

[36] Brewer, *The Sinews of Power*; Lawrence Stone, ed., *An Imperial State at War: Britain from 1689 to 1815* (London: Routledge, 1994); Kathleen Wilson, "Empire, Trade and Popular Politics in mid-Hanoverian Britain: The Case of Admiral Vernon," *Past and Present*, No. 126 (1988), 74–109; Wilson, *Sense of the People*, 152–62; David Shields, *Oracles of Empire: Poetry, Politics and Commerce in British America 1690–1750* (University of Chicago Press, 1990); Hinderaker, "The 'Four Indian Kings,'" 487–526; Richard C. Simmons, "Americana in British Books, 1621–1750," in Karen Kupperman, ed., *America in European Consciousness* (University of North Carolina Press, 1995), 361–87. Quote from Hindraker, 504.
[37] As Catherine Hall and Simon Gikandi, among others, have recently argued. See Hall, "Introduction," in Hall, ed., *Cultures of Empire* (Manchester University Press, 2000), 1–36, and *Civilizing Subjects* (London: Polity, 2002); Gikandi, *Maps of Englishness: Writing Identity in the Culture of Colonialism* (New York: Columbia University Press, 1996).

reputedly postcolonial era (although not, it must be said, from a post-colonial perspective).[38] The volumes for the seventeenth and eighteenth centuries have been justly celebrated for providing British scholars and general readers with an invaluable resource of knowledge about the official ideologies and politics of empire, the growth of an increasingly complex imperial economy, and the experiences of British imperial power for a portion of its subjects. They have also been criticized on a number of grounds: for failing to engage with scholarship on gender; for ignoring, with some exceptions, non-western perspectives; and even for providing a nostalgic view of empire that glosses atrocities and injustices in favor of achievements and ideals.[39] Most saliently for our purposes, the *OHBE* series has been questioned for its often strident hostility to postcolonial scholars, literary critics, and other "culturalist" marauders who have laid siege to the economic and political grounds traditionally held by imperial historians,[40] as well as for its conceptualization of the British empire as a series of "discrete components" of limited relevance to the study of Britain, rather than as a permeable "web" or "network," shaped by global and regional currents, that impacted metropolitan as much as colonial culture.[41] Many of these issues are addressed implicitly or explicitly not only in the chapters collected here and other current work, but also in the *OHBE*'s own multi-volume "companion" series that Roger Louis is currently organizing. But the controversy raises a different version of our initial question: if there is to be a new imperial history, then what should such a history look like?

Certainly it is warranted to question the ahistorical ways in which "empire" has been used by some writers as a shorthand to describe the entire range of global, national, and local processes set in motion by European "discovery" and settlement from the sixteenth century onwards, dramatically conflating disjunctive historical practices, intentions, and outcomes. It may also be appropriate to be skeptical of the enthusiasm with which British printed and unpublished sources have been scoured for evidence of expansionist intentions so that even the mildest expression of interest

[38] Peter Marshall, ed., *The Oxford History of the British Empire Vol. II: The Eighteenth Century* (Oxford University Press, 1998), vii.
[39] E.g., Bailyn, "First British Empire"; Kenneth Morgan, review in *JICH*, 28, 2 (2000), 117–19; Robin Blackburn, "To Settle and Rule," *Times Literary Supplement*, October 23, 1998, 5–7; Madhavi Kale, review in *Social History*, 27 (2002), 250–2; Richard Gott, "Shoot Them to Be Sure," *London Review of Books*, April 25 2002, 26–9; American Historical Association, Annual Conference 1999, "The Oxford History of the British Empire: A Forum," comments by Michael Fisher, Dane Kennedy, and Karen Kupperman.
[40] Robin W. Winks, ed., *OHBE, Vol. V: Historiography* (Oxford University Press, 1999) is most strident.
[41] Tony Ballantine, *Orientalism and Race: Aryanism in the British Empire* (Basingstoke: Palgrave, 2002); Wilson, *Island Race*, 15–20.

in the wider world, or curiosity about its wonders, is flagged as nascent colonialist ambition.[42] But it is important not to judge new initiatives by their most effusive acolytes. For the critique of the "imperial turn" in the scholarship of the past two decades was well established by the time the *OHBE* appeared, as historians, anthropologists, and literary critics strove to bring greater historical contingency and complexity into contemporary analyses of European imperialism.[43]

Indeed, the 1990s saw an explosion of nuanced and cross-disciplinary studies of nation-making and empire, variously inspired by feminist and cultural studies (in the work of such diverse scholars as Margaret Strobel, Ann Laura Stoler, Nupur Chaudhuri, and Gayatri Spivak), the political and psychoanalytic genealogies proffered by Freud, Fanon, and Foucault (of whom Said and Homi Bhabha were most influential), revisions of historical ethnography (pioneered in the work of, to name a few, Bernard Cohen, James Clifford, Mary Louise Pratt, Nicholas Thomas, and Margaret Jolly), and both subaltern studies and the "new cultural history" which, despite their divergences, shared a concern to analyze the politics of affiliation and everyday life in and through representation (on display in the scholarship of Paul Gilroy, Stuart Hall, Peter Hulme, Ania Loomba, Greg Dening, Lata Mani, Ranajit Guha, and Dipesh Chakrabarty as well as many others.). All of this work has demonstrated that the "local" and the "global" have been difficult to disentangle since 1492. It has also revealed that the contending agendas among and between metropolitan and local rulers and creole, indigenous, and enslaved populations forced cultural collaborations and exchanges shaping the tenor of imperial rule, the reach of "trade," and the meanings of Englishness, liberty, and slavery. In eighteenth-century studies, literary critics and historical anthropologists took the lead in pulling the empire back into the narrative of "national" literatures and histories, stimulating other historical, critical, ethnographic, and art historical work that has unsettled established narratives of the period.[44]

---

[42] For this critique, see Linda Colley, "The Imperial Embrace," *Yale Review*, 81 (1993), 92–8; and Dane Kennedy, "Imperial History and Postcolonial Theory," *JICH*, 24 (1996), 345–63. See also Stephen Howe, "The Slow Death and Strange Rebirths of Imperial History," *JICH*, 29, 2 (2001), 131–41.

[43] I owe the phrase "imperial turn" to Antoinette Burton, *After the Imperial Turn: Thinking With and Through the Nation* (Durham: Duke University Press, 2003). Nicholas Thomas, *Colonialism's Culture* (Durham: Duke University Press, 1994) was an early and cogent leader in this respect; see also Frederick Cooper and Ann Laura Stoler, eds., *Tensions of Empire: Colonial Subjects in a Bourgeois World* (Ann Arbor: University of Michigan Press, 1998).

[44] Felicity Nussbaum and Laura Brown, eds., *The New Eighteenth Century* (London: Methuen, 1987) was a leader; see also Margo Hendricks and Patricia Parker, eds., *Women, "Race" and Writing in the Early Modern Period* (London: Routledge, 1994); Billie Melman, *Women's Orients: English Women and the Middle East 1718–1918* (Ann Arbor: University of Michigan Press, 1992); and Further Reading at the end of this volume.

Hence obviously more is at stake in the debates about the new imperial history than its (wrongly) alleged ahistoricism or teleology. Interdisciplinarity, the impact of "theory" (especially postcolonial and gender theory), and the primacy of "culture" in investigations of empire have all come under fire as "a new form of academic terrorism" that allegedly mystifies social relations that are "really" about class, capital, or the power of the state.[45] Further, within British studies, as noted earlier, cultural analyses of empire have made incursions on the traditional grounds of imperial history, setting new agendas for research among scholars of different backgrounds who burrow into hallowed records which they read as historical documents rather than "primary sources." Above all, a "new imperial history" that defines the proliferation of British peoples, law, customs, religion, and, to a lesser extent, political institutions across the globe and the contributions of these extended territories and peoples to English culture as all part of "British history" necessarily tests and confounds the effort to write "national" history neatly demarcated by territorial lines.[46] In this context, we need to remind ourselves that the enduring fiction of moral as well as geographical separateness was forged by some of the earliest narrations of empire, and later substantiated by philosophers' and explorers' conflation of geographic distance with temporality and nationality. As new studies are emphasizing, English law and administrative regulations in British domains, although frequently a source of conflict, also aimed at maintaining the boundaries between "home" and "abroad," creating discrepant definitions of legal and national subjects and keeping the less savory aspects of imperial rule (concubinage, mixed-race progeny, violence, and other forms of "degeneracy") hidden from metropolitan view.[47]

---

[45] See e.g., Rosalind O'Hanlon and Davis Washbrook, "After Orientalism: Culture, Criticism and Politics in the Third World," *Comparative Studies in Society and History*, 34 (1992), 141–67, reprinted in Vinayak Chaturvedi, ed., *Mapping Subaltern Studies and the Postcolonial* (London, 2000, 191–219; C. A. Bayly, "Rallying Around the Subaltern," in Chaturvedi, *Mapping Subaltern Studies*, 116–26; quote from Nicholas Dirks, *Castes of Mind: Colonialism and the Making of Modern India* (Princeton University Press, 2001), 312.

[46] For a powerful critique of such national history writing, see Antoinette Burton, "Who Needs the Nation? Interrogating 'British' history," in Hall, *Cultures of Empire*, 139–40.

[47] See e.g., Lauren Benton, *Law and Colonial Cultures* (Cambridge University Press, 2002); Indrani Chatterjee, "Colouring Subalternity: Slaves, Concubines and Social Orphans in Early Colonial India," *Subaltern Studies X* (New Delhi: Oxford University Press, 1999), 49–85; Elizabeth Collingham, *Imperial Bodies: The Physical Experience of the Raj, c. 1800–1947* (London: Polity, 2001); Ann Marie Plane, "Legitimacies, Indian Identities and the Law," in Daunton and Halpern, *Empire and Others*, 217–37; Durba Ghosh, "Household Crimes and Domestic Order: Keeping the Peace in Colonial Calcutta, c. 1770–1840," *Modern Asian Studies* 38, 2 (2004); Wilson, "Empire, Gender and Modernity." A look at the parliamentary debate over the Jewish Naturalization Act in 1753 through the "imperial frame" is extremely illuminating. See *Parliamentary History of England*, Vol. XIV (1753–4), 1365–1432, and the analysis in Kathleen Wilson, "Islands of Empire: Sumatra, St. Helena and the Culture of Colonialism, 1680–1800" (forthcoming).

Perhaps as a result of these dislocations, even scholars who have been more welcoming to new approaches to imperial history remain cautious about some of their targets and goals. C. A. Bayly, whose recent work has done much to draw attention to the crucial period of 1760–1830 in British imperial studies, has also warned that the attempt to recover "the decentred narrative, the local discourse and the particular experience of the oppressed and marginalized" is

in danger of foundering in its own particularism and of becoming a form of post modern antiquarianism. For it is still necessary to ask what the "centre" was around which these decentred discourses revolved. What was the motive force of the juggernaut which rolled down on to Celtic Britain, Mediterranean Europe, Asia, Africa and North America between 1760 and 1860?[48]

Despite its cogency, Bayly's comment unwittingly illustrates the disciplinary obstacles to doing new imperial history within history itself. For the question is begged, whose center is at issue in this account? Bayly's own local studies on Indian society, as well as Jack Greene's interpretation of the "negotiated authorities" of empire in America and the recent revival of arguments about the "accidental" nature of British imperial power, have all shown the "center" to be much more vulnerable, insecure, and unstable than such a formulation suggests. The unevenness of metropolitan power, the tensions between it and local colonial states, and the disjunctures between metropolitan and colonial intentions, not to mention outcomes, are thus serious enough to warrant questioning the usefulness of such essentialist definitions of center or periphery.[49] Conversely, not only new imperial historians but also eighteenth-century colonial officials and governors, masters, merchants, planters, missionaries, and settlers would have taken issue with such an assessment: for they knew how keenly relevant such "decentered discourses" were to the success and longevity of their own particular projects and livelihoods, the maintenance of power, the control of labor, the protection of the frontiers, and thus to British rule and property. Home and Colonial Office papers, merchant venturers' archives, and family and political correspondence are filled with detailed narratives of rumors, gossip,

[48] Bayly, "British and Indigenous Peoples," 21.
[49] C. A. Bayly, *Indian Society and the Making of the British Empire* (Cambridge University Press, 1988) and *Empire and Information* (Cambridge University Press, 1996); Jack P. Greene, "Negotiated Authorities: The Problem of Governance in the Extended Polities of the Early Modern Atlantic World," in Greene, *Negotiated Authorities: Essays in Colonial, Political and Constitutional History* (Charlottesville: University of Virginia Press, 1994); and Greene, "Transatlantic Colonization and the Redefinition of Empire in the Early Modern Era," in Daniels and Kennedy, *Negotiated Empires*, 267–82; see also the works by Daunton and Halpern, Nussbaum, Sen, and Wilson in Further Reading. The "accidental" nature of British imperial power is elaborated in *OHBE*, Vol. II, as well as in Linda Colley, *Captives: Britain and the World, 1600–1850* (London: Jonathan Cape, 2002).

and guesses about the state of mind and beliefs of the indigenes or enslaved, the farmers, merchants, and others who lobbied the assemblies or East India Company courts, and the women who governed consumer practices or trudged with their men on the march. Within Britain, networks of sociability and gossip at all social levels supplemented print culture in publicizing and deliberating the facts or consequences of overseas dominions among a broader public. Similarly, familial and gossip networks maintained by the enslaved or subaltern, taken up with cosmologies and social relations whose relationship to "the center" was obscure, articulated their own notions of time, space, and power which could explode the best-laid plans of authorities. These microhistories of empire's reach and impact are central to new imperial history, no matter how difficult they may be to prise from the narratives or records of the more privileged and visible.

Moreover, where else to locate the "motive force" of the "juggernaut" of the fiscal-military state than in the networks of people, practices, values, and ideas spanning continents and oceans – in other words, in culture itself? The economic foundationalism of most imperial studies overlooks the degree to which economics, like other forms of human activity, are themselves rooted in cultural attitudes and beliefs. As scholars have argued with regard to the Atlantic slave trade, economic motives cannot fully explain the fact or patterns of enslavement, which were rooted in cultural understandings of insiders and outsiders. In this context, it is perhaps more urgent to evade what Gyan Prakash has called the "leaden understanding of colonialism as History," whereby European expansion is represented as the motor of historical progress, than it is to avoid spending too much time on women or indigenes to the exclusion of the "imperial-garrison state."[50] The point to stress here is that *all* of these sites and subjects deserve further sustained critical attention, as all are just coming to be recognized as entangled within an "imperial social formation" of the age, the specificity of each of which must be sought in its own social and geographical location.[51]

The "new imperial history" at work in this volume is organized around three themes central to a cultural history of British expansion: the impact of empire on British social and cultural practices and identities; the transoceanic networks of everyday life, cutting across the boundaries of nation and of "public" and "private," through which the traffic in people,

[50] Eltis, *Rise of African Slavery*; David Eltis, ed., *Coerced and Free Migration: Global Perspectives* (Stanford University Press, 2002), 48–9; Gyan Prakash, "Introduction," in Prakash, ed., *After Colonialism: Imperial Histories and Postcolonial Displacements* (Princeton University Press, 1995), 4.
[51] Mrinalini Sinha, "Britishness, Clubbability, and the Colonial Public Sphere: The Genealogy of an Imperial Institution in Colonial India," *JBS*, 40 (2001), 489–521.

goods, and ideas was concretized and sustained; and the role of representation in enabling, mystifying, or contesting British imperial power. As such, these chapters begin from the premise that historians and critics should address metropole and colonies as interrelated analytic fields – which is to suggest not that they are "the same," but that, despite the discrepant nature and changing relationship of specific colonial sites to the metropole, the political project of dominium and the strategies of rule were intimately linked with the projects of governance, economic prosperity, national aggrandizement, and social order "at home." Needless to say, as with all interpretive perspectives, those employed here have limitations and shortcomings. The centrality of metropolitan Britain in these queries risks re-inscribing an exaggerated importance of British developments on the rest of world history. As Ruth Frankenberger and Lata Mani have argued, if new historical analyses of empire provide just "a resource for rethinking the Western Self" then they will be incapable of displacing the dominant conceptualizations about "centers" and "peripheries" that naturalize the effects of imperial domination.[52] But the contention here is that it is precisely this European or, in this case, British Self which needs to be rethought in light of emerging studies on the costs, consequences, and possibilities of empire for the men, women, and children living across its domains. These kinds of imperial histories certainly cannot replace histories of colonial spaces, but they do emphasize the need to see the two as mutually constitutive, even in their differences, in testimony to the global systems that the British empire created, the collective and entangled collective pasts it engendered, and the exchanges and hybridities at the heart of one of the most allegedly autochthonous national cultures.

Secondly, the chapters in this volume, focusing largely on British and anglophone cultural and political practices, have the disadvantage of not pursuing the sort of transnational and transhemispheric comparisons that in other new imperial histories have proved to be so valuable.[53] Yet although in many ways the *British* empire in the eighteenth century was a fictive domain, in that its boundaries were constantly transgressed by empires, peoples, practices, and values from other cultures, British dominium – effected

[52] Ruth Frakenburg and Lata Mani, "Crosscurrents, Crosstalk: Race, 'Postcoloniality,' and the Politics of Location," *Cultural Studies*, 7, 2 (1993), quoted in Mrinalini Sinha, "Britain and the Empire: Toward a New Agenda for Imperial History," *Radical History Review*, 72 (1998), 175–84.

[53] Such as Blackburn's magisterial *Making of New World Slavery* and *The Overthrow of New World Slavery* (London: Verso, 1998); Daniels and Kennedy, *Negotiated Empires*; Hall, *Cultures of Empire*; and Clare Midgley, *Gender and Imperialism* (London: Routledge, 1998); Ann Laura Stoler, *Carnal Knowledge and Imperial Power: Race and the Intimate in Colonial Rule* (Los Angeles and Berkeley: University of California Press, 2002).

on the ground through social practices, religion, and political institutions as well as through monarchical claims recognized in international law – was a tangible reality to the subjects within its purview, both before and after the Seven Years War, when British rule came to encompass francophone as well as Native American and South and East Asian peoples. The demands of both the metropolitan British state and the polyglot and multiethnic imperial interculture shaped the tone and tenor of British dominium, and enable us to track movements of people, practices, and values across a particular territorial and conceptual space and time. The fact or possibility of British imperial power was a crucible shaping practices and aspirations of men and women across this space, for whom empire, nation, and difference were understood in unexpected and discontinuous ways. Finally, although "postcoloniality" as a descriptive label may be a chimera rather than a reality, in that neither the effects nor the era of imperialism are in the past, the historical examples of the cultural and epistemic as well as material and physical forms of domination engendered by eighteenth-century forms of empire-building are invaluable for reminding us of the nature of change over time and of the political stakes lodged in its charting.[54] The imperial histories that result seek less to "replace" narratives of politics, administration, and policy than to reconfigure them, by conceptually rethinking what empire meant from the point of view of its different partisans and opponents and its strategies and cultural technologies of rule.

That taking seriously these different points of view makes the empire look different is clear. Feminist scholars of gender and empire, for example, have been to the fore in analyzing the links between technologies of gender and national identity at home and abroad and in identifying how the history of the intimate and the "private" lay at the heart of the public projects of trade, colonization, and the "arts of discovery." In garrisons, forts, and factories, plantation societies and urban centers, the utilization of enslaved, indigenous, subaltern, and "respectable" women's bodies, the regulation of sexuality and lineage, and the demarcation of masculinity's and femininity's roles and privileges constituted in no small part the substance of imperial power and dominion. The crucial history of gender in signifying, organizing, and publicizing imperial endeavors is starting to receive its due attention, and the chapters here by Margaret Hunt, Gillian Russell, Hans Turley, Kate Teltscher, Durba Ghosh, and Kathleen Wilson

[54] Anne McClintock, *Imperial Leather* (London: Routledge, 1995), 11–12; Homi Bhabha and John Comaroff, "Speaking of Postcoloniality in a Continuous Present," in David Theor Goldberg and Ato Quayson, eds., *Relocating Postcolonialism* (Oxford University Press, 2002).

suggest some of its directions.[55] Similarly, historicizing "race," ethnicity, and identity through the analysis of the multivalent languages of temporality, performance, slavery, and freedom in Britain and the colonies reveals the hidden economies of power, sensibility, and subversion that empire galvanized amongst its subjects and objects; indeed, identity itself is reshaped by the crossings of empire, as the cultural revolutions of the age include new ways to think about self, mobility, and connection.[56] The chapters by Felicity Nussbaum, Michael Fisher, Walter Johnson, Colin Kidd, Nicholas Rogers, and Harriet Guest all suggest, from very different perspectives and locations, that empire affected the most quotidian as well as the most momentous aspects of everyday life, cultural production, sociability, and identity: imperial circuits provided some of the routes through which identifications could travel and be transformed. Moreover, the empire fostered, and provided a testing ground for, new ideas about social engineering, religious reclamation, and scientific advance, not only in colonies or territories under British control but also in lands and spaces beyond its power, which Britons from various backgrounds sought to claim, "discover," or save. The chapters by Eitan Bar-Yosef, Philip Stern, Kevin Whelan, and Sudipta Sen substantiate the impact of the eighteenth-century British empire in shaping the goals and visions of individuals and groups within the British Isles, and, conversely, the importance of their perceptions on empire, as differently calibrated projects of exploration, conquest, observation, or revolution strove to demonstrate national ingenuity or failure. Indeed, the eighteenth-century British empire may have effected a greater economic and communicative integration of globe that, as Thomas Haskell argued some time ago for the Atlantic world, shifted conventional boundaries of ethical responsibility in ways that still have repercussions today.[57] In short,

---

[55] See, e.g., Hilary McD. Beckles, *Centering Women: Gender Discourses in Caribbean Slave Society* (Kingston: Ian Randle, 1999); Wilson, *The Island Race*; Chatterjee, "Colouring Subalternity"; Joy Damousi, *Depraved and Disorderly: Female Convicts, Sexuality and Gender in Colonial Australia* (Cambridge University Press, 1997); Kathleen Brown, *Good Wives, Nasty Wenches and Anxious Patriarchs: Gender, Race and Power in Colonial Virginia* (Chapel Hill: University of North Carolina Press, 1996); Durba Ghosh, *Colonial Companions: Sexual Transgression, Racial Mixing and Gendered Order in Early Colonial India, 1760–1840* (forthcoming).

[56] See Colin Jones and Dror Wahrman, eds., *The Age of Cultural Revolutions* (Berkeley and Los Angeles, University of California Press, 2001); Kidd, *British Identities before Nationalism*; Wheeler, *Complexion of Race*; Wahrman, "Problem of English Identity"; Jonathan Lamb, *Preserving the Self in the South Seas 1680–1840* (University of Chicago Press, 2001); Joyce Chaplin, *Subject Matter: Technology, Science and the Body on the Anglo-American Frontier* (Cambridge, MA: Harvard University Press, 1999); David Waldstreicher, "Reading the Runaways: Self-Fashioning, Print Culture and Confidence in Slavery in the Eighteenth-Century Mid-Atlantic World," *WMQ*, 3rd ser., 56 (1999), 243–72.

[57] Thomas L. Haskell, "Capitalism and the Origins of the Humanitarian Sensibility, Part 2," *American Historical Review*, 90 (1985), 547–66.

the reciprocal influences of empire on individual and group perceptions, the cultural practices and circuits which produced shared or discrepant notions of time and space, or which valued different kinds of people and bodies as essential, or not, to the polity – all facilitated identifications that resulted in contradictions as well as coherences. Tracking these subjects and objects of knowledge produces an altered "map" of empire and a dissimilar set of historical issues and problems than those usually associated with imperial history. New imperial histories may thus have the effect of reinventing History itself, in that although they are archivally based, they tell a story through competing fragments, and engage with historical issues and debates emanating from a wider cross-disciplinary arena than history alone. Such histories are likely to frustrate traditionalists, but they may in fact be more truthful to the experience of the various men, women, and children caught up in the dramas of British expansion, linked together through disparate bonds of experience, identity, and practice.

THE ESSAYS

There will of course be many "new imperial histories" in the coming years. The essays collected here hint at only a few of the many emergent visions of what that imperial history may look like. They are, none the less, united by three themes, outlined above, all of which are geared towards reconnecting the histories of empire, gender, race, and nation through the compass of cultural history and criticism: the impact of empire on British culture, epistemology, and identities; the imperial networks of everyday life through which people, ideas, goods, and identities traveled and changed; and the complexities of representation in enabling or contesting national and imperial power. These themes are taken up from a variety of perspectives and in an interdisciplinary spirit, analyzed through art and aesthetics as well as political theory, quotidian social practices as well as literature, and the everyday as well as the great event. As we shall see, the authors sometimes disagree with each other (and, indeed, with the editor), but the resulting debates are lively and productive.

The chapters in Part I explore the impact of British expansion on gender, racial, and national identities and on representational and political practices in the metropole. Margaret Hunt's chapter reveals what the "fiscal-military state" looks like when women are brought into the analysis. Maritime culture and the Royal Navy depended upon women's networks on shore to feed, clothe, sustain, and enlist the men of the service, and the women, in turn, became adept at learning how to command the state into supporting their own rights to maintenance. In this way, as Hunt cogently puts it, the women and children of seamen were "on the front line of empire, though most of them never left England's shores." Gillian Russell deftly links sociability to imperial history by exposing the important role of elite women's cultural networks in promoting and publicizing British exploration in the Pacific, shaping and consuming "knowledge" about the Pacific and its people in unexpected ways. The intersections between social and theatrical performances that she reconstructs are also tracked in Felicity Nussbaum's stimulating analysis of the performance of blackness on the English stage from the eighteenth to the nineteenth century. Nussbaum discerns an evolution of racialist representation from more playful to more modern forms after the abolition of slavery (1833), when post-Enlightenment progressivism foundered on the rocks of racial and national difference. The troubled and contingent positions of colonized people of color in the English nation are also dealt with in the chapter by Michael Fisher, who examines the instrumentality of Asian autobiography at the heart of empire. Fisher's analysis of the experiences and self-representations of Asians in Britain over the eighteenth and into the nineteenth century suggests that Asians were less discriminated against in Britain than in the colonial peripheries. He thus raises vital questions, usually addressed in relation to slavery, about the degree to which legal disabilities traveled and whether notions of national and racial difference were more absolutist in some colonial and metropolitan settings than in others.

Part II examines the role empire played in shaping the aspirations, visions, and practices of a range of social groups: gentlemen scientists, plebeian millenarians, East India Company officials, and novelists all saw in England's maritime colonies, territorial outposts, or international standing opportunities to change the world or themselves; accordingly, their plans for "discovery," administration, or salvation inflected the meanings of empire for metropolitan and colonial subjects. Philip Stern takes on the interconnections between empire, gentlemanly sociability, and useful knowledge in his vivid analysis of the African Association, founded to vindicate British superiority in the arts of discovery and integrate the African interior into global networks of trade. Sudipta Sen argues for the impact of metropolitan ideas on East India Company "reform" in India in a counter to current scholarly emphases on the importance of *Indian* institutions and practices to the Company's regime. Yet he also shows that the cultural traffic flowed both ways, as the exigencies of rule in India impinged on arguments about political economy in Britain: "free trade" became the watchword of an extension and consolidation of state power, and English liberalism a means of leading denizens of "Old Corruption" in both countries into modern time. Taking a somewhat different tack from established scholarly concerns with missionary work, the chapters by Eitan Bar-Yosef and Hans Turley stress the importance of varieties of British Protestantism to evolving imperial concerns. Bar-Yosef's original analysis of the millenarian prophesying of plebeian Joanna Southcott and the Royal Navy officer Richard Brother reveals how the national and the imperial interpenetrated in their fantasies about "Jerusalem" as territory or utopia, whether located in England or the Middle East. His chapter also reminds us that it is not only in colonial spaces that God is conceived of as an actor in everyday life. Turley's trenchant and witty reading of the Crusoe trilogy and its imitators – one of the most popular motifs in European literary history – illustrates the pitfalls of historians' reductionist treatment of Protestantism, and substantiates the role of popular literature in imagining the empire and mobilizing the kind of sensibilities which supported it. New imperial histories, he argues, must move beyond bipolar studies of "self" and "other" to considerations of the mutual constitution and entanglements of modern subjects through colonialism and its cultures.

In Part III, we turn to the "Atlantic world," surely one of the most fertile areas in the field of new imperial history. From Fernando Ortiz's brilliant analysis of the transculture of the Caribbean and Eric Williams' provocative, if disputed, argument about slavery's critical role in modern capitalism to Paul Gilroy's iconoclastic model of the "Black Atlantic," the study of Atlantic history has produced immensely influential interpretations that have roused scholars to think on a grander scale.[58] The chapters in this section rise admirably to this challenge, taking on time, identity, and an Atlantic interculture that, propelled by the dark economic tides of slavery, did not begin and end at national borders. Walter Johnson brilliantly demonstrates the differential collective narratives though which Europeans and Africans shaped their experience of slavery and the slave trade. By foregrounding discrepant notions of time in the local cultures of Christian and Islamic imperialists, slave traders, and the enslaved, he illustrates how contending understandings of events and relations "shaped the historical processes in which they were joined." Kevin Whelan's bracing and kaleidoscopic tour of Irish crossings and influences in the Atlantic world takes the story of Irish westward expansion through the eighteenth

---

[58] See their works in Further Reading.

century, adding a radical "Green" Atlantic to the "Black" and "Red" ones of recent scholarship. Nicholas Rogers analyzes the different colonial and metropolitan agendas at work in apotheosizing that most English of heroes, General Wolfe, and confirms the importance of military figures in a national and imperial imaginary. Colin Kidd's provocative and perspicacious rethinking of "ethnicity" as a foundation of imperial history demonstrates the changing valences of race and nationality over the period, and makes a telling case for the longevity of theological concerns – including philosemitism – in eighteenth-century British culture and its ruminations on difference.

The chapters in Part IV privilege questions of gender and national identity in a consideration of the cross-cultural dynamics of encounter, exchange, and the production of knowledge, a convergence of activities that is taken to comprise the "arts of discovery." Kate Teltscher's fascinating look at the letters "home" from East India Company servant and British envoy to Tibet, George Bogle, conveys their role as the interface between metropole and empire, and suggests a new way to read the colonial archive. Her chapter also substantiates the performances of difference and similitude demanded by colonial encounters, the extension of the "empire of goods" to some unlikely places, and the unorthodox sexual arrangements undertaken by men in the imperial service. Durba Ghosh fearlessly takes on the issues of "colonial companions," representation, and the archive from a different perspective. Ghosh addresses the seemingly intractable problem of tracing indigenous domestic partners of English men in colonial sources, and interrogates the representational and political practices that efface such women as subjects. Her resourceful interpretation opens new paths for writing archival histories of the subaltern that manage to break free of the goals and priorities of the institutions that attempted to erase them. Finally, Harriet Guest's and Kathleen Wilson's chapters address the impact of the "arts of discovery" on England's material and imaginative relations with the South Pacific. Guest teases out new levels of meaning in contending metropolitan readings of exploration and discovery in the 1770s through textual and visual representations of Omai, the visiting Tahitian, and Captain James Cook, icon of British modernity. Wilson probes the implications of gender misrecognition on the Cook voyages for "modern" understandings of sexual and national difference. Both authors delve into a history of national and colonial interpenetration where ambiguities and lacunae in "the record" provide the spaces for Oceanic men and women to intervene in British variants of "global" knowledge and identity.

The new imperial history presented here is very much a work in progress, but its conditions of possibility are grounded in the willingness of scholars from different disciplines to take seriously questions of cultural difference and their imperial frames in the long eighteenth century. It is an exhilarating conjuncture, the full fruits of which may only be evident in a history, and a future, still becoming.

PART I

Empire at home: difference, representation, experience

Women and the fiscal-imperial state in the late seventeenth and early eighteenth centuries

Margaret Hunt

The brilliant victories, agonizing defeats, and day-to-day privations that fill the pages of traditional military history are overwhelmingly masculine ones. Yet wartime economic dislocation, the temporary, and, too often, permanent loss of fathers, brothers, husbands, and lovers, and the spiraling cost of necessities also bore with terrible force upon women, children, and other "non-combatants." Samuel Pepys, who for many years was Clerk of the Acts to the navy, knew this as well as anyone.[1] Here he is, in 1666, in the midst of the Second Anglo-Dutch War, trying unsuccessfully to avoid a confrontation with the wives of English prisoners of war:

At noon home to dinner, and then to the [Navy] office, the yard being very full of women (I believe above 300) coming to get money for their husbands and friends that are prisoners in Holland; and they lay clamouring and swearing, and cursing us . . . Then I took the opportunity when they were all gone into the fore-yard, and slipped into the office and there busy all the afternoon. But by and by the women got into the garden, and came all to my closet window and there tormented me; and I confess, their cries were so sad for money, and laying down the condition of their families and their husbands, and what they have done and suffered for the King, and how ill they are used by us, and how well the Du[t]ch [prisoners of war] are used here by the allowance of their masters . . . that I do most heartily pity them, and was ready to cry to hear them – but cannot help them . . .[2]

All manuscripts are from the Public Record Office, Kew, London unless otherwise indicated. E 112 denotes an Exchequer bill. ADM denotes navy records. HCA denotes High Court of Admiralty Records.

Thanks to Barbara Balliet, Barbara Donagan, Richard Ensor, Roger Knight, Peter Le Fevre, Maria Lepowsky, Martha Saxton, Kathleen Wilson, Kariann Yokota, and Henry Yu for their comments on various drafts of this chapter. Any remaining errors of fact or infelicities of interpretation are my own.

[1] *Diary of Samuel Pepys*, Robert Latham and William Matthews, eds. (8 vols., Berkeley and Los Angeles: University of California Press, 1972), VII, 199–200 (entry for July 10, 1666). Pepys was Clerk of the Acts from 1661 to July 1673, and thereafter Secretary to the Admiralty Commissioners.

[2] See e.g., Patricia Lin, "Fostering Fatherhood: The British National Welfare System for Soldiers' and Sailors' Families, 1793–1815," unpublished paper presented to the American Historical Association Annual Meetings, Washington, D.C., January 10, 1999.

The women Samuel Pepys describes were clearly experiencing real hardship, but they were hardly suffering in silence. Instead, they were loudly and pointedly demanding some recompense for the sacrifices they and their menfolk had made in the course of a war that is often seen as England's first modern imperial conflict. They were also quite decidedly in the public sphere and perfectly aware of the power of numbers. It is a fitting scene with which to begin an examination of the relationship between women and the military in the one of the key phases of English imperial expansion.[3]

The period from the late 1640s to the 1680s had already seen a major increase in the size, scope, and cost of the English navy. This came in response to continued royalist military resistance during the Protectorate and Commonwealth, the long and bloody rivalry with the Dutch, a more contained war with Spain, tensions with France, and expanding commercial and political interests in South Asia, the West Indies, the west coast of Africa, and North America.[4] The Revolution of 1688/9 and the outbreak of war with France – and Louis XIV's ostentatious shipbuilding program – further accelerated the rate of growth. Annual expenditure on the navy from 1689 to 1697 was already about £1.8 million; from 1702 to 1713 it leaped to £2.4 million, the largest single expenditure category in the state budget. At the same time the navy drew ever greater numbers of people into its orbit, so that by the height of the War of Spanish Succession 48,000 men were in active service, a significant proportion of the total seafaring population.[5]

War had a powerful impact upon the lives of both women and men. War expenditures pumped unprecedented amounts of money into maritime communities in the form of sailors' wages and military contracts for everything from shipbuilding and nursing care to bulk orders of hardtack and cloth. It also introduced severe constraints and burdens. A large proportion of the manpower for the wars against Louis XIV was made up of impressed men: individuals borne off forcibly from their communities (or from returning merchant ships) by the detested press gangs. Once down on a ship's rolls these men were prisoners in everything but name: the penalty for desertion was death, at least in theory, though manpower resources were so short the authorities usually settled for flogging. We have graphic descriptions from Pepys and others, as well as women's own testimonies, about the psychic

[3] I am grateful to Kathleen Wilson for recommending that I frame the question in this way.
[4] See especially John Ehrman, *The Navy in the War of William III: 1689–1697: Its State and Direction* (Cambridge University Press, 1953); and Richard Harding, *The Evolution of the Sailing Navy, 1509–1815* (New York: St. Martin's Press, 1995), 70–84.
[5] Daniel A. Baugh, "The Eighteenth Century Navy as a National Institution 1690–1815," in J. R. Hill, ed., *Oxford Illustrated History of the Royal Navy* (Oxford and New York: Oxford University Press, 1995), 120–1.

distress and material hardships created by impressment, and still more by the permanent loss or disablement of husbands, fathers, lovers, and sons that so often followed. Maritime communities paid a disproportionately high percentage of the mortality cost of the imperial state.

The prominent role women occupy in Pepys's account is indicative of their position within maritime communities more generally. In war and peace-time both, sailors' lengthy absences from home, high mortality rate, and erratic loyalties had long provided especially strong incentives for women to develop independent sources of income.[6] These were the standard early modern urban women's occupations, and they have been well described by Peter Earle, Judith M. Bennett, and others: intermittent and low-paid waged work, petty sales, taking in laundry, keeping lodgers, sewing, and, for women who had capital, running a victualing house or similar enterprise.[7] However, over and above these activities, women in seafaring communities also exercised an unusual degree of legal and moral authority, simply because their freedom of action was greater than that of their male kin (this was true in general, but far more so during wartime, when shore-leave was often out of the question). A striking symbol of this was the widespread custom of sailors conferring the right of power of attorney on their wives, mothers, or other female kin preparatory to leaving on voyages. A "power" (as East London women evocatively referred to it) might permit a woman to collect part or all of her husband's or male relative's pay from the shipowners and Navy Board, to receive money on bills, to buy and sell property, to sue in court, or to conduct business in her husband's or male relative's name. The written instrument, in turn, almost certainly derived from or ratified longstanding customary practices within maritime communities whereby wives and mothers represented their absent male relatives in a variety of legal and business transactions.

The maritime economy upon which the war economy came to be superimposed was, to use Olwen Hufton's term, an "economy of makeshift."

---

[6] I am unaware of any mortality figures for London sailors for the early eighteenth century. But for the appalling death rate among Dutch East India Company sailors at the same time see Jan de Vries, *European Urbanization, 1500–1800* (Cambridge, MA: Harvard University Press, 1984), 210.

[7] Peter Earle, "The Female Labour Market in London in the Late Seventeenth and Early Eighteenth Centuries," *Economic History Review*, 2nd ser., 42 (1989), 328–53; Judith M. Bennett, "History That Stands Still: Women's Work in the European Past," *Feminist Studies*, 14 (1988), 269–83. See also Margaret R. Hunt, *The Middling Sort: Commerce, Gender and the Family in England* (Berkeley and Los Angeles: University of California Press, 1996), 73–100, 125–46; and Ruth Wallis Herndon, "The Domestic Cost of Seafaring: Town Leaders and Seamen's Families in Eighteenth-Century Rhode Island." in Margaret S. Creighton and Lisa Norling, eds., *Iron Men, Wooden Women: Gender and Seafaring in the Atlantic World, 1700–1920* (Baltimore: The Johns Hopkins University Press, 1996), 55–69.

Let us look at a fairly typical case from the London court of Exchequer, a
court that attracted a good many sailors and sailors' families as litigants in
the 1690s and early 1700s, to see how this "economy" worked. James Paine
was a sailor who, on or around June of 1704, went as a carpenter's mate on
a voyage to the West Indies, leaving his wife, Martha, with no money, and
pregnant with their second child. Sadly, within the year Martha Paine was
dead, having succumbed to the after-effects of childbirth. In the months
before Martha's death, she and her sister, Mary Lloyd, who had moved in to
help with expenses, stayed afloat by taking in a paying lodger and a "nurse
child," and by swapping, pawning, and selling Martha's clothes and household goods.[8] We know a good deal about the disposition of these goods,
because when John Paine returned he sued his sister-in-law, Mary Lloyd,
for the return of a down bed, a sheet, a brass kettle, Martha's wedding ring,
"a fine broadcloth petticoat," and all his dead wife's other wearing apparel
and linen to the value (he claimed) of £50 or more. Lloyd's answer to these
charges reveals much about this women's economy of lending, borrowing,
distraining,[9] and rewarding. Some of the furniture was seized for the rent
by the landlord. A few things of little value were given to a female relation
"who had watched and been at great pains with [Martha] in the time of
her illness." In an affecting deathbed scene (at least as reported by Mary
Lloyd) Martha conferred the broadcloth petticoat on Mary herself, declar-
ing, before several witnesses, that "she [Martha] had nothing else worth
[Mary's] acceptance and . . . she gave [it] to [Mary] as an acknowledgment for some part of [her] kindnesses to her . . ." According to Mary,
Martha Paine never had a wedding ring of her own but "borrowed a ring
for that purpose of one Mr. Lang's Daughter." The missing sheet had actually belonged to Mary Lloyd's then master (she had, by this time, taken on
a paying job) and she took it off her own bed and lent it to her sick sister
because "[at] the laying in of the Child on which [Martha] died [she] had
but one sorry old sheet on her bed."[10]

Over the course of the second half of the seventeenth century this economy of makeshift, of scarce money, and of none-too-reliable men became
thoroughly enmeshed within a larger system, that of the Royal Navy, also
accustomed to makeshift, chronically short of cash, and dependent on
none-too-reliable MPs to vote each new supply. This hybrid system came

[8] See Beverly Lemire, "Consumerism in Pre-Industrial and Early Industrial England: The Trade in
Second Hand Clothes," *Journal of British Studies*, 27 (1988), 1–24.
[9] "Distraining" refers to seizures of goods for unpaid debts.
[10] E 112/826 Suits No. 1355 (Paine v. Lloyd) and 1356 (Lloyd v. Paine).

clearly into view after 1688 (though many of its elements were certainly much older), and because little is known about it, and it has such important implications for women, it is worth examining in some detail. At its heart was the institution of the pay ticket. During the Nine Years War (1689–97), and the War of Spanish Succession (1702–12), and indeed for many years after that, the navy experienced great difficulty in paying sailors in a timely manner. Though ships' pay, bonuses, and prize money could be substantial, sailors or their kinfolk routinely waited months or years to extract it from the navy – and private owners and large trading companies, such as the East India Company, seem to have been only a little better. In lieu of the money, the navy was in the habit of issuing numbered paper instruments that guaranteed sailors or their assignees (in the case of minors or apprentices, this was either their parent or master) payment at some generally unspecified future time. The ticket system required that sailors and their kin shoulder the burden of supporting themselves while waiting for the navy to get around to paying its bills. In practice this meant that men lived off their wives, mothers, sisters, lovers, and landladies between wage payouts or voyages, and, as a quid pro quo, authorized the women, through the power of attorney, to collect a percentage of their pay once they had shipped out.

The system also relied heavily upon professional and semi-professional discounters and moneylenders, many of them also women, to supply men and their families with cash and credit for day-to-day living expenses. In return these moneylenders accepted pawns of household goods, gained the right to all or a portion of a particular sailor's wage when it was actually paid, and, of course, pocketed hefty – some might say cut-throat – commissions for shouldering the financial risk. Those women and men who set up in or drifted into moneylending had, if they hoped to be successful, to have good contacts in the navy, in the great merchant companies, and among private shipowners so that they could be informed about when payouts were going to occur. They had to be prepared to wait through the long lines and bureaucratic delays at the pay tables, or to pay some other relatively trustworthy person to do it for them. They needed to be literate and to understand legal forms and bureaucratic procedures well enough to explain them to their often unlettered clients. They had to know their rights and be willing to insist upon them when there were problems with the papers, as it seems there often were. They needed to be alert to the venality that could sprout even amidst apparently close-knit families and friendship networks. And finally, as the load of pay ticket-related court cases in Exchequer, Chancery, and other legal venues shows, it was desirable that they have some experience with the courts and litigation. This was not a calling for the faint of heart.

When it could the navy preferred to ally with women rather than antagonize them. However, it was quite ambivalent about their involvement in ticket discounting. On the one hand, the navy saw it as being in its interest to ensure that women (especially mothers and wives) received some of the pay due to sailors. The reason for this was that the navy command believed women played an important role in persuading men to volunteer and dissuading them from deserting. It did not escape the commissioners that, if women benefited materially from the shipboard labors of their sons, husbands, and lovers (and stood to lose if their male relatives deserted and their pay was stopped), they were much more likely to apply pressure to keep them on board, and somewhat *less* likely to help them evade impressment or to harbor them if they deserted. This is why the navy positively encouraged men to allocate part (albeit a small part) of their pay to women on shore, and at times even sought to require it statutorily. Almost every new policy or proposal developed in the first half of the eighteenth century to cope with the chronic manpower shortage included some method of winning over female relatives. Thus in 1705 Peregrine Osborne proposed, "for the encouragement of their wives and children to persuade [men] to [volunteer]," that licenses for alehouses and coffee houses should go only to the widows of volunteers, volunteers disabled in service, or their wives and children. A proposal from 1709 put the issue in far starker terms. The author thought that women would be "persuaded cheerfully . . . to part from their husbands . . . and [to] encourage them to enter into the [navy], since [if his proposals for a new series of rewards for widows was to be adopted] there is such care taken of them [the wives], whether their husbands live or die . . ."[11] An act of 1728 which provided that a dead sailor's executors should be allowed immediately to receive the wages due on his ticket "without staying for the return of the ship or her general pay[out]" was actually referred to as "the Act for the encouragement of seamen to enter into His Majesty's service and to engage their wives and relations to persuade them to serve his Majesty at sea."[12]

However, there was also a good deal of public outcry – with which the navy, at least outwardly, concurred – about exploitative ticket discounters,

---

[11] J. S. Bromley, ed., *The Manning of the Royal Navy: Selected Public Pamphlets 1693–1873*, Publications of the Navy Records Society, 119 (London: Navy Records Society, 1974), 64. The proposer was a Reverend John Swanne.

[12] Ibid., 186.

often represented as female. Far and away the most common stock villain was the "wheedling landlady," said to take advantage of broke or sick sailors by extracting pay authorizations and powers of attorney from them and charging them swingeing rates to cash in their tickets. In practice, though, the navy leaned heavily upon these same landladies to provide primary medical care for the sick and injured; there were even official contracts and pay arrangements with many of them. The navy also knew that there was considerable overlap between "wives and relations," "wheedling landladies," and ticket discounters (many of these women fit all three categories) and it even went so far as to encourage some women to get into high-interest ticket discounting. The ticket office records for 1683 contain a petition addressed to the king and forwarded on to the Navy Board, from a widow, Jane Smith, claiming that she had been authorized, on account of her father and other relatives having been "great sufferers for your Gracious Father of blessed memory [Charles I]," to lend money on tickets at the rate of 12s. in the pound (a 60 percent interest rate). In fact, the purpose of Smith's letter is to complain that the navy ticket office clerk is soliciting people to sell *him* their tickets at a lower rate (a mere 40 percent) and thus undercutting her business "to the utter ruine," as she writes, "of yo[r] petitioner's Children . . ."[13] In fact, navy officialdom knew perfectly well that there had to be mechanisms in place to compensate for their own protracted pay timetables, so they both winked at discounters in their own ranks (there are repeated complaints of kickbacks and out and out solicitations by the clerks) and – if Widow Smith is any indication – actually went so far as to incorporate discounting into their byzantine system of social welfare for "deserving" navy widows.

Let us look at some of these ticket discounters at work, beginning with one Mary Herring of St. Paul Shadwell, wife of a surgeon-apothecary. In 1717 John and Avelling Hamilton of Stepney sued Mary Herring and two other women, charging that they had conspired to cheat the plaintiffs of their right to a certain sailor's pay.[14] Apparently when the ship's payout was announced both John Hamilton and Mary Herring (through her "agent," one Jane Cousins) presented competing pay authorizations to the naval pay officer, who, unsure of who was in the right, stopped payment on the tickets. The next day, however, the "agent," Jane Cousins, succeeded in persuading the pay officer to pay the money to her, because she held the instrument with the earliest date on it. Thus thwarted, the Hamiltons

[13] ADM 106/3540 Pt. 2. Brown folder marked "Petitions (Various)." Unfoliated.

[14] E 112/980 Suit No. 308 (John Hamilton and Avelling his wife v. Andrew Herring, [Mary, his wife], Jane Cousins, and Mary Holladay), 1717. The sailor was Thomas Holladay, formerly of the navy ship *Warwick*.

became convinced that Mary Herring had bribed the sailor's wife, one Mary Holladay, to give her a fraudulently back-dated pay authorization. For their part the defendants sought to establish that all had been business as usual. Mary Herring's husband, Andrew, testified that his wife "[did] frequently lend seamen money upon their wages" and also emphasized that he "left the whole management" of the moneylending business to her while "minding his own business as a surgeon" (Mary Herring was what was known as a "feme sole" trader, meaning that she carried on a business entirely independently of her husband).[15] Co-defendant Jane Cousins stated that she was employed by Mary Herring to "apply at the pay table to receive what wages was due" and that Herring had paid her a shilling in the pound "for her trouble & attendance in receiving the [money] as is usual in the like cases." And Mary Holladay, wife of the sailor whose pay everyone was fighting about, testified that Mary Herring had presented her with a properly dated assignment of pay, signed and sealed by Thomas Holladay, her husband, and had "required that she [the wife] should Impower [Herring] to receive the wages of her said husband," whereupon Holladay had delivered over to Mary Herring the power of attorney and received back her (now much-reduced) share of the money.[16]

Mary Herring and others like her clearly spent a good deal of time managing the kinship and neighborhood networks through which resources flowed. But their most important asset was their expertise in dealing with shipowners and the navy. The high value attached to an ability to navigate the shoals of the navy bureaucracy is shown in a suit from 1703 or 1704 brought against Margaret Stewart of the parish of St. John Wapping. There Stewart is described as "exercis[ing] the employ of a Solicitrix for Seamen in helping them to sell their Tickets and to receive the[ir pay] from the Treasurer or paymaster of her Majesty's Navy."[17] The records make it clear that Stewart was involved in a wide range of activities, from buying and selling pay tickets and keeping track of ships' payouts to representing sailors who had specific grievances with the Navy Office, where she is said to have "had good interest" (i.e., good connections and some influence). In this particular case Stewart was accused of obtaining various powers of attorney, pay tickets, and other financial documents from another woman, Margaret Brandon, on the pretense that "the ships from which the said tickets were due were paying off" and if "immediate care and attendance

[15] For more on the institution of the feme sole trader see Hunt, *Middling Sort*, 138–41, 269n.

[16] Most of these cases (including this one) were settled out of court, so the outcome is unknown.

[17] For another "female solicitor" from the same period see Wilfred Prest, "'One Hawkins, A Female Sollicitor': Women Lawyers in Augustan England," *Huntington Library Quarterly*, 57 (1994), 353–8.

was not given" Brandon would miss the call and the pay tickets would be past and unredeemable. Stewart also worked closely with a pawnbroker named Ann Robinson, who in turn (like Mary Herring) employed her own women "agents" to attend payouts.[18]

We are accustomed to thinking of the job of solicitor as a male monopoly.[19] Yet there is not the slightest hint here that it was considered at all unusual for a woman to represent men's and other women's interests with the Navy Office. Indeed, a perusal of other records of this sort conveys the distinct impression that dealing with importunate women – who were also often both knowledgeable and experienced at getting their way – was one of the central tasks of marine officialdom in this period.[20] Cases like this one give us a strong sense of the complexity and sophistication of these women's networks. Women brokered investments for each other (as Stewart had done with Brandon), they pawned valuables (including, very commonly, sailors' tickets) with other women and, as these cases show, they paid still other women (the "agents") to assist them in their work. Unusually, these women seem often to have been identified with their occupations (as the use of occupational terms such as "agent" or "solicitrix" clearly shows).[21] They also spent a significant proportion of their time working at these occupations, and knew themselves (and were acknowledged by others) to be offering an essential service within their communities. In effect they worked the interface between the fiscal-imperial state and the micro-economies of families and neighborhoods.

Whether they set up as "professional" discounters or not, it was very much to a woman's advantage to possess powers of attorney, authorizations, and pay tickets for more than one sailor. In its simple – and presumably original – form (one man/one ticket, with the man being a woman's husband or son) this arrangement contained real risks for the woman. It could mean disaster if the man in question died, abandoned her, revoked the power of attorney, or jumped ship – the last resulted in an immediate pay stoppage and forfeiture of arrears. The most obvious way to insure against this possibility was for women to spread out the risk by investing in pay tickets from several

[18] E 112/827 Suit No. 171 (Ann Brandon v. Mary Stewart, John Stewart, George Hopper, Anne, his wife [this was the former Ann Robinson, the pawnbroker], et al.), c. 1705.
[19] Solicitors often gained their training in fairly informal ways in the late seventeenth and early eighteenth century, which partly explains why a woman could become identified with this profession.
[20] The records of the High Court of Admiralty are extremely revealing on this point.
[21] Women were generally identified by their marital status rather than their occupation. On this see especially Michael Roberts, "'Words They Are Women, and Deeds They Are Men': Images of Work and Gender in Early Modern England," in Lindsey Charles and Lorna Duffin, eds., *Women and Work in Preindustrial England* (London: Croom Helm, 1985), 122–80.

men. Because prospective investors could "split" the pay authorizations ("buying" authorizations for, say, one or two months out of the total amount of a particular sailor's anticipated pay), women with only scant assets could still obtain them. So could those with no tangible assets at all. Undoubtedly many women's main capital was (to invoke Pierre Bourdieu's term) symbolic capital, that is, their sexuality or their ability to draw one or more men into a relationship of felt obligation to them or their children. Some "powers" and pay authorizations were presumably issued by men in return for women keeping company and having sex with them, or bearing their bastards, and because the origins of the pay authorization system lay in the notion of providing support to mothers and wives, we may surmise that transactions involving pay tickets were often overlain with much emotional complexity.

We might naturally ask what impact, if any, this system had on, first, the prevalence of female-headed households in maritime communities, and, second, illegitimacy rates. Unfortunately it is very hard to tell. We do know that female-headed households tended to be most common in poorer urban neighborhoods (over 20 percent in some locales by the early eighteenth century) and that, in the case of London, poorer neighborhoods were often those where significant numbers of sailors lived – but the direction of causality is uncertain. The evidence of illegitimacy rates is similarly equivocal: the latest figures for late seventeenth-century London suggest that illegitimacy was, overall, less common there than in many rural areas.[22] Against that, however, we must set the belief of contemporaries that sexual monogamy tended to be honored less in maritime communities than elsewhere, as well as episodic evidence from local consistory court and parish registers that sailors and their kin operated according to somewhat unorthodox sexual and marital norms.[23] If this really was the case, the pay ticket system may conceivably have encouraged such behaviors, though it certainly did not cause them.

However, even if all the social ramifications of the ticket system cannot be known, its net effect was quite clear: it made women in seafaring communities look less like female dependants and more like independent actors making (or attempting to make) diversified investments in a financial and sexual marketplace. Exchequer and Chancery cases as well as navy ticket office records from the period show that many women possessed dozens of these instruments, and that pay authorizations and powers of attorney were

[22] Richard Adair, *Courtship, Illegitimacy and Marriage in Early Modern England* (Manchester and New York: Manchester University Press, 1996), 202–23.
[23] Ibid., 218, 220.

routinely bought, sold, swapped, transferred, and pawned within neighbor-hood and friendship networks, becoming a form of circulating currency (albeit a somewhat cumbersome one) in these communities, just as clothes and other household goods had done. Most early modern and modern societies took – and take – steps to discourage women from diversifying in this way, by tying them legally and economically to one man by way of marriage, by keeping women's pay-scales very low, and by giving most financial decision-making to men. In seventeenth- and eighteenth-century maritime communities a disproportionate share of the total wealth was still initially generated by men in the form of ships' pay. However, men had considerably less than total control of the ultimate disposition of the funds since they tended to be away for such extended periods. What makes this period most interesting though (for surely some variation of this pattern had long obtained in maritime communities) is the fact that, amid the greatest naval buildup ever seen in England up to that time, women's desire to maximize their chances harmonized so readily both with the navy's desire to win women to their side, and (surely inadvertently) with the central mechanism of deferred payment, the pay ticket.

The benefits for women of this unexpected – and always partial – alliance of interests with the expanding fiscal-military state should not be exagger-ated. Individual female ticket discounters may well have made a good deal of money. Mistresses lucky enough to have a male servant could, under the right circumstances, realize a substantial proportion of their dependant's relatively paltry navy wages. But at the end of this long train of tickets, powers, authorizations, discounters, and standing in queues at the pawn-broker or the pay table, most women realized a pathetically small sum of money for their pains – though it was clearly important to them. In gender terms seafaring culture gave with one hand and took away with the other. It was unusually hospitable to strong women. But it offered men relatively few incentives to make long-term commitments to women or families. In fact, the shipboard emphasis on fraternity and autonomy from family ties[24] positively encouraged sailors to indulge in a good deal of irresponsi-ble leisure expenditure in the taverns, flop-houses, and brothels of seaport towns. Moreover men (or at least men who had reached the age of majority) could always revoke the power of attorney, or muddy the waters by issuing more than one power or pay authorization for the same money. There were a seemingly infinite number of ways for mariners to escape their financial responsibilities to the women in their lives.

---

[24] See Herndon, "Domestic Cost of Seafaring," 57, 69.

Still, one of the more interesting aspects of this system was the navy's as well as the courts' willingness, at least on occasion, to assist women in making financial claims against their husbands and other men. In the case of a wife (though not a mother, sister, or other unrelated person) the law offered some recourse if a mariner, say, revoked his wife's power of attorney: she could sue him (or have her relatives sue him) for maintenance. In practice, as we have seen, most wives expected to bring in some of the family income; in a pinch, all of it. None the less, for an absent husband willfully to remove his wife's right to represent him, with all the financial inconveniences that implied, could be a bitter pill indeed, and not every woman was prepared to tolerate it. Thus in 1716, Mary Duncan of Stepney, mother of three, went to collect the pay from two navy ships on which her husband, William, had served only to discover, to her "great surprise," that William, by then en route to the West Indies, had canceled her power of attorney. Apparently her husband was in debt to one Thomas Steer, and so transferred the "power" and pay authorization to him, leaving Mary and the children – literally – out in the cold. Mary Duncan's suit in Exchequer that same year charged William Duncan and Thomas Steer with intent "to impoverish and bring her and her poor family to utter ruin,"[25] and argued that this was all the more unjust because she had (she claimed) impoverished herself "fitting out her said husband to [go to] sea."

Other women whose husbands (or other men) failed to fulfill their responsibilities bypassed the court and went straight for the navy ticket office. Women were perpetually appealing to the navy commissioners and the ticket office to stop payment on tickets for male apprentices who had fled town (the money legally belonged to their mistresses), or men who had sold them tickets, or swapped them for services, then maneuvered to have the money for themselves. Mothers petitioned the board *not* to stop payment on their sons who had overstayed shore leave, and there are large numbers of petitions from women asking to be paid in advance of other ticket holders, because of their desperate financial straits. Here we also find wives of irresponsible or abusive men petitioning to have the money paid to them and not directly to their husbands. Thus in 1684 Ann Downe, wife of a navy shipyard worker, complained that her husband, Thomas, "being given to ill Husbandry . . . will assuredly Consume [his pay] in Extravagent Expense & Paying Ale-house Scores, and neither pay the land-lord (Soe as

[25] E 112/980 Suit 303 (Duncan v. Duncan), 1716. In equity, unlike the common law courts, women were permitted to sue their husbands, though they generally did so through a proxy, the so-called "procheine amy." Thus this case is listed as "Mary Duncan and Thomas Bowley, procheine amy, v. William Duncan and Thomas Steer."

to Keepe a house over ye head of his wife & foure small Children) nor pay the Creditters – that have furnished them with foode to Sustaine life whilst this little money hath been earning," and asked that the money be given to her or to one of her creditors directly.[26] In 1677 another enterprising woman, Hannah Roomcoyle, wife of one Captain Thomas Roomcoyle, appealed to an even higher authority, petitioning the Admiralty Commission – and King Charles II who was then sitting in on the meetings – "pretending ill usage from her husband and thereupon petitioning that, living separate from her husband, his Majesty would be pleased to oblige him out of his wages to allow her some annual support."[27] Charles actually intervened in the case to attempt some marriage counseling – which, however, proved unsuccessful. In the end Hannah Roomcoyle won her separate maintenance agreement.

It is always difficult to date the onset of notions of entitlement, still less that of "rights." There was a longstanding presumption within English law that when wives bestowed on their husbands an exclusive right to their obedience, their labor, and their reproductive powers, they might expect to receive in return a guarantee of basic maintenance. And, while this principle derived more from a desire on the part of rate payers to avoid supporting other men's wives and children than from any solicitude for the rights of women, it still had real cultural weight. As these cases show, the navy, as well as *some* courts, moved into the business of enforcing some women's right to maintenance in the seventeenth century, and one apparent result (presumably not one either the navy or the courts intended) was to undermine *some* of the more extreme manifestations of patriarchal authority. Rights are not worth much when they cannot be defended; conversely people often start to claim "rights" when some avenue of appeal exists to make them "real." It may well have been that the existence of newly codified and regularized avenues of appeal in both the courts and the military bureaucracy bolstered some women's confidence in their ability both to be rights bearers and to act as rights defenders.

But one gains the impression from reading the navy material, in particular, that more was at work than simply the presence of new forums in which to fight for married women's customary entitlements. War has often acted as a catalyst for expanding notions of rights. Linda Colley, Kathleen Wilson,

[26] ADM 106/3540 Pt. 2. Brown folder marked "Petitions (Various)."
[27] J. R. Tanner, ed., *A Descriptive Catalogue of the Naval Manuscripts in the Pepysian Library at Magdalene College, Cambridge*, Publications of the Navy Records Society, 57 (London: Navy Records Society, 1923), 524, 526 (Petition of November 10, 1677). Thanks to Peter Le Fevre for revealing the end of the story.

and others have emphasized the ways in which the eighteenth- and early nineteenth-century wars encouraged new groups including artisanal and middling men, and, on occasion, women, to symbolically "join" the political nation through parades, electioneering, fund-raising, and enthusiasm for British territorial expansion.[28] New and evolving notions of citizenship and rights run through their accounts, among them the right to parliamentary representation, a free press, and freedom of association – though Wilson, especially, also finds goodly amounts of xenophobia and efforts on the part of some to keep real power in the hands of small groups of relatively prosperous white men.

Important as these evolving "rights" were and are, they are fundamentally political in conception. The heavy demands – in terms of blasted lives, crippling taxes, consumer dearth, the ruination of trade, and lengthy arrears of pay – that early modern wars placed upon both combatants and civilians also gave rise to other kinds of demands and a different species of empowerment. The navy wives and mothers who afflicted Samuel Pepys's conscience in 1666 were not the first to conclude that the sacrifices they and their menfolk had made entitled them to a better deal in material terms from the government than they were getting. Moreover, as virtually every recent study of women and the rise of the welfare state has shown, they would not be the last.[29]

In fact, the vociferous engagement of women with the fiscal-military bureaucracy – increasingly seen by John Brewer and others as the main engine of the evolving modern state – belies the claim that the state was, or was becoming, a male-only event.[30] Instead it marks the beginning of a long dialog between some groups of women and the state that continues to this day, and that has had the utmost importance in defining modern conceptions of entitlement, resource allocation, sacrifice, and gendered citizenship within the imperial nation.

A central (if often unstated) plank of older conceptions of the modernizing state is the claim that, whereas men learned, somewhere around the time of John Locke (or for the more humble, around the time of the French Revolution), to join together to defend common "rights" (in the process

[28] Linda Colley, *Britons: Forging the Nation, 1707–1837* (New Haven: Yale University Press, 1992); Kathleen Wilson, *The Sense of the People: Politics, Culture and Imperialism in England, 1715–1785* (Cambridge University Press, 1995).
[29] Theda Skocpol, *Protecting Soldiers and Mothers: The Political Origins of Social Policy in the United States* (Cambridge, MA: Belknap Press of Harvard University Press, 1992); Anna Davin, "Imperialism and Motherhood," *History Workshop Journal*, 5 (1978), 9–63.
[30] John Brewer, *The Sinews of Power: War, Money and the English State, 1688–1783* (New York: Alfred A. Knopf, 1989).

creating "politics" and the "modern political subject"), women, "confined to the home," or at least to a neighborhood, were too cowed and isolated from one another to do anything of the sort. What then are we to make of the copious evidence of late seventeenth- and eighteenth-century English-women joining together in collectivities of various sorts in an attempt to bend the navy – and, as we will see, other large corporate entities – to their will? Certainly it is true that the navy sources do not support facile notions of "sisterhood" any more than most male groupings (except for rhetorical purposes) do notions of "brotherhood." They contain far too much evidence of women defrauding or exploiting each other, denouncing friends and even relatives to the Navy Board, and pursuing their own or their immediate family's interests at everyone else's expense. On the other hand, there is a good deal of evidence in both the navy and legal records that women from seafaring communities were very conscious of the benefits of collective action, and that, when they had to, they knew perfectly well how to engage in it.

An especially suggestive example of this is women's growing involvement in parliamentary lobbying from the 1690s on. The central reason why the Royal Navy was so often in arrears was that it had to depend upon Parliament to vote the money. As a result, sailors and their female kin were often drawn into campaigns – ranging from clubbing together to employ a paid lobbyist to staging loud demonstrations – intended to encourage the government to do its duty by the people who fought its wars, whether aboard ship or at home. Probably fairly typical of the former group was Sarah Hill, a woman named as defendant in a case brought in Exchequer in 1714. Hill, a navy widow, probably of "middling" status, was owed in excess of £500 by the navy for service rendered by her late husband. She was sued by her parliamentary lobbyist, one Jones, because she refused to pay him 5 shillings in the pound for every pound he recovered for her through "agitating" in Parliament. In her response to his complaint she accused him of gradually upping his rate by "pretending others had done the same" (that is, others in the loose grouping that had hired him) and finally of taking advantage of her advanced age and infirmities (she claimed to be "very Ancient near eighty years of age") to fraudulently insert 5s. in the pound into the contract instead of the 2s. 6d. upon which the two had agreed verbally.[31]

Less genteel efforts to influence Parliament came in the form of noisy demonstrations by distressed navy wives and widows. During some of the

---

[31] E 112/980 Suit No. 275 (Jones v. Hill), 1714.

early eighteenth-century debates about navy pay protocols, groups of "old women" took to hanging about Parliament and, "grown peevish by old Age and want of food" (as one sympathetic broadside had it), began "foolishly abus[ing] . . . such Members . . . as are the Commissioners of the Admiralty, Navy or Victualling, imagining them the Causes of their misfortune."[32] This writer attributed their actions to a combination of "Feminine Imprudence" and desperate want, and it is clear that demonstrations like these formed part of larger public relations campaigns that may or may not have been initiated by the women themselves. But though the context is cloudy, it is unlikely that such women were as naive as some contemporaries felt compelled to claim. Sarah Hill and the poor navy wives and widows had behind them a lifetime of dealing with the military bureaucracy. It is not surprising that they would attempt to seize an instrumental role with respect to the central political institution of the land.[33]

This chapter began with women mobbing the Navy Office during the Second Anglo-Dutch War. I want to end with a spectacular case (actually a series of cases) that commenced early in the reign of William and Mary and lasted well into the reign of Anne. The issue was a familiar one – non-payment of sailor's wages – but this time the culprit was the East India Company rather than the navy. The story is as follows: in March of 1692 an East India Company ship, the *Modena*, went down in a hurricane with all hands aboard. When news of the tragedy reached London a massive effort got underway to try to identify the ship's shareholders and get them to pay out the back wages of the drowned men to their surviving relatives. The ship's shareholders included Sir Josiah Child, former chairman of the East India Company, George Bohun, Sir Thomas Grantham, Sir Samuel Dashwood, and several other well-known City personages. For the most part these were extremely rich and certainly very powerful men; however, they had already suffered a significant loss in the *Modena*, so they balked and stalled over paying.

During the next fifteen years the affair was fought out over at least three different court jurisdictions. The precise terms of the dispute are not easy to reconstruct from the surviving records, but the level of indignation the whole affair stirred up on the part of the relatives is plain to see. Incensed

---

[32] *The Objections against Taking Off the Q's and R's from the Sailors Fully Answered*. London: broadside, early eighteenth century (copy in London Guildhall Library).

[33] Parliamentary lobbying by navy widows was so common that it became a fertile area for graft, as is shown by several cases of men defrauding navy widows of money by claiming to be engaged in lobbying Parliament for early payment of navy arrears. See e.g., ADM 1/5115/1 Accounts and Papers relating to the Widows Charity, 1733–44 for an elaborate scam perpetrated by one David Scott in 1742 on at least six navy widows.

and grieving mothers and widows brought actions for debt at Queen's Bench, and succeeded in having some of the owners arrested for debt. The shareholders retaliated with countersuits. In one Exchequer case Sir Thomas Grantham tried to claim that it was customary for the men to be paid their wages on board and that, with the ship lost, no records could be recovered to say what, in fact, had been paid out. To this the defendants, all of them mothers, sisters, or wives of *Modena* sailors, retorted tartly that they had their wage authorizations and that there was no custom, when ships went down, that the seamen's wives stopped receiving the wages.[34] After years of litigation the women won the case in Admiralty Court, but the shareholders continued to pull strings to evade actual payment. One of several petitions to the latter court came in 1706 from "Sarah Christie, Jane Logan, Catherine Petill, Elizabeth Anderson, Sarah Adie, Grissill Adie, Ann Creswell and about seventy more[,] most of whom are poor Widows whose husbands were lost in the ship Modena . . ." objecting to a delay in filing papers by Sir Richard Child (Sir Robert Child's son and executor), and complaining that the petitioners were thereby kept from receiving their just due "which by reason of their poverty they are in great want of."[35] Another from 1707 on behalf of "several . . . poor widows whose husbands was [*sic*] cast away and destroyed in the good ship Modena" complained that the petitioners "have just reason to believe that their proctor, Mr. Sears, has an understanding with the owners" and was colluding with them to avoid payment and pervert the course of justice. The petition finished by urging that the court "in pity and justice to the poor widows and fatherless children would be pleased to examine thoroughly into their just cause to the end they may immediately obtain justice otherwise they and their poor families must inevitably perish."[36]

CONCLUSION

The affair of the *Modena* (whose final outcome I have so far been unable to discover) was unusually dramatic but, as I have shown, it was hardly unique.[37] These women's strong sense of distributive justice sprang from lifetimes of wheeling and dealing, working bureaucracies, going to court

[34] E 112/826 Suit No. 133 (Thomas Grantham v. Martha Knowles, Christian Addey, and Martha Standard alias Knott.), 1703.
[35] HCA 15/31 (Instance Papers, 1700–17, K-O), Petition of November 21, 1706.
[36] Ibid., Petition of July 7, 1707. The proctor was responsible for steering other lawyers' cases through the court.
[37] See e.g., cases involving the following ships: the *William* and *Sheppa* (1704), the *Good Hope* (1704), the *Hawke* (1705), and the *Victory* (1716), all in HCA 3/63.

and fighting for their right to pay and other material benefits against other women as well as against men and male institutions. Undeniably the evolving relationship between women and the fiscal-imperial complex of the late seventeenth and early eighteenth century had its pathological side. The delayed payment schemes by which most early modern naval wars were fought were policies carried out on the backs of those least able to resist. Men on board were at least fed and clothed, albeit poorly; there were no such benefits for their kin. Scams, rip-offs by weak people against even weaker people, betrayal of friends and family members for sometimes pathetic sums of money, semi-institutionalized extortion (like the ticket discounting system): all these testify to families and communities pushed to the limit by forces that were often completely beyond their control. On the other hand the system was clearly empowering for at least some of the people in it. Many of these women did learn the ways of large state bureaucracies, becoming among the earliest Europeans to do so. At least some carved out occupations, bodies of expertise, and even substantial incomes for themselves in the process. Exploitative as it was, the discounting system at least kept the money within the community, and, at least some of the time, in the hands of women.

Histories of women and the military often stress the way the routinizing and professionalizing of national armies and navies in the course of the eighteenth and nineteenth centuries tended to exclude women, whether the old style camp follower or the woman sailor. This chapter takes a different tack. The Royal Navy in the late seventeenth and eighteenth century saw no reason to reform longstanding practices within maritime communities that gave women considerable economic authority; indeed it sought to cooperate with them and even to turn them to its own ends. It seems that the navy, far from excluding women, came to see certain advantages to forging a rough and ready alliance with them in order to get the job done. The evidence suggests that, to be successful, expansionist states have, in some way, to enlist *both* women and men in the costly enterprise of warfare, and that, in the case of England, this can be seen almost from the beginning of the early modern imperial project.

But it could also be said that these women met the navy halfway. Over time they developed a new understanding of the relationship between that state and their communities, a body of practical knowledge about how bureaucracies worked, and a rhetorical style that aided them in extracting at least some of the benefits to which they believed themselves entitled. As one broadside of the period evocatively put it, the women and children of naval officers were "always ready and willing to hazard their lives in the Service of their King and Country."[38] By eliding the sacrifices made by women and children with those of men in battle, these and other productions honored the real-life struggles of the people left at home while British war and merchant ships expanded the boundaries of the empire – and then went on to demand justice from the state on that basis.

The sheer scale of the late seventeenth- and early eighteenth-century naval buildup, along with the exigencies of war, forced large numbers of poor to middling women to deal in new ways with the navy bureaucracy, the East India Company, and Parliament. Clearly passivity was not what these women were about. Just as clearly they were not free agents in a laissez-faire universe of pure choices. For most of them the state and its foreign wars were a source of disruption and economic and personal hardship. The privations they suffered were chosen neither by them *nor* by their male relatives. On the other hand, the ways in which they came to terms with a changed environment are of the utmost importance for the early history of both the modern British military and the modern welfare state. These women and their children were on the front line of the empire, though most of them never left England's shores.

---

[38] *The Case of the Distressed Widows of the Commission and Warrant Officers of the Royal Navy* (London, 1751). I am grateful to Kathleen Wilson for bringing this broadside to my attention.

CHAPTER 2

An "entertainment of oddities": fashionable sociability and the Pacific in the 1770s

Gillian Russell

The British encounter with the South Pacific that began with John Byron's expedition of 1764 and culminated in Cook's three voyages of 1768–71, 1772–5, and 1776–80 coincided with the tremendous expansion in the mechanisms and forums of publicity in metropolitan culture in this period. This accounts for the unprecedented scope of its impact in a variety of spheres: in voyage literature, newspapers, periodicals, drama, poetry, paintings, engravings, and aesthetic theory, as well as in the social and natural sciences and ethnology.[1] The voyages of Cook were "celebrated," in Glyndwr Williams's term, partly because of the new journals and newspapers and the recently opened venues for display and dissemination such as the British Museum and Sir Ashton Lever's Holosphusikon which facilitated that celebration.[2] In turn, the cultural phenomenon of the voyages shaped the discourses circulating within the sphere of publicity concerned with the intersections of luxury, gender, commerce, exoticism, civility, custom, and nature. It is not my intention, nor is it possible, to engage here with debates in relation to these discourses in eighteenth-century Pacific studies, which have been ably addressed by a number of scholars.[3] What I would like to address are the intersections between representations of the Pacific

---

[1] Glyndwr Williams, "The Pacific: Exploration and Exploitation," in P. J. Marshall, ed., *The Oxford History of the British Empire, Vol. II: The Eighteenth Century* (Oxford University Press, 1998), 552–75, at 564.

[2] Williams, "The Pacific," 555.

[3] Bernard Smith, *European Vision and the South Pacific*, 2nd edn. (New Haven: Yale University Press, 1985) and *Imagining the Pacific: In the Wake of the Cook Voyages* (New Haven: Yale University Press, 1992); Greg Dening, *Mr. Bligh's Bad Language: Passion, Power and Theatre on the Bounty* (Cambridge University Press, 1992); Harriet Guest, "The Great Distinction: Figures of the Exotic in the Work of William Hodges," *The Oxford Art Journal*, 12 (1989), 36–58; Harriet Guest, "Curiously Marked: Tattooing, Masculinity, and Nationality in Eighteenth-Century British Perceptions of the South Pacific," in John Barrell, ed., *Painting and the Politics of Culture: New Essays in British Art, 1700–1850*, (Oxford University Press, 1992), 101–34; Nicholas Thomas, *Entangled Objects: Exchange, Material Culture, and Colonialism in the Pacific* (Cambridge, MA: Harvard University Press, 1991); Neil Rennie, *Far-Fetched Facts: The Literature of Travel and the Idea of the South Seas* (Oxford: Clarendon Press, 1995).

48

and fashionable sociability in the 1770s. In an attempt to contribute to the reconfiguration of imperial history in this volume as a whole, this chapter argues that the sociability of the female elite played a key part in the formation and reception of unstable imperial discourses in this decade. It introduces sociability as an analytical category to imperial history, and ultimately suggests a new perspective on the role that the Pacific continues to play within eighteenth-century studies.

The term "fashionable sociability" is derived from Peter Clark's *British Clubs and Societies 1580–1800: The Origins of an Associational World*. Clark describes an "intricate tessellation" of social activity in Georgian Britain of which he distinguishes three broad categories: the "private" sociability of the home, where "the greatest volume of social contact took place"; an "old-style" sociability based around the church, Parliament, the court, and the street; and a "new-style" sociability engendered by the commercialization of culture in venues such as the coffee house, the inn, the tavern, the alehouse, the proliferation of forms of voluntary association, theatres, pleasure-gardens, dancing assemblies, and so on.[4] Within this last category Clark notes but does not substantively analyze distinct gender differences between what he calls "fashionable sociability" "influenced by sensibility and the public presence of women" and the sociability of the club, coffee house, and tavern, which was strongly identified with male homosociality. A significant figure in the development of fashionable sociability was Teresa Cornelys, an Austro-Italian who in 1760 established Carlisle House in Soho Square in London as a meeting place for people of fashion.[5] She held balls and concerts there as well as reviving the masquerade. Her assembly, or "Society" as it was known, was run on the basis of private subscription under the auspices of a group of fashionable aristocratic women, a method which allowed Cornelys to avoid the scrutiny of the laws regulating entertainments that were open to the paying general public. However, to all intents and purposes Carlisle House was a commercial enterprise and Cornelys an entrepreneur in the business of pleasure. The founding of her "Society" in 1760 was a significant development in public culture because it represented a commodification of the sphere in which elite women exerted a powerful role – their own household. The development of Carlisle House, followed by Almack's assembly rooms (1765), the Ladies' Coterie (1770), and ultimately the Pantheon on Oxford Street (1772), together represented

---

[4] Peter Clark, *British Clubs and Societies 1580–1800: The Origins of an Associational World* (Oxford: Clarendon Press, 2000), 192, 39, 451.

[5] For a discussion of Cornelys and fashionable sociability in general see my *Schools for Scandal: Women, Sociability and Theatre in Late Eighteenth-Century Britain* (in progress).

an amplification of this sphere of influence for women, with far-reaching consequences for the male homosocial identity of the associational world described by Peter Clark. In this chapter I wish to discuss the relevance of these developments to the Pacific voyages, focusing firstly on the significance of the Pacific as a subject of talk in the context of the domiciliary sociability of women of fashion. (The term "domiciliary sociability" is designed to circumvent some of the connotations of "private" or "domestic." These gatherings were not necessarily intimate affairs nor were they cut off from the wider social world.) I then go on to analyze how the reconfiguration of the masculinist public sphere signified by a specific development of these years – the Ladies' Coterie of 1770 – both reflected on and was in turn mediated by some of the satiric poetry that emanated from Cook's voyages.

THE VOYAGERS AT HOME

After the return of the *Endeavour* to England in July 1771, Joseph Banks and Daniel Solander re-acculturated themselves to metropolitan life partly through the promotion and consolidation of the achievements of the voyage. The newspaper press was the main instrument of this: the *London Evening Post* reported on July 20–23 that "we learn by the Endeavour, from the South Seas, that they discovered a Southern Continent . . . From this voyage we expect many discoveries and much entertainment." Coverage of the return of Banks and Solander included reports of their reception by the king and queen at St. James's Palace and later Richmond. The *Public Advertiser* questioned the propriety of the royal couple being subjected to such an "entertainment" (implicitly questioning royal taste): "it is too great a Liberty to take with such sacred Characters, to suppose they would Day after Day stare at the Pictures of some useless Weeds, or gape over the Slippers and Habits of poor Savages, fit only to add to the like Curiosities at Don Saltaro's Coffee-house."[6] These encounters were described as "private" conferences as befitted the status of Banks and Solander as gentlemen rather than official servants of the crown, but descriptions of them in such terms also reflected an uncertainty as to the nature of George III's interest, something which the *Public Advertiser* clearly set out to exploit.[7] Was he responding to the *Endeavour* voyage as a private individual, motivated by curiosity, or as the King of England, interested in the progress of his empire? Were the interviews concerned with the pursuit of knowledge or the mutual "entertainment" of both parties?

---

[6] *Public Advertiser*, September 3, 1771.   [7] *Gentleman's Magazine*, August 1771, 375.

Elsewhere Banks moved in a variety of social circles, being confirmed as a member of the Royal Society Club, meeting Dr. Johnson (possibly for the first time), and relaxing at a house party at the country seat of his patron the Earl of Sandwich at Hinchinbrooke in Huntingdonshire.[8] It was on this occasion, as Frances Burney noted in her diary, that her father, Charles Burney, secured a place for his son James on the next voyage to the Pacific, an indication of the importance of such sociability in establishing and promoting patronage networks.[9] The social circuit of Banks and Solander in late 1771 also included women of fashion. Lady Mary Coke commented: "the people who are most talk'd of at present are Mr Banks & Doctor Solander: I saw them at Court & afterwards at Ly Hertford's, but did not hear them give any account of their Voyage round the world, which I am told is very amusing."[10] Another prominent woman to be entertained by Banks and Solander was Margaret Cavendish Bentinck, née Harley, the Duchess of Portland, "the paradigmatic aristocratic woman collector" of the period, according to Ann B. Shteir.[11] She followed the example of her father, whose Harleian collection of manuscripts was acquired for the British Museum in 1753, but her interests went beyond the family's focus on books and manuscripts to encompass shells, fossils and minerals, botanical specimens and exotic artifacts of all kinds, including birds and animals. In 1785 she became famous for her purchase of the Barberini Vase, subsequently known as the Portland Vase, from Sir William Hamilton. The duchess was an active botanist, often in collaboration with her close friend Mary Granville Pendarves Delany. Delany was herself notable as a botanical artist who specialized in intricate paper collages of flowers.[12] The Duchess of Portland had been an early sponsor of Daniel Solander's career in London, employing him to classify her natural history collection at her country seat of Bulstrode, and thereby encouraging the dissemination of the controversial principles of Linnaeus.[13] Her enthusiastic account of the flowering of one of the exotic plants brought back to England by the

---

[8] E. H. McCormick, *Omai: Pacific Envoy* (Auckland: Auckland University Press and Oxford University Press, 1977), 25–8.

[9] *The Early Diary of Frances Burney 1768–1778*, ed. Annie Raine Ellis (2 vols., repr. New York: Books for Libraries Press, 1971; first pub. 1889), I, 138–9.

[10] Lady Mary Coke, *Letters and Journals* (4 vols., Bath: Kingsmead Reprints, 1970; first pub. 1889–96), IV, 435.

[11] Ann B. Shteir, *Cultivating Women, Cultivating Science: Flora's Daughters and Botany in England, 1760–1860* (Baltimore: The Johns Hopkins University Press, 1996), 47.

[12] Shteir, *Cultivating Women*, 43–4.

[13] John Gascoigne, *Joseph Banks and the English Enlightenment: Useful Knowledge and Polite Culture* (Cambridge University Press, 1994).

voyagers, cited by Bernard Smith, testifies to her enduring interest in Banks's discoveries and continuing dialog with him.[14]

The duchess was one of the people with whom Banks consulted after his return from the South Seas in July 1771. In November Mary Delany informed Mrs. Port of Ilam that Banks and Solander were "preparing an account of their voyage," but that a separate "Natural History" was to be published and that Dr. John Hawkesworth had been engaged to write "the history." "As this was *private* talk," Delany added, "perhaps it should not be mentioned in general."[15] The letter also includes some gossipy news: an update on the health of the Princess of Wales, a contradiction of a newspaper report that Lord Villiers was to marry Lady Stanhope, and an account of the progress of the new Pantheon in Oxford Street – "I suppose Almack's and Soho must *hide their diminished heads*" (374) (Delany was referring to Almack's assembly room and Carlisle House in Soho Square). This letter was followed by two from London describing a visit that Mary Delany had made with the duchess to Banks's house in New Burlington Street on December 17, 1771 "to see some of the fruits of his travels." They were shown paintings of plants from Tahiti, most of the "views" having "gone to be engraven for the history of their travels to come out next year" (384). Another letter to Mrs. Port described the visit as "a charming entertainment of oddities" which included the display of an "Otaheite dress" (387).

These letters indicate a neglected context in which knowledge of the Pacific voyages was defined and circulated – the social circles of elite women. Delany and the Duchess of Portland were both prominent women with extensive familial, social, and intellectual networks that included the court, the church, and belles-lettres. In Delany's letters news of the publication of the voyages is represented as being equivalent to that of the Villiers engagement, the health of the Princess of Wales, and the current state of building work on an assembly rooms, the Pantheon. It circulates in the form of gossip between women, first orally articulated in a sociable context and then relayed in the form of epistolary conversation. Moreover, there is evidently a close relationship between this "private talk" and print culture: Mrs. Delany contradicts newspaper reports of the Villiers engagement as well as implicitly commenting on press coverage of the building of the Pantheon. Contextualized in such a way, the publication of the account of the *Endeavour* voyage partakes of the same permeable boundary between

---

[14] Smith, *European Vision*, 166.
[15] *The Autobiography and Correspondence of Mary Granville, Mrs. Delany*, ed. Lady Llanover, 2nd ser. (3 vols., London: Richard Bentley, 1862) [hereafter referred to by page number in parenthesis in the text], 1, 372.

"private talk" and print with implications for its epistemological status: it has not yet acquired sanction as a form of legitimate knowledge and as such is open to contradiction and rewriting. Banks's "entertainment" of the Duchess of Portland and Mrs. Delany was therefore occurring at a crucial time in the publicization of the "fruits" of the *Endeavour* voyage, when he was working to secure the reputation of the voyage and of himself and Solander in a variety of spheres – the court, the Royal Society and Admiralty, the club and the coffee house, and print culture. The Duchess of Portland's influence and patronage was undoubtedly of direct value to him, but his engagement with her also signified that women like her mattered in a larger sense, that the discursive permeability of such "private talk" had to be taken into account.

Harriet Guest has highlighted contemporary uncertainty as to the aims and motives of Pacific exploration and the destabilizing effects that followed from this: "the underdetermined nature of European interest in the South Pacific produces or enables moral conflicts and inversions . . . The prospect of expansion seems to disclose the moral and political ambivalences of the 'culture of civilized life.'"[16] Like Nicholas Thomas and others, Guest has noted that the concept and practices of curiosity underpinning Pacific exploration were highly unstable. According to Thomas, curiosity was "not fixed but morally slippery . . . its associations with legitimate authority and inquiry are disputed and ambivalent." It was "infantile, feminine, somehow tarnished, and licensed in the sense of licentiousness rather than authorization."[17] The curiosity that motivated the aristocratic male virtuoso was both a reflection of and to some extent legitimated by the effeminized character of the upper class of both genders. In the latter half of the century, however, this view was complicated by the increasing professionalization of the natural sciences and their reconfiguration away from a variety of amusement to a form of socially useful knowledge that was, moreover, increasingly valuable to the fiscal-military state. As John Gascoigne and others have argued, Banks was a crucial figure in both actively promoting this change and functioning as its object in the highly unstable nature of his public identity or identities.[18] In the early 1770s Banks was variously the libertine dilettante motivated by licentious curiosity, the man of science and agent of empire, and the macaroni man of fashion. The latter persona, exemplified by his representation as the fly-catching

[16] Guest, "Curiously Marked," [hereafter referred to by page number in parenthesis in text], 105.
[17] Nicholas Thomas, *In Oceania: Visions, Artifacts, Histories* (Durham, NC: Duke University Press, 1997) [hereafter referred to by page number in parenthesis in text], 106, 107.
[18] Gascoigne, *Joseph Banks.*

macaroni by the caricature publishers Matthew and Mary Darly in July 1772, was particularly significant as a commentary on Banks's celebrity in the period 1771–2, of which the evening's "entertainment" of the Duchess of Portland and Mary Delany had been a part.[19] In being represented in this way Banks joined a diverse group of men, also caricatured as macaronies, which included Charles James Fox, the fashionable portrait painter Richard Cosway, and the failed Scottish banker Alexander Fordyce, as well as other emergent men of science such as the entomologist and engraver Moses Harris.[20] These men shared a complex project of self-promotion in a variety of spheres, including print culture. They allowed themselves both to promote and to be the object of "private talk," in contexts such as the evening at New Burlington Street and in the pages of new journals such as the *Town and Country Magazine* (established in 1769). As such these men not only risked their own effeminization but also potentially amplified the cultural impact of women such as the Duchess of Portland and the fashionable world in which she moved. The macaroni phenomenon was both a critique of the effeminizing power of publicity and an expression of it. As Gascoigne suggests, Banks shucked off the chrysalis of fashionability in a "metamorphosis from virtuoso to botanist" but his macaroni celebrity of 1771–2 was none the less a crucial stage in his transformation.[21]

Guest has productively contrasted the visual representation of Banks in Sir Joshua Reynolds's *Memoirs of the Society of Dilettanti* of 1779 with Benjamin West's portrait of 1771, engraved in 1773 (figure 1). In both paintings Banks is "portrayed as a collector and connoisseur of curiosities" but, as Guest interestingly points out, the Reynolds painting emphasizes the "conviviality" and "bonds of social affection and affiliation" that unite these men, and which served as a "shield" against the effeminizing "intrusions of curiosity" (116). In contrast, the West portrait depicts Banks in isolation surrounded by a "litter of curiosities" – "it is as though Banks at once celebrates and stares down the more frivolous aspects of his dilettantism, and of his reputation as a macaroni" (116). The "ambiguity of gender" in West's portrait of Banks, Guest argues, which makes him "a curious spectacle

---

[19] "The Fly Catching Macaroni," pub. M. Darly July 12, 1772, BM 4695. See also BM 5046, BM 4696.

[20] See "The Original Macaroni," May 20, 1772, BM 5010 (Fox); "A Macaroni Gambler," July 2, 1772, BM 5016 (Fordyce); "The Macaroni Painter, or Billy Dimple sitting for his Picture," 1772, BM 4520 (Cosway); "The Aurelian Macaroni," July 5, 1773, BM 5156 (Harris). For macaronism see Miles Ogborn, "Locating the Macaroni: Luxury, Sexuality and Vision in Vauxhall Gardens," *Textual Practice*, 11 (1997), 445–61, and his *Spaces of Modernity: London's Geographies 1680–1780* (New York: Guildford Press, 1998); Philip Carter, *Men and the Emergence of Polite Society: Britain 1660–1800* (Harlow: Longman, 2001).

[21] Gascoigne, *Joseph Banks*, 66.

Figure 1   Benjamin West, *Joseph Banks* 1773 (National Library of Australia).

comparable to Reynolds's Omai," should be ascribed to "the absence of a visible and defining network of social relations" (118). I would like to suggest that the "defining network of social relations" for this painting is the fashionable world and its association with the power of publicity. The male sociality which Guest rightly identifies as so important in Reynolds's *Society of the Dilettanti* is predicated on a different kind of female sociality, that of the fashionable milieu of the Duchess of Portland and Mary Delany in which "private talk" of the Pacific is integrated with gossipy news. The West portrait dates from 1771, the year in which Banks entertained the duchess and Delany, and thus relates to the crucial period of his assertion of a public role in the wake of the *Endeavour* voyage. To consider the Duchess of Portland as part of the milieu in which Banks was defining himself intensifies the "ambiguity of gender" which Guest discerns in the West portrait, for the duchess, in her role as collector, had herself complicated the gendered identity of the virtuoso. The duchess's collecting exaggerated the "infantile" or effeminizing tendencies of the male virtuoso's curiosity by extending the interests of her male Harleian forebears into areas such as botany and fossil collecting that were usually associated with women. At the same time she compromised the traditional amateurism of the male virtuoso by contributing to the professionalization of science through her sponsorship of Solander. She also enhanced her own position by using income derived from her mother and not the Portlands to elaborate the fabric of Bulstrode as her personal museum, and by pursuing her interests in such a way that might be construed as a form of excessive consumption. The duchess had "checked her purchases" in the 1780s, according to Walpole, but like an addictive shopper had been unable to resist the temptation of the Barberini Vase.[22] It is clear too that the duchess's collecting was partly a sociable practice, something that was integrated with visiting, entertaining, conversation, and, in particular, her intimate female friendships. Frances Burney reported how Mary Delany's memorializing of her friend after the duchess's death in 1785 had focused on two artifacts – two dried leaves in an envelope on which was inscribed "picked at Bolsover, by the duchess and myself, in September 1756, the 20th year of our most intimate and dear friendship," and an African weaver bird, the only memento which Delany would take from the duchess's vast collection.[23] In inscribing her collection with such affective significance, the duchess and her friends were countering the negatively feminized connotations of curiosity by recasting

---

[22] Horace Walpole, *The Duchess of Portland's Museum* (New York: The Grolier Club, 1936), 7.
[23] *Diary & Letters of Madame D'Arblay*, ed. Charlotte Barrett and Austin Dobson (6 vols., London: Macmillan, 1904), II, 295, 305.

curiosity as a mode of sensibility. The figure whom the representation of Banks in the West painting may be said to "stare down," therefore, is not so much his own later incarnation as a macaroni but the Duchess of Portland, the woman of fashion as virtuoso. But as Guest herself suggests by offering the alternative of celebration, "stare down" perhaps exaggerates the drama of Banks's expression. The face of the returned voyager is expectant, frank, and gentle, in the sense of expressing both tenderness and gentility. His stance is one of welcoming movement towards the viewer rather than defensive recoil or confrontation. Dressed in the "fruits" of his discoveries, he is offering himself as a curiosity to be mediated, and perhaps made powerful, on the terms of the fashionable world of the Duchess of Portland and Mary Delany. He himself is part of the sociable "entertainment."

Nicholas Thomas has claimed that it is "contextualization in human action – action that is accorded some moral or historical significance – that is at the greatest remove in the images of curiosities" (101). He uses the frontispiece of the *Catalogue of the Portland Museum* of 1786, the catalogue of the auction of the duchess's collection after her death in 1785, as an illustration of this "decontextualizing mode" (103). It is clear from the Delany letters that what was entailed in the initial response to the *Endeavour* voyage was in fact a complex *recontextualization* of its products, both material and ideological, within the networks of elite metropolitan sociability.[24] Indeed we could say that it was only by reinvesting the curiosities of the *Endeavour* voyage with "human action" in such a context, circulating, talking about, and looking at them, that the venture into the Pacific could be properly assimilated and activated. As Thomas makes clear, the problem with the kinds of artifacts with which Banks surrounds himself in the West painting (and implicitly Banks himself) is that they

were not specimens in any meaningful sense; they were not the objects of any theoretical discourse or symptomatic inquiry. There was, in this period, nothing like Linnean classification that could be applied to artificial curiosities: they were not drawn into any comparative study of technology or craft; they played no significant part in the ethnological project of discriminating and accessing the advancement of the various peoples encountered . . . (111–13)

This lack of a classificatory framework made the curiosities of the *Endeavour* voyage an appropriate topic of gossip. Writing from the perspective of feminist philosophy, Lorraine Code has argued that analyses of gossip "that overemphasize its 'private' dimension fail to capitalize on the political

---

[24] For a similar "recontextualization" of Omai, the Raiatean "product" of the second voyage who came to London in July 1774, see chapter 15 by Harriet Guest in this volume.

power of this practice – this art – whose efficacy extends far beyond the artifical confines of 'the private.'" Code appeals to the "unruliness" of gossip: "Because it circulates outside the boundaries of formal deliberative systems, it can neither be contained or controlled . . . Its eruptions depend, for their epistemic success, on exact, interested specificity – on an attunement with the location, the historical moment, and the circumstances that comprise it."[25] The "private talk" of New Burlington Street constitutes one of these moments of gossip's "epistemic success." The expanding discursive domain of fashionable sociability, through print culture and the development of sites such as the Pantheon, enabled Banks and Solander to publicize their enterprise. At the same time, the Pacific voyagers amplified the domain of women like the Duchess of Portland and Mary Delany by giving them something to talk about. The ramifications of this for the emerging disciplines of natural science and for male homosociality as a hegemonic form of talk are clear in Reynolds's portrait of the members of the Society of Dilettanti. The sociality depicted here not only constitutes a shield against the "intrusions" of feminized curiosity, as Guest suggests, but also resists the dangerous possibility that the "fruits" of the Pacific voyages could only be socially and culturally articulated as "girl talk."

THE COTERIE AND THE "ARREOY" [ARIOI]

The most powerful challenge to elite male homosociality in this period was the formation of the Ladies' Club or Coterie in 1770.[26] In the early months of that year rumors had begun to circulate in the metropolis about a new site of sociability located in one of Almack's rooms in Pall Mall. This development followed Almack's successful attempt in 1765 to compete with Cornelys's Carlisle House by establishing his assembly rooms just to the north of Pall Mall in King Street.[27] The membership of this new gathering or assembly was said to consist of the cream of the young Whig elite, both male and female, and its organization was based on that of the gentleman's clubs in St. James's.[28] Horace Walpole "outed" himself as a member.[29] For

---

[25] Lorraine Code, *Rhetorical Spaces: Essays on Gendered Locations* (New York and London: Routledge, 1995), 152–3.
[26] For a more detailed discussion of the Coterie see Russell, *Schools for Scandal*.
[27] See *Survey of London, Vol. XXIX: The Parish of St. James Westminster, Part One South of Piccadilly* (London: The Athlone Press, 1960), 327–34.
[28] See *Autobiography and Correspondence of Mrs. Delany*, I, 261–3; Cecil Aspinall-Oglander, *Admiral's Widow: Being the Life and Letters of the Hon. Mrs. Edward Boscawen from 1761 to 1805* (London: The Hogarth Press, 1943), 28.
[29] Horace Walpole, *Correspondence*, ed. W. S. Lewis (47 vols., New Haven: Yale University Press, 1937–83), x, 305.

a contemporary commentator such a development was "a Convulsion in the moral World . . . as extraordinary as any former Change or Revolution in the natural or political System . . . the Ladies of the first Quality . . . have arrogated the old Salic Laws of Libertinism, and openly set up a Tavern in protest Rivalry of Boodle's, Arthur's and Almack's."[30] The name "coterie" derived from a label attached to a group of anti-ministerial Whigs, known as Wildman's club, which met at a house at Albemarle Street in 1764.[31] The recurrence of this term in relation to the association of ladies and gentlemen at Almack's in 1770 reflected a desire to classify this grouping politically by linking it with the Albemarle Street Whigs, to stigmatize it as modish, foreign, and intrinsically unstable in meaning – "coterie" was said to derive from the French – and last but not least, to distinguish it clearly as a different formation to the club or coffee house. Much of the discourse on the Coterie in the newspaper and periodical press of 1770 was concerned not only with naming but also with locating it: reports speculated that it was to be found in the Thatched House tavern, at the Duchess of Bedford's headquarters in Bloomsbury Square, at the home of Elizabeth Montagu in Hill Street, at Sir Sampson Gideon's, or at the London Tavern in the City.[32] The Coterie was potentially everywhere because of its resemblance to the domiciliary sociability of elite women which had no institutionalized existence, apart from commercial establishments such as Cornelys's and Almack's. The Coterie therefore represented a significant threat to the culture of male homosociality identified with the tavern and the coffee house. The importance of these institutions to political culture had been accentuated in the 1760s by the role they played in the mobilization of Wilkite radicalism: the incursion of fashionable sociability into the masculinist domain of the club, represented by the Coterie, was interpreted as signifying elite women's claims to comparable rights and liberties.

The nature of the threat which the Coterie represented was conveyed by one commentary in the *Public Advertiser*, a letter from "A. Z.," "Historiographer to the Ladies Society." Its critique was framed in the familiar context of an attack on the current lack of patriotic virtue, expressing a concern that Britain had overreached itself as a result of the Seven Years War and needed to increase the birth rate in order to sustain the empire.

---

[30] *Public Advertiser*, June 8, 1770.
[31] Paul Langford, *A Polite and Commercial People: England 1727–1783* (Oxford University Press: 1989) 356. See also *Address to the Remaining Members of the Coterie* (London: J. Wilkie, 1764); *Answer to the Budget. Inscribed to the Coterie* (London: E. Sumpter, 1754); also commentary in the *Public Advertiser*, November 12, 1764; November 26, 1764.
[32] *General Evening Post*, May 22–24, 1770; *Lloyd's Evening Post*, May 9–11, 1770; *Lloyd's Evening Post*, May 21–23, 1770; *Lloyd's Evening Post*, June 25–27, 1770.

Where "changling and changeable" "Statesmen," the writer claims, had failed to address the crisis facing Britain, "a Junto of patriotic Ladies" had stepped into the breach. The purpose of the "Ladies Society," in short, was illicit sex in the service of the empire. The persistent use of "Society" rather than coterie or club may have been designed to suggest associations with the goals of philanthropic organizations such as Hanway's Marine Society, founded in 1765 to recruit poor lads and men into the navy. The letter suggests that in "Days of Ignorance our Gothic Ancestors," knowing little of the "Value of Commerce" and the "Benefits of a quick Transition of Property," had made marriage indissoluble on the grounds of "some antiquated Notions of Christianity." However, attitudes were different in 1770. With the cooperation of the ecclesiastical courts contemporary women of fashion had established the "Ladies Society" with the aim of rendering the "useful Evasion of old Laws easy to Individuals, and universally beneficial to the Nation." The ladies' example is conceived as extending far beyond London to encompass the political nation as a whole: "when by the noble Example of this Society all ranks of People in every part of the three Kingdoms, shall have formed themselves into like Clubs, on a very modest Calculation we must suppose 50,000 new Subjects will be annually sent to the Colonies."[33]

The mode of Swiftian irony which the writer deploys here is designed to highlight the perversion of the ideals of patriotism and service to the public good which the Coterie represents. Toleration of such a development, the letter suggests, would amount to a legitimation of adultery and the admission of the sexual licentiousness associated with women into the (masculine) public sphere. Lust would be nothing more than an instrument of social utility. But the highly unstable ironic register of the letter means that it is also possible that it is the discourses and practices associated with commerce that are to blame for the legitimation of female sexuality, not female sexuality per se. A. Z.'s reference to the more rapid transition of property being one of the social benefits of adultery suggests that the primacy of commerce in the polis has the potential to distort traditional moral values, characterized as "the Ignorance of our Gothic ancestors" when "antiquated" notions of Christianity prevailed. Moreover, because of commerce's investment in female sexuality as a mode of exchange, it has the capacity, like the Coterie itself, to problematize existing systems of knowledge and forms of social and political organization by making a discursive and material space for women – hence the correspondence between the

[33] *Public Advertiser*, May 19, 1770.

Ladies Society and the Marine Society. The "populate or perish" argument of men like Hanway entailed, as A. Z. suggested, an acknowledgment of women's role in producing bodies to man the empire and hence a form of legitimation of women in the public sphere: the Coterie was the sociable corollary of such a development.

Like Banks's voyages, the Coterie was the subject of Mary Delany's epistolary gossip. Banks, Solander, and Cook may have learned of it on their return to London in 1771, possibly in the drawing room of Lady Hertford or even in the royal palaces. If so, they may have reflected on the analogies between the Coterie and a Pacific social institution that had fascinated them – the arioi, or arreoy as it was often rendered in contemporary texts. The arioi was a group, comprising mostly men but with some women, which traveled throughout the Society Islands "performing ceremonies and entertainments in exchange for lavish hospitality and within the context, largely, of 'Oro worship."[34] Arioi performances were notable for "their employment of sexual and especially copulative imagery, and their uninhibited lampooning of prominent persons." The arioi also practiced infanticide, a number of explanations for which have been given, the most widely canvassed being that it was a form of population control. Western observers in the late eighteenth and early nineteenth centuries variously described the arioi as a society of warriors, as young male libertines or freemasons, or as a group of "comedians" or strolling players.[35] These terms indicate the frameworks in which the arioi was being interpreted – those relating to the theatricality, caste-defined male homosociality and associational culture in general that were crucial to the identity and functioning of the British male elite, both military and civilian. As Christopher Balme has indicated in his discussion of the theatricality of sexual encounter between the British and Pacific islanders, adapting Edward Said, theatricalization was a tool of colonial power: "a particularly Western style of thought that ultimately was brought to bear on most of the colonized world . . . [it was] closely connected with containment and circumscription."[36] Sociability played a similar role in colonization that has been hitherto neglected by scholarship, as a practice and language of cross-cultural encounter as well as informing its ideology. Early eighteenth-century periodicals such as the *Tatler* and the *Spectator* and the work of Scottish Enlightenment philosophers elaborated

---

[34] Douglas L. Oliver, *Ancient Tahitian Society* (2 vols., Honolulu: University of Hawaii Press, 1974), II, 914.

[35] Ibid., I, 923, 942–3, 913–14.

[36] Christopher B. Balme, "Sexual Spectacles: Theatricality and the Performance of Sex in Early Encounters in the Pacific," *TDR: The Drama Review*, 44 (2000), 67–85, at 69.

sociability as a civilizing value, an emanation of the increased mobility and circulatory social practices attendant on trade which in turn refined trade itself. The extent to which such a view of sociability conditioned eighteenth-century imperialism's view of its civilizing purpose is illustrated by the terms in which Arthur Phillip was instructed to encounter the Aborigines of New South Wales: he was to "open an *intercourse* with the natives, and to *conciliate their affections*, enjoining all our subjects to live in *amity* and *kindness* with them" (my emphasis).[37]

It is important to recognize, however, that sociability, like theatricality, was not an unchanging tool of hegemonic colonial power but was itself historically contingent and unstable in its meanings. This was particularly the case in the 1760s and 1770s when, as I have suggested, the male homosocial identity of the institutions of the public sphere, such as the tavern and the coffee house, was threatened by the emergence of the Coterie and fashionable sociability in general. This context can be traced in accounts of the arioi in the journals of Cook and Banks culminating in Hawkesworth's *Account of the Voyages* (1773). The passage dealing with the arioi in Cook's *Journal* begins with a description of "a very indecent dance," the "timorodee," performed by young girls. "One half of the better sort of inhabitants," according to Cook, enjoyed "free liberty in love" and the offspring of such unions were "smother'd at the moment of their birth." This group of people was called "Arreoy's" who "have meetings among themselves."[38] Banks's account is similar to Cook's: both men refer to the arreoy as "they," whom they describe as having "meetings."[39] Hawkesworth's version of both Cook's and Banks's descriptions of the arreoy is significant for introducing the term "society" which, as we have seen, featured in the newspaper controversy concerning the Coterie. Hawkesworth, unlike the voyagers, had been present in London in 1770 when the dispute about the Coterie was at its height and his account is redolent of some of the newspaper attacks on the Coterie at this period:

there is a scale in dissolute sensuality which these people have ascended, wholly unknown to every nation whose manners have been recorded from the beginning of the world to the present hour, and which no imagination could possibly conceive. A very considerable number of the principal people of Otaheite, of both sexes,

[37] Quoted in Williams, "The Pacific," 568.

[38] *The Journals of Captain James Cook*, ed. J. C. Beaglehole (4 vols., London: Hakluyt Society, 1955–74), I, 128.

[39] *The Endeavour Journal of Joseph Banks 1768–1771*, ed. J. C. Beaglehole (2 vols., Sydney: Public Library of New South Wales and Angus and Robertson, 1962), I, 44.

have formed themselves into a society, in which every woman is common to every man . . . These societies are distinguished by the name of *Arreoy*.[40]

While Banks and Cook gave priority in their accounts to the practices of free love and infanticide, and less to the arioi as an institution that promoted such behavior, Hawkesworth suggests that the forming of this heterosexual "society" was the principal cause of such "dissolute sensuality" of which infanticide is the most heinous manifestation. Greg Dening has said that "The British possessed Tahiti by compressing the complexities of their ethnographic moment into a few experiences made memorable because they displayed Tahiti as a mirror for themselves."[41] In displaying the arioi, Cook and Banks, but particularly Hawkesworth, had thrown up the grotesque mirror of the Coterie.

Contemporary fascination with the arioi, inspired, I would suggest, by recent experiments in heterosexual sociability in the metropolis, led to the relevant passage in Hawkesworth being widely disseminated in journals such as the *Westminster Magazine*.[42] It also featured significantly in the explosion of satirical poetry known as the Oberea–Banks cycle which was given further impetus after 1774 by the fashion for Omai.[43] This poetry has received increased attention recently from scholars who have emphasized how Otaheitan sociality was used as a weapon by which to discipline metropolitan femininity.[44] I wish to argue the historical specificities of that attack in relation to both the Pacific and the metropolis by suggesting that this literature relates to particular developments in fashionable life. Moreover, there has been a tendency in this scholarship perhaps to overestimate the cultural authority and formal stability of such writings. Combining classical allusion with the topical raciness of the *Town and Country*, muck-raking erotica with the high ground of satirical purpose, at the same time cannibalizing and debasing Hawkesworth's account as a spurious legitimacy for their endeavors, these poems are highly unstable

---

[40] John Hawkesworth, *An Account of the Voyages and Discoveries in the Southern Ocean* (London, 1773), quoted in Jonathan Lamb, Vanessa Smith, and Nicholas Thomas, eds., *Explanation and Exchange: A South Seas Anthology, 1680–1900* (University of Chicago Press, 2000), 81.

[41] Greg Dening, *Performances* (Melbourne: Melbourne University Press, 1996), 152.

[42] *Westminster Magazine* I (June 1773), 334–6.

[43] For an account of the cycle see Colin Roderick, "Sir Joseph Banks, Queen Oberea and the Satirists," in Walter Veit, ed., *Captain James Cook: Image and Impact* (Melbourne: The Hawthorn Press, 1972), 67–89. See also McCormick, *Omai*.

[44] Guest, "The Great Distinction"; Bridget Orr, "'Southern Passions Mix with Northern Art': Miscegenation and the *Endeavour* Voyage," *Eighteenth-Century Life*, 18 (1994), 212–31; Dening, *Performances*.

artifacts, hybrid offspring of belles-lettres, the scandal sheet, and "private talk."[45] Their salacious intertwining of the more notorious "scenes" from Hawkesworth with allusions to famous adulteresses and sites of scandal such as Cornelys's Carlisle House has the effect of amplifying the status of South Seas knowledge as a sociable entertainment, a form of unruly gossip. At the same time, these texts attempted to regulate the very construction of the Pacific in such terms. The encounter with Pacific sociality, particularly the arioi, is represented in these poems not in terms of the exotic or the new but as a yawn-inducing confirmation of what was already known about the feminized licentiousness of the metropolis. Thus the introduction to *A Second Letter from Oberea, Queen of Otaheite, to Joseph Banks*, attributed to Major John Scott, claims that the arrival of Oberea's plenipotentiary in London "has greatly contributed to revive the spirits of every member of the fashionable societies in the neighbourhood of St. James's. Almack's, Boodle's, Scavoir Vivre, &c. are all in raptures, and particularly that distinguished under the appellation of the English AROUAI, in Pall Mall" (i.e. the Coterie). A note to "AROUAI" states: "This Society takes its name from one in the Island of Otaheite, where persons of both sexes indulge themselves in freedoms not consistent with decency to mention here but may be met with in Dr. Hawkesworth's Voyages."[46] Scott adapts that aspect of the discourse surrounding the Coterie concerned with its naming and location to announce the finding of its proper name and home. In a reversal of one of the tropes of colonial encounter, the British learn to name themselves in the language of the Other, rather than vice versa. The apotheosis of the Coterie as the "English AROUAI" is a measure of its universalizing potential as a model for sociality and also its exceptional status as a space mediating between London and Otaheite, combining the English and Pacific "primitive."

The topical immediacy of Pacific sociality, its perverse familiarity in the context of the early 1770s rather than its exoticism, was stressed in another poem from 1774, *An Epistle (Moral and Philosophical) from an Officer at Otaheite. To Lady Gr*s**n*r*, which has been attributed to Major John Courtenay. Its addressee, Lady Henrietta Grosvenor, was the most notorious adulteress of the period. The case brought by the Duke of Grosvenor against the king's brother, the Duke of Cumberland, for criminal conversation with Lady Henrietta and the subsequent parliamentary divorce were widely reported in the newspaper press and magazines between 1769 and 1772.

[45] The idea of cannibalizing is derived from Dening, *Performances*, 153.
[46] *A Second Letter from Oberea, Queen of Otaheite, to Joseph Banks, Esq.* (London: T. Carnegy, n. d. [1774]), 3.

Some of the reporting, notably in the *Middlesex Journal*, exploited the affair as part of a Wilkite critique of court corruption and as a test of the boundaries of press freedom. A denizen of Almack's and Soho, Lady Grosvenor exemplified the association for contemporary commentators between the development of such institutions and the rise in adultery.[47] Throughout the 1770s she continued to flaunt her notoriety by attending masquerades and her name became a byword of female licentiousness in the print media. The reference to Lady Grosvenor in *An Epistle* therefore had the effect of mobilizing, in the context of the Pacific voyages, the discourse linking adultery and fashionable sociability. Moreover, in doing so, the poem added another dimension to the problem of fashionable sociability, amplifying its significance as a discourse of empire, and also implicitly drawing attention to uncertainties in the imperial enterprise, manifested most powerfully in anxieties of gender.

Such anxieties are apparent in the highly digressive structure of the *Epistle*, its almost febrile moving to and fro between Europe and the Pacific in a way which makes it impossible to determine the poem's true locus. Constructing a mock authority for itself in an apparatus of notes, mostly from Hawkesworth but also referring to Diderot and Priestley, the poem parodies Hawkesworth's construction of his own authority. It mimics his mediation of the journals of Cook and Banks in the form of the gentleman speaker's sentimental education, via salacious anecdotes from Hawkesworth, of a female addressee, "Emma." (Although the *Epistle* is addressed to Lady Grosvenor she is not the addressee within the text.) The poem rehearses the tropes of Hawkesworth's narrative by which the voyages had become known (and which continue to feature in a similar tropological way in Pacific eighteenth-century studies) – the stealing of Banks's breeches, Queen Oberea's tattooed bum, the performance of a sexual act between a young girl and a young man witnessed by the Tahitians and Cook's "people," the dancing of the timorodee, the use of nails to obtain sexual favors from Tahitian women, the introduction of venereal disease to Tahiti by the French, the debate about custom and nature articulated by Hawkesworth, and finally, the arioi, free love, and infanticide. The *Epistle* was not unusual in this respect: as Greg Dening has suggested, the poems of the Oberea–Banks–Omai cycle were notable for coming "back again and again to the same incidents on the voyage. They made simplicities by repetition . . . They played the ironies every way . . ."[48] Dening identifies this strategy

---

47 See Russell, *Schools for Scandal*, for a discussion of adultery and fashionable sociability.
48 Dening, *Performances*, 153.

as crucial to the act of possessing Tahiti, which is undoubtedly the case, but the containment entailed in this compulsive ironizing was also directed at the complexities of the imperial enterprise itself. Considered within the specific context of the early 1770s the strategies of texts such as the *Epistle* reveal a profound skepticism about the meanings of empire, produced partly by the new contexts in which knowledge of places such as the Pacific was being formed and disseminated – the highly feminized sphere of publicity in which print and the sociable milieux of talk were interimplicated. By foregrounding the production of knowledge of the Pacific as a series of curious anecdotes, an "entertainment of oddities," the *Epistle* both critiques the contexts in which such knowledge was being produced and participates in them. The author's product – a literary commodity, costing one shilling and sixpence – is itself part of the entertainment, like Banks's presentation of himself to Mary Delany and the Duchess of Portland. The potentially compromising position in which this places the masculine authority of the writer can be related to the profound anxiety which the poem reveals about the security and stability of the imperial center. Relating the Pacific to what the British had failed to achieve in India, the speaker addresses Liberty, "Britannia's guardian pow'r": "Tho' gath'ring clouds, the thunder storm presage,/ *Draw down the light'ning*, ere it burst in rage." The clouds are forming over America:

> O'er Albion's realms in majesty preside,
> Nor let th' Atlantic wave, thy sons divide;
> Unite *them*, Goddess, in ONE glorious cause,
> Who share thy rights, religion, and thy laws.
> In peace preserve Britannia's sacred rest,
> Restore her children to a mother's breast . . .[49]

It is in this context that the culminating "curious anecdote" of the poem, the account of the arioi, gains particular significance. "Still must I sing the lewd promiscous joy,/Which boundless reigns amidst their *Arreoy*," the speaker states (28). He then refers to the practice of infanticide among the arioi, making an ironic contrast between "such black scenes" and the reproductive enterprise of the Coterie:

> Far different scenes in Briton's isle I see,
> Where shines conspicuous the fam'd *Coterie*.
> Their social orgies, genial love admit,
> And brisk Champaign improves their sparkling wit.
> Low at their feet elected members stand,

---

[49] *An Epistle (Moral and Philosophical) from an Officer at Otaheite. To Lady Gr*s***n*r* (London: n.d.), 21, 22, hereafter referred to by page numbers in parenthesis in text.

And population teems around the land;
As thorn-trees by inoculation bear
The juicy apple, and the luscious pear:
So the stale Countess, by a *strange* embrace,
Yields to her Lord and unresembling race;
Joyous he sees the '*olive branches*' spread,
And wreaths the nuptial honours around his head.   FINIS.
                                                           (30–1)

The population control practiced by the arioi is contrasted with the Coterie's status as a child factory for the nation, a revival in the context of the Pacific voyages of one of the prominent attacks on the Coterie in 1770. The echoing of the suggestion that clubs like the Coterie would be set up to populate the empire therefore has the effect of discursively integrating the Pacific with broader concerns about commerce as intrinsically effeminized and effeminizing and with racialized constructions of empire focused on the reproductive capacities of the female body. As Felicity Nussbaum has shown, discourses of empire from the early modern period were mapped on to discourses of the sexualized female body, in particular that of the "savage" mother capable of infanticide: "the invention of the 'other' woman of empire enabled the consolidation of the cult of domesticity in England and, at the same time, the association of the sexualized woman at home, with the exotic, or 'savage,' non-European woman."[50] In the discourses surrounding the Cook voyages, the "other" woman of the South Seas renders visible the sexualized identity of the British woman of fashion (and vice versa). As the references to the grafting of fruit and to the "stale Countess" producing an "unresembling race" suggest, the adultery signified by the Coterie threatens the security of patriarchy through a miscegenation of rank, a prospect as appalling as racial miscegenation. The "fond mothers" of Otaheite acting Medea's part, the "stale" figure of Lady Grosvenor producing an "unresembling race," and the invocation to Britannia to offer succor to her sons are variations on the dominant theme of the poem – its fear of the annihilating power of the feminine, as galvanized in the 1770s by the intersections of commerce, empire, and fashionable sociability. In this sense, Lady Gr*s**n*r's relevance to the poem is not peripheral or incidental – she is the perverse Britannia of her age, the autochthonous imperial mother whose reign extends from Soho to Otaheite.

The savage mothers of the metropolis are also the subject of the final poem of the Oberea–Banks–Omai cycle that I wish to address: *Seventeen Hundred and Seventy-Seven: or, a Picture of the Manners and Character of the*

---

[50] Felicity A. Nussbaum, *Torrid Zones: Maternity, Sexuality and Empire in Eighteenth Century English Narratives* (Baltimore: The Johns Hopkins University Press, 1995), 1.

Age (1777). The poem has been attributed to the Irish poet and dramatist William Preston (1753–1807) and was published in Dublin and London.[51] It takes the form of an address from "a lady of quality" in England to the absent Omai, who returned to the Pacific with Cook on the second voyage. Omai is reminded of the pleasures he had enjoyed in London – Cornelys's masquerades, the gardens of Vauxhall, and the amorous instruction of the brothel madam Charlotte Hayes's "mystic school" (p. 2). The poem offers an image of the metropolis, and indeed of Britain as a whole, as colonized by a licentious femininity. The old-fashioned "dame" who was devoted to her household and never scorned her husband has been usurped by the gadding woman of fashion who is maddened by the "thirst of pleasure":

> Here *Circe's* train, and routs of *Comus* dwell,
> And tipsey Revel hears the midnight bell,
> In secret orgies of the witching hour,
> When zealous Cot'ries deep libations pour . . .
> (p. 8)

The references to Circe, to Milton's *Comus* which was a trope of luxurious entertainment, and to the pagan rites of the "zealous COT'ries" firmly situate the poem within contemporary critiques of fashionable sociability. In this context, fashionable women are the metropolis's true primitives, behaving "As Indians frank – as Indians naked too" (p. 12). Corrupted by such an example, male macaronies can offer no resistance. "Rise and be MEN," the poem demands of them, enjoining a general "cry" of "joy" that would "rend" the temple of fashion – the Pantheon (p. 13).

The fulcrum of fashionable sociability's transgressive energy, the engine room of the empire of luxury, is Carlisle House or "NAT'RAL-ARTIFICIAL grove," where

> . . . happy Nabobs plume their silken wings,
> And British rapine wears the spoil of kings;
> Where, imp'd by fashion, Grubs from 'Change aspire,
> And Jews converted ape the Christian's fire . . .
> There let Cornelys wave her potent wand,
> And scenes of Faëry rise at her command.
> Be monstrous shapes of fabled legend there,
> Let motly nations in her train appear.   (pp. 15–16)

51 [William Preston], *Seventeen Hundred and Seventy-Seven: or, a Picture of the Manners and Character of the Age. In a Poetical Epistle from a Lady of Quality* (London: T. Evans, 1777), hereafter referred to in parentheses in text.

In this context, Otaheite serves as the supreme confirmation of the licentious feminized energy at the heart of the metropolis, the South Seas counterpart of Cornelys's realm of faery. More than any other poem in the Oberea–Banks–Omai cycle, *Seventeen Hundred and Seventy-Seven* offers a comprehensive analysis of the crisis of the times as the effect of the effeminization of public culture, epitomized by institutions such as Carlisle House. It also makes a rhetorically complex analogy between the Coterie and the arioi, which is not named but described as an Otaheitan "commonwealth of joys" (p. 20). A note to this latter phrase refers the reader to Hawkesworth's account of "a most extraordinary association," i.e. the arioi (p. 20). Like Hawkesworth's use of the term "society," the mention of "association" and "commonwealth" has the effect of invoking the politically charged meanings of these words in contemporary Britain, and the threat which the Coterie represented to male homosociality. The writer ironically commends the arioi as an example which "our modish dames" could follow – "They [i.e. the arioi] give the ton, o'er etiquette preside,/ Direct amusements, and opinions guide" (p. 20). The transparent allusion to the Coterie in these lines aims at an effect of déjà vu by suggesting that British women of fashion were already "savage" before this model of savage "civility" was "discovered" by Cook. Once more the encounter with the peoples of the Pacific is constructed in these satiric poems as a bathetic confirmation of what was already known. Moreover, the strategy of pretending not to be alluding to the Coterie – extending the discourse of naming in relation to the Coterie to a refusal to name it – has the effect of making it more profoundly exotic and potentially threatening than anything that Cook might have encountered. But perhaps the most powerful effect of the poet's irony here is that it enables him recursively to inscribe the Coterie with the crime of infanticide. The children of the arioi are the "little tell-tales" of sexual pleasure that, bleeding, free the "couch of love" from vile restraint (p. 20). If the arioi resemble the Coterie in so many ways, why not in this respect too?

The affiliation of the arioi and the Coterie, not only in textual production but also in forums such as the theatre,[52] exemplifies the specific configuration of the Pacific in the early 1770s that I have been addressing in this chapter – as fashion, as topic of conversation, as a form of sociable entertainment, as an excuse for a performance – varieties of knowledge that enhanced the social, political, and cultural spheres in which elite women

---

[52] See George Colman the Elder's prologue to Thomas Hull's tragedy, *Henry the Second* (London: John Bell, 1774), which makes an analogy between the Coterie and the arioi.

in particular were prominent. The isomorphism of the Coterie and the arioi serves to disclose profound anxieties not only about the feminization of the metropolitan public sphere as evidenced by fashionable sociability, but also concerning the effeminizing tendencies of the imperial project itself. These poems neutralize Pacific alterity in a way which simultaneously annihilates the threat of Oberea and her metropolitan doubles – most strikingly Grosvenor, but also Portland and Delany. As Bridget Orr and Harriet Guest have suggested, Captain Cook's later apotheosis as paragon of patriotic virtue and of British manliness was a response to the unruliness of "talk" about the Pacific in the 1770s, and the profound anxieties about empire, gender, and Enlightenment progressivism which it had exposed.[53] This chapter has been an attempt to explain some of the contexts of that "talk" and to introduce the category of sociability as part of the framework in which a cultural history of the British empire in this period could be conducted. The reaction against the feminization of knowledge of the Pacific in the 1770s was profoundly influential on later conceptions of the imperial enterprise and indeed on the discipline of imperial history itself, shaped as it has been by the model of Cook's mythologization.

By returning to the sociable contexts in which knowledge of the Pacific was shaped, by tracing the genealogy of that knowledge on the beach or ship as well as in the drawing room, the print shop, the club, or lecture room, we (by which I mean the Anglo-American-Australasian-Pacific academic community) can perhaps gain a better understanding of the politics of our own dialogue about the Pacific and the metropolis. West's portrait of Banks, for example, like the story of Omai, continues to be recontextualized in academic publications such as this, in conference papers, and in exhibitions.[54] Granted, this represents a different context from the drawing rooms of the early 1770s, but one which none the less is equally as concerned with the institutionalization of knowledge and the promotion of careers. Only by returning to the cultural contexts in which the Pacific was "celebrated" in the 1770s can we begin to acknowledge the complex ways in which the Pacific continues to entertain.

[53] Orr, "'Southern passions,'" 228–30; Harriet Guest, *Small Change: Women, Learning, Patriotism, 1750–1810* (Chicago: Chicago University Press, 2000), esp. ch. 10.
[54] For Omai exhibitions see *The Two Worlds of Omai* (Auckland: Auckland City Art Gallery, 1977) and *Cook & Omai: The Cult of the South Seas* (Canberra: National Library of Australia, 2000).

CHAPTER 3

The theatre of empire: racial counterfeit, racial realism

Felicity A. Nussbaum

Literary studies of the long eighteenth century are increasingly shaped by the recognition that the history of the empire penetrated Britain in ways that transformed the poetry, fiction, and drama of the period including texts such as Aphra Behn's *Oroonoko* (1688), Daniel Defoe's *Robinson Crusoe* (1722), Samuel Johnson's oriental tale *Rasselas* (1759), and Laurence Sterne's *Sentimental Journey* (1768). These texts address issues of slavery, captivity, commerce, and imperial authority. The metropole itself evolved into a contact zone where the empire persistently intruded into domestic affairs, and the consequences for the nation were palpable. One popular public manifestation of this penetration of people from elsewhere occurred in England's theatres. The drama incorporated colonial encounters onto the skins, gestures, and dialogue of white actors at once to fabricate the representation of racial difference, to celebrate and worry it, and finally to grant it a recognizable reality. In particular, impersonations in blackface helped formulate the racial politics that came to predominate around the Atlantic and later the Pacific, though even as imperial designs expanded, calls for the abolition of slavery grew more intense near the end of the century. Concerned about the moral corrosiveness of slavery, England struggled to reconcile its notions of a "free and virtuous empire"[1] with an emerging conviction about its national and racial supremacy.

Ignatius Sancho (1729–80) was among those who offered a serious contest to assumptions of black inferiority. Though he was born on a slave ship headed for the West Indies, Sancho became extraordinarily accomplished as the first Afro-British playwright, theatre critic, art critic, composer, and patron of the arts.[2] One "first" that Sancho did not manage to achieve was

---

[1] See Kathleen Wilson, *The Sense of the People: Politics, Culture and Imperialism in England, 1715–1785* (Cambridge University Press, 1995). I am especially grateful to Jenny Sharpe, Rachel Lee, and Judith Jackson Fossett for their insights relevant to this paper.

[2] Ignatius Sancho, *Letters of the Late Ignatius Sancho, An African*, ed. Vincent Carretta (New York: Penguin Books, 1998), back cover.

to become the first black actor on the British stage. Joseph Jekyll, Sancho's eighteenth-century biographer, suggests that the author

loved the theatre to such a point of enthusiasm, that his last shilling went to Drury-Lane, on Mr. Garrick's representation of Richard. He had been even induced to consider the stage as a resource in the hour of adversity, and his complexion suggested an offer to the manager of attempting Othello and Oroonoko; but a defective and incorrigible articulation rendered it abortive.[3]

Jekyll does not seem to recognize the monumental significance of Sancho's aspiration, but the fact that the first African black did not appear on the British stage until Ira Aldridge's London debut in the early nineteenth century means that such a performance in the 1760s or 1770s would have been an unprecedented event in theatre history. That Aldridge chose to leave America and its all-black theatre troupe, the African Theatre, suggests that the history of black performance was very different in England from that of the New World. Among the reasons for his self-imposed exile was that Aldridge's appearance on the stage coincided with the creation of a sufficient number of black parts to allow him to make a living as an actor in England.[4]

Throughout the eighteenth century the black heroes of Shakespeare's *Othello* and Southerne's *Oroonoko* continued to be presented on stage, and adaptations proliferated in the abolitionist years of the 1770s and beyond.[5] This chapter will consider turning colors in the British theatre of the eighteenth century, especially as that transformation can be understood from the dramatic repertory of black roles. When Aldridge first performed in England as Oroonoko at the Coburg (now the Old Vic) in October 1825, his acting inspired both derision and applause. He performed in numerous plays familiar to eighteenth-century audiences who were accustomed only to the greasepaint, lampblack, smeared cork, pomatum, and woolly-wigged caricatures of blackness by white English actors who affected nativism.

---

[3] Sancho, *Letters of the Late Ignatius Sancho*, 7.

[4] David Krasner, "Perspectives on American Minstrelsy," *Nineteenth Century Theatre*, 27, 2 (Winter 1999), 142, suggests that Aldridge left the American stage because "race played a significant role in his lack of opportunities." The history of black actors in America deserves much more critical attention. See, e.g., Clifford Ashby, "A Black Actor on the Eighteenth Century Boston Stage?" *Theatre Survey: The American Journal of Theatre History*, 28, 2 [1987], 101–2.

[5] In America between 1716 and the mid-nineteenth century, there were 425 performances of *Othello* from its first performance in 1751, 101 of McCready's farce *The Irishman in London: The Happy African*, beginning in 1793, and 66 performances of Bickerstaff's *The Padlock* after 1769. These plays were among the ten most frequently performed works. See Dale Cockrell, *Demons of Disorder: Early Blackface Minstrels and Their World* (Cambridge University Press, 1997), and James V. Hatch, *The Black Image on the American Stage: A Bibliography of Plays and Musicals, 1770–1970* (New York: DramaBook Specialists Publications, 1970).

Touring in the provincial theatres, Aldridge was best known for roles in *The Ethiopian, or the Quadroon of the Mango Grove* (*The Slave*), Hassan in M. G. Lewis's *The Castle Spectre*, Zanga in Edward Young's *Revenge*, and Mungo in Isaac Bickerstaffe's *The Padlock*, all of which were parts written exclusively as black characters. Aldridge also blanched himself for other roles in order to play, for example, a white-bearded, bewigged, and chalked King Lear, Macbeth, and Shylock. In the year in which slavery was abolished in the British colonies, Aldridge's inaugural appearance at Covent Garden (one of two patent theatres) as Othello on April 16, 1833, received mixed reviews. After another appearance that week, he was exiled instead to minor London theatres, as well as to tours in Scotland, Ireland, Europe, and Russia, until twenty-five years later when he returned to the West End as Othello.[6] In the minor theatres, perhaps as early as 1838 as a black minstrel in a composite of his major roles, Aldridge competed with the white minstrel shows that popularized impersonations of black actors from the African Theatre.

I

In addition to appearing in the familiar tragedies *Oroonoko* and *Othello* that featured African nobility, blackfaced players most notably in the later eighteenth century took comic parts as slaves, servants, or the working class in plays such as *The Padlock*, *The Blackamoor Wash'd White*, and *Harlequin Mungo*. These plays, attended by visiting luminaries from around the emerging empire, provided dramatic figurings of blackness that vied with, and perhaps superseded, the real Indian kings and African princes occasionally reported to be in the audience, as well as the increasingly well-known Afro-British abolitionists Cugoano, Sancho, and Equiano. These plays provide, like minstrelsy, an opportunity to display "the fetishized mark of genuineness . . . one big wink,"[7] to celebrate black male bodies by simulating them. The effect reduces actual blacks to sexualized stereotypes and occludes their slave labor while seeming to share the romantic views of abolitionists who strongly sympathized with the plight of the oppressed. The tragedies, comedies, and pantomimes deal with two major

---

[6] Aldridge's third performance at Covent Garden was canceled, and he did not appear on the London stage until 1858 after playing on the continent, according to Herbert Marshall and Mildred Stock, *Ira Aldridge: The Negro Tragedian* (Carbondale, IL: Southern Illinois University Press, 1968), 133. He returned to the West End as Othello in 1865.

[7] W. T. Lhamon, Jr., *Raising Cain: Blackface Performance from Jim Crow to Hip Hop* (Cambridge, MA: Harvard University Press, 1998), 16.

cultural fears that intensified in the later eighteenth century: that miscegenation brought contamination to a nation seeking a purified identity
distinctly different from its imperial peoples, and that burgeoning numbers of free blacks arriving in the country would take the jobs of English
domestics.

If this early public counterfeit of blackface defused the threat of black
masculinity and helped regulate race relations in ways similar to nineteenth-
century American minstrelsy, then what difference does it make when an
actual black male enters the theatre after British slaves in the colonies
were finally emancipated in 1833? How, we might ask, is black masculinity
configured in a theatre that is attempting to reconcile the anxieties of empire
with evolving national myths? If, as Hazel V. Carby suggests, "Society
has relied upon affirmations of masculinity to resolve social and political
crises," does the appearance of the first black man on the English stage
when slaves are freed negotiate this cultural turning point principally by
replicating existing power relations by acting in plays in which white men
had performed racial stereotypes?[8] By figuring blackness in this way on the
metropolitan home stage, the plays celebrate blackness while easing the
path to continued exploitation in the periphery. These plays, in spite of
being produced as the abolition movement gathers force and succeeds, are
not really anti-slavery plays.[9] Black parts (as acted by white men) on the
eighteenth-century stage may occasionally serve the goals of abolition but
more often, as this chapter argues, the parts heighten the instabilities and
contradictions surrounding race in eighteenth-century culture, attempt to
cleanse England of its racial impurities and its slave history, and work toward
a racism located principally in the skin and in the physiognomy. Through
an analysis of Aldridge's repertory, I examine a nation's ability to distract
itself from the violence perpetrated on the real black male body through
its investment in the public performance of counterfeit black masculinity.
The theatre of empire isolates a contact zone within the painted white
actor's body and in that incorporation glosses over the bogus nature of the
encounter.

Blacking up in the eighteenth-century theatre, as I have argued elsewhere, was almost exclusively masculine since very few women of color

---

[8] Hazel V. Carby, *Race Men* (Cambridge, MA: Harvard University Press, 1998), 37.
[9] Here I agree with Wylie Sypher who states that "Strictly, there is no drama of anti-slavery; there are
   only a number of plays in which the Negro plays his part," *Guinea's Captive Kings: British Anti-Slavery
   Literature of the 18th Century* (Chapel Hill: University of North Carolina Press, 1942), 232. It is the
   nature of that "part" that this chapter investigates.

were represented in drama.[10] The history of black men on the eighteenth-century stage is a very short history indeed since I know of no African male (or female) performers on the London stage until Aldridge's appearance. Instead the black history in this period is one of blackface, of costume and disguise, other than the very few exceptions which record sightings of black performers at fairs and carnival gatherings. Blackface – a white man who pretended to be a black man – emphasized performance as an important element of race; but in reassuring the viewer that the actor was actually white beneath the make-up, the practice also reflects elements of racist essentialism. In becoming black, the white man can participate in the sublime thrill of blackness, yet in the very act of presenting it, he exerts some control over its effects. This impersonation of black men is more fluid than creolization or miscegenation. Blackface establishes a border between cultures which encourages an irreverence about complexion's consequences that makes blackness appear to be decorative and alien.

There are few recorded instances of black street performers during the period. In the late seventeenth century the account of the grocers' tribute in the Lord Mayor of London's pageant mentions a negro boy holding exotic fruits and mounted on a camel. Another is described as wearing a garland of feathers on his head, flanked by a goddess of plenty and by two "West-Indian princes" with three other "Black-Moors" grotesquely dressed in bright silks and outlandish feathers, all of whom attend a black-faced king.[11] In the entertainments set forth by the company of drapers in the Lord Mayor's procession for 1675, "two Negro's in Robes of Silver . . . represent Strength and Concord" to parade through the streets of London.[12] It seems likely that these men were blackface representations adorned with exotic props rather than actual blacks since an observer comments that the imperial being in the grocers' pageant has "a Face black, and likewise his Neck and Arms, which are naked to the Elbows; on his Head a Crown of various coloured Feathers, a rope of Pearl about his Neck, Pendants in his Ears, short curl'd

[10] Notable exceptions are Yarico and the lesser known Cubba. Southerne's Imoinda in his adaptation of Aphra Behn's novella *Oroonoko* is of course white. See Felicity Nussbaum, *The Limits of the Human: Fictions of Anomaly, Race, and Gender in the Long Eighteenth Century* (Cambridge University Press, 2003) for a fuller account of points made in this chapter.

[11] Thomas Jordan, *London Triumphant: or, The City in Jollity and Splendour: Expressed in various Pageants, Shapes, Scenes, Speeches and Songs . . . for Sir Robert Hanson Knight, Lord Mayor of the City of London. At the Cost and Charges of the Worshipful Company of Grocers* (London, 1672), 3.

[12] Thomas Jordan, *The Triumphs of London, Performed on Friday, Octob. 29. 1675, for the Entertainment of the Right Honourable, and truly Noble Pattern of Prudence and Loyalty, Sir Joseph Sheldon Kt, Lord Mayor of the City of London . . . all set forth at the proper Costs and Charges of the Worshipful Company of Drapers* (London, 1675), 13.

black wool-like-Hair, a Coat of several painted Feathers."[13] Other accounts tell of two negroes dressed in "Indian" habits mounted on griphons. It is not exactly clear whether these performers would have been Africans, though it seems most likely that whites in black greasepaint participated in these pageants.[14]

There were, however, growing numbers of actual Africans in England during the Restoration and eighteenth century. The count of blacks visible in English streets continued to expand until it reached a conspicuous critical mass in the last two decades of the century. Observers suggest that black servants tended to congregate together, and that domestics of both sexes held fashionable gatherings in which they "supped, drank, and entertained themselves with dancing and music, consisting of violins, French horns, and other instruments . . . till four in the morning. No Whites were allowed to be present, for all the performers were Blacks."[15] In the centers of the black slave trade, including Manchester, Liverpool, Birmingham, and Bristol, other private entertainments probably sprung up as well. Freed blacks in England worked in the streets as entertainers, sweepers, or beggars. Most of the slaves sold in London were children, but there were also elite Africans who sent their free young children to be educated in Europe.[16] At the same time the number of blackface roles in the theatre slowly increased even though Africans and East or West Indians themselves were not accepted as principal actors on the London stage.

It is easy to forget that white men performed all the black parts in eighteenth-century drama. English playwrights and actors are able to define racial identities. Early on in tragedy blackface performers exhibit passion along with heroic savagery, and the characters are usually displaced Africans of rank. At mid-century blackface performers are introduced into farce, pantomime, and comedy, all interludes which evolved while the full-scale blackface tragedies continued to be produced. These slaves, servants, and other working-class characters – unlike their princely tragic counterparts – sing, dance, play the guitar, and speak in dialect. These increasingly codified

---

[13] Jordan, *London Triumphant*, 4.
[14] Sybil Rosenfeld, *The Theatre of the London Fairs in the 18th Century* (Cambridge University Press, 1960), 110, quoted by Alfred Jackson, "London Playhouses, 1700–1705," *Research in English Studies*, 8 (1932), 301.
[15] *London Chronicle* 15/1116, February 14–16, 1764, 166, cited in Peter Fryer, *Staying Power: The History of Black People in Britain* (London: Pluto Press, 1984), 69. *The Servants Pocket-Book* (1761) remarks that black servants were known to "herd together." See J. Jean Hecht, *Continental and Colonial Servants in Eighteenth-Century England*, Smith College Studies in History, Vol. 40 (Northampton, MA: Smith College, 1954), 18.
[16] Fryer, *Staying Power*, 60.

racial markers are less an indicator of racial authenticity than a malleable disguise that shifts according to the generic context. Second, such plays allow white men to inhabit black men's bodies, to shape and mold the culture's perceptions of them, while simultaneously implying through racial simulation that race is as ephemeral as paint. The core beneath the racial counterfeit, and perhaps even the core of black men themselves, is imagined as "white." Thus complexion seems nominal if black, and essential if white. Third, these black parts also permit white men to attempt a kind of interracial male bonding that smooths over differences in rank and geographical origin in the interests of Enlightenment humanism.[17] The bond between black and white men seems most urgent to cement at times of significant cultural shifts in race relations, as in the case of the later decades of the eighteenth century when England turned from slavery to abolition. Further, the immigrant population of laborers from Ireland, Scotland, and Wales would have surged, allowing for the identification of disenfranchised groups subject to internal colonization with blackface. Blackface may have provided significant cohesion around shared goals in spite of dissension amongst the groups, and blackface allowed escape into another identity, or the possibility of a hybrid one.[18] Finally, the male bonding between black and white men in these plays seems both to evoke a dynamic homoerotic miscegenation and at the same time to effect a misogynist racism that marginalizes white women and largely eradicates black women from the stage. These plays and others were critical in the formation of national white masculinity at the beginning of modernity, and in unifying that masculinity when liberal white feminism began to gain a public voice.

Here I can only begin to speculate on the cultural functions such characters and plays served. Though Ignatius Sancho remained a member of the audience in the eighteenth-century theatre rather than a performer on stage, his life is reflective of major historical changes for black men and of the awful threat that they posed in the imaginations of many white British men and women. Sancho's life story reflects the danger that former slaves arriving in England posed since he progressed from being a servant without wages to a man who competed with English domestic servants for paid employment, and who finally became a producer of wealth in his own right. Though his letters were published only posthumously (1782), his writings

[17] Robyn Wiegman, *American Anatomies: Theorizing Race and Gender* (Durham and London: Duke University Press, 1995), 126, argues this point in relation to America.
[18] Lhamon, *Raising Cain*, 55, applies the term "vernacular struggle" to the *lumpen* of New York minstrelsy in the 1830s. North American blackface musical performance dates from about 1767, and it was encouraged in Albany at the time of the building of the Erie Canal.

were among the very first to voice anti-slavery sentiments.[19] As Sancho
became better educated and more economically self-sufficient, he aspired
to appear in the two most popular plays with black protagonists, *Othello*
and *Oroonoko*. The "defective articulation" which prevented the realization
of this dream has sometimes been interpreted as stuttering, but more likely
it may have been his speaking with an inflection or dialect that reflected his
origins and his very early years in New Granada.[20] Sancho himself married
a black woman. If he had succeeded in mounting the boards, he would
also have afforded a stark reality to the threat of miscegenation since the
central characters in both tragedies are, of course, black men and white
women.

   Othello and *Oroonoko* continued to be presented throughout the century
in racial counterfeit, and adaptations proliferated along with the increased
consciousness of the cruelty of colonial slavery in the 1760s and 1770s.
In addition to these very familiar tragedies, comic blackfaced characters
appeared most notably in Isaac Bickerstaff's *The Padlock* (1768) and Rev.
Henry Bate's *The Blackamoor Wash'd White* (1776). Perhaps the first minstrel show on the English stage, *The Blackamoor Wash'd White* was booed
from the stage after three performances and never performed again; but
The Padlock was frequently revived, and the name of its blackfaced character, Mungo, entered the language as a synonym for a black man. The
central male characters in these dramas were all acted by white men in
blackface. These precursors of minstrelsy provide, I suggest, an example of
what Eric Lott has called "minstrelsy's mixed erotic economy of celebration
and exploitation"[21] and of a white culture's fascination with black skin.

   A critical view of minstrelsy now largely out of favor suggests that by
robbing a culture to exploit it, blackface is simply a form of white dominance over blacks. In the two eighteenth-century comic plays by Bickerstaff
and Bate we can see that the blackface characters certainly display important elements of cultural robbery – an exaggerated dialect, a performance of
African dancing or singing – but the concept of such thievery is more exactly
descriptive of the nineteenth century.[22] If not principally the pillaging of

[19] See Sancho, *Letters of the Late Ignatius Sancho*.
[20] When P. T. Barnum exhibited a macrocephalic African American as a man-monkey, "Zip, the What-
   is-it?" was alleged to lack language. See Bernth Lindfors, ed., *Africans on Stage: Studies in Ethnological
   Show Business* (Bloomington: Indiana University Press, 1999), ix. The ability to speak was often a
   critical issue in determining the relative humanity or bestiality of Africans.
[21] Eric Lott, *Love and Theft: Blackface Minstrelsy and the American Working Class* (Oxford University
   Press, 1993), 4.
[22] David Dabydeen, *Hogarth's Blacks* (Manchester University Press, 1985), 50, notes representations of
   African dancing in Settle's *Empress of Morocco*, Southerne's *Aaronic*, D'Avenant's *The Playhouse to*

a foreign domain, then what other functions do these blackface comic men absorb on the eighteenth-century stage? Lott remarks with reference to American minstrelsy of the nineteenth century, "The blackface mask is less a repetition of power relations than a *signifier* for them – a distorted mirror, reflecting displacements and condensations and discontinuities between which and the social field there exist lags, unevennesses, multiple determinations."[23] This instability of meaning and its entangling with power relations requires much nuanced decoding when it is transposed to minstrelsy's English prehistory where the fuzzy borders of "white" and "black" were being drawn on stage, a border which W. T. Lhamon, Jr. (building on Mary Louise Pratt) has called a "contact zone" between cultures, and a contact zone which I have suggested incorporates racial difference and empire within white men's bodies.[24] In fact, *The Padlock* and *The Blackamoor* offer important alternatives to the dominant dramatic images of the black prince and the noble savage, and make troubling issues such as miscegenation and slavery potentially ludic, less horrifying, and at the same time represent claims both for and against racial codes. An appearance of harmless hybridity substitutes for the menace of sexual intermixture and interlaces the absurdities of blackface romance. Blackface seems to make *whiteness* essential to the skin while blackness is easily washed off. With Aldridge's arrival on stage that claim is contested because his blackness obviously cannot be erased. But he in turn raises the question of whether *whiteness* is not also contingent by daring to play roles in whiteface.

The Blackamoor Wash'd White is a two-act comic opera first performed at Drury Lane in February 1776. Though the minstrel show was a nineteenth-century American "fiction about blacks that pleased its perpetrators,"[25] blackface comedy in England a century earlier was slow to satisfy an audience. When the production was first mounted, reportedly it was loudly scorned: "Much hissing and Crying out no more no more!" The audience was temporarily appeased only to repeat the response the following night: "Mr. Garrick was on and off the Stage several times nothing would content them."[26] The farce closed after three nights. It is not clear exactly what produced such a pronounced reaction, though the play was certainly unusual

---

be let, Foote's *The Patron*, and Bate's *Harlequin Mungo*. George Colman the Younger's *The Africans* is also ethnographically realist, presenting an imagined Africa with references to groundnuts and couscous, "broil'd ostrich" and "antelope's brisket," tigerskin robes and bird of paradise feathers.

[23] Lott, *Love and Theft*, 8.   [24] Lhamon, *Raising Cain*, 3.

[25] W. T. Lhamon, Jr., "Core is Less," *Reviews in American History*, 27 (1999), 566.

[26] George Winchester Stone, Jr., ed., *The London Stage 1660–1800, Part 4: 1747–1776* (Carbondale, IL: Southern Illinois University Press, 1960), 1948–50.

in its topic and approach. Perhaps the audience was providing a critical response to a weak script, but it may as likely have been responding to the particular treatment of racial and class intermixture that the play advanced, and its portrayal of white women's fascination with black men.

The Blackamoor Wash'd White deals with the cultural anxieties mentioned earlier – that increasing numbers of free blacks would spoil the labor market for English domestics, and that their positions within an urban domestic space might hazard miscegenous unions. There is convincing evidence that when slaves first came to England their wages were paltry or non-existent, and their pay often amounted to shelter and clothing in exchange for their services, their devotion, and the visible display of themselves as part of their owner's wealth. Native-born English servants were more likely to demand monetary remuneration, and earlier in the century blacks had been legally prevented from gaining upward mobility and from competing with whites by serving as apprentices: "The Proclamation by the Lord Mayor of London . . . in September 1731 . . . forbidding as it did the employment of blacks as apprentices in the city" was intended to prevent blacks from usurping white British jobs among the working class.[27] Britain's Committee for the Relief of the Black Poor had convinced the British government to deport its black poor to Sierra Leone in the 1780s. *The Blackamoor Wash'd White* and *The Padlock* are poised between these two legal attempts to limit upward mobility for the poorest of Britain's immigrants. At the end of the Seven Years War (1763) large numbers of the British military returned home to find themselves in a sea of surplus labor. The surge of British soldiers seeking jobs corresponded to the time of black servants' increased resistance to working without wages and not only produced a crisis in employment but provoked persistent difficulties in shaping a postwar masculinity.[28]

A parody of the *Othello* plot, *The Blackamoor Wash'd White* explores the cultural confusions about sexual interaction between the races and the consequences of locating race in social class. In the play the delusional Sir Oliver Oddfish, suspecting that his wife and daughter are attracted to their white male servants, creates a moat around his estate and sacks his staff. Invoking the tradition of washing the Ethiop white, the play comically shows that the blackamoor is only a British soldier masked and painted after all, and that white womanhood will not be sexually threatened by black butlers, footmen, or valets.[29] Blacks were associated almost exclusively with

[27] Fryer, *Staying Power*, 119.   [28] Ibid., 71.

[29] Kim F. Hall, *Things of Darkness: Economies of Race and Gender in Early Modern England* (Ithaca: Cornell University Press, 1995) argues for the ubiquity of the "whitewashed Ethopian" in Renaissance literature: 115.

the servant class and chastized in print for their alleged unwillingness to be employed in other capacities. While class issues appear right on the surface of the play, conversations about the labor of black servants in England help to distance the forced labor of negro slaves in the colonies. Blackface in the eighteenth century (as well as in later minstrel shows) invoked social class so forcefully that the language of race also helps us to map the concept of the working class as these blackface performers, for the first time comic, replicate the troubles of the laborers on stage.[30] It is not completely clear in the play as to whether the sexual intermixture with blacks, or the unstable social class attributed to their seeking employment, is more troubling to the emerging consciousness of a middling class.

The play sexualizes both white and black male servants because they have easy access to women in the boudoir, and it treats the difference in status between lady and attendant as irrelevant in the face of desire. As the play progresses, Sir Oliver Oddfish asks his nephew Grenville to replace the white servants with blacks, "a regiment of Blackamoor Devils," so that his womenfolk will be safer from sexual temptation.[31] The play mocks Oddfish's naivete about the reputed sexuality of black men, though the joke rests on blackface – that a white man pretending to be black, not an actual African, expresses desire for his daughter. Grenville coaxes his friend Frederic to disguise himself as the black Amoroso in order to court Sir Oliver's daughter Julia. That the disguise, a discarded masquerade costume, is a readily available prop indicates the pervasiveness of racial impersonation in the broader culture. The comedy in *Blackamoor* rests in part on Frederic's speaking dialect, one of the earliest examples of racialized speech, with genuflections to "massa," as well as offering the opportunity for malapropisms and *double entendres*.

A taleteller like Othello, Frederic recounts the story of an Egyptian man who, like Sir Oliver, zealously hovers over the white and red fruit of his cherry tree, an obvious allusion to Julia's complexion. The tale is also vaguely linked to the garden of Eden in that a cherry tree figures as the fatal apple tree, and the blackened Frederic is likened to the devil. Sir Oliver is "blackened" too when, in an allusion to Othello, he puts a handkerchief over his head to spy on his wife whom he suspects of cuckolding him. The allegory allows for titillating allusions to a woman's sexual part, her cherry, ripe for picking. The comedy arises from averting an Othello-like tragedy; but this Othello is not really black, the sexual threat is merely a ruse, and the

---

[30] Lott, *Love and Theft*, 69.
[31] The play in Larpent MS 400 is cited from the Henry E. Huntington Library, San Marino, California.

pretend "black" servant rises to become a white gentleman. To black up has been "the most fortunate metamorphosis of his life" since it has won him Sir Oliver's approval. In washing the blackamoor white, the comic opera offers cultural reassurance that white British men will not be contaminated by the threat of black servants, by miscegenous offspring, or by the working class. Blackface is a convenient vehicle that allows a white man to win his beloved and to be judged on virtue rather than rank. This play underscores the way that class, like race, for white men is tentative and impermanent, and that race might be provisional for black men as well.

Though the character Frederic is not a member of the white working class as later minstrels often were, the one white servant remaining, Jerry, gives voice to working-class anxieties about black freemen and even East Indians taking English jobs: "Why surely the times are turn'd topsey turvey, that white Englishmen should give place to foreign Blacks." Suggesting that "the Devils bastard" will "sculpt a body in one's sleep," the first act of the comic opera ends with a song because, although Frederic (Amoroso) pretends to be black and alien and working class, he turns out to be a white soldier. In short, black reassuringly proves to be white:

> Must a Christian man's son born & bred up,
>   By a *Negar* be flung in disgrace?
> Be asham'd for to hold his poor head up,
>   'Cause as how he has got a white face?
>   – No never mind it little *Jerry*,
>   Let your honest heart be merry;
>   British boys will still be right,
>   Till they prove that *black is white*!

In this play black *is* reassuringly white since Frederic blacks up and pretends to be a servant, but his core remains white. The wish that blacks will prove to be white, that skin is merely a costume which can be discarded to reveal a white heart and soul, is a constant theme of eighteenth-century representations. In this comic opera, being black is a whimsical habit to put on, a mere costume easily removed, rather than a skin color or geographical origin with real consequences. *The Blackamoor* thus introduces a precursor to American minstrelsy in a singing blackface trickster who engages in comic routines to contest authority in the person of a dominant, if easily duped, patriarch. The humor in the concluding acts of the play focuses on the grotesqueness of the blackened Frederic courting the lovely white Julia. She returns the affection while repeatedly reassuring them that the disguised Frederic is white underneath, both as a character and as a man.

This play and others like it trifle with the connotations of "black" as it can be variously applied to suggest that the word itself carries hilarity. *The Blackamoor* also allows the characters unselfconsciously to utter racisms against the counterfeit black, including making allusions to a black mazzard (a wild cherry), ugly devil, blackey man, raven, magpie, Satan, and calling attention to "saucer" eyes. Like later minstrelsy, it displays "the power of 'blackness' while deriding it."[32]

Another black part occurs in an anonymous one-act Christmas pantomime employing stock characters, *Furibond; or, Harlequin Negro*, in which a chorus celebrates England as the home of liberty. Applauding the end of the slave trade, this play, first performed at the Theatre Royal in Drury Lane in 1807, follows the well-established harlequinade form with its sequential scenes of comic trickery.[33] A West Indian plantation owner and collector of museum exotica, Sir Peevish Antique, is about to return to England. His daughter Columbine resists her father's plan to marry her to Furibond, a Caliban-like Jamaican enchanter wishing for a white skin who exercises his magic to pursue her and to reappear in England as the Dandy Lover.

"Black" is again an inherently comic concept associated with discomfort or embarrassed laughter. For example, a comic black female servant absconds with a basket laden with food, and the strokes of the Harlequin's magic sword turn a lottery bill into one for "shining japan blacking" (294). The Clown acting the part of a shoe-black applies the blacking to Furibond's white stocking. When a scuffle ensues, the Clown blackens Furibond's face, clothes, and legs in his disguise as "a Buck," a patronizing term for a young black man.

This pantomime is, then, in its comic revelry, a fulfillment of the potential intermarriage between black servant and white master's daughter that was booed from the stage decades earlier in *A Blackamoor Wash'd White*. Yet the white man as Harlequin is more ambiguous than a white man acting as a black servant. In fact, the original complexion color of the black-masked Harlequin covered in black tunic and tights is even more difficult to determine since his disguised person benignly unites black and white

---

[32] Lott, *Love and Theft*, 26.
[33] See the introduction to *Furibond; or Harlequin Negro* (London, 1808) in Jeffrey N. Cox, ed., *Slavery, Abolition and Emancipation: Writings in the British Romantic Period* (5 vols., London: Pickering and Chatto, 1999), v, 281–305. The play is cited from this edition.

men and in particular conjures up signs of mixed race. These comic plays make the ornamental nature of race the subject of ludicrous clowning and stage business. The performance of race is a laughing matter, blackness a pliable concept, and the easy union of black and white, especially black and white men, becomes a cause for revising national hymns to celebrate a white masculinity that can simply fold blackness into itself.

II

The plays of the later decades of the eighteenth century and into the nine-teenth century – many of which I do not have the space to discuss here – increase the number of blackface roles played by white men. In the late eighteenth century, I suggest, the masking and unmasking of white actors eventually substitutes for the confusion between geographical identities and hues – between Indian and African, between copper and mahogany – more typical of the earlier period. White actors in blackface reassured their audi-ences that race is as easily removed as washing or smudging, but the point was also to reveal the reassuringly ineradicable whiteness within. Lacking a language and a cultural context for asserting that a black "heart" or "core" could be virtuous, some blacks submitted to the indignity of claiming they possessed white hearts under their black skins. Yet when Ottabah Cugoano argues for an "essential" man, the core of character and worth is devoid of color instead of unveiling a pithy whiteness beneath the surface. He writes,

It does not alter the nature and quality of a man, whether he wears a black or a white coat, whether he puts it on or strips it off, he is still the same man. And so likewise, when a man comes to die, it makes no difference whether he was black or white, whether he was male or female, whether he was great or small, or whether he was old or young; none of these differences alter the essentiality of the man, any more than [if] he had wore a black or a white coat and thrown it off for ever.[34]

For Cugoano men have an essential humanity *sans* tincture rather than possessing a black surface which can be removed to reveal the white kernel of the spirit.

The eighteenth-century stage then provides a peculiar interlude between the presumably all-white, all-male stage of Shakespeare and the appearance of the first black male actor in a patent theatre in 1833.[35] Throughout the

[34] Quobna Ottobah Cugoano, *Thoughts and Sentiments on the Evil of Slavery* (1787), ed. Vincent Carretta (New York: Penguin, 1999), 41.
[35] See the important biography from which I have derived much information on Aldridge, Marshall and Stock, *Ira Aldridge*, 37, 53.

time after white women appear on stage for the first time, frequently in breeches roles, white male actors appear in blackface. But during these years when actual black men do not mount the boards, and white women often act transgressively in breeches roles, the parts of black women are erased even when the story would seem to command their presence. Sexual realism precedes racial tension. Women and blacks were excluded from being "themselves" on stage. The initial appearance of female bodies on the Restoration stage opened the possibility of a theatre career for women, stimulated the writing of crossdressed roles, and at the same time clarified gender difference. In being crossdressed *women* for the first time after the Renaissance rather than boys in women's clothing, actresses were able to taunt audiences to imagine their heterosexual difference under men's clothing. Thus they performed difference and subjected themselves to its regulation at the same time. The case of black actors is a unique instance. A literal connection between representing a black body and an actual black body on stage was delayed by a full century and a half after white women had been admitted to the English stage. The popularity of black parts encouraged playwrights to invent such roles as they had done in the case of breeches parts, but it seems likely that black characters acted by a black man both stabilized "race" in a way that had not occurred before – since he could not reveal his inherent whiteness – and solidified fears of miscegenation. Yet a real black man also forced rethinking of whether (masculine) whiteness was fundamental.

In the years immediately preceding abolition in England, the counterfeit black man came to coexist with the embodied black man on the early nineteenth-century English stage. Ira Aldridge, most probably born in New York of Fulah ancestry from Senegal, was known as "the African Roscius," and he first acted in the African Free School in New York. As noted earlier, his roles ranged from Othello and Oroonoko to the violent Zanga in Young's *Revenge* and Hassan in Lewis's *Castle Spectre*.

Young's *Revenge* (combining *Othello* and Aphra Behn's *Abdelazer, or the Moor's Revenge*) was first produced on stage at Drury Lane in April 1721. The play makes untenable the potential links between black man and white, slave and colonizer, which were so prominent in the comedies. The hero Zanga's princely status gives his revenge efficacy and strength while avoiding any direct criticism of England's slave trade or arousing concerns about Othello-like mixed-race liaisons while it reconciles England to Africa. His rage (mitigated by sentiment and love of a lost country) may also be interpreted as the representation of the legitimate reprisal of all Africans for their captivity. Miscegenation is not at issue, and the theme adds bite to the *Othello* plot in making Zanga's revenge representative of more than a black man's jealousy. The noble but murderous Zanga avenges a parricide and in so doing, retaliates for the murder of all Africans and their displacement from their country by Spain rather than England. If played by Ira Aldridge the anti-slavery message might have seemed especially powerful to the English audience. On the other hand, when Zanga was played by Edward Kean as he was in 1815, the black man's revenge may have appeared less terrifying since the Moor was, after all, simply a painted white man whose enslavement was only as permanent as the greasepaint on his skin. These plays offer versions of slavery that attempt to reconcile Africa and England in various ways.

In *The Revenge* and also in *Castle Spectre* the black male character is at once violent, sentimental, and heroic – a noble African slave, or a former slave, whose captivity seems especially heinous because of his princely status while, as we have seen, the black characters of eighteenth-century comedy are largely working-class servants. *The Padlock*, first performed very successfully at Drury Lane Theatre in 1768, was often paired with *Oroonoko* or *Othello* as Aldridge's most frequently acted roles, but Mungo was his principal comic part. The latter offered him an early minstrel role in which he sang and played the guitar as the crafty slave of a West Indian planter.[36] The story involves an aging Don Diego who ponders marriage with his sixteen-year-old poverty-stricken ward Leonora, who is in love with the young Leander. Padlocking Leonora and Mungo into his home to guard her purity in his absence, Don Diego tells of having "banish'd all that had the shadow of man, or male kind" (30), apparently excluding Mungo from the category of humankind and ignoring his masculinity. Like *The Blackamoor Wash'd White*, *The Padlock* is filled with masculine dominance and racialized violence. Yet the play also displays a compromised black masculinity aligned with disability, white slavery, and passive white femininity.

The African character Gambia in Thomas Morton's *The Slave* (1816), adapted from the novel *Sélico* (1793) by Florian, differs substantially from other serious plays with black parts in charging that "there is a state worse than slavery" (314) since Gambia is himself an enslaver of his fellow man, and he does not support the slave rebellion that occasions the play. *The Slave* also questions whether the hybrid woman's allegiance should lie with England or with Africa, and racial romance is a means of refining national and racial

---

[36] Isaac Bickerstaff, *The Padlock, A Farce* (London, 1823). This edition in the William Andrews Clark Memorial Library is the only edition existing which is faithfully marked with the stage business and stage directions, as it was performed at the Theatre Royal. There is a modern reprint in Cox, *Slavery, Abolition and Emancipation* v, 73–108.

loyalties. In a series of reversals, Clifton and Gambia, white man and black, become brothers whose bonds supersede Clifton's love for Zelinda: "If we are not brothers, let the white man blush that he is alien to the blood that mantles in that noble breast" (353). Enslaving Africans turns out to be a contest of masculinity: "These fetters are too large – the forger of these bonds thought they were to control manly vigour." After Clifton quells the rebellion with mercy – "The sword achieved much, but clemency more" (343) – Zelinda willingly agrees to freeing Gambia from slavery rather than herself. The black and white man are reconciled, slavery and its violence forgotten, and the quadroon woman selflessly accepts remaining a slave so that the men can be together. The freed Gambia will accompany Clifton while Zelinda stoically remains in Surinam with her child: "England! Shall I behold thee? Talk of fabled land, or magic power! But what land, that poet ever sung, or enchanter swayed, can equal that, which, when the Slave's foot touches, he becomes free!" (380). Rather than haunting white men, or embodying the African man's loss, here the woman of color accedes to her own self-sacrifice and that of her child to free black *men* and, in the process, strengthen the male bond across color lines at her expense. But the play does not end with this lesson. All are finally freed when even the most reprobate of white men reforms. In turn, because of his devotion to Zelinda, Gambia, his very name an African country, frees Clifton from debtor's prison and from the guilt of past wrongs. In fact, in *The Revenge*, *Castle Spectre*, and *The Slave*, the African tutors the white man in moral law and in civility.

The Slave may provide a partial explanation for the demise of the Inkle and Yarico story at the end of the eighteenth century. In that popular cultural fable, of course, an English sea captain mercilessly sells his pregnant mistress, variously African or American Indian, into slavery. Zelinda, unlike Yarico, embodies the hybridity within herself rather than shifting from one tinctured or geographical identity to another since she would have been played by a white woman. At the historical moment of abolition, however, the freed black man – without much sympathy for slave rebellion and heroically rejecting the quadroon woman he loves – is encouraged to join hands in brotherhood with the white man. Both men desire her, yet both willingly relinquish her. Together they abandon the mixed-race woman and the hybrid child who provide all too public evidence of the white man's sexual desires. No longer a story of Inkle's misogyny and racism, the racial romance evolves into a tribute to the capacity of the black man to save the white man from himself. *The Slave* successfully desexualizes the black male as sexual competition and sentimentalizes him. Here as in *The*

Blackamoor Wash'd White the relationship between black and white man may be interpreted homoerotically since the noble Gambia was sometimes played by a black actor.[37] *The Slave* justifies freeing the black man because he will continue to serve the white man and his interests even without his fetters – all the more crucial when an actual black man is playing Gambia the Slave, one of Aldridge's most popular roles. In addition the play offers reassurance that the discomfiting hybrid woman and her offspring will be appropriately abandoned and forgotten like Africa, slavery, and the miscegenation which she represents.

Aldridge's certifiable blackness in the role of Gambia would have emphasized the importance of color and questioned the easy equation of whiteness with virtue. In short, the various hues are less flexible and assigned hierarchical meaning in *The Slave* and in later plays including *The Africans*. The cultural function which color-shifting figures played evaporates with abolition; racial categories and their relationship to geography and nation harden; and the playfulness with which actors inhabited variously colored bodies becomes a matter of great seriousness.

III

If masquerade is "both a displacement of empire and an embrace of it," and if it is "an almost erotic commingling with the alien"[38] that offers a celebration and adoration of otherness, it is also worth noting that the alien who is presented as a racial fabrication on the eighteenth-century stage is almost invariably male until the performance of Colman's *Inkle and Yarico* in 1787. Blackface in the theatre is the masculine counterpart to the bewitchingly supple colorings and origins of female characters in fiction and popular lore such as Imoinda and Yarico. In the early nineteenth-century theatre, costumed and painted white women playing women of color absorb slavery's contradictions to reform or enoble men, both African and English. Black women were both more malleable because they, like other women, possessed no character at all, and more terrifying because of their capacity to reproduce slaves as valuable commodities. This insistence on the "masquerade of race" seems to lessen the fear of miscegenation as white men become one with their object of oppression in the contact zone of the imperial theatre. The history of Aldridge's repertory and of other black parts allows us to witness the blackface representation of men

[37] Lott, *Love and Theft*, 57, writes of the "homoerotic charge" of nineteenth-century American minstrelsy.
[38] Terry Castle, *Masquerade and Civilization: The Carnivalesque in Eighteenth-Century English Culture and Fiction* (Stanford University Press, 1986).

of color as a spectacle to wash the blackened *Englishman*, not the actual blackamoor, white. Whiteness is portrayed as fundamental and permanent while blackness is ornamental and temporary until a black actor takes the stage, and the white spectator freshly confronts the fictive nature of race while attaching blackness to a real body.

Both the noble and the ignoble negro in these plays with blackface parts are manipulated to fortify a white English masculinity as blackface, like minstrelsy, is enlisted for racist, misogynist, and class-related purposes. Rather than determining whether racism preceded slavery or the reverse, I am arguing that racism itself is enormously flexible in its historical manifestations. Various blackface roles define blackness as noble *and* savage, as prince *and* slave, as heroic *and* comic, as blank verse *and* speaking dialect, as being threatening to white women *and* forming a racial alliance against them, as being both black and white. Yet I am also charting a shift from the eighteenth century to the early nineteenth century which would make blackness less "both/and," less separable from skin, hair, and facial features and progressively rather more locatable. The representation of blackness by white actors makes the difference of complexion essential since white men can perform race, but black men cannot perform themselves on the English stage until Aldridge.

Once Aldridge took the stage (though blackface of course continues into contemporary times on stage and colorblind casting is an increasingly common practice), in an important way neither the Englishman *nor* the blackamoor could be washed white as convincingly.[39] What is being staged is that unlike the case for whites, for blacks, race is not a performance that can be discarded. In fact, Aldridge's later performances in the 1860s as Othello made blatantly obvious the corporeality of "race" as illustrated in a memoir by his Desdemona, Mrs. Madge Robertson (Kendal):

Mr. Ira Aldridge was a man who, being black, always picked out the fairest woman he could to play Desdemona with him, not because she was capable of acting but because she had a fair head. One of the great bits of "business" that he used to do was where, in one of the scenes he had to say, "Your hand, Desdemona," he made a very great point of opening his hand and making you place yours in it, and the audience used to see the contrast. He always made a point of it and to a round of applause, how I do not know. It always struck me that he had some species of . . . real intelligence. Although a genuine black . . . the fairer you were the more obsequious he was to you.

[39] Aldridge's appearance on stage is historically parallel to the increase in ethnographic shows such as the Hottentot Venus and of the European march toward scientific racism. See Z. S. Strother, "Display of the Body Hottentot," in Bernth Lindfors, ed., *Africans on Stage: Studies in Ethnological Show Business* (Bloomington: Indiana University Press, 1999), 1–61.

When Aldridge stages the constructedness of race in his whiteface performance of blackness, at the same time he challenged the impermeability of
whiteness by making *it* seem to be something that could wash off. Aldridge,
like Equiano and Sancho before him, understood that color – if it is determined by corporeal elements – is at the crux of English culture in spite of
white men's wish to make it appear to possess a contingent quality, and that
whiteness cannot easily be transferred. Once the white man in blackface –
the simulated Other, the almost but not quite native – becomes instead a
material presence, a black body to deal with on the streets, in the parks, in
the living museums of London, and on the stage, masqueraders no longer
rush to emulate aliens of color with such regular and studied pleasure.[40] In
fact the public masquerade with its license for racial disguise largely disap-
peared in England at about the time of the abolition of slavery. Instead, a
new racial realism slowly makes a place for the first black actor whose dark
skin and specifically African origins become a crucial part of his appeal on
the English stage.[41] Freeing the slaves paradoxically exacerbated the racism
that had fostered black slavery in England of the early nineteenth century,
and abolishing the slave trade encouraged racism's evolution into newer,
more modern, and more firmly located forms of credible fictions which the
first black actor on the English stage took pains to exploit and to contest.

[40] The phrase "almost the same, but not white" appears in Homi Bhabha's classic essay, "Of Mimicry
and Man: The Ambivalence of Colonial Discourse," *October*, 28 (1984), 125–33. I have obviously
altered the meaning of Bhabha's phrase.
[41] On the subcontinent of India, "The wearing of Indian dress in public functions by employees of the
[East India] Company was officially banned in 1830." Bernard S. Cohn, *Colonialism and its Forms
of Knowledge: The British in India* (Princeton University Press, 1996), 112.

CHAPTER 4

Asians in Britain: negotiations of identity through self-representation

Michael H. Fisher

ASIANS ENTERING BRITAIN

By the late eighteenth century, Asian men and women of a variety of classes had established themselves in Britain.[1] At this time, many Britons believed their own "modernity" was evinced by their participation in the institutions and practices of public culture, including the rapidly emerging capitalist print media.[2] Yet British ideas about "modernity," as about "race" and "nation," were developing in the context of early European imperialism in Asia.[3] Thus, as early Asian settlers or visitors moved to Britain, they had access to the evolving media and forms of public discourse to represent themselves directly to British audiences. To do this, Asians had to negotiate, adapt, accommodate, or refuse British efforts to shape "Oriental" or "Asian" racial and national identities.

While "Orientalism" no doubt eventually dominated public discourse in Britain, Asian voices thus continually challenged it.[4] Edward Said's early work particularly, however, overlooks the agency of Asians, tending rather to make them appear mainly as victims.[5] Tanika Sarkar critiques this omission of Asian agency in the colonies:

---

[1] In this chapter the term "Asian" is used to designate people coming from south, southeast, central, west, and east Asia, rather than the more perjorative term used commonly in the eighteenth century, "Asiatic." The concepts of "Indian" nationality and "East Indian" ethnicity were not yet established, although specific "nations" like Chinese were used.

[2] For "modernity" and South Asians, see Arjun Appadurai, *Modernity at Large* (Minneapolis: University of Minnesota Press, 1996).

[3] See Benedict Anderson, *Imagined Communities* (London: Verso, 1983), especially 41–9, and Kathleen Wilson, *The Sense of the People: Politics, Culture and Imperialism in Britain 1715–1785* (Cambridge University Press, 1995), especially 29–54.

[4] See John M. Mackenzie, "Empire and Metropolitan Cultures," in Andrew Porter, ed., *Oxford History of the British Empire, Vol. III: The Nineteenth Century* (Oxford University Press, 1999), 270–93; Mackenzie, *Orientalism: History, Theory, and the Arts* (Manchester University Press, 1995); D. A. Washbrook, "Orients and Occidents," in Robin W. Winks, eds., *Oxford History of the British Empire, Vol. V: Historiography* (Oxford University Press, 1999), 596–611.

[5] Said's later works, and those of other scholars, have recognized Asian and African agency in self-representations. Edward Said, *Culture and Imperialism* (New York: Alfred A. Knopf, 1993); Ibrahim

Most recent works on cultural developments in the colonial period tend to assume the operations of a single, monolithic colonial discourse with fully hegemonistic capabilities. All that South Asians could possibly do was to either form a secondary, derivative discourse that simply extended the message of the master-text, or refuse and resist its positions and language . . . This position . . . necessarily robs colonized Indians of effective agency and evacuates an especially complicated historical problem of all complexities . . . [B]oth complicity and resistance of Indians would equally and exclusively shape themselves around a colonial agenda and be eternally parasitic upon it.[6]

Even more so in metropolitan Britain, Asians used Britain's developing print capitalism to project their self-portrayals to a largely anonymous anglophone, socially mixed audience.

The concept of "Asian" in most British minds at first carried few of the negative connotations that colonialism would gradually infuse into it. Further, in early modern Britain, "'race' was identified and signified through religion, cultural practice, custom, language, climate, aesthetics and historical time, as much as physiognomy and biology."[7] Since Asians, who so chose, could adapt themselves to British norms in all these categories except physiognomy and biology, this left room, albeit limited room, for diverse Asians to reshape identities within British society. Asians and their hosts negotiated relationships and roles that, while based on their constantly changing but usually unequal economic and political power, none the less reflected to some degree the agency of both. Some Asians pioneered new forms of cultural entrepreneurial activity which, as a result of their Asian origin, presented them as different from, yet attractive to, European audiences: employers, employees, social or sexual partners, and/or patrons. Nevertheless, British definitions over time increasingly stressed ascriptive factors like biological "race," diminishing Asian assimilation into the host culture. Nor was assimilation necessarily their desire or in their interest. Out of these asymmetrical dialogues between diverse Asians and varieties

Abu-Lughod, *Arab Rediscovery of Europe* (Princeton University Press, 1963); Muhammad As-Saffar, *Disorienting Encounters*, ed. and trans. Susan Miller (Berkeley: University of California Press, 1991); Mushirul Hasan, "Resistance and Acquiescence in North India," in Mushirul Hasan and Narayani Gupta, eds., *India's Colonial Encounter* (Delhi: Manohar, 1993), 39–63; Bernard Lewis, *The Muslim Discovery of Europe* (London: Weidesfeld and Nicolson, 1982).

[6] Tanika Sarkar, "A Book of Her Own," *History Workshop Journal*, 36 (Autumn 1993), 61.

[7] See Kathleen Wilson, "The Island Race," in Tony Claydon and Ian McBride, eds., *Protestantism and National Identity* (Cambridge University Press, 1998), 267; Roxann Wheeler, *The Complexion of Race: Categories of Difference in Eighteenth-Century British Culture* (Philadephia: University of Pennsylvania Press, 2000), 7; Mark Harrison, *Climates and Constitutions* (Delhi: Oxford University Press, 1999).

of indigenous Britons came shifting Asian self-representations and social roles.[8]

An Asian's scope for self-representation, and the reception of those auto-biographical utterances by the British public, varied by the author's class and gender, as well as by the medium selected – for example, printed books or mass-distributed newspaper advertisements. Conversely, the presuppositions of the self-representational medium and the public reception of an Asian's use of it clearly reshaped his or her own sense of self.[9]

Some recent scholars have argued powerfully for recognition of the diversity of metropolitan Britain's past, not as a "mere pluralizing gesture . . . [but rather to] rematerialize the movement of colonial subjects from the so-called peripheries to the ostensible center."[10] Stressing the identities embodied in the distinctive cultures of Asians or Africans in Britain, these writings advocate reconceptualization of Britain as a diverse society. Postmodernist thought, with its problematizing of all categories and dichotomies, resonates with the strand of writing that depicts Britain as filled with a variety of shifting, unstable, and unclassifiable peoples with multiple and contingent identities.[11] Less explicitly oriented toward the present situation in Britain, some excellent historical scholarship has already begun to emerge which studies the history of the complex and changing relationships among Asians, Africans, and Britons in Britain and the participation of each of these in public culture.[12]

---

[8] Asian self-representations in Indian languages lie outside of the scope of this chapter. See Gulfishan Khan, *Indian Muslim Perceptions of the West* (Karachi: Oxford University Press, 1998); Juan Cole, "Invisible Occidentalism," *Iranian Studies*, 25, 3–4 (1992), 3–16; Kumkum Chatterjee, "History as Self-Representation"; and my "Representations of India," *Modern Asian Studies*, 32, 4 (1998), 891–948; Simon Digby, "Eighteenth Century Narrative," in Christopher Shackle, ed., *Urdu and Muslim South Asia* (London: SOAS, 1989), 49–65.

[9] For a scintillating account of the "conflictual discourses" used by marginalized subjects in the inherently bourgeois genre of autobiography, see Felicity Nussbaum, *The Autobiographical Subject* (Baltimore: The Johns Hopkins University Press, 1989), 10.

[10] Antoinette Burton, *At the Heart of the Empire* (Berkeley: University of California Press, 1998), 6–7.

[11] See Panikos Panayi, *Immigration, Ethnicity and Racism in Britain* (Manchester University Press, 1994); see also Salman Rushdie's extensive works; Prafulla Mohanti, *Through Brown Eyes* (New York: Penguin Books, 1989); Farokh Dhondy, *Bombay Duck* (London: Jonathan Cape, 1990); Hanif Kureishi, *Buddha of Suburbia* (New York: Viking, 1990), *London Kills Me* (London: Faber and Faber, 1991), and *Intimacy* (New York: Scribner, 1999).

[12] E.g., Laura Tabili, *"We Ask for British Justice"* (Ithaca: Cornell University Press, 1994); Tabili, "The Construction of Racial Difference," *Journal of British Studies* 33, 1 (January 1994), 54–98; Antoinette Burton, "Making a Spectacle of Empire," *History Workshop*, 42 (1996), 126–46; Ruth Lindborg, "'Asiatic,'" *Victorian Studies* 37, 3 (Spring 1994); Ron Ramdin, *The Making of the Black Working Class* (Aldershot: Gower, 1987); Frank Reeves, *British Racial Discourse* (New York: Cambridge University Press, 1983); Paul Rich, *Race and Empire*, 2nd edn (Cambridge University Press, 1990).

Thus, eighteenth-century Asian autobiographical assertions in the metropole complicate our understanding of British imperialism and the development of Britain itself. This chapter examines these issues, highlighting a much traveled Asian, Emin (1726–1809), who lived nearly a decade in Britain and later made himself the first Asian to write autobiographically and publish a book in English. It embeds analysis of Emin in a larger survey of Asians in early modern Britain.

A DIVERSITY OF ASIANS IN BRITAIN

Despite official British efforts to limit the number of Asians coming to Britain, contain them after their arrival, and expel them quickly thereafter, many resisted these constraints and created spaces for themselves within British society. Some settled for considerable lengths of time, a few for the rest of their lives. Occasionally Asians achieved considerable upward social mobility in Britain. For example, Emin and Dean Mahomed both became gentlemen and professionals, even if they had once been manual laborer and servant respectively.[13] Abu Talib, a scholar and official, successfully sustained his celebrated (albeit inaccurate) identity as "Persian Prince" during three London seasons (1800–2).[14] Indian aristocrats and diplomats also found places for themselves with the corresponding classes in Britain.

As Britain's links to India expanded from the mid-eighteenth century onward, increasing numbers of working-class Asians arrived. Asian sailors (lascars) worked on ships which brought Asian goods to Britain.[15] Various Europeans brought with them Indian servants, as did elite Asians traveling to Britain for business, politics, legal disputes, or pleasure. Figure 2, Official return of "black servants" and lascars from Britain to India, indicates that over 1,500 working-class Asians traveled to and from Britain between 1748 and 1768. Of these working-class people, all the lascars were male, about half the servants were female.[16] By the early nineteenth century, over a

---

[13] See my *Travels of Dean Mahomed* (Berkeley: University of California Press, 1997).

[14] See my "Representing 'His' Women," *Indian Economic and Social History Review*, 37, 2 (2000), 215–37.

[15] See Rozina Visram, *Asians in Britain* (London: Pluto Press, 1992) and N. Benjamin, "British and Indian Sailors," in P. M. Joshi and M. A. Nayeem, eds., *Studies in the Foreign Relations of India* (Hyderabad: State Archives, 1975), 485–96.

[16] This chart, complied from East India Company records, British Library [hereinafter BL], understates since more reached England than returned or returned unofficially. For these records, the East India Company designated all people of Asian and mixed Asian and European descent as "Black," although most British authorities and public opinion generally distinguished between Africans and Asians, and used "Black" in inconsistent ways during this period.

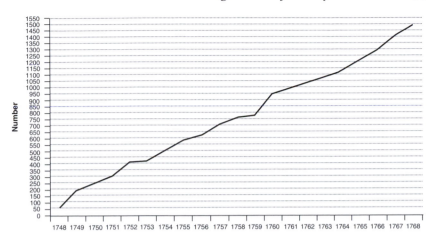

Figure 2   Official return of "black servants" and lascars from Britain to India, cumulative total by year, 1748–68. Compiled from East India Company records, British Library.

thousand Asians arrived annually in Britain. Such a counter-flow complicates established notions both of European imperialism as entirely white intrusion into non-white territories and of Britain as an exclusively white society until post-World war II Asian and African immigration.

Relatively far fewer Asian women than men made the journey to Britain, and women tended to scatter more into British society. The largest number of Asian women came as nursemaids and other servants. A few Asian wives or mistresses of Europeans accompanied their partners to Europe, basing their social class on that of their European male, indexed by the type of relationship they had with him.[17] Indeed, until about the mid-nineteenth century, when Anglicized and Christian, the children of such mixed marriages or relationships found different degrees of acceptance in British society. For example, Lord Liverpool, prime minister from 1812 to 1827, was of mixed Asian-European descent.[18] Others, including women, fared less well, as chapter 14 in this volume by Durba Ghosh suggests.[19] Yet within Britain, informal sexual relationships and recognized marriages between Asian (or African) men and British women within their respective social classes remained relatively frequent and commonplace well into the nineteenth

[17] See Abu Talib Khan, on Haleme Banu, the Asian wife of General DeBoigne in London *c.* 1800: *Masir Talibi fi Bilad Afranji*, ed. Hosein Khadive-Jam (Tehran: Islamic Revolution Publication and Educational Organization, 1983, reprint), 100–1.
[18] See Norman Gash, *Lord Liverpool* (Cambridge, MA: Harvard University Press, 1984), 10.
[19] Christopher Hawes, *Poor Relations* (London: Curzon, 1996).

century.[20] The British male establishment, however, increasingly objected
to such relationships. Indeed, many British authorities regarded British
prostitutes and 'fallen women' as threats to Asian men, rather than the
reverse.[21]

From the late eighteenth century onward, "Oriental quarters" developed
in Britain's major port cities. Here Asian sailors and other transient visitors
found lodging, food, and companionship, while providing income to their
hosts. Many of the male rooming-house and tavern-keeping hosts were
Asian settlers in Britain who thus catered to Asian visitors as their own means
of economic advancement. Almost all of the host women in this mixed
society were British, the consorts of Asian men.[22] Such British women
both adapted some Asian identity (such as names) but also retained some
British identity that they conveyed to their Asian partners (such as nominal
Christianity). As in colonized spaces on the subcontinent and elsewhere,
the negotiation of identity through naming was an important instrument
in claiming subjectivity and national status.[23]

Overall in the metropolis, indigenous British systems of patriarchy
tended to favor male Asian settlers over European females. Asian men could
often control property and enter public discourse more easily there than
could married British women, including British women they themselves
married. Conversely, in the colonies, British colonial attitudes tended to
"feminize" all Asians: empowering European men, and women as well, over
Asian men and women.[24] Related, but not identical, to relations between
males and females were the contested cultural concepts of gender which
again followed different trajectories in metropolis and colony.[25]

Most Asians in Britain came disproportionately from the minority populations of Muslims, Armenians, Parsis, and Christians; orthodox Brahman-
ical restrictions on travel and life overseas proved an additional obstacle for
high-born Hindus. A significant proportion of Asians who settled in Britain
became Christian there – at least in name if not necessarily by conviction,
accepting "Christian" names in Britain without any religious conversion.
Others, like Dean Mahomed, became Christian but retained an explicitly

[20] See Stephen Braidwood, *Black Poor and White Philanthropists* (Liverpool University Press, 1994),
148, and Douglas A. Lorimer, *Colour, Class and the Victorians* (Leicester University Press, 1978).
[21] Society for the Protection of Asiatic Seamen, advertisement, *The Times* (London), December 9,
1814.
[22] See Joseph Salter, *Asiatic in England* (London: Seely, Jackson, and Halliday, 1873), 26–7.
[23] See chapter 14 by Ghosh in this volume.
[24] See Mrinalini Sinha, *Colonial Masculinity* (Manchester University Press, 1995). This created a particularly problematic role for later British feminists dealing with Indian issues. See Antoinette Burton,
Burdens of History (Chapel Hill: University of North Carolina Press, 1994).
[25] See Kumkum Sangari, "Relating Histories," in Svati Joshi, ed., *Rethinking English* (Delhi: Oxford
University Press, 1994), 32–123.

non-Christian name. In the 1750s, Emin Anglicized his name from "Ameen son of Hovsep" to "Joseph Emin," to make it easier for Britons to recognize and pronounce. Further, he made his Armenian Christianity a special marker of self-identification with Britons, and explicitly distanced himself from the Catholic French as well as Muslims and Jews.[26] The relatively high social standing of such Asian men reflected signs of cultural status valued by most Britons: respectable social class, non-Catholic Christian associations, male gender, and English literacy and deportment. British approval of those non-whites who embodied these characteristics diminished over the nineteenth century, however, heightening the barriers against later Asian upward mobility in British society.

The translation of Asians from one cultural arena to another inevitably altered not only their self-perception but also the media and forms available to them for expressing and publicizing these new identities. British legal and legislative systems differed in values and procedures from those in India, often according more effective juridical agency to Asians in Britain than in their homeland. Many Asians, including lower-class sailors and servants, found that they could deploy their personal testimony to defend their individual and property rights successfully in British courts against Asian or British adversaries.[27] Influential Asians gained access to the British Parliament when other bodies, like the East India Company, rejected their appeals.[28] As Asians learned to write and publish in English, they also gained access to that language's literary forms, including autobiographical genres – which many British conceptualized as prime features of modernity. These genres were not traditionally part of Asian linguistic cultures. Further, British innovations in the technologies of mechanical mass production and ever wider distribution of newspapers and books created a large public readership in Britain from the late eighteenth century onward. In contrast, literacy rates in South Asia remained much lower, printing technology less advanced and more costly, and established elites more reluctant to allow mass access to print media.[29]

[26] *Gentleman's Magazine*, 37 (January 1767), 3–7. Joseph Emin, *Life and Adventures of Joseph Emin, An Armenian Written in English by Himself* (London: The Author, 1792): 2nd edn. A. Apcar (Calcutta: Asiatic Society of Bengal, 1918), 11.

[27] See Proceedings of Old Bailey, Sessional Papers.

[28] See Parliamentary Papers, Select Committee Reports, Second Report, 1772, 265–89; Fifth Report, 1773, 546–49; Reports on Justice in Bengal, 1781–1782, First series, 4, Report on the Administration of, 1783, 39–40, 124.

[29] See B. S. Kesavan, *History of Printing and Publishing in India* (New Delhi: National Book Trust, 1985); Francis Robinson, "Islam and the Impact of Print," in Nigel Crook, ed., *Transmission of Knowledge* (Delhi: Oxford University Press, 1996), 62–97; and C. A. Bayly, *Empire and Information* (Cambridge University Press, 1996).

Various Asians in England used these developing British media and published self-advertisements widely through newspapers and/or books to advance their own cultural assertions. Often they sought employment or patronage by highlighting the author's putative training, ability, and identity as desired by potential employers or patrons. For example, an Asian woman advertised herself in the *Morning Chronicle* (April 1, 1795):

WANTS PLACE: As a servant to a family going to Bengal, a native of that country, where she lived two years with the Lady she is going to leave, who brought her to England, and has kept her here for eight years; she does not quit her place for any fault, but because it no longer suits the Lady to keep her; She can speak French tolerably, having accompanied her mistress to France, and remained there twelve months; can dress hair, cook plain victuals, make bread, wash well, and will endeavour to make herself useful to any lady who may be going to India, or with children. Her mistress with whom she still lives till she can otherwise be provided for, will recommend her.

In such self-representations, Asian servants showed themselves to be accomplished individuals, worthy of the trust of the reader. Less based on Asian agency, other "place wanted" or "for sale" advertisements were placed by their European masters or, in the case of slaves, their owners.[30]

Asian authors of books in English often explicitly intended their demonstrations of literacy to prove their intellectual capacity for such accomplishments to Europeans. Most conventionally highlighted their distinguished patron (to whom the book was dedicated) and listed their prominent subscribers (each of whom had trustingly paid part of the purchase cost in advance of publication, with faith in the author's ability to complete the work). Virtually all early non-white book authors in English therefore explicitly indicated their own agency, stating on the title page "Written by Himself" or "Herself."[31] As many scholars have shown, Asians and Africans often regarded their power to narrate and represent their own experiences in their own terms as powerful modes of resistance to European cultural domination.[32] This assertion remained particularly salient, since many white supporters of slavery defended that institution on the basis that

[30] See Visram, *Asians*, and Peter Fryer, *Staying Power: The History of Black People in Britain* (London: Pluto Press, 1984) for other advertisements.

[31] In addition to Joseph Emin and Dean Mahomed, these include Olaudah Equiano, *Interesting Narrative of the Life of Olaudah Equiano*, ed. James Nichols (1814). Some British authors, including women writers, also asserted their agency through this convention.

[32] See Martin Daunton and Rick Halpern, eds., *Empire and Others: British Encounters with Imperial Peoples, 1600–1850* (London: UCL Press, 1999); Homi Bhabha, *Location of Culture* (New York: Routledge, 1994); Henry Louis Gates, "James Gronniosaw," in James Olney, ed., *Studies in Autobiography* (New York: Oxford University Press, 1988), 51–72; and Said, *Culture and Imperialism*.

"blacks" lacked this very capacity. Even some British abolitionists presupposed that Asians and Africans were incapable of writing for themselves in cultured English.

British assertions of imperial power, however, made their relations with Asians increasingly asymmetrical. In South Asia, the East India Company began in 1757 a century-long conquest that would bring the entire subcontinent under its military domination.[33] Nevertheless, most people in eighteenth-century Britain, including those in the centers of power, did not yet accept such imperialistic assertions.[34] Testimony before Parliament by Asians and their supporters such as Edmund Burke (1729–97) reinforced the British government's aversion to Company aggression in India.[35] Notably, Pitt's 1784 India Act forbade further Company political involvement there. Parliament's disapproval of Governor-General Warren Hastings's unauthorized territorial expansions and abuses of Asians led to his resignation (1784), then impeachment and trial in Parliament (1786–95, with Edmund Burke taking a leading prosecuting role).[36] Thus, Asians who entered eighteenth-century Britain did so before most people on either continent recognized or approved of "British imperialism" in Asia. Not until well into the nineteenth century would leading figures in London come largely to accept and even to advocate the expansion of British rule over India. To project full-blown "imperialism" or "colonialism" into the mid-eighteenth-century perceptions of early Asians in Britain, or into attitudes held by most Britons toward Asians there, would therefore be anachronistic. Nevertheless, we must simultaneously highlight the underlying asymmetrical power relationships that would eventuate in British imperialism.

The growing force of British imperialism, even if not yet articulated fully, continued to change British cultural attitudes toward Asian and African cultures. Britons of many classes, both in provincial towns and in port cities, came to believe passionately in the economic benefits of empire.[37] Particularly from the 1770s onward, much of the information and values about the "Orient" eventually came to Britain through European "Orientalist"

---

[33] In 1757, the British conquered an area three times the size of England; by 1857 they held 1 million square miles. See my *Politics of the British Annexations* (New Delhi: Oxford University Press, 1997).
[34] See Wilson, *Sense of the People*, 137–205.
[35] See Sudipta Sen, *Empire of Free Trade: The English East India Company and the Making of the Colonial Marketplace* (Philadelphia: University of Pennsylvania Press, 1998), 64, and chapter 6 by Sen in this volume.
[36] See P. J. Marshall, *Impeachment of Warren Hastings* (London: Oxford University Press, 1965), and Sara Suleri, *The Rhetoric of English India* (Chicago: University of Chicago Press, 1992).
[37] See Wilson, *Sense of the People*, and H. V. Bowen, *Elites, Enterprise, and the Making of the British Overseas Empire, 1688–1775* (New York: St. Martin's Press, 1996).

scholars and officials as they began to filter, distort, or suppress Asian voices.[38] Said, by examining the ways in which Europeans appropriated the Orient in public discourse, has done much to bring vital issues about representation and its relationship to colonialism to the fore.[39] Mary Louise Pratt also has linked Orientalism and imperialism: "books by Europeans about non-European parts of the world went (and go) about creating the 'domestic subject' of Euroimperialism [and] . . . have engaged metropolitan reading publics with (or to) expansionist enterprises whose material benefits accrued mainly to the very few."[40] In this view, orientalizing European elites made even their general public support imperialism, against its better interests, through the picture of the colonized which these works exclusively paint. Significantly, many of those in late eighteenth-century British society most dismissive of and hostile to Asians and Africans collectively were those Britons who had experience in the colonies and who imported colonial attitudes into Britain. In particular, British slave owners largely identified African, Afro-Caribbean, and other non-white peoples as sub-human commodities.[41] The massive slave trade in Africans, but limited in Asians, often led to British distinctions among "blacks," particularly in the period when slavery was still legal.[42] Thus, we must seek to keep in mind the continued tensions among these various factors as they changed at different rates in the colony and metropole respectively. These appropriations of "the Orient" certainly affected, but did not always translate directly into, British attitudes toward the Asian individuals living among them, however.[43]

Thus, British colonialism created and enhanced inequities between Europeans and Asians. Nevertheless, because of the new networks of transport and communication that imperialism created, Asians coming to Europe encountered new cultural forms and media, with all their challenges and

---

[38] See Said, *Culture and Imperialism*; S. J. Al Azm, "Orientalism and Orientalism in Reverse," *Khamsin*, 8 (1981), 5–26; Lisa Lowe, *Critical Terrains* (Ithaca: Cornell University Press, 1991); MacKenzie, *Orientalism*; Heidi J. Holder, "Melodrama, Realism and Empire on the British Stage," in J. S. Bratton, ed., *Acts of Supremacy* (Manchester University Press, 1991), 29–32; and Tejaswini Niranjana, "Translation, Colonialism and the Rise of English," in Svati Joshi, ed., *Rethinking English*, 124–45.

[39] Edward Said, *Orientalism* (New York: Vintage Books, 1978).

[40] Mary Louise Pratt, *Imperial Eyes: Travel Writing and Transculturation* (London: Routledge, 1992), 4.

[41] See Anthony J. Barker, *African Link* (London: Frank Cass, 1978); Christine Bolt, *Victorian Attitudes to Race* (London: Routledge and Kegan Paul 1971); and Rich, *Race and Empire*, 3–5.

[42] Asians were only sometimes legally and culturally distinguished from Africans. *Public Advertiser*, January 5–19, 1786. See Fryer, *Staying Power*, 115–26.

[43] See Nabil Matar, *Turks, Moors and Englishmen in the Age of Discovery* (New York: Columbia University Press, 1999).

opportunities for autobiographical assertion. A striking example worthy of extended consideration is that of Emin.

AN EARLY ASIAN AUTOBIOGRAPHER

Emin (1726–1809) has left us several substantial self-representations from the 1750s to the 1790s, products of his encounters with British culture in the metropole. They stretch from the precolonial period (prior to any extensive British territorial expansion in South Asia) until a time when the British had already conquered and annexed about 250,000 square miles and were poised for one of their periods of most rapid imperialism there. Through Emin's writing and that of the Britons with whom he dealt, we can examine how they negotiated a mutually attractive "Oriental" identity for him. This identity – publicized mainly through his autobiographical constructions in British public discourse – portrayed him as a self-made individual, a freedom fighter for his nation's liberation from imperialist control.[44]

Although Emin spent most of his life (more than forty years) in Calcutta, he was not by birth South Asian. An Armenian born in Hamadan, Iran, Emin immigrated at age eighteen to Bengal in 1744, where he joined his family and the other 3,000–4,000 Armenians ensconced there. His family offered him an education and he presciently decided to study English, rather than Portuguese, Danish, Dutch, or French; at this time, few would have predicted a British empire in India. In 1751, Emin moved to England, working his passage as a sailor in the company of an Armenian friend.[45] Like many Asian sailors, he left his ship when it reached London, entering British society with £4 11s. 4d., his net pay for the six-month voyage.[46]

While some Asian sailors located themselves among other Asians in a portside neighborhood, Emin, like others, gradually merged into British society. Although Emin initially depended on the patronage of an Armenian jewel merchant, Stephan Cojagian, and occasionally had contact with other Armenians in London, he did not settle among them. Rather, he eventually chose social situations where he was the only Asian present, and he largely adapted himself to British social and sartorial norms, but without losing his

[44] Research into Emin's life by his great-great-granddaughter, Amy Apcar, and unpublished literary analysis by Loretta T. Nassar have added considerably to our understanding of Emin. See also A. R. Ioannisian, *Iosif Emin* (Erevan: Armenian SSR Government, 1989).
[45] Log of Walpole, L/MAR/B/293H, BL.
[46] Receipt book of Walpole, L/MAR/B/293FF, BL.

Figure 3 *Portrait of Emin*, attributed to Arthur Pond, 1756/8. Presumed
destroyed in a fire at Hagley Hall, 1925.

distinctive Armenian identity.[47] Over the next three years in London, Emin
learned lessons about British values through a variety of social situations. At
first, he studied English culture and sciences at Mr. Middleton's Academy
for Boys in Bishopsgate. Unable to continue paying his fees, he then sought
employment as an unskilled laborer (a bricklayer in Drury Lane and a
grocer's porter in the City). In desperation, he agreed to sign indentures for
a Jamaica plantation (which he then repudiated). After returning briefly
to Middleton's Academy as a servant-student, he worked as a load-carrier,
but injured himself. Next, he found semi-skilled employment as a law clerk
copying cases.[48]

[47] See Beth Fowkes Tobin, *Picturing Imperial Power: Colonial Subjects in British Painting* (Durham:
Duke University Press, 1999), 22ff.
[48] Emin, *Life and Adventures*, 16, 31.

Like most Asians in Britain, Emin had a guaranteed passage home waiting for him should he fail in the metropolis. Asian sailors and servants learned that autobiographical petitions submitted to the East India Company's Court of Directors, soliciting its financial aid or its intervention against their employers, could bring relief or redress.[49] When persuaded by such petitions of the individual's worthiness and need, the Company's Directors customarily ordered them lodged, fed, and clothed in its barracks, and then shipped back as passengers, all at the expense of the shipowner who initially brought them to England. In Emin's case, his father (a Calcutta merchant) offered to pay his passage home, should Emin give up his aspirations in England.[50] Emin, despite his suffering, refused to return with his personal transformation incomplete.

While moving through British society, Emin found scope to negotiate his identity, since many Englishmen with whom he dealt had few preconceptions about his Armenian ethnicity, or much awareness of lands east of England generally. When Emin approached one potential employer, a master bricklayer, this man at first took Emin for a Frenchman and cursed him for it. When Emin denied being French and began to explain what being an Armenian meant, the man identified him as German. Finally, the man accepted Emin into his employ, concluding "Well, well, Germans and Armenians are all alike, as long as you are not a Frenchman."[51] Thus, Emin could shape his particular status among the range of "foreigners" whom Englishmen ranked hierarchically; being a non-Catholic Christian privileged him over some Catholic Europeans, like Irishmen and Frenchmen. Indeed, he broke with his former Armenian patron in London, Stephan Cojagian, when that man converted to Catholicism; Emin denounced him (using, strikingly, epithets that conflated Catholics and Jews through a Shakespearean reference), as a "papist . . . turn-coat . . . [as greedy as] Shylock the avaricious Jew in the Merchant of Venice."[52]

Emin learned from more-educated and politically aware Britons that his Armenian identity could be made a mark of distinction. In 1755, while strolling in St. James's Park, Emin met Edmund Burke, then a struggling young attorney. Their chance encounter developed into an enduring friendship. Both Burke and Emin recorded that Burke consistently regarded Emin as a "gentleman" despite his poverty. Emin copied out Burke's work as he

[49] See L/MAR/1, "Minutes of the Committee of Shipping," BL.
[50] Emin's father had sent £60 for Emin's passage home. Emin, *Life and Adventures*, 47 and *passim*. See also C. Manningham, Calcutta, to William Davis, February 20, 1754, manuscript MO 1511, Huntington Library.
[51] Emin, *Life and Adventures*, 34.   [52] Ibid., 32, 37.

wrote it, including "On the Sublime and Beautiful" and *Vindications of Natural Society* (both 1756). Throughout, Burke guided Emin's education like a "dear uncle" and they held long political discussions, as well as playing chess and drinking together.[53] This warm personal relationship lasted even as Burke entered Parliament and rose to become one of its leading lights. Burke would continue his personal engagement with Asians throughout his life. In 1781, he hosted three Indian diplomatic emissaries to London representing the Maratha Peshwa; they lived in his greenhouse at Beaconsfield.[54] As noted above, Burke took a leading role in the impeachment and trial of Warren Hastings in Parliament for abuses of the human and political rights of Asians.[55] From his first encounter with Burke, Emin learned that he gained British respect and continued sponsorship through his expression of his individual and indomitable quest for liberty for his oppressed Armenian people, seeking to win them a nation-state free from Turkish or Russian imperial domination.

Emin's recognition of solidarity with a fellow Armenian, albeit transitory, let to his entrée to his most powerful patrons. Emin later described his chance encounter with another Armenian in 1755:

[He] met a young man in a Turkish habit, and had the curiosity to speak to him in that language, as he found him to be an Armenian; both parties were glad to see each other. Emin after inquiry, was informed that the man had been sent over with an Arabian horse, as a groom, by the English merchants of Aleppo, for his Grace [Hugh Smithson] the late Duke (at that time Earl) of Northumberland.[56]

Emin's immediate bonding with a fellow Armenian suggests how networks of Asians in Britain could quickly develop. Nevertheless, the bonds did not endure. Emin regarded himself as superior in class and education to the Armenian groom, refusing to eat at his table with the stablemen but rather demanding to dine among the duke's upper servants.[57] The duke elicited Emin's story of his militant ambitions as an Armenian nationalist, encouraged him in 1756 to write an autobiographical epistle, and then

---

[53] Burke to Emin, *c.* August 7, 1757 and March 29, 1789 in *Correspondence of Edmund Burke*, ed. Thomas W. Copeland (10 vols., Cambridge University Press, 1958–78), I, 120–2, V, 455–7; Emin to Mrs. Montagu, August 7, 1785, in Emin, *Life and Adventures* 486.

[54] Burke thus respected a Brahmanic desire for purity in cooking and eating entirely separately from his British hosts. Burke to Hillsborough, July 12, 1781 and Burke to Ragunath Rao, draft, August 1781 in *Correspondence of Edmund Burke*, IV, 367–8.

[55] Further, William Burke had an Indian body servant, "Tombee," who lived with them at Beaconsfield and was William's main heir. Philip Magnus, *Edmund Burke* (London: John Murray, 1939), 288. See William Burke's will in Dixon Wecter, *Edmund Burke and his Kinsmen* (Boulder: University of Colorado, 1939), 94.

[56] Emin, *Life and Adventures*, 54.   [57] Ibid., 55.

circulated this political manifesto among 300 of the British social and political elite, including the royal Duke of Cumberland.[58]

Emin wrote to generate support among the British aristocracy, describing his feelings and aspirations as an individual and a liberator-in-training for his Armenian nation. As Emin represented himself, he had only moved to England in order to learn European military technology and moral virtues which he could then deploy in the emancipation of his persecuted people in their Asian homeland. Emin's ardent nationalist rhetoric apparently resonated with Britons who were striving to imbue nationalist sentiments among their own people.

Emin also stressed his membership in a collective non-Catholic Christianity, which both Armenians and the English shared. Further, he and the English both struggled against Muslims and other non-Christians, whom he described as "wild and barbarous nations."[59] Nevertheless, he accepted that Armenians, and therefore he himself, lacked the full military merits (and literary conciseness) of the English:

[In 1744 in Calcutta] . . . I saw the Fort of the Europeans and the Soldiers Exercise, and the Shipping and that they were dextrous and perfect in all things, then I grieved with myself, for my Religion and my Country, that we were in Slavery and Ignorance like Jews Vagabonds upon Earth . . . but I resolved I would go to Europe to learn Art Military and other Sciences to assist that Art; and I was sure that if I would go into Armenia like an European Officer, I may be usefull at least in some degree to my Country . . . I am afraid I am too trouble some in my Accounts to your Lordship but we people of Asia can't say little and a great deal like Scholars . . .[60]

Touched by this appeal, Northumberland and others promised advancement; the royal Duke of Cumberland enrolled Emin as a cadet officer in the military academy at Woolwich.[61]

Subsequent autobiographical letters from Emin to various British elites consistently reveal Emin to be a self-reflective individual, aware of how others have regarded him, and aspiring to enhance their valorization of him and his culture.[62] Revealing his education by Burke and others, his articulated aspirations were thus on terms he and his European hosts could all respect. Indeed, most British contemporaries described Emin as an enlightened and self-dedicated leader of his oppressed people, noting his intellect,

---

[58] Elizabeth Montagu, *Elizabeth Montagu . . . Correspondence*, ed. Reginald Blunt (2 vols., London: John Murray, 1906), II, 101.
[59] Emin, *Life and Adventures*, xxix, xxxii, 431.   [60] Emin to Northumberland, 1756, 58–60.
[61] Northumberland to Emin, 1756; Emin, *Life and Adventures*, 58–60.
[62] E.g. Emin to Pitt, March 1758; Emin, *Life and Adventures*, 91–2.

his squint, but only occasionally his darker skin color: "This Prince, while in *England*, was known by the name of *Imene*. His person was of the middle size, had a slight cast in his eyes, of a sprightly disposition, very intelligent and entertaining in his conversation, and exceedingly fond of discoursing on the sciences."[63]

Emin's British patrons included numerous elite women who apparently regarded his cause as a romantic nationalist quest. Among them, Lady Yarmouth sponsored his correspondence, and then meeting, with William Pitt (later Earl of Chatham).[64] In particular, Elizabeth Robinson Montagu, a leading literary figure, made herself his champion in high society. Emin regularly addressed Mrs. Montagu as "My Queen of Sheba," both showing her respect and identifying her with eastern culture at the same time.[65] He identified himself in the male role, as inspired by his patroness, yet never aspiring to possess her: "Your Persian Slave whom you have been pleased to honour with the Title of a Hero . . ."[66] Emin's recorded interactions with various classes of European women remained chaste.

In all, Emin served about five years with the English and Prussian royal armies, periodically fighting on the continent against the French during the Seven Years War. Although regarded as a gentleman officer, he remained an outsider, never formally entering the British officer corps. Then, making good on his pledge to fight on behalf of his Armenian nation, Emin made several expeditions to west Asia, subsidized by Northumberland. For two years (1759–61), he traveled and made alliances among Armenians living under Ottoman rule.[67] After a brief visit to England, he returned to the battlefield and spent another eight years (1761–9) fighting for Armenian liberation from the Russian and Turkish empires. Emin later claimed that he once raised and led a force of 18,000 Armenian mountaineers into combat. As with so many other Armenian liberation struggles, however, his efforts proved bloody but futile.[68] Following his withdrawal from his fruitless Armenian campaigns he returned to Calcutta in 1770.

[63] Letter to the Editor, *Gentleman's Magazine*, 36 (1766), Supplement, 583–4. See *Annual Register 1767*, 10: Chronicle, 204–10. Another writer remarked descriptively and without prejudice on his "brown complexion." *Gentleman's Magazine*, 37 (January 1767), 3–7.
[64] Mrs. Montagu to Her Husband, March 1758; Emin, *Life and Adventures*, 91–2.
[65] E.g., Emin to Mrs. Montagu, May 10, 1757; Mrs. Montagu to Her Husband, 1757. Montagu, *Correspondence*, II, 102, 107–8; William Jones to John Macpherson May 6, 1786, in John Shore Teignmouth, ed., *Memoirs of . . . Sir William Jones* (London: John Hatchard, 1804), xxi–xxiii, 277; MO 1575 Emin to Montagu in Messenger Monsey, St. James, to Montagu October 22, 1757, Huntington Library.
[66] Emin to Mrs. Montagu, September 14, 1757, in Emin, *Life and Adventures*, 80.
[67] Emin, *Life and Adventures*, 133–61.   [68] Ibid., 168–423.

Emin chose not to rejoin the Armenian community in Calcutta immediately but rather sought to pursue a military career in the East India Company's Bengal Army.[69] Yet he ran up against stronger social and racial barriers in Bengal than those he had faced in London. The East India Company maintained strong national requirements for its regular commissioned officer corps: by regulation, Catholics and non-Europeans could not hold such army commissions except under special dispensations.[70] Emin sought the influence of his powerful English patrons, the dukes of Northumberland and Cumberland, to have him officially nationalized as British and therefore able to get an appointment with an officer's commission; they confessed their inability to arrange this from London.[71] Burke lamented that "a man once countenanced by the first people of this kingdom as well as of Germany, should . . . pass his life in misery and contempt in an English settlement. I know many think him an impostor, but I can bear witness to the truth of what he asserted . . ."[72] Thus, Emin could gain entry into the Bengal Army only at the most marginal officer's rank: brevet ensign in the irregular cavalry.[73] After two years of thankless military employment, Emin lost active service status in 1772 when the irregular cavalry demobilized. Eventually, Emin was retired to the Third European Invalid Unit in Calcutta.[74] Yet, because of his anomalous status, he had to petition the Company for twenty-five years before he received his back pay and pension.[75]

Thereafter Emin retained relations with both British and Armenian worlds. He continued to sustain a correspondence with female as well as male British elite through the 1790s. Yet he spent the remainder of his life largely among the struggling Armenian community in Bengal. His final major assertion of his identity in British public discourse was his autobiographical book.

Emin sent drafts of this 640-page work to Mrs. Montagu and Warren Hastings in London and Sir William Jones in Calcutta, requesting them

[69] Ibid., 429.
[70] French officers and men of mixed ancestry faced similar barriers. See Rosie Llewlyn-Jones, *A Very Ingenious Man, Claude Martin* (Delhi: Oxford University Press, 1992).
[71] Northumberland to Emin, May 17, 1771; Emin, *Life and Adventures*, 440–1.
[72] Burke to John Stewart, October 30, 1772 in *Correspondence of Edmund Burke*, II, 359–60.
[73] Bengal Army List, National Archives of India. V. P. C. Hodson, *List of the Officers* (4 vols., London: Constable and Phillimore, 1927–47), II, 137; Emin, *Life and Adventures*, 439, 483.
[74] Emin to Hastings, Bassrah, March 3, 1774, Warren Hastings General Correspondence, Addl. 29134 ff. 322–3, BL. See also Mustaffa A. al-Najjar, Muhammed A. al-Amin, and Abdul W. Khan, eds., *Bussorah Diaries* (2 vols.: University of Basra, 1980), I, 325, February 6, 1774, diary no. 202, 86–9; Emin, *Life and Adventures*, 441–55.
[75] Emin, *Life and Adventures*, 483, 513.

to solicit subscribers (at two guineas each) and also asking for their advice
on revisions.[76] In response, Mrs. Montagu complimented him on how
well he retained his English diction.[77] Jones, in contrast, adopted a tone
that demonstrated the higher degree of separation between Britons and
Asians that prevailed in the colonies than in England at this time. Jones
urged Emin to make the tone of his work less "Asiatick," at least as far as
Emin, as an Asian, was able: "strike out every passage that may favour of self-
approbation . . . [D]iscard forever the Asiatick style of panegyrick, to which
you are too much addicted . . . [T]he Asiatick style . . . is utterly repugnant to
English manners, which you prefer, I know, to those of Persia." Nevertheless,
Jones himself made only minor modifications, editing mistakes that he
presupposed an Asian would be incapable of getting right: "I have corrected
only these errors in language and orthography, which were unavoidable in
an English work written by a native of Hamadan . . ."[78] Emin used the
authority of Jones and his other subscribers to show his approach to, and
yet distance from, English culture: "My guardian Angel Sir William Jones
has been so good as to correct the wrong spelling and false English of
it . . ."[79] Thus sponsored by Britons, in 1792 aged sixty-six, Emin published
his autobiographical book in London: *The Life and Adventures of Joseph
Emin, An Armenian, Written in English by Himself.*[80]

Emin wrote his book primarily for a British – not Asian – audience,
although he advertised its sale in English newspapers in Calcutta as
well.[81] Throughout, he sought to make his identity comprehensible and
respectable to Britons, yet he located himself as an aspiring outsider to
the culture of his British readers. As he narrated his life chronologically,
he retrospectively described himself in the third person, making himself as
author the intermediary between Britons as his readers and himself as his
subject.

Emin accepted the definitions of authorial voice and content inherent in
this British genre (at the time). It was customary to attribute, as did Emin
in his preface, the impetus for writing the account to the author's friends

[76] *Calcutta Gazette*, January 1, 1789; Emin, *Life and Adventures*, 489–90; Emin to Hastings, Calcutta,
January 15, 1789, Warren Hastings General Correspondence, Addl. 29171 f. 255, BL.
[77] Emin to Mrs. Montagu, August 15, 1791; Emin, *Life and Adventures*, 493–6.
[78] Sir William Jones to Emin, August 10, 1788; Emin, *Life and Adventures*, xix–xx.
[79] Emin to Mrs. Montagu, January 15, 1789; Emin, *Life and Adventures*, 490–2.
[80] Emin wrote: "my reason for not publishing it here [in Calcutta] was to avoid the dearness of the
Press." The initial printing cost in London was £50. Emin to Hastings, Calcutta, January 15, 1789,
Warren Hastings General Correspondence, Addl. 29171, f. 255, BL.
[81] My analysis of the book's seventy-three subscribers indicates 80 percent were European (five of these
European women) and the remainder Asians. Emin, *Life and Adventures*, 489.

and supporters, whom the author humbly obeyed. His self-deprecating remarks about his own limited literary abilities reflected these conventional requirements but also his own distinctive situation: unlike his contemporary British authors, Emin consistently ascribed his self-alleged inadequacies to his own "Asiatic" nature, including his "wild Asiatic temper."[82] As Emin explained to Mrs. Montagu: "I ... cannot avoid mixing an Asiatic tincture in my writing, I indeavour much to naturalize my sentiments to the English."[83]

Yet while Emin represented himself as a member of his own culture, at the same time he also asserted his just pride in his own unique individual accomplishments. He declaimed that he alone among Armenians studied modern English military science, fought to awaken his dormant nation, and wrote "his own history, which is a novelty never before attempted by any of his richest [Armenian] countrymen."[84] Indeed, his work was apparently the first book written in English and published by an Asian. While, he asserted, such personal accomplishments would not be outstanding in an Englishman, they were his marks of individualistic distinction as an Armenian:

The singularity of his sufferings would, in his opinion, scarce excite curiosity had he been an Englishman . . . but, considering that he is the only Armenian, out of several thousands, and in thousands of years, who has had an inexpressible thirst for improvement and liberty, it is natural that the world should wish to know the particulars of his life: yet he is at a loss in what manner to proceed, since, if he should write every thing, much will appear fabulous to many persons who are not well acquainted with his character; but, if too concisely, he is afraid of disobeying his benevolent friends. However, he intends to preserve the medium, in hopes to meet the approbation of his candid readers, who condescend to indulge, and kindly pass over, any impropriety in his work; and will consider the difficulty and labour by which he has attained the noble language of a foreign country, and that without either a friend or money.[85]

Thus, Emin distinguished his personal identity from his European patrons and audience but also, on occasion, as an individual apart from the rest of his Armenian community.

The autobiographical genre that he selected shaped his enterprise in distinctive ways, different from how genres produced by Asian cultures would have done. Emin was certainly multilingual in Armenian, Persian, English, and Portuguese, and probably Bengali as well. He would have been familiar with indigenous Asian literary forms of history-writing or travel

---

[82] E.g., Emin, *Life and Adventures*, xxix–xxx, 2, 41.
[83] Emin to Mrs. Montagu, August 15, 1791; Emin, *Life and Adventures*, 493–6.
[84] Emin, *Life and Adventures*, xxxii.   [85] Ibid., xxviii–xxx.

literature current during his years living in India, but little in his book reflected those genres. Rather, his stress on his individuality, his nationalism, and his progressive use of military science to bring his nation to progress all accorded with the British autobiographical genre of his day.

The central argument that runs throughout Emin's narrative reveals the position which he and his elite British patrons in London had negotiated. He stressed throughout his family's martial traditions, not its current mercantile vocation. Emin also presented the English conventional belief that the English striving for learning – history, science, and particularly military science – marked their superiority over other cultures, including his own: "if Europeans had not been industrious in point of learning, and that in their smallest quarter of the world, they could not have stood against Asia and Africa, nor have found America to civilize."[86] Thus, to Emin, British success in colonial expansion was proof of its virtues. He accepted that for "us Asiatics," there were deficiencies in science, ambition, and individual achievement not found among the English.[87] Emin must have known that such words would resonate with his British patrons and cause them to look favorably upon him in the role they had mutually constructed.

CONCLUSION

The British empire contained cultural negotiations at home as well as overseas. Asians of various classes who entered late eighteenth-century Britain deployed the developing media of print culture and Enlightenment notions of identity, individuality, and nationality. These Asians made public discourse in Britain a contested terrain, struggling with Orientalists over their disparate representations of Asia and Asians. Seen from the perspective of Asian settlers and visitors, that is, regarding Britain as approached from the outside and, often, by members of the working class, we can see how they encountered new opportunities for self-definition and self-representation, as well as faced unexpected challenges. The multiplicity of voices in British public discourse should not be overlooked. Such a perspective contrasts with established historiographic representations of the British empire, which are often largely from the top down and center out.[88]

The new media of British public culture provided opportunities for these Asians' own progress and advancement. Asian servants learned that

[86] Ibid., xxix, 2, 58–60.   [87] Ibid., xxx.
[88] For a recent example, see the magisterial *Oxford History of the British Empire*, ed. William Roger Louis (5 vols., Oxford University Press, 1998–9).

personal advertisements in mass-produced and circulated newspapers could obtain them employment. Asian sailors learned that individual petitions laying out their worthiness and needs could provide them with support and transportation home from the East India Company. Even impoverished Asians learned that sworn testimony in court could sometimes secure redress of their legal grievances or free them from incarceration by the state. Educated Asians, like Emin, learned that they could acquire the patronage of the powerful if they represented themselves autobiographically as aspiring individuals with patriotic ambitions for the liberation of their nation.

While distinctive, Emin's career was not unique. His project of shaping his self-representations of his Armenian nationalist identity for a British audience resonated with powerful elements of the British establishment. His experience in the colonies, however, proved far more limiting, based on his racial identity as a non-white. The different meanings of "race" and nationality that he experienced at British hands in the metropole and the colony respectively highlight the complexity of the imperial process, warning us against bifurcating between the monoliths of "the colonizer" and "the colonized."

Over the period under consideration in this volume, cultural concepts and valuations of race, class, and gender shifted, both in metropolitan Britain and in colonial India. The very definition of "British" changed profoundly, for example concerning English Catholics, Jews, Irish Protestants, and people of English or mixed ancestry living in colonies.[89] Issues such as citizenship versus subjecthood, and the idea of a nation-state, all proved subjects of interest and debate in metropolitan and colonial Britain. Economic changes also brought social cleavages and conflict.[90]

Each of these changing cultural categories defined Asians in Britain in cross-cutting ways. Empowered as upper class, an Asian woman settler might simultaneously have been subordinated by gender to the British men of that class. The largest group of Asians in Britain, male sailors and servants, proved able in many cases to form domestic liaisons with European women of the working classes, a relationship that tended to empower them over their European female partner. All these categories, further, varied among different classes and groups of Britons. While elite British men increasingly criticized what would eventually become known as "interracial marriages,"

[89] See Linda Colley, *Britons: Forging the Nation, 1707–1837* (New Haven: Yale University Press, 1992).
[90] See E. P. Thompson, *The Making of the English Working Class* (New York: Pantheon Books, 1964), and Dror Wahrman, *Imagining the Middle Class* (Cambridge University Press, 1995).

the British women who participated in them seem to have favored them by choice.[91]

Despite various cultural and social assertions by early Asian settlers, the weight of British public opinion and the force of expanding imperialism shifted against Asians during the nineteenth century. The British empire, with its inequities of power, shifting notions of race, and growing Orientalism, meant that Asians increasingly faced exclusions, constraints, and prejudices from Britons. To succeed even partially, Asians often needed to negotiate, adapt, or accommodate their values and self-representations in light of British expectations. Often, this also meant refusing British presuppositions about or limits on them.

By the 1850s, the concept of biologically based racial difference found application in many aspects of British imperialism, both overseas and domestically. Increasing numbers of Britons returned from the colonies with colonial attitudes toward colonized peoples. These British colonial attitudes gradually infused into the metropole, to the detriment of Asians living there. The bloody conflict in India in 1857, among other anti-colonial struggles, followed by their no less violent suppressions by British forces, seemed to make biologically defined race the basis for identity on both sides. Many Britons interpreted social Darwinist theories of evolution as giving a scientific validity to these evolving concepts of race as inherited and immutable in individuals. Thus, Asian sojourners in late imperial Britain interacted within a quite different social matrix than did earlier Asians like Emin.[92]

---

[91] For a later period, see Philippa Levine, "Race, Sex, and Colonial Soldiery in World War I," *Journal of Women's History*, 9, 4 (Winter 1998), 104–30.

[92] See Burton, *At the Heart of the Empire*, 6.

PART II

Promised lands: imperial aspirations and practice

"Rescuing the age from a charge of ignorance": gentility, knowledge, and the British exploration of Africa in the later eighteenth century

Philip J. Stern

Thunder, Death & Lightning; – the Devil to pay: lost by disease M. Scott, two sailors, four carpenters & thirty one of the Royal African Corps, which reduces our numbers to seven, out of which Doctor Anderson & two of the soldiers are quite useless, the former from one disease or other has been four months disabled – we every day suppose he'll kick it.[1]

With these words from the banks of the Niger in late 1805, Lieutenant John Martyn, the chief Royal African Corps soldier on Mungo Park's second expedition to Africa, painted a vivid picture of the miserable, ultimately insurmountable conditions Park's crew faced. Even before Martyn posted this news home, Anderson and another did in fact "kick it" and soon after, the rest, including the explorer himself, perished sailing down the Niger.

Park's experience was no anomaly. Facing disease, thieves, hostile states and merchants, and warring kingdoms, most early explorers in Africa never returned. Such intimidating obstacles, and the great profits already reaped from a well-established coastal trade in men and goods, prevented Europeans from organizing ventures into the interior. So, despite the self-proclaimed heroism of individual adventurers and the aspirations of the Enlightenment, a late eighteenth-century English geography primer still lamented that "The interior parts of [Africa] . . . are very little known by Europeans, so that they may almost be ranked with undiscovered countries."[2]

This chapter has benefited immeasurably from, and I am immensely grateful for, the comments and advice of David Armitage, Nicholas Dirks, Richard Elphick, Daniel H. A. Maksymiuk, Kimberly Stern, Deborah Valenze, Ben Vinson III, and Kathleen Wilson.
[1] Lt. Jn Martyn to Megan [Martyn?], November 1, 1805, British Library, [hereinafter BL] Add. MS 37232 f. 63.
[2] *Geography for Youth, or a Plain and Easy Introduction to the Science of Geography for the Use of Young Gentlemen and Ladies* (London: T. Lowndes, 1782), 106.

As if responding to such a challenge, on June 9, 1788 an elite London dining club known as the Saturday's Club announced itself "desirous of rescuing the age from a charge of ignorance, which, in other respects, belongs so little to its character" and formed an Association for Promoting the Discovery of the Interior Parts of Africa, popularly known as the African Association. In an oft-quoted declaration, they

> Resolved, that, as no species of information is more ardently desired or more generally useful than that which Improves the Science of Geography; and as the vast Continent of Africa, not withstanding the efforts of the Ancients, and the wishes of the Moderns, is still, in a great measure unexplored, the Members of this Club do form themselves into an Association for promoting the Discovery of the Inland parts of that quarter of the world.[3]

For several generations of scholars, the Association's quest for geographical knowledge was captured in that one word "useful." Many historians in the 1950s and 1960s, whose concerns were doubtlessly influenced by decolonization, argued that the Association was motivated by industrial, commercial, or humanitarian (i.e., anti-slave-trade) interests.[4] Robin Hallett offered the most comprehensive arguments about the Association and British interest in Africa generally,[5] but also described the Association's members and leaders as "men of affairs" with a pragmatic interest in Britain's economic development. While explorers may have been driven by adventure, the Association's members possessed a curiosity much more "rational, practical, and assured."[6]

A more social and cultural perspective on the Association renders arguments stressing such "practical" motives insufficient. While the African Association was founded amidst a growing debate over the slave trade, its members included prominent individuals on both sides of the issue, and in pursuing its aims maintained ties with humanitarians, slavers in West Africa, and Jamaican plantation owners alike.[7] The contention that

[3] *Proceedings of the Association for Promoting the Discovery of the Interior Parts of Africa* (London: W. Bulmer and Co., 1810), repr. ed. Robin Hallett (2 vols., London: Dawsons of Pall Mall, 1967), I, 9. [hereinafter *Proceedings*].

[4] See A. Adu Boahen, *Britain, the Sahara, and the Western Sudan, 1788–1861* (Oxford: Clarendon Press, 1964), 1–2 for an extensive historiographical review of these early works.

[5] Robin Hallett, *Records of the African Association, 1788–1831* (London: Thomas Nelson, 1964) and *The Penetration of Africa: European Exploration in North and West Africa to 1815* (New York: Frederick A. Praeger, 1965).

[6] Robin Hallett, "The European Approach to the Interior of Africa in the Eighteenth Century," *Journal of African History*, 4 (1963), 195, 202.

[7] Boahen, *Western Sudan*, 3–4; John Gascoigne, *Joseph Banks and the English Enlightenment: Useful Knowledge and Polite Culture* (Cambridge University Press, 1994), 40; Bryan Edwards to Joseph Banks, June 14, 1796, Correspondence of Sir Joseph Banks, Kew Gardens Collection [hereinafter Kew], II, 140.

the Association was preoccupied with commercial or strategic gain, on the other hand, largely underestimates the complexity of its motivations and the discretion of its leaders. In the second half of the eighteenth century, the African coast was certainly integral to an Atlantic, even global, system linking commercial and military interest to territorial expansion, but this semi-private effort by gentlemen to send explorers into the deserts and jungles of Africa stands apart from a ubiquitous "blue water" commercial policy or "the need to finance and provision imperial armies from local resources."[8] Under the *de facto* leadership of the eighteenth century's most prolific patron of science and exploration, Sir Joseph Banks, the Association became, as John Gascoigne has argued, an "informal structure of empire," but how it came to "promote imperial ventures" is inseparable from its cultural context.[9]

The Association was concerned primarily with acquiring geographical knowledge. Of course, the usefulness of that knowledge was one aspect of its appeal. Some of the Association's founders, like Banks and Sir John Sinclair, were among the great "improvers" of their age, and, as several scholars have shown,[10] science in this period was intimately united with commerce and empire. Yet the material benefits of the African interior were hardly axiomatic nor were they "discovered" through exploration. Geographical knowledge had to be actively created and defined as *useful knowledge*. While the curiosity of the men behind the African Association was certainly rational, practical, and assured, their ostensible desire to rescue their age from ignorance raises certain unavoidable questions: what were they looking for, why did they want it, and what did they do with it once found?

THE GENTLEMAN AND GEOGRAPHICAL KNOWLEDGE

In 1788, exploring the interior of Africa was an audacious, almost quixotic, pursuit. Lacking a reliable malarial prophylactic and an effective knowledge of the course of major rivers, a late eighteenth-century European had between a 30 and 70 percent chance of death in his first year on the coast,

---

[8] C. A. Bayly, "The British and Indigenous Peoples, 1760–1860: Power, Perception, and Identity," in Martin Daunton and Rick Halpern, eds., *Empire and Others: British Encounters with Indigenous Peoples, 1600–1850* Daunton and Rick Halpern (London: UCL Press, 1999), 23.

[9] John Gascoigne, *Science in the Service of Empire: Joseph Banks, the British State and the Uses of Science in the Age of Revolution* (Cambridge University Press, 1998), 178–82; R. E. R. Banks et al., eds., *Sir Joseph Banks: A Global Perspective* (Kew: Royal Botanic Gardens, 1994).

[10] See, among others, Gascoigne, *Science*; Richard Drayton, *Nature's Government: Science, Imperial Britain, and the "Improvement" of the World* (New Haven: Yale, 2000); David Mackay, *In the Wake of Cook: Exploration, Science & Empire, 1780–1801* (London: Croom Helm, 1985).

and moving about the interior dramatically increased the hazard.[11] Nevertheless, the men of the Association unhesitatingly felt the effort worth the sacrifice: "it is by similar hazards of human life alone," wrote Banks in 1803, "that we can hope to penetrate the obscurity of the internal face of Africa."[12] Regardless of the funds spent and the lives lost, the Association was committed to sending explorer after explorer, relishing every scrap of information and often promoting it as if it had discovered the keys to the kingdom of Prester John.

To be sure, the Association's founding members were practical men – members of Parliament, fellows of the Royal Society, great landowners, commercial investors, and a future Governor-General of India. Yet, given the odds involved in African exploration, these men were clearly motivated beyond the limits imposed by sensible expectation or mercantile calculation. And here one must remember that these "men of affairs" were also patrons, poets, scholars, and spendthrifts. Their interests were manifold, and their politics were diverse. In the end, what primarily bound these men together was not a single objective to be found in Africa but a set of cultural practices found at home: in a word, gentility.

Gentility was a flexible and composite category: the ethos of a landed elite defined within a shared social world to which demonstrations of refined and exclusive education, taste, leisure, and wealth gave access. Yet, if gentility was a shared identity, it was also a form of power, which centered, as Roy Porter has argued, on "cultural hegemony, a conspicuous show of the good life, the excitation of envy and emulation."[13] That is, gentlemen were consumers. Even the most abstemious of gentlemen demonstrated a "collecting mentality" that set him apart from others, flaunted his wealth, claimed his authority over men and nature, and revealed the learning and leisure afforded (even required) by his station. Thus, knowledge and consumption went hand-in-hand, and through the eighteenth century natural history and the exotic became standard fare for the gardens, libraries, and clubs of the elite.[14]

[11] Philip Curtin, "'The White Man's Grave': Image and Reality, 1780–1850," *Journal of British Studies*, 1 (1961), 95.
[12] Quoted in Gascoigne, *Banks and the Enlightenment*, 19.
[13] Roy Porter, "Material Pleasures in the Consumer Society," in Roy Porter and Marie Mulvey Roberts, eds., *Pleasure in the Eighteenth Century* (New York: NYU Press, 1996), 20.
[14] Barbara M. Benedict, "The 'Curious Attitude' in Eighteenth-Century Britain: Observing and Owning," *Eighteenth-Century Life*, 14 (1990), 59, 77–78; "Introduction," in David Philip Miller and Peter Hanns Reill, eds., *Visions of Empire: Voyages, Botany, and Representations of Nature* (Cambridge University Press, 1996), 3; John Gascoigne, "The Ordering of Nature and the Ordering of Empire: A Commentary," in ibid., 108; Drayton, *Nature's Government*, ch. 4.

The Association, true to form, was built upon an ethos of conspicuous wealth, exclusivity, and civility. Its annual subscription fee of five guineas (about £375 today) was no doubt prohibitive, and, in Robin Hallett's words, "only the socially established would find themselves at ease in so assured and aristocratic an assembly."[15] Additionally, all of the leaders of the Association reflected this cultural currency of learning. One had previously held a Cambridge chair in chemistry, and another was typically eulogized as having "distinguished himself for Greek and mathematicks."[16] Most demonstrated a facility with the ancients, from parliamentary speeches to their publications, two founding members were self-styled poets, and several took their turn with histories of various sorts. Joseph Banks too was no doubt a "literary man" (as the Orientalist William Jones called him); if nothing else, as Neil Chambers has observed, he was a literal man of letters – collecting correspondents much like he did plants.[17]

This custodianship over knowledge and its artifacts was part of this genteel ethos. As Steven Shapin has argued, as establishing the reliability of sense experience became increasingly more crucial in the inductive, experimental science of the later seventeenth century, gentlemen came to be the bearers of empirical knowledge, particularly through collective bodies like the Royal Society. Liberated from material wants and adhering to a particular code of behavior, the landed were seen to be disinterested and autonomous, and that endowed their observations with accuracy and their words with the power of truth.[18] The explorer, however, did not have this authority: at root, his report consisted in empirical evidence gathered (usually) by a non-gentleman outside the European institutions that gave such findings authority. While seen to be a heroic and intrepid act, traveling away from the reassuring structures of civil society to places seen as exotic and seductive none the less cast doubt on any explorer's trustworthiness, putting him in what Jonathan Lamb has called the "unstable position of the eyewitness." In sum, faith in an explorer's account depended upon faith in the explorer himself.[19]

[15] Hallett, *Records*, 21.   [16] *Gentleman's Magazine*, 62 (1792), 1218–19.

[17] Neil Chambers, "Letters from the President: The Correspondence of Sir Joseph Banks," *Notes and Records of the Royal Society of London*, 53, 1 (1999), 44; Garland Cannon, "Sir William Jones, Sir Joseph Banks, and the Royal Society," *Notes and Records of the Royal Society of London*, 29 (1975), 206–7.

[18] Steven Shapin, *A Social History of Truth* (University of Chicago Press, 1994).

[19] Simon Schaffer, "Visons of Empire: Afterword," in Miller and Reill, *Visions of Empire*, 340; Dorinda Outram, "On Being Perseus: New Knowledge, Dislocation, and Enlightenment Exploration," in David N. Livingstone and Charles W. J. Withers, eds., *Geography and Enlightenment* (University of Chicago Press, 1999), 283–4; Jonathan Lamb, "Eye-Witnessing in the South Seas," *The Eighteenth Century: Theory and Interpretation*, 38 (1997), 202, 206.

The Association assuaged this epistemological crisis by interceding in the production of geographical knowledge. Its leaders institutionalized exploration. Selecting explorers, directing expeditions, and redacting and publishing information, it put explorers' knowledge into the context of a trustworthy scientific structure, and turning *exploration* into *geography*, its leaders lent the exploration of Africa their authority as gentlemen.

Method, however, was as important as status. Antiquarianism, civil and natural history, and mathematics were pursuits particularly reserved for the eighteenth-century gentleman,[20] and all of these united in the "moral geography" (essentially a combination of topography, political geography, ethnography, and history) practiced by James Rennell, Britain's foremost cartographic authority and the geographer to the Association. Mathematical precision based on contemporary findings was juxtaposed to the authority of Greek and Roman accounts, and both "the ancients" and "the moderns" were summoned as the sources of specific geographical problems to be solved. In fact, while engaged with the Association, Rennell both won the Royal Society's prestigious Copley Medal for establishing a reliable translation of time on a journey into distance (based on the rates at which camels crossed the desert) and authored a magisterial two volumes on Herodotus' "geographical system." A combination of induction, deduction, and Rennell's personal reputation appealed to the gentleman and contributed to the authority of the Association's work.[21]

None the less, the Association did not dispense with the need for creating faith in the explorer himself, which required "trust in his moral integrity and trust in his perceptual accuracy."[22] The deportment of its "geographical missionaries," the Association's leaders seemed to believe, could make or break an expedition. Its first West African expedition, for example, failed to achieve its ends because, as Henry Beaufoy, the Association secretary, wrote to the membership, the explorer had not been "a traveller of good temper and conciliating manners."[23] An ideal explorer combined physical strength with moral and mental acuity, or, as Beaufoy punctuated a recommendation

[20] Steven Shapin, "'A Scholar and a Gentleman': The Problematic Identity of the Scientific Practitioner in Early Modern England," *History of Science*, 29 (1991), 312.
[21] See Michael T. Bravo, "Precision and Curiosity in Scientific Travel: James Rennell and the Orientalist Geography of the New Imperial Age (1760–1830)," in Jas Elsner and Joan-Pau Rubiés, eds., *Voyages and Visions: Towards a Cultural History of Travel* (London: Reaktion Books, 1999); Philip J. Stern, "'Not Withstanding the Efforts of the Ancients and the Wishes of the Moderns': The Authority of Cartography in the Origins of the Modern British Exploration of Africa," *The Portolan*, 40 (Winter 1998), 7–26.
[22] Outram, "On Being Perseus," 283.   [23] *Proceedings*, I, 303–4.

of a would-be agent for the Association, his "attainments are Classical &
in some degree Scientific; & his Understanding, as far as I can judge, is
of no ordinary Class."[24] Given the right combination of status, method,
and source, the Association was in a remarkable position to situate itself as
author of geographical knowledge.

The same elements that made the Association capable of producing
knowledge also made it attractive to subscribers. Efforts at "improving" –
from agricultural production to the "fund of human knowledge" – brought
not only material progress, but, also, as Sinclair boasted for himself, domestic and international renown.[25] More importantly, though, the Association
aimed to turn Africa into one of the gentleman's leisured pleasures. In fact,
as early as 1790, Beaufoy predicted that the Association would open Africa
itself to gentlemanly investigation, even as a replacement for the Grand
Tour:

> The powerful empires of Bornou and Cashna will be open to his investigation;
> the luxurious city of Tombuctou, whose opulence and severe police attract the
> merchants of the most distant states of Africa, will unfold to him the causes of
> her vast prosperity; the mysterious Niger will disclose her unknown original and
> doubtful termination; and countries unveiled to ancient or modern research will
> become familiar to his view.[26]

Africa was becoming something to be devoured by the elite,[27] due, in part,
to the Association. James Cook's first voyage in the Pacific, on which Banks
the naturalist had cut his teeth, had intensified Britons' global ethnograph-
ical and geographical interest,[28] sensibilities tantalized by these "countries
unveiled to ancient or modern research." There was a modern aspect, one
that would certainly mark later nineteenth-century empire, of anthropological and cartographical inquiry, but this scintillating new world became
accessible through a more familiar one, the gentleman's club. This is essential to understanding its appeal and its development.

---

[24] Beaufoy to Banks, n.d., Sir Joseph Banks Collection, California State Library, Sutro Branch
[hereinafter SP], A2:52.
[25] Sir John Sinclair, *The Correspondence of the Right Honourable Sir John Sinclair, Bart.* (London: Henry
Colburn and Richard Bentley, 1831), xxiv.
[26] *Proceedings*, II, 199–200.
[27] Felicity Nussbaum, "Polygamy, Pamela, and the Prerogative of Empire," in Ann Bermingham and
John Brewer, eds., *The Consumption of Culture, 1600–1800: Image, Object, Text* (New York: Routledge,
1995), 218.
[28] Richard Grove, *Green Imperialism: Colonial Expansion, Tropical Island Edens and the Origins of
Environmentalism, 1600–1860* (Cambridge University Press, 1995), 316.

THE ECONOMY OF GENTILITY

The Association was formed amidst a "throng of society activity under George III,"[29] in an environment in which "clubability" was a crucial pre-requisite for access. And although learned societies in this period often "stressed the practical utility of their ideas,"[30] they too were sites of socia-bility. Clubs of all forms were places of pleasure – from the intellectual to the hedonistic – which reinforced a set of cohesive practices and behavior. Conversation, essential to the club, was the heart of gentlemanly knowledge and the ligament of genteel society, and the Association fostered it in per-son, through its meetings, and at great distances, through the distribution of its materials.[31]

However, the gentleman's position in eighteenth-century British society was not as indisputable as it may have been a century earlier. The growth of consumerism was slowly eroding his monopoly on leisure while he simul-taneously faced charges of weakness and (French) effeminacy for his attach-ment to such luxury.[32] Gentlemen were often objects of ridicule: Banks was as well known for his sexual exploits as for his scientific achievements on his voyage with Cook to Tahiti, and even the less salacious renderings in the press often depicted him as much as a member of "the Macaroni Club" fop-pishly chasing butterflies as President of the Royal Society soberly pursuing affairs of science and state.[33] The Association's desire to "rescue the age" then was emblematic of the elite's retrenchment against, as Linda Colley has described it, growing accusations of "unBritish" practices and of being a "separate and malign interest in the nation."[34] While the elite maintained its position through etiquette and social cohesion as a group, it also consoli-dated its power by reasserting an involvement with the state. Most founding members of the Association, including Banks, followed suit.[35]

[29] Peter Clark, *British Clubs and Societies, 1580–1800: The Origins of an Associational World* (Oxford: Clarendon Press, 2000), 118.
[30] Ibid., 112.
[31] Shapin, *Social History of Truth*, xxx, 81, chs. 5–7; Michèle Cohen, *Fashioning Masculinity: National Identity and Language in the Eighteenth Century* (London: Routledge, 1996); Marie Mulvey Roberts, "Pleasures Engendered by Gender: Homosociality and the Club," in Porter and Mulvey Roberts, *Pleasure in the Eighteenth Century*, 75, 50.
[32] Amongst others, see Cohen, *Fashioning Masculinity*, 6–12 and *passim*.
[33] Bridget Orr, "'Southern Passions Mix with Northern Art': Miscegenation and the *Endeavour* Voy-age," *Eighteenth-Century Life*, 18 (1994), 114–28; Gascoigne, *Banks and the Enlightenment*, 62.
[34] Linda Colley, *Britons: Forging the Nation, 1707–1837* (New Haven: Yale University Press, 1992), 164–5.
[35] David Cannadine, *Aspects of Aristocracy: Grandeur and Decline in Modern Britain* (New Haven: Yale University Press, 1994), 18–25; Jorge Arditi, "Hegemony and Etiquette: An Exploration on the Transformation of Practice and Power in Eighteenth-Century England," *The British Journal of Sociology*, 45 (1994), 177–93; Gascoigne, *Science*.

Yet, while two founding members had led troops against the American colonies, Association leaders by and large eschewed the martial personae described by Colley,[36] opting for a more restrained form of armchair swashbuckling. His wealth put to "penetrate" the African interior, the Association patron created not only entertainment, but also the impression of virtue in service. James Cook himself had created "a new kind of national hero" in the imperial activities of the explorer, idealized as a representative of the achievements of British religious, scientific, and national character amidst the anxieties over "Britishness" and empire occasioned by the close of the Seven Years War and war with the American colonies.[37] While the gentleman added authority to the content of explorers' knowledge, the explorer buttressed the Association's claim to service to science and nation and provided a connection to the non-aristocratic "alternative masculinity" and national heroism of the explorer.[38] Or, as the Association leadership boasted in its first official publication for the public-at-large, such pursuits manifested "that persevering spirit which ever distinguishes manly minds, engaged on sound principles, and for noble purposes."[39]

If the connection with exploring buttressed the gentleman's position, the process also reinforced his traditional role as patron. The Association opened opportunities for explorers and also provided some of the practical perquisites offered by the well connected: leaves of absence from other engagements, government and Association-funded pensions, and publicity, to name a few. Almost a decade after the death of their third explorer, Daniel Houghton, his children were still drawing on Association funds for their education.[40] Explorers were distinct from their patrons, and only one was ever invited to join the Association: an honorary membership offered in lieu of payment by an Association then in straitened circumstances. But this should be unsurprising; as Richard Drayton has noted, "in the accumulation of learning, as in that of wealth, the 'volunteer' was often the exploiter of others' labour and expertise."[41]

---

[36] Colley, *Britons*, 177–93.
[37] Kathleen Wilson, "The Island Race: Captain Cook, Protestant Evangelicalism and the Construction of English National Identity, 1760–1800," in Tony Claydon and Ian McBride, eds., *Protestantism and the National Identity* (Cambridge University Press, 1998).
[38] Ibid., 271–2.
[39] *The Journal of Frederick Horneman's Travels, from Cairo to Mourzouk, the Capital of the Kingdom of Fezzan, in Africa, in the Years 1797–8* (London: 1802; repr. Darf Publishers 1985), x.
[40] African Association Minute Books, General Meetings, University Library, Cambridge, MS Add. 7085 [hereinafter GM], ff. 23, 29; SP 2:40a, 2:59.
[41] Richard Drayton, "Knowledge and Empire," in P. J. Marshall, ed., *Oxford History of the British Empire, Vol. II: The Eighteenth Century* (Oxford University Press, 1998), 237; Shapin, *Social History of Truth*, ch. 8.

In many ways, in fact, the accretion of learning had much in common with that of wealth: the Association was a gentlemanly business. Its leaders were not the "gentlemanly capitalists" P. J. Cain and A. G. Hopkins have described fueling nineteenth-century empire,[42] but rather they functioned within what can better be understood as an *economy of gentility*. Eighteenth-century gentlemen certainly participated in the market and had material stakes in empire,[43] but to view their behavior on that basis alone would be to miss an essential characteristic of their activities. Patronizing African exploration was both business and pleasure – two elements in this case that are virtually indistinguishable. "Social enjoyment," Roberts has noted, was the "stock-in-trade" of the gentleman's club,[44] but this economy preserved much more than pleasure. Knowledge, the Association's asset, produced status, access, influence, and was invested (like money) to make more knowledge. Club life assembled "charmed circles of power," valuable personal connections that reinforced genteel "prestige and authority." Sinclair, for one, credited his political alliance with Rawdon to the Association.[45] Yet the Association's business extended well beyond dinners at St. Alban's or the Star and Crescent Tavern, and the "enlightened moral economy" of scientific exchange[46] advanced more than learning. The gentlemen of the Association were in the business of producing knowledge and, if things went right, national heroes. Its value secured, knowledge not only illuminated the uncovered mysteries of the globe; it was capital to accumulate and deploy within a cultural market that measured its dividends in terms of achievement, prestige, and power. To these ends, the project's continuing success became its defining purpose.

INTERNATIONAL AND NATIONAL NETWORKS

The African Association reinforced gentlemanly exclusivity beyond the financial requirements, particularly through stipulations restricting access to its findings. Its products, like the printed *Proceedings*, were supposed to be the particular fruits of membership. In fact, the Association had only two inaugural rules: that the Committee keep all information from explorers private, and that it convene the Association at large to communicate any

[42] See P. J. Cain and A. G. Hopkins, *British Imperialism: Innovation and Expansion 1688–1914* (London and New York: Longman, 1993).
[43] See H. V. Bowen, *Elites, Enterprise, and the Making of the British Overseas Empire, 1688–1775* (Basingstoke and New York: Macmillan and St. Martin's Press, 1996).
[44] Roberts, "Pleasures," 49.
[45] Cain and Hopkins, *British Imperialism*, 26; Clark, *British Clubs*, 150; Sinclair, *Correspondence*, 133.
[46] Schaffer, "Visons of Empire," 339–40.

"interesting Intelligence" it received, if it did not endanger the welfare of the travelers.[47] Such covert practices were not only practical; they enhanced the ethos of privilege.

However, the collection of knowledge for men like Joseph Banks also depended upon, as Chambers has shown, "web-like networks" of information, and, as David Philip Miller has argued, Banks, as a center of British science, disciplined manifold resources, people, and institutions into a single system of "accumulation, calculation, and exercise of power."[48] Thus, although it had only one hundred subscribers in 1790, the Association ordered five hundred copies of its first *Proceedings* to be printed.[49] The governing Committee distributed extras to friends, to associates, and particularly to potential sources of African intelligence, such as officials of the Royal African Company and explorers not in Association employ.[50] In recognition of his geographical work, James Rennell was given several copies of the 1798 *Proceedings*, which he was told "to distribute amongst [his] friends."[51] The Association also worked to extend its reputation abroad. Banks, who was very much involved in the Atlantic and European scientific communities, often updated European colleagues on the progress of exploration. One German botanist, although aware that Rennell's 1790 map was "only destined for the Members of the African Society," requested a copy from Banks and was sent one.[52] The Association envisioned a chapter in Calcutta, and in the early nineteenth century boasted itself the "origin, head, and model of every succeeding [European] plan of discovery in Africa," including an ill-fated French Société de l'Afrique. And in perhaps the strangest moment of this exchange, the Committee took advantage of the short-lived Peace of Amiens to send Napoleon a copy of Friedrich Hornemann's journal, in appreciation of the passport the French leader had given the Association's fifth explorer when in Egypt.[53]

As knowledge was made useful, Miller stresses, "it was the ability to deploy the information thus gathered together which was crucial."[54] For the Association, nothing could accomplish this more swiftly than stimulating

[47] African Association Minute Books, Committee Meetings, University Library, Cambridge, MS Add. 7087 [hereinafter CM], f. 9.
[48] Chambers, "Letters from the President," 27–8; David Philip Miller, "Joseph Banks, Empire, and 'Centers of Calculation' in Late Hanoverian London," in Miller and Reill, *Visions of Empire*, 25.
[49] SP A1:93.
[50] E.g., Thomas Shootbred to Joseph Banks, February 23, 1791; SP A2:15; J. Gray to Banks, June 30, 1795, SP A3:14.
[51] Rennell to Warren Hastings, August 18, 1798, BL Add. MS 29176, f. 141.
[52] Schlanbusch to Banks, June 10, 1791, BL, Add. MS 8098, ff. 87–8.
[53] GM, f. 103; *Proceedings*, II: 325–6; Hallett, *Penetration of Africa*, 292.
[54] Miller, "'Centers of Calculation,'" 32.

commerce and empire. On the one hand, its leaders buttressed their authority by articulating their project in terms of civic advantage. Yet, as geography
served empire, empire served geography. The Association routinely called
on merchants, slave traders, diplomats, and other individuals involved with
Africa to assist explorers and to supplement their findings. Merchants and
manufacturers, who often "wrapped their quest for gentility in the cloak
of improvement,"[55] could be brought into the Association's fold and sometimes its dues-paying membership. Virtue demanded that gentlemen attend
to the nation, but commerce and state likewise governed resources that the
Association could discipline to its project.

A little over a year after its founding, the Association reached out directly
to capital for support. Through Thomas Ivatts, the Association's first clerk,
Banks kept an ear to the Africa Coffee House, a gathering place for those
involved in the Africa trade,[56] and in 1789, the Committee, stressing the
"large quantities of European and Indian goods" traded in Timbuktu,
resolved to undertake a joint venture with a group of traders led by Philip
Sansom, a prominent merchant and abolitionist. Yet the Association's actual
commitment to the commercial end of the venture was at least circumspect.
When Sansom suggested that the Association might contribute £100 to
support the supercargo, it declined. While "truly sensible of the propriety
of giving to the Commercial Adventure . . . the most liberal aid in their
power," the Committee insisted its contribution "must depend on the future
state of their funds,"[57] even though sixty-one new members had joined in
that year alone.[58]

Citing complications with its three explorers, the Association eventually abandoned this expedition, but three years later, it received the initial
reports of Daniel Houghton, its first explorer in West Africa. The Committee hastened to approach the government with a proposal to render his
discoveries "serviceable to the Commercial Interests of the Empire,"[59] and
in 1793, it resolved to discuss with Henry Dundas the appointment of a
temporary Consul to Senegambia. The British had once before tried such
a colony, which would have unified their posts in Upper Guinea and on

[55] David Hancock, *Citizens of the World: London Merchants and the Integration of the British Atlantic Community, 1735–1785* (Cambridge University Press, 1995), 281.
[56] Thomas Sharpless to Thomas Ivatts, November 29, 1796, SP A3:23a; Ivatts to Banks, April 19, 1796, SP A3:24.
[57] CM, ff. 27–9.
[58] Saturday's Club Minute Books, University Library, Cambridge, MS Add. 7086, ff. 9–22.
[59] GM, f. 13.

the Gambia, but the venture ended in administrative and financial ruin.[60] Houghton's voyage, of course, had been a dramatic failure too – he had not made it very far inland and had faced several calamities, ultimately disappearing somewhere in the interior – but with his "scattered notices" organized by Rennell into a lucid narrative,[61] the Association advertised an "extensive and lucrative trade" to be expected on the Gambia and the Niger, with complementary, but distinct, advantages: "the Establishment of such a commerce would equally promote the Interest of the Public *and facilitate the Geographical Improvements that are the peculiar objects of this Association.*"[62]

Again, public interest could be turned to enhance knowledge, and government involvement was the surest route to such success. The Association and its explorers already relied on British diplomatic stations in North Africa; a West African consulate, which was estimated to cost in excess of £3,000, the Committee felt "would strengthen the probability of success in an expedition that may otherwise depend on the chances of a single life."[63] And where government went, capital would follow. As Beaufoy reported to Banks, "several merchants of great wealth in the City had offered to vest a large sum in the adventure to Bambouk [Bambuk], as soon as they were assured that the countenance and protection of Government would be given to the Plan."[64] Yet, when Dundas suggested that the Association help subsidize the Consul, the Committee responded that it would be irresponsible to spend subscription money on a project not within the Association's "express purposes."[65] It did agree to pay £400 for a vice-consul, but only if it was satisfied with the *geographical information* he provided.[66]

Given the financial and military strain of war with France, the Committee ultimately recommended postponing the plan. In the same year the Association had proposed it, William Gilbert from the Sierra Leone Company approached Joseph Banks privately to suggest that the African Association take part in establishing an inland colony, which he argued would lead to the "improvement of the natives," which in turn would lead Europeans to the "riches" of the continent. Gilbert's proposal was based on the very fact that imperial and commercial venture was not the Association's mandate – as much as he felt it should be. While the Sierra Leone Company was interested in trade and settlement,

[60] J. D. Fage, *A History of West Africa: An Introductory Survey*, 4th edn (Cambridge University Press, 1969), 77–8.
[61] *Proceedings*, I, 263–94.   [62] GM, ff. 17–18. Italics mine.   [63] CM, ff. 81–2.
[64] Hallett, *Records*, 142–3.   [65] CM, ff. 131–2.   [66] Ibid., ff. 81–2.

The Association, on the other hand, have nothing to say to the Coast. They wish to discover . . . Surely there must be something more at bottom, & there *is*. It is a Discovery with an intent to benefit if not the Africans, yet, at least, their own Country – to receive the Riches, the Luxuries, of Africa. But it is said, this is an after Object.

It was only through uniting the two in common purpose that a settlement in the interior could be envisioned, one which would "at one & the Same Time direct its views to the Commerce of the Coast, the Object of the Company, & to the . . . Exploration of the Country, the object of the Association."[67] Banks deferred the offer immediately, and while he could envision a day when such a colony might be established, he wrote in his notes for the day, Gilbert's "decision tended to colonisation & civilization of the people of Africa. It did not in my opinion concede with the purpose of the Association in its present state."[68] This is not to argue that the Association was not imperial in its reach, but rather that it was not self-consciously so in its grasp. Its considerable promotion of empire and commerce served primarily to involve others in exploration, maintaining the Association's status in the center as the proprietor and promoter of a certain kind of knowledge.

PUBLICATION AND PUBLICITY

Five years after its founding, the Association had funded three expeditions, two from the north and one from the west. Two explorers dead, the other largely unsuccessful, and its efforts to involve commerce and state amounting to little, the Association none the less represented itself as having made great progress. By 1791, there were 109 subscription-paying members[69] and its activities were building towards a crescendo. In 1794, convinced that the Niger could be reached from the west, Banks and Beaufoy hired their next explorer, a Scottish physician recently returned from India named Mungo Park.

Park arrived at the Gambia in June 1795 and two years later returned to London an instant celebrity. He had found the River Niger (the first known modern European to do so), putting the question of its eastward direction, in Rennell's words, "*for ever* at rest." Park became a favored, albeit awkward, guest at clubs and coffee houses throughout London, and his *Travels in the Interior Districts of Africa*, published in 1799, was even more popular. Its narrative, Association secretary (and historian of Jamaica) Bryan Edwards

---

[67] Gilbert to Banks, August 19, 1792, SP 2:29.
[68] SP 2:28. Cf. Gascoigne, *Science*, 180.   [69] Hallett, *Records*, 24.

privately boasted, had "most strongly fixed the public attention,"[70] and the book sold an astounding 1,500 copies, warranting four editions before the end of the next year. The first edition alone earned Park over one thousand guineas in its first week.[71]

Printed materials, particularly the *Proceedings*, were physical manifestations of the Association's network of knowledge. Park's journal was, in this sense, no different. Edwards had edited the work, and James Rennell contributed an essay and a map to the volume. Park made the role of his "noble and honourable employers" clear in his preface, regretting only that "it is so little commensurate to the patronage I have received. As a composition, it has nothing to recommend it but *truth*."[72] The latter claim, however, was dependent upon the former – the authority of his text was directly related to the invocation of his patrons. Added to the narrative, which reported not only Park's geographical findings but the various forms of adversity he faced with confidence and his never-failing Protestant moral character, the import was clear: the Association had produced its first hero.

The leadership wasted no time in promoting Park's accomplishments. Edwards wrote to the Association at large that Park's discoveries gave "great room to hope that the original purposes of the Association will be speedily accomplished"; before long the Association's Committee would disclose, "to the wonder and contemplation of Europe, those vast and unexplored regions of the African continent, which the spirit of discovery, both in ancient and modern times, has hitherto sought after in vain."[73] In a speech to the Association in May 1799, which Robin Hallett called "one of the most significant utterances of the age,"[74] Banks gloried that Park had "opened a Gate into the Interior of Africa, into which it is easy for every Nation to enter & to extend its commerce and Discovery from the West to the Eastern side of that immense Continent."[75]

Although some remained unconvinced of the economic possibilities of the interior,[76] Banks spoke of a gold trade worth over a million pounds a year and was calling for permanent colonial trading posts and complete European commercial intercourse with Africa. While Park's narrative was

[70] Edwards to Banks, August 28, 1799, Kew 2/227.
[71] George Nicols to Joseph Banks, May 8, 1799, SP A4:33; Kenneth Lupton, *Mungo Park the African Traveler* (Oxford, 1979), 115–20; Hallett, *Penetration of Africa*, 242–9.
[72] Mungo Park, *Travels in the Interior Districts of Africa Performed under the Direction and Patronage of the African Association in the Years 1795, 1796, 1797* (London, 1799; repr. London: The Folio Society, 1984), xxi.
[73] *Proceedings*, I, 317.   [74] Hallett, *Records*, 165.   [75] GM, ff. 53–6.
[76] For example, James Rennell to John Sullivan, October 17, 1802, Public Record Office, London, Colonial Office (hereinafter CO) 2/1, ff. 46–7.

by no means unequivocal on the state of African civilization and despite his refusal of Gilbert's proposal several years earlier, Banks insisted the time had come to introduce "these ignorant savages" to science. With a detachment of five hundred troops and an investment of £30,000, the state must seize a great portion of the coast, he argued, so that a trading company might be established inland. Banks, who opposed the anti-slave movement precisely because it mixed religion with politics,[77] indicated that among other things such a company could in time rule the natives more justly than their "arbitrary Princes," converting them to the "tenets of our faith" and abolishing slavery. "That these Effects are likely to take place," he wrote his friend Lord Liverpool, President of the Board of Trade, "may be seen by the whole sense of Mr. Parke's Book."[78]

He seemed, as E. W. Bovill put it, "quite carried away by Park's account," so much so that some historians have argued that this was the very moment when the Association became a convinced agent of empire.[79] Yet if Park's publication was a watershed, it was certainly no rupture. The Association had always somewhat hyperbolically promoted the success of its ventures and the great benefits to be achieved by intercourse with the interior. The rhetoric, though, had become more urgent, the proposals more drastic, and the "suggestions" much more emphatic. Banks, to be sure, was well aware of the power of persuasion and representation, and his correspondence, as Chambers has noted, reveals the ability deftly to judge his various audiences and "modulate accordingly."[80] But what were his purposes here?

Not denying his genuine excitement at Park's success, the rest of the speech offers two other ends. Following his rousing oration, Banks led the Association in renewing its request to the government to establish a Consul at Senegambia,[81] which, as envisioned six years earlier, would have been a great furtherance for the Association. He then delivered to the meeting an alarming report on the state of the Association's funds. Clubs in this period faced fierce competition for membership,[82] and the Association had always been driven by the need to present itself as vibrant, useful, and successful. Now, twenty-three members had died, twenty-one were in arrears, and forty-two had discontinued their subscriptions. New membership was declining as well, and the Association, which had once

---

[77] Gascoigne, *Banks and the Enlightenment*, 37–55.
[78] Banks to Lord Liverpool, June 8, 1799, CO 2/1, f. 10.
[79] E. W. Bovill, *The Niger Explored* (Oxford University Press, 1968), 1.
[80] Chambers, "Letters from the President," 40; Gascoigne, *Banks and the Enlightenment*, 17; Patricia Fara, "The Royal Society's Portrait of Joseph Banks," *Notes and Records of the Royal Society of London*, 51, 2 (1997), 199.
[81] *Proceedings*, II, 5.   [82] Clark, *British Clubs*, 140.

had 142 members, now had 57.[83] Its funds stood at a little over £119, "a Sum," Banks admonished, "very inadequate to that which always ought to be ready in case the misfortune of your traveler being taken prisoner by the Moors, and a ransom demanded for His liberty."[84] He warned "that under such circumstances, the Committee were restricted in directing their expeditions, by the narrowness of resources; and considering what were their funds, might justly indeed, appeal to the Meeting, and to the public at large, if their scheme of enterprize was not fully commensurate with their means."[85]

It is hard to tell what was more horrifying for Banks: the inability to support their explorer or the possibility they might have to solicit the public for support. In any event, the Association had already resolved "to suspend any attempt at further Discoveries in Africa by way of the River Niger," and Banks was forced in November 1799 to decline an offer of service, citing both the expense of Friedrich Hornemann's continuing journey and the recent drop in membership.[86]

Hornemann, who had tried to reach Timbuktu and the Niger from the north, was never heard from after 1801. In the following year, the Association assembled a journal from what he had sent back, publishing it along with selected correspondence, a six-part appendix, and Rennell's revised map. Association secretary William Young prefaced the journal by relating Hornemann's accomplishments to Park's and by reiterating Banks's sentiments on the Association's finances from three years earlier. Careful to point out that the Association could not "condescend to solicitation," he appealed to the "generosity and patriotism" of his audience and reminded them again that "the extent of our undertakings can only be commensurate with our means."[87] Asking for money was ungentlemanly; struggling to maintain its gentle character amidst a crisis in gentility itself, the Association needed to highlight its successes every way possible if it was to be sustained.

Armed with these two books, this funding drive evidently worked. Five years after the publication of Park's journal, the Committee reported to the Association of the "flourishing" treasury, which stood at a significant £1,836, and accepted a proposal from Henry Nicholls to travel to the Niger. He was immediately instructed to read Park's *Travels*.[88] Nicholls arrived on the coast of what is today Nigeria in January 1805, and died three months later, never having ventured inland. None the less, the Committee's

---

[83] GM, f. 56.   [84] Ibid., f. 57.   [85] *Proceedings*, II, 15.
[86] GM, ff. 38–42; Hallett, *Records*, 279.   [87] *Horneman's Travels*, xiv, xv.
[88] GM, f. 113; CM, f. 192; Hallett, *Records*, 268.

rejuvenation campaign had not only temporarily bolstered the Association's membership and treasury. Its crucial effect had been to involve the crown and the Colonial Office permanently in the cause of exploration.

THE STATE AND THE ORIGINS OF EMPIRE

In 1802 (a year after the Association had gratefully sent Napoleon its publication) Banks wrote John Sullivan at the Colonial Office to tell him that he had "met with a book written with the clear intention to induce the French to colonise the whole of the Senegambia Country," referring to S. M. X. Golberry's recently published *Fragmens d'un voyage en Afrique*. State involvement in scientific endeavor was often impelled by competition with France,[89] and again Banks used a book as powerful ammunition. Golberry, he wrote, had "drawn a picture, which every poor and industrious man in France cannot but contemplate with a wish to enjoy the comforts of so productive and so agreeable a country . . . *I am clear that his Majesty's Ministers should be aware of the contents . . .*" and then offered to lend Sullivan his copy and told him where he could buy his own.[90] Banks's concerns likely struck a chord, and Sullivan began in that year to consult several individuals, including Rennell, on an expedition to Africa.[91] After a few years of planning, interrupted briefly by the reorganization of Colonial Office leadership, Park set sail in 1805. He again reached the Niger, this time never to return.

Although a "spectacular failure which added very little to existing knowledge" as Philip Curtin has argued, it was "nevertheless a new kind of expedition."[92] Until then, the business of African exploration remained in the hands of gentlemen and a club; with the state's direct involvement, the nature of the project changed. While the Association spent £767 on Nicholls's ill-fated voyage, the Colonial Office paid almost double that amount to one merchant alone in preparation for Park's expedition.[93] Originally supposed to lead an entourage of about three hundred, mostly troops, Park eventually took with him thirty-five Royal African Corps soldiers and more than ten others – still a far cry from his first voyage's retinue of two.

[89] Drayton, "Knowledge and Empire," 244–5.
[90] Banks to John Sullivan, August 1, 1802, CO 2/1, ff. 7–8; Boahen, *Western Sudan*, 29.
[91] Rennell to Banks, October 7, 1802, Dawson Turner Collection, Natural History Museum, London, vol. 13, ff. 268–9; CO 2/1, ff. 14–29, 30–45, 50–62.
[92] Philip D. Curtin, *The Image of Africa: British Ideas and Action, 1780–1850* (Madison, WI: University of Wisconsin Press, 1964), 150–1.
[93] CM, ff. 227–9; CO 2/2, ff. 19, 21, 68–92.

Whereas travelers like Hornemann had relied on anonymity, Park complained of the difficulty of disciplining soldiers and of finding Africans willing to join so conspicuous an expedition. Yet he also reported proudly that "Nothing could exceed [the King of Kai-ai's] amazement when he saw the soldiers *march*"[94] – a type of hubris typical of nineteenth-century empire.

Park still kept Banks updated, writing him and requesting the Colonial Office show him the accounts sent back from Africa,[95] but the Association was no longer the only player in the game. The posthumous account of this voyage was published not by the African Association, but by the African Institution, an anti-slavery group incorporated in 1807. The slave trade now illegal, exploration became associated with uncovering sources of "legitimate trade," commerce to replace the profits of slaving. Missionaries, whose efforts would come to define Victorian expeditions in Africa, were also finding their way to Africa in greater numbers, particularly through the efforts of the London Missionary Society, the Church Missionary Society, and the Sierra Leone colony.[96]

Within the state, exploration also acquired a different sort of patron, perhaps the most important of whom was John Barrow. Barrow, FRS and Bart., was the new generation's Joseph Banks, but much unlike his friend, Barrow made his career *within* government. Serving Macartney's embassies in China and the Cape of Good Hope and at the Admiralty for forty years, he promoted and advised government voyages around the world. Eighteen books and over two hundred articles later, Barrow had guided, in Nigel Penn's words, "his (or his country's) project of "mapping" the globe for the British Empire."[97] Another very different influence came from the British administration in Africa. The consulates had always been integral to exploration, but in 1814, when Hanmer Warrington was appointed Consul-General at Tripoli, he became a particularly keen advocate of British involvement in the interior, and a crucial contact for the second generation of British explorers in sub-Saharan Africa. After all, geographical discovery, the charismatic and often self-involved Warrington predicted, "certainly will be an honor to England which will be appreciated by after ages."[98]

---

[94] Park to Earl Camden, April 26, 1805, BL, Egerton MSS, 3009, f. 43.
[95] Park to Banks, November 16, 1805, BL, Add. MS 37232, ff. 64–5.
[96] Hallett, *Penetration of Africa*, 347–50.
[97] Nigel Penn, "Mapping the Cape: John Barrow and the First British Occupation of the Colony, 1795–1803," in Jeffrey Stone, ed., *Maps and Africa* (Aberdeen University African Studies Group, 1994), 121.
[98] Warrington to A. G. Laing, October 10, 1825, Royal Society MS 374, f. 100.

CONCLUSION

In 1788, the material interests of the British empire had seemed more or less content to confine themselves to the African coast, and despite abortive attempts in the seventeenth and eighteenth centuries to penetrate sub-Saharan Africa, it was far from inevitable that this largely maritime empire would begin to involve itself in the continent's interior. Not two decades later, the African Association's deliberate and assiduous attention to African discovery had already transformed European contact with the continent. Collecting, deploying, and promoting its knowledge, the Association had defined the African interior as a project of state and as a subject of inquiry germane to gentlemen, commerce, and empire alike.

As a form of imperial activity that resided in a club, however, its destiny was intimately tied to the rising assault upon polite society. In the realm of science, early modern notions of genteel "improvement" were giving way to a more modern concept of "progress,"[99] putting knowledge within the purview of the "expert" who, in Shapin's words, left "both the 'scholar' and the 'gentleman' as almost empty linguistic shells, roles well on their way to losing their institutions, their legitimacy, and ultimately, their members."[100] Such was the fate of the African Association. As government gradually took over, the Association found its focus changed, its membership declining, and with Banks's death in 1820, its leadership enervated. It never again achieved the influence it had had in the last decade of the eighteenth century. The Association penned its final resolution in 1831, incorporating itself into another club recently turned exploration society, which embodied an almost ecumenical alliance of state, church, and commerce: the Royal Geographical Society.

Knowledge, like money, has value only by common consent; to achieve the status of *useful knowledge*, and thus to have power in a commercial and imperial sense, the geography of Africa was first milled through a cultural process particular to its time: the expectations of metropolitan club life, the networks of institutionalized science, and an *economy of gentility*, which ordered and maintained the power of a gentlemanly class through the changing financial and political fortunes of its individual members. Knowledge was indeed power, but it was at root a power that can only be understood within this social and cultural context. Attention to the strategies and impulses by which the Association put the interior of Africa into

---

[99] Gascoigne, *Banks and the Enlightenment*, 261–5.
[100] Shapin, "A Scholar and a Gentleman," 314.

the imperial frame of reference provides – in a way that linear concepts of "discovery" and economic development cannot – a picture of the Association, and eighteenth-century empire generally, as distinct from its modern nineteenth- and twentieth-century descendents while simultaneously showing the continuities implicit in that lineage. Conversely, it locates this British "domestic" culture in its much wider context, within a gentlemanly network of objects of knowledge around the globe. Under these cultural conditions, the Association both fed upon and shaped the multiplicity of processes that we call, by shorthand, "empire" in the late eighteenth century. The small group of men who led this Association, and Joseph Banks in particular, thereby fathered a process that could only flourish once its parent had withered away, but which identifies the later eighteenth century as a critical moment in the story of British contact with Africa.

CHAPTER 6

Liberal empire and illiberal trade: the political economy of "responsible government" in early British India

Sudipta Sen

When merchants of the English East India Company after decades of traffic and skirmish with local powers became the unexpected rulers of India, they had to lay down the foundations of a lasting colonial dependency in a state of exigency. The new responsibilities of rule quickly exceeded its subordinate and delegated status: the charter upon which it had been conceived could not provide for the evolving structure of its polity and economy. In the last decades of the eighteenth century the Company thus embarked on a bold venture to craft its own version of a colonial state, aspects of which derived from statecraft in contemporary England, but which were also shaped inevitably through peculiarities of the struggle to make India amenable to British rule.

To contemporary observers the Company represented the best and worst of mercantilism: a commercial monopoly with a prodigious appetite for irregular political expansion wherever it saw the possibility of future markets. I propose in this chapter, nevertheless, that the colonial state in India was founded on conflicting visions of political economy: the immediate demands of profit and conquest as opposed to wider liberal ideas of rule. I excavate a few significant contradictions of ideology in the formation of the colonial state played out in the realms of policy and governance, inherited no doubt from the historical development of the "fiscal-military" state of Great Britain itself. Prevalent interpretations of British expansion in India tend to ignore such connections, focusing instead on the overwhelming force of indigenous Indian institutions and practices in the formation of the East India Company's regime.[1]

---

[1] Eric Stokes, *The Peasant and the Raj* (Cambridge University Press, 1978); C. A. Bayly, *Rulers, Townsmen and Bazaars: North Indian Society in the Age of British Expansion, 1770–1870* (Cambridge University Press, 1983), and *Indian Society and the Making of the British Empire* (Cambridge University Press, 1988); D. A. Washbrook, "Progress and Problems: South Asian Economic and Social History, c. 1720–1860," *Modern Asian Studies*, 22 (1988), 57–96.

This study eventuates from a deliberate splicing of British and Indian ends of the history of empire, an exercise that may appear to many as defying conventional boundaries of national histories.[2] It highlights the conflict of interests between authoritarian and liberal imperialism on the subject of the freedom of trade and economic improvement in eighteenth-century British India. I argue that the distinctions usually drawn between mercantilism and free trade, open and captive markets, do not readily obtain in this period. While aware of the benefits of unrestricted trade between nations, the East India Company was also concerned with the regulation of commerce for the advancement of public property and private fortune.

The Company did not expect its Oriental subjects to appreciate the virtues of unrestricted commerce: Indian kingdoms were hardly built on the foundations of liberty and property. Instead they represented sordid examples of medieval tyranny reminiscent of the Dark Ages in Europe. Rather than a civil society composed of free and conscientious subjects, the original inhabitants of India were scarcely better off than slaves.[3] The English (Dalrymple, Orme, Mill) did not consider Indians truly cognizant of the institution and entitlements of property, and thus by implication the mechanics of trade. *Prima facie*, the consent of Indians to legislation pertinent to the advancement of commerce was of little use to policy.

The colonial fiscal-military state, however, was subject to adaptation in India, especially where it was involved in the dismantling and reconstruction of vast remnants of the Mughal imperial order. Such a predicament demanded reformulations of policy in quick succession: the "cares and embarrassments of this various state" – as Warren Hastings put it to the Court of Directors in 1773 – "the miscellaneous heap which each day's exigencies present . . . points on which the general welfare of your affairs most essentially depends."[4] None the less, as I argue below, policymakers took a great deal of trouble to ensure a "responsible government" to secure what Bolts saw as "an interest in the hearts of the subjected natives."[5]

This urge for moral governance on the part of a monopolistic and warlike corporation seems puzzling in the heyday of Old Corruption and political

[2] On the nationalist strictures of British and imperial history see Antoinette Burton, "Who Needs the Nation?" *Journal of Historical Sociology*, 10 (1999), 227–48. For an argument in favor of opening up the boundaries of British history, but restricted to the settler colonies, see J. G. A. Pocock, "The Limits and Divisions of British History: In Search of the Unknown Subject," *American Historical Review*, 87 (1982), 311–36.

[3] Alexander Dalrymple, *A General View of the East India Company* (London: 1772), 19–21.

[4] Warren Hastings to the Court of Directors, November 11, 1773, in *Speeches and Documents on Indian Policy, 1750–1921*, ed. A. B. Keith (3 vols., Delhi: Anmol Publications, 1985), I 36.

[5] William Bolts in his preface to *Considerations on Indian Affairs* (1772), cited in Ramsay Muir, *The Making of British India 1756–1858* (Manchester University Press, 1923), 101.

influence of the crown back home in England. Recent histories of economical reform, spearheaded in this era by Pitt, suggest that such measures were designed above all to preserve the legitimacy of the old and entrenched elite.[6] The Company-state in India, subject to parliamentary inquiry and public accountability, initiated a similar course, attentive to public outcry during the trial of Clive, impeachment of Hastings, opposition to the passage of Fox's India Bill (1783) and also Pitt's India Act (1784). While exigencies of rule in India impinged on political and economic ideology emanating from Britain, charges of Oriental excess against Company servants in India fueled the debate over permissible spoils of political office at the heart of British parliamentary politics. Meanwhile in India, six months away by sail, a liberal ideology of governance enchanted with the idea of free and unrestricted trade across the Indian countryside helped pave the way for a radical restructuring of native society, particularly as such ideas were inimical to established norms of local commercial and political culture. This chapter is thus an attempt to fathom the cross-traffic of ideas and practices that both join and separate the British and the Company-state in India, passages where more than one set of archives seem entangled.

COMMERCE, EMPIRE, AND FREEDOM

Bernard Semmel's well-known study of the free trade debate begins with the quarrel between David Hume and Dean Josiah Tucker over the question of rich nations preying on poorer ones for advantage over oceanic trade.[7] Although the affinity between mercantilist enthusiasm and the push towards the acquisition of colonies does not always seem clear – Tucker being an arch opponent of the colonial system in opposition to Burke during the American Revolution – it seems reasonable to suppose that the idea of free trade had gained a degree of currency a few years before the publication of the *Wealth of Nations*. Although Semmel himself discounted the English experience in India and also Ireland as "atypical,"[8] the controversy over free trade remains crucial to our understanding of the popular and conscious image of chartered corporations such as the East India Company,

---

[6] See especially Philip Harling, *The Waning of "Old Corruption": The Politics of Economical Reform in Britain, 1779–1846* (Oxford: Clarendon Press, 1996), 7; also Michael J. Turner, *British Politics in an Age of Reform* (Manchester University Press, 1999), 38–9.

[7] Bernard Semmel, *The Rise of Free Trade Imperialism: Classical Political Economy and Empire of Free Trade and Imperialism* (Cambridge University Press, 1970), 14–19.

[8] Ibid., 2.

and the manner in which they attempted to run their affairs in the era of parliamentary supervision.[9]

Adam Smith, one may recall, questioned the legitimacy of all monopolies as counter to the natural laws of the market, arguing against the "exclusive privileges of corporations, statutes of apprenticeship, and all those laws which restrain . . ."[10] He singled out the East India Company as the one which "oppresses and domineers in the East Indies."[11] The Company in India was "perfectly indifferent about the happiness or misery of their subjects,"[12] and such a government was really the worst for any country.[13] Yet he argued that the unprecedented expansion of the world market through the opening of trade in Asia and the Americas outweighed the drawbacks of colonial warfare, expansion, and monopoly.[14] As Semmel noted, it is very difficult to pin Smith down as a true partisan of either physiocracy or mercantilism, or even as a beacon of latter-day classical political economy. The contemporary distribution of the wealth of nations suggested to him that a greater autonomy for Britain's colonies, and a system of free trade, would greatly benefit the people of the kingdom, while the question of national interest and security discounted such a possibility in the immediate future.

Smith did not advocate that the East India Company relinquish its territorial responsibilities and competitive interests in India. Instead, he called for more public governance, pressing for a much greater convergence between the benefits of commerce and the interests of the inhabitants of India. His attitude was in many respects far more representative of the era than has been acknowledged. In the decades immediately after the transfer of revenue collections in northern India from the Mughal empire to the Company, liberal ideas of political economy with mercantilist and physiocratic undercurrents were running through administrative agendas and infected even the most recently recruited servants in the Company administration in the period after the 1770s.

[9] See for instance the Petition of the City of London against Lord North's Regulating Act, May 28, 1773, in P. J. Marshall, *Problems of Empire: Britain and India 1757–1813* (London: George Allen and Unwin, 1968), 107.
[10] Adam Smith, *The Wealth of Nations* [1776] (London: Penguin Books, 1986), 164.
[11] Ibid., 176.
[12] Adam Smith, *An Inquiry into the Nature and Causes of the Wealth of Nations*, 5th edn, ed. Edwin Cannan (2 vols., London: Methuen, 1930), II, 243. See also William J. Barber, *British Economic Thought and India 1600–1858: A Study in the History of Development Economics* (Oxford: Clarendon Press, 1975), 98.
[13] Smith, *An Inquiry*, 140.   [14] Semmel, *Rise of Free Trade Imperialism*, 26–7.

My case for liberal imperialism in India is based on a history of the ruling ideologies of the Company-state that advocated – at least for the public record – a great deal of concern for social and economic reform, culminating in the consolidation of customs in the 1770s and far-reaching land revenue and market reforms in the 1790s urged in particular by Cornwallis as the Governor-General. On a larger scale, however, I follow the concern of Uday Mehta, who suggests that the emergence of empire and liberal thought in historical coincidence do not necessarily point to a singular contradiction; rather they reveal many intriguing and circuitous links.[15] It was through the contingency of empire that liberal ideas found a new and unfamiliar context, and it is possible to demonstrate some of their claims and limitations in the very workings of the early colonial administration. As Mehta puts it, the Indian question was "paradigmatically the issue of how a body of ideas that professed a universal reach responded to the encounter with the unfamiliar."[16] Some of these modes found their expression in concerns that were at the center of the early political and economic enterprise of the British in India.

LEGITIMATE TRADE AND THE MEANS OF IMPROVEMENT

In 1776, before the devastations wrought by the great Bengal famine had fully passed, Warren Hastings, the Governor-General, had urged the formation of a Commission of Inquiry into the land revenue arrangement of British territories in order to secure to the primary producers a "perpetual and undisturbed possession of their lands."[17] The welfare of the cultivator, Hastings held forth, "ought to be the immediate care of the Government," but the only way to reduce the influence of the interposing landholders (the notorious *zamindars*) was by enforcing regulations "so framed as to produce their own effect without requiring the hand of Government."[18] In a minute that followed, Richard Barwell of the Council attempted to sum up the grand objective of revenue reform, that "personal property ought to be held as sacred in the pittance of the poor as in the possessions of the rich."[19] The rhetoric of this memorandum should be of interest to historians of colonial political economy:

---

[15] Uday Singh Mehta, *Liberalism and Empire: A Study in Nineteenth-Century British Liberal Thought* (University of Chicago Press, 1999).
[16] Ibid., 8.
[17] *The Fifth Report from the Select Committee of the House of Commons on the Affairs of the East India Company*, ed. W. K. Firminger (Calcutta: R. Cambray and Co., 1917), 1, cccxi.
[18] Ibid.   [19] Ibid., cccxiv.

The wealth of every country is to be found in the wealth of the commonality alone, especially in this country, where the particular manners and superstitions of the higher class either influence them to secrete their acquisitions, to dissipate it in religious endowments out of the provinces, or in the ostentatious folly of giving daily food and subsistence to a number of idle dependants, who are by such means totally separated from the bulk of the people, and who must have otherwise been employed in the manufactures and cultivation of the country.[20]

This is perhaps one of the earliest declarations of the Company as an agent of progress in India, even though one may note that the very language of governance was inflected in this age of Whiggish improvement with the promise of social change by fiat. In the spirited debates of the next two decades led by Alexander Dow, Philip Francis, Thomas Law, and a host of other administrators on the spot, the sentiments above were expressed repeatedly. Ranajit Guha has demonstrated how these arguments took place in the context of the Permanent Settlement of land revenue in eastern India aimed at the creation of a class of landlords diligent in the collection of revenue and dependent on the British.[21] But the appeal of progress, and confidence in the indictment of the current ruinous state of affairs in India, was widespread. The moral enlightenment had advised framers of political economy that agriculture and commerce were indices of the penultimate stage of human advancement, while industry was the hallmark of truly polished nations such as Britain. Indian civilization in this respect seemed to have reached a considerable state of advancement in the remote past, but through despotism and anarchy had fallen short thereafter.[22]

In the plans for what Hastings had called the "improvement of the British interests"[23] in India a great deal of attention was paid to the conditions of the primary tillers of the land. But there was also concern over the unsettled state of inland trade and commerce to the detriment of the average trader and manufacturer. While ideological cross-currents leading to the settlement of land revenue, especially in Bengal, have been well studied, less has been said about the modes in which the British set about reforming practices of trade and commerce in the north Indian countryside.

The use and abuse of inland trade in India after all had been the immediate cause of the wars with the last Bengal Nawabs leading to the annexation of territory by the East India Company, once in 1756–7 and again in 1763–4.

[20] Ibid.
[21] Ranajit Guha, *A Rule of Property for Bengal: An Essay on the Idea of the Permanent Settlement* (Paris: Mouton, 1963).
[22] Ronald Meek, *Social Science and the Ignoble Savage* (Cambridge University Press, 1976), 1–4.
[23] Warren Hastings to Lord Mansfield, March 21, 1774. Keith, *Speeches and Documents*, 60.

The story of these conflicts is well known and thus not worth repeating here at any length.[24] Servants of the Company had been indulging in private trade in certain key items crucial to the regional court and favored merchants: salt, betel nut, tobacco, and opium. They did this by bending the clauses of a favor (transcribed as the "Phirmaund") given to the English by the Mughal Emperor Farruksiyar in 1717, granting a general and unspecified leave for the Company to buy and sell without local interference in items valuable to their overseas trade. The Bengal Nawabs accused Company servants of shielding their own goods of trade intended for personal profit under this leave, undermining local authority over markets and traders along with the fortunes of many prominent merchants loyal to the court. As the East India Company gathered the reins of administration, it was generally accepted that not only ensigns and cadets, but also senior officers had violated the spirit of agreement between the English and the local rulers dating back to the beginning of the century. The abuse of internal trade became a *cause célèbre*, leading to public condemnation of the depravity of private interests in India and the career of servants employed by the Company. At the same time it provided the administration with a foil for a new crusade to put an end to all restrictions in the way of commerce, English or native. Some of the ways in which this particular construction of mercantile probity came about, especially through a clash with native Indian practices, will be discussed at length below.

The Court of Directors, prior to the passage of the Regulating Act (1773), had disparaged all prohibitions and restrictions on trade in India. They had noted in their proceedings that while customary duties had been part of the revenue of Indian regimes since ancient times, "exemption from the payment of these duties became one of the first objects of the Company on the commencement of their influence with the native powers."[25] These being secured by treaty, letters of exemption (known as the "dustuck"[26]) passed goods duty free through the customs houses, tolls, markets, and bazaars while the same duties were rigorously exacted from the natives. Such

[24] P. J. Marshall, *East Indian Fortunes: The British in Bengal in the Eighteenth Century* (Oxford: Clarendon Press, 1976), and also his *Bengal: The British Bridgehead* (Cambridge University Press, 1987); B. K. Gupta, *Sirajuddaullah and the East India Company, 1756–1757: Background to the Foundation of British Power in India* (Leiden: E. J. Brill, 1962); Sukumar Bhattacharya, *The East India Company and the Economy of Bengal from 1704 to 1740*, 2nd edn (Calcutta: Firma K. L. Mukhopadhyay, 1969); Sudipta Sen, *Empire of Free Trade: The East India Company and the Making of the Colonial Marketplace* (Philadelphia: University of Pennsylvania Press, 1998).
[25] India Office Records [hereinafter IOR], Home Miscellaneous [HM] 216, 2. A summary of the proceedings of the Court of Directors, the Supreme Council and the Board of Customs at Calcutta, in and since the year 1773.
[26] Hindusthani *"dastak"* (hand-written pass).

letters had been "converted into instruments for evading the customs of the prince" much to the advantage of the servants of the Company. Having acquired the "abuse of immunity and indulgence" they had sheltered private merchandise under the Company letter and flag. The Directors, having examined the affairs of government customs in 1771, declared the practice as having had a very deleterious effect on "the freedom of trade of the country."[27]

The Directors knew, as all contemporaries did, that profits from the "country trade" supplemented the meager salary of many Company servants, and that the end of such privilege would deprive them of a staple source of income.[28] Some senior members in recognition of their ranks were given certificates at selected outposts as an "incitement to their diligence and to their faithful discharge of several duties."[29] Notwithstanding such conditional remedies, servants of the Company expressed their "disappointment" and "mortification" at having been deprived of the one favor that "gave them a superiority to the free merchants and sojourners."[30]

Given the scale and intensity of the legendary "shaking of the pagoda tree" in this part of India, it seems rather surprising that almost immediately after conquest the succession of individual windfalls became such an object of public concern in Calcutta, Madras, and London. Within ten years of the assumption of territorial rule and revenue collection in India, avenues of spectacular private enrichment were being closed off in favor of a more responsible approach to trade, commerce, and governance in north India. This was in no small part due to the greater vigilance of Parliament over affairs as evident in Lord North's Regulating Act of 1773, aimed at strengthening the Court of Directors against servants of the Company in India.[31] It was also apparent in the very arrangements that affirmed and extended the Company's charter that the era of Oriental excess had come to a close. Article XXIV of the Regulating Act instructed that no person holding or exercising any civil or military office under the Company should accept gifts or rewards from Indian rulers and their agents.[32]

The regulation of profits points to the accretion of responsibility to officers of the Company who had now become agents of a new colonial state. While the phrase "responsible empire" may exaggerate the intentions of the

27 IOR, HM 216, 7. General Letter to Bengal, April 10, 1771.
28 Marshall, *East Indian Fortunes*, 109; also Holden Furber, *John Company at Work* (New York: Octagon Books, 1970), 14–15.
29 IOR, HM 216, 11.
30 Ibid. 13–14. Bengal Board, Revenue Letter, February 7, 1773.
31 See Marshall, *Problems of Empire*, 34.
32 The East India Company Act, 1773 in Keith, *Speeches and Documents*, 52.

various contending factions in the extended patronage of the Company and Parliament, the business of state-building and revenue-gathering in India had by all accounts become a more solemn undertaking.

MEASURES AGAINST INDIAN "DESPOTISM"

It was clear to harbingers of economic reform in India that the society in question was in many ways unsympathetic and even undeserving of the reforms being proposed. War with the Bengal Nawabs had already proved to the English that Indian rulers were untrustworthy, capricious, vindictive, and for the most part inconsistent. A tyrannical attitude of Indian potentates to the regular trader and to commonly accepted rules of commerce was something that the policymakers of the Company often took for granted.

It is clear that Indian rulers did not share the same principles of reciprocity between merchants and the polity. Affairs of the state, especially land revenue collection, were the genuine and legitimate concerns of an aristocratic Mughal culture, while trade and commerce, though necessary for the wherewithal and prosperity of the realm, were not. An ideal association between the imperial body politic and the realm of merchants and their goods had been elucidated in the celebrated text of Abul Fazl dedicated to the exalted court of Akbar the Great. In the opening passages of Abul Fazl's *Edicts* the emperor appears as divinely ordained with the ability to bring together and regulate various denominations of subjects.[33] He thus constitutes all who dwell on earth by an even ordering of their various ranks. These appear as four elemental divisions: warriors are likened to fire, merchants and people of various professions to air, people of learning to water, and peasants and cultivators to earth itself.

Quite apart from such an ideal conception of rank and order, merchants foreign and native in the late medieval period in India were subject to the authority of rulers and their agents in a very direct sense. The Bengal Nawabs mistrusted the increasingly martial bearing of European traders, and it is worth noting that it was precisely the military intentions of the English in Calcutta that drove Siraj to war against them. In the period under consideration the Company still ruled through a Mughal investiture, and in Bengal, their stronghold, through the so-called "puppet Nabobs": Mir Jafar and Mir Kasim. As the British attempted to legislate and implement

---

[33] *The Ain-i-Akbari by Abul Fazl 'Allami*, ed. H. Blochmann (Calcutta: Asiatic Society of Bengal, 1872), 3. The reference here is that of Yunani medicine derived from Galenic conception of the flows of different humors.

new modes of commerce, they were endlessly frustrated by what appeared to be the very inability of Indian rulers and Indian subjects to uphold the virtues of equitable taxation, standard prices, and the principles of free and fair trade. Some of these views were a direct result of the conflict with Mir Kasim, the "puppet" Nawab who rebelled against the British.

The proliferation of internal trading among Company servants discussed above, which would be declared illegal in the 1770s, led to the fateful war with Kasim involving the neighboring kingdom of Awadh and even the forces of imperial Delhi. This was the battle of Baksar (1763–4), far more important in its outcome than Plassey. In fact it was the rout of the Mughal forces in this skirmish that precipitated the title of Diwan for Clive handed out by Emperor Shah Alam, whereby the English became collectors of revenue for eastern India and thus, to all intents and purposes, the rulers. The main cause of conflict between Kasim and the British was the issue of trade and sovereignty, and the impasse over the very terms and meanings of legitimate commerce provides a fascinating glimpse of the clash of material cultures as well as the changing conceptions of the role of the state in Indian society.

Judging from his letters, it is clear that Kasim understood that the British were violating their *own* codes of conduct and terms of their treaty by continuing to indulge in private trade in the manufactories and marketplaces of greater Bengal. Kasim complained bitterly to Henry Vansittart, the governor of Fort William, about the behavior of Company servants and their Indian dependants (the *gumashta*s). "It is true indeed," he wrote, "that a country does prosper from the exertions of traders and from the comings and goings, the selling and buying of merchants."[34] But these were strange times, where everyone tried his luck in the country trade. Kasim remonstrated in particular against native agents of the English who on behalf of their new masters went about purchasing and selling goods above and below the market rate in contravention of legitimate authority and without any heed to protests of the common people. They scouted markets and granaries, setting themselves up as landlords and leaseholders in the face of the Nawab's officers; they passed the merchandise and effects of others along with their own, abusing their licenses and permissions, and thus causing the loss of rightful revenue.[35]

---

[34] Letter of Kasim Ali Khan to Nawab Nasir-al-mulk Shams-ud-daulah Bahadur Tahawwur-i-jang, Mr. Henry Vansittart, Governor of Fort William, Calcutta. Hermann Ethé Collection of Persian Manuscripts, IOR, E 481, f. 10.

[35] Ibid., f. 13.

In view of such violations Mir Kasim in 1763 abolished all duties on trade for two years, at the end of which period, he declared, privileges formerly enjoyed by the English based on the Mughal grant of 1717 would be subject to further examination.[36] Merchants were "no one's servants, but for the sake of a very small profit, deal one with the other."[37] In effect, he deprived the English of their advantage by promoting a free market: "let every man for his own fancy buy and sell whatever he pleases – I shall interrupt no one."[38]

Officers Aymatt and Hay who were dispatched to make amends with the Nawab demanded that they had a "right to a free trade" and that the privileges of the English derived from the Mughals could not be interfered with.[39] They denounced the act of lifting all duties as "entirely repugnant to their interests."[40] Kasim replied that such exemptions had deprived the government of the annual receipts of 3 to 4 million rupees per year, for the past three years. Moreover, the English had proceeded against the Nawab's officers with "utmost indignity" and thus insulted his authority.[41] The lines were thus drawn on the sand in 1763.

As the Company deposed Kasim and assumed charge in Bengal, they relinquished for the most part a pursuit of private fortunes. Company servants had now become agents of a much more autonomous state, and their covenants clearly forbade involvement in local trading practices. In the immediate aftermath of the war with Mir Kasim, Company stalwarts acknowledged that they had knowingly violated the intent of the Mughal grant of 1717. Kasim was the victim of this "yoke of imperious commerce."[42] The English had acted as both traders and magistrates in the markets under his authority; it was the "unwarrantable and licentious manner" in which private trade had been carried on by the agents that had led to the political crisis in Bengal.[43] The English interlopers suffered not from a lack of judgment, a directive from London put it, but from a lack of "virtue to withstand the temptation of suddenly amassing a great fortune." This led to widespread abuse. The English and their lackeys "exacted by violence a sanction for a trade to enrich themselves without the least regard or advantage to the Company whose forces they employed to protect them in it."[44]

---

[36] IOR, Bengal Public Consultations [hereinafter BPC], range 1, 36: 56. Fort William, Calcutta, May 9, 1763.
[37] Ibid., 60. [38] Ibid. [39] Ibid., 56. [40] Ibid., 57. [41] Ibid.
[42] IOR, HM 216, Bengal Government Customs, 2.
[43] IOR, HM 92, Extract of General Letter to Bengal, February 8, 1764.
[44] Ibid., Extract of the General Letter to Bengal, April 26, 1765, 85–6.

As Clive himself pointed out, the office of the Governor-General of Bengal had to be well appointed and well rewarded, for anyone acquainted with the riches of Bengal was aware of the "prodigious emoluments within the reach of gentlemen high in the service."[45] He proposed that the conscience of delinquent servants would only be "awakened by the legal consequences of perjury and pecuniary punishment," and punitive sanctions would be the surest means of preserving the honesty and the covenant of the entire lot. Clive was worried about their "conduct in a state of temptation"[46] and hoped that these strictures for service would not be construed as an "affront to religion and to morality," but rather, seen as a necessary device for the preservation of a legitimate empire.[47] But then corruption was endemic to the East and had to be contained for the honor of the Company and the nation. The issue of just and unjust commerce in a peculiar sense, then, helped lay the new constitution of the ruling corporation. Paradoxically, some Englishmen had behaved much like the Oriental despots they reviled in the years of conquest.[48]

A FREE AND A FAIR TRADE

Now that the question of mercantile adventurism had been resolved and participation in internal trade of the country declared "illicit" and "illegal" by the lawyers of the Company, various ancient levies, duties, and privileges from trade that characterized indigenous society came under the purview of administrators.[49] The Select Committee directed that such duties had to be adjusted with regard to

the good of the natives whose interests and welfare are now become our primary care; & we earnestly recommend it to you that you take the most effectual method to prevent these great necessaries of life from being monopolized by the rich and great amongst themselves, & by that means the poor and indigent becoming liable to those grievances & exactions, which we mean to prevent, our own people from being guilty of.[50]

Sentiments of welfare persisted in the next decade, when, as I have discussed above, the administrative responsibilities of the Company were being re-examined by Parliament. The liberty of trade in this era was more than

[45] Ibid., Extract of a letter from Lord Clive, President and Governor of Bengal, September 30, 1765, 117.
[46] Ibid., 117.   [47] Ibid., 118.
[48] See, for example, Alexander Dow, *The History of Hindostan* (London: Vernor and Hood et al., 1803), cxxx.
[49] IOR, HM 92, 129, Extract of General Letter from Bengal, September 30, 1765.
[50] Ibid., 130.

just a rhetorical turn. Whether implemented or not, it became the stuff of
official policymaking aimed at improving the lot of average subjects in the
new dependency.

In their letter of November 3, 1772, the Committee of Circuit, having
made a thorough investigation into revenue from commerce, attempted to
identify dues that appeared "most oppressive to the inhabitants"; among
these were duties arbitrarily levied by rural landholders (*zamindars*) and
revenue-farmers on "all goods and necessaries of life passing by water
through the interior part of the country." They observed that these deduc-
tions would decrease the rent roll, but "would doubtless in time be productive of the most salutary effects as they would tend to encourage manufactures and trade." They would repair lives and pursuits devastated by
the late famine, and "free the people from vexatious prosecutions and promote general ease; whereby the revenue would virtually be supported and
improved."[51]

Some of these ideas were carried into effect shortly. Newly appointed
collectors in the various districts of Bengal were asked in the 1770s not
to allow any further levies at river quays on boats carrying merchandise
between Benares and Dhaka, a measure that alienated rural landholders
and chiefs, leading to sporadic defiance of the Company's authority in years
to come.[52] In the 1780s these duties were all consolidated under the head of
government customs, which had established several designated outposts in
the key cities of the Bengal–Benares region: Calcutta, Hugli, Murshidabad,
Dhaka, Patna, and Benares.[53]

In 1790, during the Governor-Generalship of Lord Cornwallis, a
momentous decision was taken to abolish all and sundry market duties
throughout the territories of the East India Company, a decision that had
serious consequences on the limits and nature of patronage, authority, and
exchange in Indian society.[54] Cornwallis asserted that the Company was
exercising a prerogative, one which had always been claimed in the past,
but never successfully implemented by the Mughals or the Nawab's administration, that the imposition and collection of internal duties were the

---

[51] IOR, HM 216, 11.
[52] IOR, HM 216, *passim*; also Murshidabad Council to William Harwood, Collector of Rajmahal,
April 23, 1772, Bihar State Archives, Collectorate of Bhagalpur, 1771–2. See also Notification of April
7, 1786, Regulation No. XXI, *Regulations in the Revenue and Judicial Departments enacted by the
Governor General in Council for the Government of the Territories under the Presidency of Bengal AD
1780 to 1792* (London: 1834), IOR, range v/8/15.
[53] West Bengal State Archives [hereinafter WBSA], Proceedings of the Board of Revenue (BOR),
Customs, Vol. I, Fort William Revenue Department, letter of June 20, 1788.
[54] I have discussed these at length in *Empire of Free Trade*.

"exclusive privileges of government."[55] No one could hereafter establish a marketplace without the express sanction of government; the power of imposing and collecting duties was taken away from landholders. These measures were expected to end "vexatious duties" on articles of "internal manufacture and consumption" and on exports and imports. Framers of the new policy hoped that the "natural effects" of these reforms would benefit trade and bring "ease to the inhabitants of the country."[56]

Cornwallis wrote to the Court of Directors in August 1789 that he had purposely withdrawn markets from the charge of the *zamindars* and placed them in the custody of government, so that the Company might retain the "unrestrained power to raise or lower internal taxes."[57] This measure was also conducive to the "security of property," restoring confidence in each individual subject residing under British dominion that he would be "allowed to enjoy the fruits of his own labors," as well as an incitement to "exertion and industry."[58]

As the lower basin of the River Ganges passed under a new regime of commerce initiated by the Company in the years between 1770 and 1795, and networks of trade spread beyond their immediate territorial jurisdiction, neighboring rulers were also urged to bring their economies in order and lift the age-old strictures on merchants and goods traversing their kingdoms. The Nawab Wazir at Lucknow, Shuja-ud-Daulah, ruler of the principality of Awadh, had been repeatedly reprimanded for refusing to intercede on behalf of merchants, and also for not enjoining his officers to keep their hands clear of the newly emerging trading center of Benares.[59]

The Nawab, however, was not entirely convinced of such benefits to trade in his kingdom from the presence of the English or the merchants they favored.[60] He was keenly aware of the previous hostilities just a few years before, and observed that whenever English merchants arrived in Awadh from the Company territory they set up houses and factories, and employed soldiers to secure their effects and residences. Agents of the English "*sardars*" (chiefs) had oppressed artisans and common people, and disregarded officers of the customs. It was inevitable, he wrote, that the officers of duty in his kingdom would demand their share from the merchants,

---

[55] IOR, Bengal Board of Revenue, Proceedings, Sayer [hereinafter BORS] 1790: Extract, Governor-General in Council in the Revenue Department, June 11, 1790.
[56] Ibid.
[57] Earl Cornwallis to the Court of Directors, August 2, 1789. Keith, *Speeches and Documents*, 158.
[58] Ibid.
[59] IOR, HM 201, 27. Council to the Nabob Shujah Ut Dowlah [*sic*], March 28, 1770 (Letters from the Bengal Government 1770–2).
[60] IOR, HM 203, 85–7.

and the merchants would refuse by force to accede to such demands, and this would then lead to further increase of violent confrontations.[61] The Nawab demanded that no merchants from the English dominion travel to his kingdom without formal written sanction from the government of Calcutta, and in the event of any misunderstanding there would be a just recourse in documentation.

The intended beneficiaries of these fiscal reforms were unlikely to appreciate measures undertaken in their interest. If India continued to remain mired in despotism, as many later critics following Mill would unfailingly point out, who were these measures ultimately directed at? While the average trader and the average cultivator emerged as the archetypal objects of improvement in the official discourse of colonial political economy, the immediate offenders and suspects were surely the various intermediary representatives of traditional rule in India, in particular the *zamindar*s. The purported altruism of the colonial state in the era of regulation and reform in India went hand in hand with the redefinition of its terms of domination. As the administration of revenue was extricated from the precolonial bearings, it was possible for the Company-state to establish its distance from Indian society and formalize the limits of concourse.

THE ENDS OF COLONIAL LIBERALISM

The terms and meaning of "free trade" kept changing in the latter half of the eighteenth century. Before and during the period of conflict with Indian rulers and landholders over access to the marketplaces and manufactories of greater Bengal, many agents construed "free trade" as simply the license to pursue private ends under the leave of a chartered corporation that had earned a right to trade through war and treaties.[62] In the same decade, though, after the infamous "rape" of Bengal, the "freedom" of trade became a benchmark of fiscal reform: the English and their agents had taken too much liberty with the country trade, and it was time to ameliorate the effects of anarchic commercial practices.[63] In a letter to the Select Committee (1768), the Directors wrote approvingly of the regulation that had been established for "the freedom of the inland commerce of the natives," confident that in a few years the measure would prove to be

---

[61] Ibid.
[62] The construction "freedom to trade" based on letters from the indigenous powers appears even in the first decade of the eighteenth century. See IOR, BPC 1704–9, range P/1/1, 85.
[63] IOR, HM 92, 121, Extract of Select Committee's letter from Bengal, September 30, 1765.

"the means of diffusing a general opulence throughout the provinces" and ultimately increase the revenues as well as the "attachment of the people."[64]

A similar bent of reform was at work in deliberations that resulted in the consolidation of internal revenues in northern India in the 1790s, protecting marketplaces in the countryside from the pernicious influence of indigenous landed elements and religious institutions.[65] It was the very character of the native landholders that rendered them unfit to maintain established markets. As one district collector put it, it was inevitable that they would try to evade rules, "not sensible that their own interest will be materially affected by any discouragement to commerce and that losing the benefit of frequented markets their estates must necessarily decline."[66] Thomas Law of the Board of Revenue, one of the chief architects of the settlement of markets, was convinced that these measures "must expeditiously promote manufactures and commerce." They would further encourage, he thought, the growth of urban centers of "lasting convenience" emulated by natives across the countryside.[67] Cornwallis communicated to the Court of Directors in 1793 that the trade and manufactures of India had indeed become accessible to British subjects and a wider European market through the adoption of "very liberal measures."[68]

This last statement brings us to the heart of the vexing question that has been posed in this chapter: why was the fledgling colonial state in India already commending itself on its liberal achievements within a mere two decades of its conception? The clash between liberal and mercantilist ideas, between colony and empire, has so far been largely an Atlantic, Anglo-American story. Jonathan Clark has urged that questions of liberty and property as part of a libertarian and hegemonic "English myth" appeared on both sides of the Atlantic, drawing taxation and trade into the center stage of political and constitutional controversy.[69] Taxation in the Indian context did not involve the question of fair representation; neither did it lead to disaffection with the "common good" – a result of administrative distance and political dissent in British North America as elucidated by

---

[64] Ibid., 667, Extract of the Company's letter to the Select Committee, November 11, 1768.
[65] Sen, *Empire of Free Trade*, 134–43.
[66] IOR, BORS, P/89/36, Letter of the Collector of Purnia to Fort William, September 1, 1790.
[67] Ibid., Fort William, September 24, 1790.
[68] Cornwallis to the Court of Directors, Fort William, March 6, 1793. See the *Correspondence of Charles, First Marquis Cornwallis*, ed. Charles Ross (3 vols., London: John Murray, 1859), III, 556.
[69] J. C. D. Clark, *The Language of Liberty 1660–1832: Political Discourse and Social Dynamics in the Anglo-American World* (Cambridge University Press, 1994), 1–4. For another version see J. R. Pole, *Political Representation in England and the Origins of the American Republic* (London and Melbourne: Macmillan, 1966).

Peter Miller.[70] Instead, debates over reform in significant ways *advanced* the cause of empire in India.[71] Because Indian rulers appeared to the British as resigned to habits of tyranny and despotism, their resistance to imperial expansion could be seen as acts only of rebellion, and not of legitimate dissent.

A preliminary answer to the question of economic reform may be found in the rising demand for what John Brewer calls the "orderly collection of public moneys" in eighteenth-century England.[72] The engine of the fiscal-military state was stoked above all by war, which as Braddick shows, employed not only increasingly large numbers of men as instruments of carnage, but parliamentary taxation to meet shortages in times of crisis.[73] The extension of the Seven Years War in the Indian arena invites a similar appraisal of the Company-state in India, which, even after the removal of the French threat, was surrounded by potentially hostile powers. As Thomas Law asked in his familiar rhetorical style dismissing the case for indigenous landed elite gathering market revenues: "Had the Sovereign of Great Britain relied till now upon his nobles' support, and had those nobles exercised the power of imposing duties would not oppression and poverty have still prevailed? What has occasioned her internal prosperity and external security, but a specific land tax, & distinct taxation to support army and independent Courts of Justice?"[74]

E. P. Thompson suggested, in passing, a related explanation for the particular ideology of land revenue reforms in India with specific reference to Cornwallis: as the product not of Smith or of the physiocrats, but of the "Whiggish, improving outlook" of the British gentry.[75] The observation merits further consideration, especially if Whiggism should be seen as a general and widespread body of attitudes, prejudices, and beliefs that set

[70] Peter N. Miller, *Defining the Common Good: Empire, Religion and Philosophy in Eighteenth-Century Britain* (Cambridge University Press, 1994), 1, 9.
[71] A somewhat comparable case may be made for fiscal measures (stamp duty) imposed on settlers on the turbulent western frontiers of North America who in turn forced them on the native population. See Francis Jennings, "The Indian's Revolution," in Alfred Young, ed., *The American Revolution: Explorations in the History of American Radicalism* (DeKalb: Northern Illinois University Press, 1976). On this possible comparison I am indebted to my colleague Jim Glassman.
[72] John Brewer, *The Sinews of Power: War, Money and the English State, 1688–1783* (New York: Alfred A. Knopf, 1989), 91.
[73] Michael J. Braddick, *The Nerves of State: Taxation and the Financing of the English State, 1558–1714* (Manchester University Press, 1996), 91–103; see also Jonathan Scott, *England's Troubles: Seventeenth-Century English Political Instability in European Context* (Cambridge University Press, 2000), 399–400; cf. Brewer, *Sinews of Power*, 38.
[74] IOR, BORS, P/89/36, Fort William, December 29, 1790.
[75] E. P. Thompson, *Customs in Common: Studies in Traditional Popular Culture* (New York: New Press, 1993), 170.

the normative standard for political and social order in Georgian England.[76] The case for progressivism in India becomes even more persuasive when one considers how important the criterion of property was for membership in civil society, and autonomy of the legislature for a rule of law.[77]

The history of the conversion of the East India Company from a predatory, mercantilist political entity to a settled and fiscally responsible state mirrors the passage from "Old Corruption" in England to the economical reforms of the 1780s and beyond.[78] This transition helps explain the changing disposition of the colonial administrators in India in the aftermath of the first wave of conquests, acutely aware of corruption in the ranks and abuse in the highest offices, and increasingly answerable to Parliament.[79] Public inquiry into the affairs of Clive and Hastings exposing the spoils of a chartered monopoly was perhaps a part of that larger transformation in governance resulting in the rise of administrative efficiency and the diminution of royal influence based on patronage.[80] While the full extent of this historical link remains beyond the range of this chapter, we cannot ignore in this case the reciprocal significance of English and colonial history in the restructuring of north Indian political economy.[81]

Why a monopolistic corporation rife with corruption and sustained by patronage would become the willing agent of a regime of colonial reform in India, in the era of what one historian called the "wholesale bribery and jobbery that turned the Commons into a market-place,"[82] is not an easy question to answer. One would have to consider in this context how narrowly we must construe the means of "corruption" for as J. H. Plumb did remind us, the political battles, factional strife in the Houses of Parliament, and financial scandals were all indicative of the increase in government

[76] For a general discussion of Whiggish ideas see H. T. Dickinson, "Whiggism in the 18th Century," in John Cannon, ed., *The Whig Ascendancy: Colloquies on Hanoverian England* (New York: St. Martin's Press, 1981), 29.
[77] Ibid., 37, 40–1; see also H. T. Dickinson, *Liberty and Property: Political Ideology in Eighteenth-Century Britain* (New York: Holmes and Meier Publishers, 1977).
[78] See Philip Corrigan and Derek Sayer, *The Great Arch* (Oxford: Basil Blackwell, 1985), 110–11.
[79] See, for parliamentary intervention in the Atlantic sphere, Philip Lawson, ed., *Parliament and the Atlantic Empire* (Edinburgh University Press, 1995), 1–4.
[80] E. P. Thompson saw in this change the greater currency of libertarian ideas and autonomy of the arena of the free market that had the effect of whittling down some of the "parasitic functions" of the state. See "Eighteenth-Century English Society: Class Struggle Without Class?" *Social History*, 3 (1978), 141.
[81] Henry Parris, "The Origins of the Permanent Civil Service, 1780–1830," *Public Administration*, 46 (1968), 146–7; John Torrance, "Social Class and Bureaucratic Innovation: The Commissioners for Examining the Public Accounts, 1780–1787," *Past & Present*, no. 78 (February 1978), 57–81.
[82] Louis Kronenberger, *Kings and Desperate Men: Life in Eighteenth-Century England* (New York: Vintage Books, 1942), 207.

activity.[83] Such proliferation, in a world run by patronage, was inevitable, argued Plumb, for the "political nation" was always larger than what birth and influence would allow; and "this was true," he wrote, "even at the greatest extension of our Empire."[84]

A different way to approach the problem, however, would be to consider how far libertarian and imperial sentiments were interspersed with the discourse of a national empire. Kathleen Wilson has outlined how the consolidation of the first empire under Pitt called for an extension of the birthright of all Englishmen to its farthest colonies.[85] This larger backdrop provides a basis for judging how the misgovernment of those colonies eventually became the barometer of an imperial nation's political institutions. More importantly for the purposes of the present exercise, the salience of a moral concern in political-economic affairs allows for an appraisal of the ideology of colonial conquest and state-formation in the era of frenetic commercial activity in India. In its effort to consolidate the collection of revenue, and realize a new era of unrestricted internal commerce, the Company also went about extending police and custom outposts throughout the empire.[86] By the end of the century, the Company had successfully secured the avenues of commerce and exchange from the despotic and corrupt influence of indigenous authority. Ironically, by the same token, it had also laid out the foundations of a surprisingly resilient, functional, and structured political and economic organization.

---

[83] J. H. Plumb, *The Growth of Political Stability in England 1675–1725* (London: Macmillan, 1967), 127.

[84] Ibid., 188.

[85] Kathleen Wilson, *The Sense of the People: Politics, Culture and Imperialism in England, 1715–1785*, (Cambridge University Press, 1995), 200–1.

[86] I have dealt with the establishment of the regulative framework of the Company-state extensively in *Empire of Free Trade*, 89–119.

CHAPTER 7

"Green and pleasant lands": England and the Holy Land in plebeian millenarian culture, c. 1790–1820

Eitan Bar-Yosef

The millenarian movements that flourished in England in the late eighteenth century have received much scholarly attention in recent decades. Centering around the charismatic leadership of Joanna Southcott and Richard Brothers, and envisioning a New Jerusalem of social justice, these movements have often been seen as precursors of Owenism, Chartism, even the Labour Party.[1] It is rarely noticed, however, that this millenarian hope of building Jerusalem in England was rekindled just when England was moving closer and closer to the actual, geographical, Jerusalem in the Middle East. In June 1799, in a decisive battle near Acre, the Royal Navy assisted Ottoman forces in defeating Bonaparte's troops; henceforth the British empire, anxious to protect the route to India, was increasingly drawn towards Palestine, with strategic, commercial, and religious interests always enmeshed together.

A rereading of Southcott's and Brothers's visions of the millennium, this time in the context of Britain's expanding involvement in the Middle East, serves two main purposes. On the one hand, their work offers an insight into the changing boundaries of the geographical imagination, in or about 1800. Torn between the anticipation of a New Jerusalem in England's green and pleasant land, and the growing recognition that the apocalyptic scenario must be performed in a much broader geographical sphere – the Levant – the prophets' extensive writings allow us to perceive how a poor working woman from Devonshire or a retired Royal Navy officer imagined a remote geographical region, part of the disintegrating Ottoman empire.

On a more fundamental level, Southcott's and Brothers's work exposes cross-exchanges between class, nation, and empire. British social historians

---

[1] See E. P. Thompson, *The Making of the English Working Class* (London: Penguin, 1972), 877–87; J. F. C. Harrison, *Robert Owen and the Owenites in Britain and America: The Quest for the New Moral World* (London: Routledge, 1969), 91–139; W. H. Oliver, *Prophets and Millennialists: The Uses of Biblical Prophecy in England from the 1790s to the 1840s* (Auckland University Press, 1978), esp. 197–217; Barbara Taylor, *Eve and the New Jerusalem* (London: Virago, 1983), esp. 161–72.

have long pointed to the pivotal role played by the Protestant biblical vocabulary – in which these millenarian visions were embedded – in the emergence of class consciousness. *"Pilgrim's Progress* is, with *Rights of Man*, one of the two foundation texts of the English working-class movement," E. P. Thompson has written; after all, the connecting notion between religious revivalism and radical politics (tinged with revolutionary millenarianism) "is always that of the 'Children of Israel'"[2] – and, we might add, the "Land of Israel." More recently, scholars have turned to examine how Protestant culture – and the conviction that Britain was God's favored nation, the New Israel – shaped the construction of Britain's imperial ethos: *The Pilgrim's Progress* may have inspired generations of dissenting radicals, Linda Colley has recently pointed out, but it also contributed to a more conventional mass patriotism.[3] What still remains to be explored, however, is the relationship between these metaphorical appropriations of the "Promised Land," in both the domestic and imperial spheres, and the actual Promised Land in the Middle East: how did the growing recognition of the earthly Holy Land, and Britain's ambitions there, shape the language available for the articulation of working-class grievances? What happened to the biblical imagery when it fell back on the geographical sphere from which it had originally emerged? And, looking ahead to the nineteenth century, how did the socialist-millenarian vision of *Jerusalem in England* shape the imperial vision of *England in Jerusalem*?

The Holy Land, as both territory and utopia, stood at the heart of English Protestant culture. With their extreme biblical literalism, the millenarian movements of the late 1790s allow us to narrate the story of Britain's imperial expansion from below (or from within), precisely because they problematize the neat dichotomy between the colonial and the domestic, between the academic and the plebeian. By examining the multiple, often contradictory, representations of "Jerusalem" we can thus come closer not only to a new imperial history of British interests in the Middle East, but also to a new understanding of the meaning of "empire" in the metropolitan center.

I

English millenarianism, which burgeoned during the Civil Wars and the Interregnum, did not die out with the Restoration. Rather, it persisted

---

[2] Thompson, *Working Class*, 34, 429.
[3] Linda Colley, *Britons: Forging the Nation, 1707–1837* (New Haven: Yale Univeristy Press, 1992), 28. Also see Tony Claydon and Ian McBride, eds., *Protestantism and National Identity: Britain and Ireland, c. 1650–c. 1850* (Cambridge University Press, 1998).

throughout the eighteenth century, significant at all social levels.[4] The 1790s, in particular, saw a great millenarian outburst: the French Revolution was perceived by many as the first in the prophied series of events which would dispatch the millennium, the Second Coming and the Kingdom of God on earth. Within this broad cultural climate, however, two distinct trends could be outlined: one was respectable, orthodox, learned, the other rooted in popular culture and folk customs.[5]

The polite, or academic, tradition was associated with eminent scholars like Joseph Priestley, George Stanley Faber, Samuel Horsley, and James Bicheno, who often turned to the work of mid-seventeenth-century divines like Joseph Mede and Thomas Brightman. Many were Dissenters, others affiliated to the Church of England, but they all approached the question of the millennium with the same scientific sobriety. The conversion of the Jews to Christianity and their restoration to the Holy Land – the exact order of events was much disputed – had long been seen as crucial phases in the apocalyptic design;[6] and the failure of the Jewish Naturalization Act in 1753 merely reinforced the conviction that the Jews, rather than being assimilated, were awaiting their restoration to Palestine.[7] Many of these luminaries believed that England had been providentially chosen to be the agent of restoration, Isaiah's "Tarshish" that would "bring my sons from far" (60:9). Palestine's strategic position, as a passage to India, was central to these millenarian calculations; it was expected that the Jews, grateful for their restitution to Jerusalem, would remain indebted to the British empire. However, as Napoleon was advancing towards Egypt and Palestine in 1798–9, the question of whether the Antichrist himself was to restore the Jews acquired much more than just exegetical interest.[8] A failure to persuade Turkey to give up Palestine and to prepare the Jews for their great migration "would prove most fatal to our government and commerce," warned Bicheno.[9]

---

[4] Oliver, *Prophets and Millennialists*, 17.

[5] J. F. C. Harrison, *The Second Coming: Popular Millenarianism, 1780–1850* (London: Routledge, 1979), 3–10, 207–8. For a more subtle view see Iain McCalman, "New Jerusalems: Prophecy, Dissent and Radical Culture in England, 1786–1830," in Knud Haakonssen, ed., *Enlightenment and Religion: Rational Dissent in Eighteenth-Century Britain* (Cambridge University Press, 1996), 312–35.

[6] See, among many others, Mayir Vereté, "The Restoration of the Jews in English Protestant Thought 1790–1840," *Middle Eastern Studies*, 8 (1972), 3–50; Mel Scult, *Millennial Expectations and Jewish Liberties: A Study of the Efforts to Convert the Jews in Britain up to the Mid-Nineteenth Century* (Leiden: Brill, 1978).

[7] N. I. Matar, "The Controversy over the Restoration of the Jews: From 1754 until the London Society for Promoting Christianity among the Jews," *Durham University Journal*, 82 (1990), 30.

[8] Oliver, *Prophets and Millennialists*, 60.

[9] James Bicheno, *The Restoration of the Jews, The Crisis of All Nations . . .* (London, 1800), 96.

That these scholarly millenarian speculations became intertwined with imperial and commercial calculations suggests that in explaining the emergence of Britain's colonial interests in the Middle East, Edward Said's model of a secularized (if not secular) Orientalism, emerging from mid-eighteenth-century philology, is inadequate. It is typical of Said to select Napoleon's invasion of Egypt in 1798 as the keynote for the Orientalist project – accompanied by a full-scale academy which produced the *Description de l'Egypte*, the Egyptian expedition was "the very model of a truly scientific appropriation of one culture by another"[10] – and not Napoleon's invasion of Palestine, a year later, which resonated a completely different set of apprehensions and expectations. The Holy Land, too, attracted much scientific interest; however, the very purpose of scientific interest in Palestine was to corroborate religion, not to undermine it.[11] As early as 1805, a Palestine Association was established in London to promote "the knowledge of the geography, natural history, and antiquities of Palestine and its vicinity" by "imitating as closely as possible the meritorious exertions made by the African Association" (discussed by Phillip J. Stern in chapter 5 of this volume). Nevertheless, unlike the *terra incognita* which was Africa, Palestine was the *terra sancta*; and the objective of the new society was to promote "biblical and historical knowledge," "with a view to the illustration of the Holy Writings," "a pursuit worthy of the attention of Christians."[12] To ignore this religious energy, or to claim simply that it had been "reconstituted, redeployed, redistributed"[13] in a secular framework, it is to overlook the extent to which the divine promise shaped not only the English encounter with Palestine, but also the British imperial ethos as a whole.

I will return to Said later on. First, however, we must turn to the opposite end of the millenarian spectrum, to the plebeian millenarians with whom this chapter is primarily concerned. Stemming from the radical sects of the Civil Wars, these were "the enthusiasts, the fanatics, the come-outers."[14] What distinguished them from their respectable contemporaries was very often the zealous literality that characterized their interpretation of prophecy. Notwithstanding their obvious political differences, Priestley and Horsley, Bicheno and Faber, all agreed that the apocalyptic scenario was to be enacted in the Levant, and that prophecies regarding Israel should

---

[10] Edward Said, *Orientalism: Western Conceptions of the Orient* (1978; London: Penguin, 1995), 42.
[11] Billie Melman, *Women's Orients: English Women and the Middle East, 1718–1918* (1992; 2nd edn, London: Macmillan, 1995), 29.
[12] *Palestine Association 1805* (London, 1805), 3, 7, 10, 4. Because of the risky conditions of travel and research, the association was essentially inactive. In 1834 it was absorbed into the Royal Geographical Society.
[13] Said, *Orientalism*, 121.   [14] Harrison, *Second Coming*, 6.

be applied to the Jews.[15] Plebeian millenarians, on the other hand, were much more likely to think of themselves as God's chosen people. Centering around the charismatic figure of a prophet who conveyed the heavenly communications directly to them, they tended to be premillenarian, believing that salvation would be achieved through divine intervention which would destroy the existing evil order and bring about the millennium.

Since popular revolutionism often found expression in the values and conceptions of traditional culture, revolutionary ambitions frequently merged – at least discursively – with the millenarian impulse.[16] For example, the flexibility of Thomas Paine's political rhetoric is demonstrated by his preparedness to turn to the language of popular religion when he seeks to appeal directly to the disenfranchised reader.[17] We should not, however, confuse the usage of this terminology as a rhetorical device in the service of radical/infidel politics with a genuine inclination to implement the millenarian vision in its most literal and localized terms: *we* are the Chosen People, and *here* is where our Jerusalem is to be established.

In mid-seventeenth-century England, this internalization of the biblical vocabulary generated various millenarian projects, such as the Diggers' cultivation of the common land at St. George's Hill. Gerard Winstanley, who told Thomas Fairfax that he was of the race of the Jews, believed that "all the prophecies, visions and revelations of scriptures, of prophets and apostles, concerning the calling of the Jews, the restoration of Israel and making of that people the inheritors of the whole earth" referred to the New Jerusalem that the Diggers were building in Surrey.[18]

Nowhere was this hope of building Jerusalem in England articulated more imaginatively, and influentially, than in John Bunyan's *The Pilgrim's Progress* (1678). With its emphasis on the glories of the afterlife, Bunyan's allegory rejected the Diggers' expectation of an imminent, terrestrial, New Jerusalem. And yet it did share the millenarian fantasy of reaching a Jerusalem that would adhere to the most familiar and palpable of terms: Jerusalem in Bedfordshire. Depicting a Chosen Child of God on his way to Mount Zion, Bunyan reads the landscape of Old Testament Canaan typologically, but only to literalize it as a muddy, poorly signposted seventeenth-century English road. The immense popularity of *The Pilgrim's Progress*

[15] Oliver, *Prophets and Millennialists*, 62.
[16] Clarke Garrett, *Respectable Folly: Millenarians and the French Revolution in France and England* (Baltimore: The Johns Hopkins Univeristy Press, 1975), 225.
[17] Jon Mee, *Dangerous Enthusiasm: William Blake and the Culture of Radicalism in the 1790s* (Oxford: Clarendon Press, 1992), 5.
[18] Christopher Hill, "Till the Conversion of the Jews," in *Collected Essays, Vol. II: Religion and Politics in Seventeenth-Century England* (Brighton: Harvester, 1986), 277.

during the eighteenth century suggests how the tradition of imagining "Jerusalem in England" persisted in popular Protestant culture. Like numerous hymns, sermons, and Sunday school textbooks, Christian's journey to Zion encouraged laboring men and women to think of themselves as God's elect, passing in this world on their way to the Promised Land: "Jerusalem, my happy home/When shall I come to thee?"[19] But it also provided the language with which new generations of radicals could imagine their own Jerusalem in England, here and now.

To be sure, the same sources which could invite a close identification with the biblical vocabulary – for example, Protestant almanacs – often implied that the earthly Jerusalem, "out there," must also play a central role in the apocalyptic design. A popular eighteenth-century chapbook, *The Wandering Jew, or The Shoemaker of Jerusalem*, describes how the mythical Jew travels through Asia and Africa, America and Europe, before reaching Hull, where he prophesies "that before the end of the world the Jews shall be gathered together from all parts of the world, and return to Jerusalem, and live there, and it shall flourish as much as ever."[20] Texts like these complicated the almost instinctive urge to envision the apocalypse in indigenous terms. The *Jews* are to return to Jerusalem and live *there*: what, then, is to become of us, and of the Jerusalem here?

Throughout the eighteenth century it was perhaps easier to overlook these questions, but as the British empire was drawn towards the Middle East, the existence and significance of the geographical Jerusalem was becoming increasingly difficult to ignore. Following centuries in which it was eclipsed by the heavenly Jerusalem, the earthly city was once again gaining greater cultural visibility. And yet its location and appearance must have remained obscure for many, first and foremost for the distinguished prophetess herself.

II

Joanna Southcott was born in 1750 and brought up in the village of Gittisham, Devonshire.[21] Having worked on her father's farm, she entered domestic service in various households in Exeter and eventually became a skilled upholstress. Raised an Anglican, she gradually became associated

---

[19] This version of the late sixteenth-century hymn is by Joseph Bromehead (1796).

[20] *The Wandering Jew, or The Shoemaker of Jerusalem* (n.p., 1810), 7.

[21] On Southcott see James K. Hopkins, *A Woman to Deliver Her People: Joanna Southcott and English Millenarianism in an Era of Revolution* (Austin: University of Texas Press, 1982); Harrison, *Second Coming*, chs. 5–6; Garrett, *Respectable Folly*, ch. 9; G. R. Balleine, *Past Finding Out: The Tragic Story of Joanna Southcott and Her Successors* (London: SPCK, 1956); Thompson, *Working Class*, 420–8, 878–9; the *Dictionary of National Biography* (*DNB*).

with the Methodist circle in Exeter; and although she received little or no formal education, she was not illiterate. In 1792 her housework was interrupted by a mysterious voice informing her that she was the "Woman clothed with the Sun" mentioned in Revelation 12. At the age of forty-two, an unmarried domestic servant, Southcott became a prophetess, ordered by the spirits to set their communications down in writing. In 1802 the spirit directed Southcott to begin the sealing of believers: thousands signed the petition calling for the overthrow of Satan, and received the seal with her signature. In 1814, Joanna aroused an enormous sensation by announcing that she herself, a 64-year-old virgin, was to give birth to Shiloh, the new Messiah, who would gather the Jews and restore them to the Promised Land. She died later that year, the autopsy revealing no evidence of pregnancy. Despite her death, the movement persisted throughout the century under the leadership of various self-proclaimed prophets.

The approach of the Kingdom of God was the most significant element in Southcott's teaching, but her writings do not offer a detailed blueprint of the millenarian utopia.[22] Rather, they depict the millennium as the ultimate state of blissful existence. Jerusalem represents spiritual regeneration and material prosperity in terms that shift from the sparkling metals and precious stones of Revelation to the organic-Edenic qualities that feature in the Old Testament prophecies. Southcott seems to appeal particularly to the poor by stressing the material rewards that await them:[23]

> I told thee I had gold in store,
> To build Jerusalem's ruins here:
> I said my kingdom should come down,
> With every splendor man to crown,
> I said My vines should clusters bring,
> And every happiness should spring . . .[24]

Or in another passage, this time in prose:

for the new Heavens and the new Earth, is a heaven here *below*, that they never *yet* possessed. The new Earth, is making all things new, and I will so improve the earth, that it shall be as the Garden of Eden to man, for every barren mountain shall become a fruitful field! And I will throw down and build up, until every house is made pleasant for man: gardens and vine-yards shall join to their houses . . . Such shall Jerusalem and all the borders be new built.[25]

---

[22] Hopkins, *Woman to Deliver*, 145.
[23] The social composition of Southcottianism remains unclear; Hopkins, in the most authoritative study to date, claims that the "poor and oppressed" were prominent in her following: ibid., 215.
[24] Joanna Southcott, *The Second Book of Visions* (London, 1808), 8.
[25] Joanna Southcott, *Answer of the Lord to the Powers of Darkness* (London, 1802), 112.

James Hopkins has remarked that the forthcoming "golden days" are described in terms easily understood by Joanna's audience.[26] But these were also the terms with which Joanna herself was most familiar: a roof, good crops, rest, land. These material assurances challenge the Methodist image of the believer as an impoverished yet happy pilgrim – "No foot of land do I possess,/ No cottage in this wilderness"[27] – awaiting his or her allotment at the heavenly Canaan. Southcott echoes the yearning for land which, particularly after the massive land enclosures, "rises again and again, twisted in with the outworker's desire for an 'independence', from the days of Spence to the Chartist land plan and beyond," as E. P. Thompson has noted: "Land always carries associations – of status, security, rights – more profound than the value of its crop."[28] This is precisely what Southcott promises her followers, as she transforms the image of the Promised Land to, simply, the promise of land.

When Southcott envisions "gold of ophir, that shall come/ To build Jerusalem up again,"[29] the millenarian utopia is not assigned a specific geographical location. And yet it is intimately associated with the fate of Southcott's followers, and therefore with England itself. "To build Jerusalem's ruins here," says the spirit, and surely there was no reason to suspect that it would happen anywhere else but here. A hymn, adapted from Southcott's texts for the use of her congregation, declares:

> If to GOD'S VOICE men could hearken,
> And obey His strict command,
> They will find, from what HE'TH spoken,
> This shall be "a happy Land".*
>   "A happy Land".

And in case of doubt, the note at the bottom of the hymn-book page states, explicitly: "England."[30]

The proclamation of the birth of Shiloh, who was to lead the Jews to the Holy Land, made this question more pressing. "Happy are those that are longing for my coming," the spirit declared, "and to see the CHILD born, that I shall set upon my holy hill of Zion."[31] But where was this

[26] Hopkins, *Woman to Deliver*, 145.
[27] "How Happy is the Pilgrim's Lot!" in John Wesley, *A Collection of Hymns for the Use of the People Called Methodists* (1779; 3rd edn, London, 1802), 71.
[28] Thompson, *Working Class*, 254.
[29] Joanna Southcott, *A Continuation of the Prophecies . . .* (Exeter, 1802), 15.
[30] Philip Pullen, *Hymns, or Spiritual Songs, Composed from the Prophetic Writings of Joanna Southcott . . .* (London, c. 1814), 87.
[31] Joanna Southcott, *Prophecies Announcing the Birth of the Prince of Peace . . .* (London, 1814), 37.

Zion? Southcott herself was not quite sure. Commenting on Revelation 21 in *The Third Book of Wonders* (1814) she asserts that the approaching Kingdom of God has no direct relationship to the earthly Jerusalem: "The new Jerusalem, coming down from heaven, meaneth where the visitation is made known: it does not mean Jerusalem where it stood . . ."[32] In *The Fourth Book of Wonders* (1814), however, Southcott implies that the old city is fundamental to the eschatological plan: "for I shall cast out all the heathens for their sakes, and now establish the THRONE OF DAVID for ever in Jerusalem, as I have promised. For, *where I was crucified, I will be exalted; where I died for MAN, my SON shall reign over MAN*."[33]

Nevertheless, even when Southcott does allude to the earthly Jerusalem, it is always to the ancient city depicted in the Scriptures. So, although a certain ambiguity does exist in her teaching in relation to the situation of Jerusalem, the tension is not so much between England and a present-day reality in the East, but between England and a textual representation that can always be applied, yet again, to the happy land that is England. Southcott views biblical texts as "types and shadows" which must be understood allegorically. "But, *Jerusalem doth not mean barely the spot where it once stood*," she writes: "the meaning of the word is, the NEW JERUSALEM that comes down to men, which signifieth *the paradise they were created in at first*." The old city was a type of the new city, which in itself is merely a reflection of the Edenic original.[34]

All this is highly reminiscent of Bunyan, of course (though, unfortunately, without the humor or the invention). And, just as in *The Pilgrim's Progress*, Southcott's vision of "Jerusalem in England" is inseparable from the notion of the English as Chosen People. Once again, Southcott does not allude specifically to the English, but the identification of her followers with God's elect – her assertion that "the house of Israel . . . is the HOUSE OF FAITH"[35] – makes this absolutely clear. The question of faith, in turn, is closely linked to the familiar promise of land: "So all they that will inherit the Promise must catch hold of MY WORDS, and say, *"I am of the seed of ISRAEL, as the seed of faith is sown in my heart"*: and these are the people that I will plant in the land, and they no more shall be plucked out of their land."[36] Southcott refers to the prophecy of the Jewish restoration

[32] Joanna Southcott, *The Third Book of Wonders, Announcing the Coming of Shiloh; with a Call to the Hebrews* (London, 1814), 16.
[33] Joanna Southcott, *The Fourth Book of Wonders, Being the Answer of the Lord to the Hebrews* (London, 1814), 51.
[34] Joanna Southcott, *A Continuation of the Controversy with the Worldly Wise* (London, 1811), 31.
[35] Joanna Southcott, *The True Explanation of the Bible . . .* (London, 1804), 435.   [36] Ibid., 435.

to Palestine, but only to dismiss its literal interpretation: "doth not my Bible affirm, that the fulfilment thereof is called to the restoration of the Jews? But what restoration doth that mean? Not a Jew outwardly by form or name; but a Jew inwardly by faith . . . for I now tell thee, the restoration of the Jews doth not so much allude to the Jews, that they all will be converted and brought in, as it alludes to the restoration of faith."[37] Faith transcends all other difference, racial or national, but it is not an abstract conception; rather, it is associated directly with the identity of her followers. Southcott collapses the Jew/Gentile dichotomy, only to create a "sameness" from which a new distinction emerges: believers/infidels.

This notion of "sameness" seems to have its rhetorical equivalent in Southcott's highly repetitive, almost numbing, style. The sheer bulk of her writings – sixty-five books and pamphlets, some 4,500 printed pages, and perhaps twice as much again in unpublished manuscripts[38] – sometimes reads like an attempt to silence, simply suffocate, all other voices.[39] Southcott's Jerusalem is not merely described by words: it is essentially made of words. "The building of the walls, and the beauty of the city, that is said to come down to men below, is the beauty and fulfilment of my words and promises, *much greater* than it is described by the beauty of the city," she explains: "But men are not to suppose that the cities will be made of pure gold; and yet, they will be filled with MY PURE WORD . . ."[40] It is not the actual City of God, or even the textual description of it, but rather the existence of the text itself which represents the millennium. The words are both promise and fulfilment, means and end. This self-contained element can explain why Southcott's teaching has often been understood as a call for resignation.[41] And yet it is precisely this self-referential tone which allows Southcott to secure her audience's attention by always balancing the ethereal with the tangible; her formulations always fall back, eventually, on the terms most familiar to both her followers and herself. The Holy Land as a geographical reality that might contradict or complicate her interpretation of prophecy did not seem to trouble the prophetess. This was hardly the case with Richard Brothers.

---

[37] Ibid., 407, 169.   [38] Harrison, *Second Coming*, 88.
[39] This rhetorical maneuver could be traced back to John's Revelation. See Steven Goldsmith, *Unbuilding Jerusalem: Apocalypse and Romantic Representation* (Ithaca: Cornell University Press, 1993), esp. 27–84.
[40] Joanna Southcott, *London, November 7th, 1808* (London, 1808), 26–7.
[41] See Thompson, *Working Class*, 424.

III

Brothers was born in 1757 in Placentia, Newfoundland.[42] His father, a gunner in the local garrison, sent the boy back to England to join the navy. Brothers entered Woolwich, became a midshipman at the age of fourteen, fought in several battles, and was promoted to lieutenant. Following the Peace of Versailles, he retired on half-pay, which allowed him to visit France, Spain, and Italy. Since he refused, on religious grounds, to take the oath required for the receipt of his pension, he soon fell into debt, was sent to a workhouse, and later to prison. In 1792 – the same year Southcott first heard the spirit – Brothers had decided to leave England, when he was suddenly notified by God that he was the Prince of the Hebrews and the Nephew of the Almighty: as his surname clearly revealed, he was descended from King David through James, one of the *brothers* of Jesus. In 1794 he published *A Revealed Knowledge of the Prophecies and Times*, in which he anticipated that the Kingdom of Christ was at hand. For a short time, his activity overlapped with Southcott's, but her following was considerably larger. Sympathetic at first, Southcott soon claimed that his work was written under the influence of the devil.

Considering the many months he spent in the workhouse, the prison, and the asylum, it is hardly surprising that Brothers's writings are often critical of the rich and powerful and attentive to the needs of the poor.[43] Despite his passionate denials, some aspects of Brothers's teaching – like his claim that the king should abdicate and pass the throne to the appointed King of the Hebrews – clearly provoked revolutionary sentiments. He was arrested in March 1795, examined by the Privy Council on suspicion of treason, and was eventually committed to a lunatic asylum, where he continued to elaborate his millenarian designs. Most of his supporters, however, soon became devoted Southcottians. He was released in 1806 and resided with a few faithful followers until his death in 1824.

Central to Brothers's eschatology is the "departure of the Hebrews from all nations, and their return to Jerusalem," which, he calculated, would take place in 1798.[44] He urged the Jews to "collect all their property and

---

[42] On Brothers see Garrett, *Respectable Folly*, esp. chs. 8–9; Harrison, *Second Coming*, esp. ch. 4; Thompson, *Working Class*, 127–9; Cecil Roth, *The Nephew of the Almighty: An Experimental Account of the Life and Aftermath of Richard Brothers, RN* (London: E. Goldston, 1933); John Barrell, "Imagining the King's Death: The Arrest of Richard Brothers," *History Workshop Journal*, 37 (1994), 1–32; the DNB.

[43] See especially Richard Brothers, *The New Covenant Between God and His People* (London, 1830).

[44] Richard Brothers, *A Revealed Knowledge of the Prophecies and Times* . . . (2 vols., London, 1794), I, 12, 14.

depart in great haste from all nations to their own land."[45] It was Brothers
himself, as King of the Hebrews, who would lead them back and undertake
the building of the New Jerusalem. "It is fifteen hundred years since my
family was separated from the Jews, and lost all knowledge of its origin,"
he explained.[46] Only divine intervention allowed him to discover his real
identity, as a descendant of the House of David.

While Southcott follows the Bunyanesque tradition of imagining
England as that "happy land," Brothers's geographical imagination is considerably broader: his New Jerusalem is to be built on the devastation of
the present Jerusalem in the Middle East. England, far from being happy,
is described as "this Egyptian land"[47] which must be forsaken: "It was in
this manner that God directed the departure of the Hebrews from Egypt
at first under Moses, and it is now in the same manner for the last time
he will direct their departure from England under me."[48] Brothers's entire
corpus is an elaborate effort to address the endless technicalities demanded
by this new Exodus. His task is mighty indeed:

you must be thoroughly informed from history and the accounts of late travellers,
that the whole land of Israel is now quite a desert, and that on entering it, I have
first to divide it into numerous portions, then get it cultivated with the plough
and the shovel, to sow feed and plant trees; I have harbours to make for shipping,
and store-houses for immediately receiving what is landed from them; high roads
to make; and water-courses to form; materials to provide, and cities to build . . .[49]

To accomplish all this, Brothers appeals to numerous nations, from
Abyssinia to Japan, presenting each ruler with a detailed list of provisions
required to establish the new "Hebrew empire."[50] Russia, for example, is
requested to send 400 shiploads of timber ("with a proportionate quantity
of nails"), 6,000 barrels of beef, 40,000 tents "with kettles and ovens in proportion," in addition to the 300 shiploads of timber, 100 large wagons, 800
wheelbarrows, and so forth, required from each country. England should
contribute 100,000 tons of coal, 10,000 tons of beef, 90,000 sacks of flour,
and so forth, in endless detail.[51] At first, Brothers's plans seem to reflect the
urgency of the project, but the list soon loses all sense of operative meaning
and becomes a mere textual construct, echoing similar biblical inventories.

[45] Ibid., II, 129.   [46] Ibid., I, 78.   [47] Ibid., II, 124.
[48] Richard Brothers, *A Letter from Mr. Brothers to Miss Cott . . . With an Address to the Members of His Britannic Majesty's Council* (London, 1798), 48.
[49] Brothers, *Miss Cott*, 134–5. Brothers refers explicitly to the travel accounts by Wood and Bruce, who visited the East in the mid-eighteenth century. See his *A Description of Jerusalem: Its Houses and Streets, Squares, Colleges, Markets, and Cathedrals, the Royal and Private Palaces, with the Garden of Eden in the Centre, as Laid Down in the Last Chapters of Ezekiel* (London, 1801), 68, 74.
[50] Brothers, *Miss Cott*, 23.   [51] Ibid., 90–1, 89, 123.

Since the present desolation of the land and its future restitution are both foretold in the Bible, it is only by mimicking the Scriptures textually that Brothers can hope to realize prophecy.

In some instances, Brothers claims that prophecy should be understood allegorically. Revelation 7 and 19, for example, are merely "a metaphorical representation of the last judgement."[52] In Revelation 21, John "is so struck with wonder at being shewn, in a vision, the appearance of this matchless city and its fine buildings, that he compares the walls to Jasper, the city itself to fine gold!", but the description "must be taken in a metaphorical sense."[53] More often than not, however, Brothers insists on a thoroughly literal realization of prophecy. Southcott, as we have seen, shifts effortlessly between Jerusalem as a textual construct and the palpability of "Jerusalem in England." Brothers, on the other hand, attempts to reconcile the textual prophecy with Palestine's actual geography; but it is the textual prophecy that must always prevail.

A typical example concerns New Jerusalem's "river of water of life." In both Ezekiel's and John's visions, there is a wide river flowing through the city, a fact which simply does not correspond with the topographical reality of the old Jerusalem. According to Brothers's *A Description of Jerusalem* (1801), the present-day city stands on the original site of the Garden of Eden, which had "a fine river flowing through it." During the Deluge, God "found it necessary" to alter

the surface of that part by destroying the river and garden, and raising high hills to surround where the garden originally was, and where Jerusalem now stands . . . It now solely belongs to God to restore it at least to some part of its original level and beauty: for otherwise, unless the present form was altered to a necessary level by sinking the Mount of Olives, or removing it, and by bringing again a good river of water through that ground, the great and splendid city I gave the plan of, alluded to by all the prophets, and most beautifully described by St. John in his 22d chapter of Revelation, could never be built by man. But to remove every apprehension of that kind, and every difficulty that opposes the undertaking, God expressly says by Ezekiel, in the 47th chapter, that a deep navigable river shall flow through the city, dispensing fertility to the land, livelihood and wealth to the people.[54]

The Mount of Olives must be removed, and a river must be brought in, to realize the biblical vision: the existing topography must yield to the text.

---

[52] Ibid., 199.
[53] Richard Brothers, *A Letter to the Subscribers for Engraving the Plans of Jerusalem* . . . (London: G. Riebau, 1805), 38.
[54] Brothers, *Description of Jerusalem*, 16–17.

On the one hand, this plan suggests an undiminished premillenarian reliance on divine power, which seems to contradict Brothers's obsession with the human effort required to establish the New Jerusalem. On the other hand, it is an attempt to respond to the challenges provoked by prophecy with yet another textual maneuver: since Palestine's landscape is constructed on the basis of biblical phrases, it is only natural that Brothers, too, would toy with and reassemble these textual building-blocks.

Brothers devotes much thought to the transformation of Palestine into a European, green and pleasant woodland: "According to every hundred acres divided there must be an equal number of trees planted, of oak or ash, elm, beech . . . in such a manner as will set off the land to appear lively and delightful."[55] His detailed blueprint of Jerusalem, based on the descriptions in Ezekiel and Revelation, presents a perfectly proportioned city. With a Garden of Eden – a glorified Hyde Park – at its center, and buildings and streets reminiscent of Nash's work in Regent Street,[56] Jerusalem would easily eclipse the capitals of Europe: "Look at London and Paris, those two great and wealthy cities, there are no such regular streets in either, or healthy accommodation as in ours."[57]

This determination to Occidentalize the Orient is most evident in Brothers's plans for Egypt, which has been assigned "to me and mine for ever." Following Isaiah 19:20, Brothers promises to deliver the Egyptians "from all oppression, and they shall revive, live, and be my people." However, they must first "reform from sloth and indolence to industry and cleanliness; the streets of the cities must be widened, and all houses in future must be built in the English manner, as more cool and better adapted than yours to preserve health." Brothers orders the great pyramids to be "levelled with the ground": "They were raised as idle monuments of ostentation; God at the time permitting the indulgence of this vanity, foreseeing that at the restoration of the Jews in the latter days I should want the material for real purpose of utility."[58] By leveling the pyramids to the ground, and using the stones for building cities "in the English manner," Brothers is erasing the Oriental landscape and transforming East into West, literally.

These geographical and architectural transformations had their racial equivalent, which brings us to the most radical aspect of Brothers's teaching. It was not only Brothers himself who was of Hebrew descent; numerous other English men and women – even the king and several members of

---

[55] Brothers, *Miss Cott*, 81.   [56] See Roth, *Nephew of the Almighty*, 84.
[57] Brothers, *Description of Jerusalem*, 34.   [58] Brothers, *Miss Cott*, 111, 113, 112.

the Privy Council – were of similar lineage. Those closest to Brothers were lucky enough to belong to the prestigious House of David. Others were the descendants of the lost ten tribes, those Israelites captured by the Assyrians, exiled, and eventually scattered throughout Europe, "having lost all remembrance, either by tradition or genealogical manuscript, of such a distinctive origin." That they were now "different in dress, manners and religious ceremonies from the visible Jews" should not deceive the students of prophecy:[59] "For I declare, by his sacred command, that the visible Jews are but few in number, compared to the great multitude professing Christianity, but all descended from the former Jews in the land of Israel, the forefathers of the present visible ones . . ."[60] In other words, most of the Hebrews who would be restored by Brothers to Palestine were actually English Christians: "It is plain that it is not the visible Hebrews that are meant, because they are known as such already; but it is the invisible Hebrews, descended from the old, that are to be singled out and distinguished from the strange people they live amongst."[61]

The conviction that the English were God's chosen nation could be traced all the way back to Foxe's *Book of Martyrs*. Brothers's outstanding contribution to this tradition was in his ability to accommodate two contradictory traditions. In his claim that prophecies about "Israel" refer to the Jews, Brothers joins Faber, Priestley, and their eminent colleagues who see the Jews as the object (and the English as agents) of conversion and restoration. At the same time, by insisting that the "real" Jews are in fact the English, Brothers shares with Southcott – if not Winstanley and Bunyan – the fantasy of belonging, literally, to God's elected race. Of course, whereas Southcott's interpretation is essentially spiritual, Brothers's argument is genealogical (even though he, too, dismisses the Jewish ritual of circumcision and emphasizes the spiritual aspects of belief instead).[62] Just as he bends the topography of Jerusalem to allow the literalization of prophecy, Brothers develops a racial theory which allows him to literalize the familiar analogy between England and Israel. Brothers can thus voice grievances associated with specific class-oriented aspirations – particularly the want of land – but resolve them by shifting to a colonial framework:

All the families which I have recognized as of Hebrew extraction, are, independent of me by the virtue of that recognition, entitled, as well as the visible professed Jews, to reside in their native land, whether in the city or country, or alternately

---

[59] Richard Brothers, *Wrote in Confinement. An Exposition of the Trinity . . .* (London, 1796), 25.
[60] Brothers, *Revealed Knowledge*, II, 124–5.   [61] Brothers, *Miss Cott*, xii.   [62] See ibid., 76–7.

in both if they like: although the distribution of the land belongs to me, yet as brethren our right of inheritance is general.[63]

While polite millenarians approached the restoration of the Jews to Palestine as a project that could benefit British imperialism, Brothers's proto-British-Israelism made the "Hebrew empire" a British colonial project par excellence.

From this fusion of millenarian vocabulary, colonial visions, and working-class aspirations, a distinct narrative emerges:

Palestine, 3211 years ago, when the Hebrews entered it from Egypt, abounded with springs and rivers, corn, wine, and oil, which were afterwards improved in the time of David to be the finest in the world . . . but now all is barren, as if never inhabited by our ancestors, the very sand of the desert has narrowed the old limits of the land by its constant encroachments, there are no meadows or cornfields, no trees for fuel or building, no pastures filled with cattle or sheep, neither are the hills clothed with vines or olives . . . [However] . . . many of these difficulties [are] easily conquered, by a wise people fortified with courage and perseverance; for it is our own country, and the only one we can live free in. Therefore, every man and woman must call up to their assistance every energy of patience, virtue, and industry, to settle the foundation of all future praise and all future benefit, by putting as many parts of the country as possible into a state of cultivation . . .[64]

All this sounds remarkably familiar: the barren land restored to its former glory; the appeal for patience and industry; and, above all, the conviction that "it is our own country, and the only one we can live free in." Indeed, Brothers's narrative is conspicuously similar to the official Zionist version which would emerge almost a century later (relying heavily on both millenarian and colonial imagery). Like the Zionists, Brothers explains that the Hebrew empire would initiate a commercial burst of growth, "so that no one can lose by the change, but, on the contrary, all will materially gain."[65] But he, too, never stops to consider the fate of the present inhabitants of the Holy Land who are to give way to the colonizers. It is Palestine's indigenous population that remains truly invisible.

IV

Southcott and Brothers imagined very different Jerusalems. How can these incompatible visions be explained? To what extent did they reflect broader undercurrents? And where can we locate their enduring political and cultural effects?

---

[63] Ibid., 80.   [64] Brothers, *Description of Jerusalem*, 43–4.   [65] Brothers, *New Covenant*, 6.

There is little doubt that the single most significant experience which molded Brothers's perception of the world – and which made him, in many ways, an exceptional figure among plebeian millenarian circles – was his long service in the Royal Navy. It enabled him to translate abstract textual or cartographical descriptions into geographical detail and to grasp the practical implications of travel.[66] Only an awareness of Palestine's topographical reality, and a seaman's mentality, can explain those endless inventories of supplies needed to blossom the desert. In both scholarship and expression, then, Brothers was much closer to Priestley and Bicheno than he was to Southcott;[67] what distanced him from the respectable millenarians was essentially his insistence on the personal role assigned to himself (and to the rest of the "invisible" Jews). Challenged with Palestine's irrepressible existence, Brothers adopted the radical working-class appropriations of "Holy Land" and "Chosen People," but transferred them back to the geographical region in which they were initially forged. The result is a pseudo-jingoistic attempt to solve working-class grievances by turning to the colonial framework: the promise of land, Brother explains, is only possible in the Promised Land.

This imperial vision of "England in Jerusalem," which also employs the intimacy of "Jerusalem in England," was in fact much less eccentric than it might appear. Consider, for example, the Palestine Exploration Fund (PEF), established in 1865 on the same principles that guided its predecessor, the Palestine Association of 1805. The PEF was one of the institutions which, according to Edward Said's influential model, supported and sustained the Orientalist discursive apparatus.[68] The PEF's cartographical surveys of Palestine – which facilitated the British take-over in 1917 – were carried out by Royal Engineers, lent by the War Office; among them were future eminent "imperial agents" like H. H. Kitchener and T. E. Lawrence.[69] Still, it would be a gross over-simplification to read all this in terms of a scientific, secularized Orientalism. In 1865, the Archbishop of York, who would

[66] See Marcus Rediker, *Between the Devil and the Deep Blue Sea: Merchant Seamen, Pirates, and the Anglo-American Maritime World, 1700–1750* (Cambridge University Press, 1987), esp. 10, 294.

[67] Deborah M. Valenze, "Prophecy and Popular Literature in Eighteenth-Century England," *Journal of Ecclesiastical History*, 29 (1978), 89. One of Brothers's most ardent followers was the distinguished Orientalist Nathaniel Brassey Halhed MP (1751–1830), author of *A Code of Gentoo Laws* (1776) and *A Grammar of the Bengal Language* (1788). He raised the issue of Brothers's arrest twice before a baffled House of Commons, but neither of his motions was seconded. He went on to become a loyal Southcottian. See Rosane Rocher, *Orientalism, Poetry, and the Millennium: The Checkered Life of Nathaniel Brassey Halhed, 1751–1830* (Delhi: Oxford University Press, 1983).

[68] Said, *Orientalism*, 2.

[69] On the PEF see John Moscrop, *Measuring Jerusalem: The Palestine Exploration Fund and British Interests in the Holy Land* (Leicester University Press, 1999).

serve for many years as the PEF's president, defined the goals of the new society:

This country of Palestine belongs to *you* and to *me*, it is essentially ours. It was given to the Father of Israel in the words: "Walk through the land in the length of it, and in the breadth of it, for I will give it unto thee". *We* mean to walk through Palestine in the length and in the breadth of it, because that land has been given unto us . . . It is the land towards which we turn as the fountain of all our hopes; it is the land to which we may look with as true a patriotism as we do to this dear old England, which we love so much.[70]

The justification of the PEF's work was based not on the series of binary oppositions which underlie Said's work – East/West, Same/Other – but rather on the blurring of these oppositions: like "this dear old England," Palestine already *belongs* "to you and to me." This unequaled sense of possession, which seems to characterize the depiction of no other Oriental province but Palestine, suggests that it is impossible to perceive the distinct nature of British imperial interests in Jerusalem without taking into account the millenarian image of Jerusalem in England. Since Brothers's views were merely extremely literal interpretations of ideas which had been part and parcel of Protestant culture, it is perhaps not surprising that his unique claim over Palestine – "it is our own country" – actually anticipated the nineteenth-century English encounter with the Holy Land.

Southcott, in contrast, had never left England. Even though she could read, there is little evidence that books, other than the Bible, exerted any significant influence on her work. In one of her pamphlets she makes a rare reference to a scholarly work, *Knowles's History of the Turks*,[71] and another pamphlet includes an attack on Paine's *Age of Reason*, but these were exceptions: "I never read any books, at all," she claimed.[72] Her upbringing, education, and occupation all link her to old, provincial, traditions; no wonder that Southcott was much less knowledgeable about the outside world. Her Jerusalem continues to function as a Bunyanesque utopian existence, closely associated with English life, customs, and landscape. And while Napoleon looms large over many of her prophecies, the emphasis is always on England's safekeeping, rather than on any expansionist vision. Indeed, the soothing familiarity of Southcott's Jerusalem – as opposed to Brothers's fantasy in the desert – may explain why her following was

---

[70] "Report of the Proceedings at a Public Meeting," June 22, 1865 [leaflet], 8, PEF/1865/2, Palestine Exploration Fund Archive, London.

[71] Joanna Southcott, *The Continuation of the Prophecies of Joanna Southcott* . . . (London, 1802), 7.

[72] Cited in Hopkins, *Woman to Deliver*, 10.

considerably larger. The Holy Land was simply too far away to demand any real consideration.[73]

It is useful to conclude with another contemporary visionary, William Blake, and his beautiful lines from the Preface to *Milton*, a work he began writing and etching in 1804:[74]

> I will not cease from Mental Fight,
> Nor shall my Sword sleep in my hand:
> Till we have built Jerusalem,
> In Englands green & pleasant Land.[75]

This theme was elaborated in another great poem which Blake began composing in 1804: *Jerusalem*. Here we once again encounter the familiar fantasy of discovering the Promised Land in one's own vicinity, "The fields from Islington to Marybone,/ To Primrose Hill and Saint Johns Wood" (171). His rearrangement of the scriptural geography in the English land-scape, the allotment of the British Isles between the twelve tribes, the image of Golgonooza which fuses Ezekiel's vision with the brick and mortar of London – all these are a masterly reworking of the Bunyanesque tradition. And yet, emerging more than a century later and from a very different intellectual climate, it is more of a simulacrum. "The Beauty of the Bible is that the most Ignorant & Simple Minds Understand it Best," he wrote (667). Blake was not ignorant and hardly simple-minded, but his prophet-ical books are a colossal exertion to mimic such a plebeian reading. It seems that just like Brothers, whose genealogy affirmed the desire of belonging to God's elect, Blake devised a complex mythology simply to recover the naive childhood fantasy of Jerusalem in London. Between 1797 and 1804 he became convinced that Britain, not Palestine, was the original Holy Land. "All things Begin & End in Albions Ancient Druid Rocky Shore," Blake wrote in his address "TO THE JEWS" in *Jerusalem* (171). This should be understood in its most literal sense, just like the short poem from the

---

73 This was probably true of her followers as well. See *An Interesting Account of the Proceedings of the Followers of the Late Joanna Southcott, Shewing the Folly of Their Intended Departure for the City of Jerusalem with a Full Description of That Ancient and Celebrated City, Its Laws, Government, etc.* (London, 1817), in which the anonymous author explains that Southcott's disciples cannot grasp the palpable dimensions of the journey to Jerusalem because they "have not, in the course of their reading, paid much attention to the situation of Palestine" (12).

74 The literature on Blake's millenarianism is enormous; but see in particular Morton D. Paley, "William Blake, The Prince of the Hebrews, and the Woman Clothed With the Sun," in Paley and Michael Curtis Phillips, eds., *William Blake: Essays in Honour of Sir Geoffrey Keynes* (Oxford: Clarendon Press, 1973), 260–93; Mee, *Dangerous Enthusiasm*, 28–9, 33–5, 46–7 and *passim*.

75 William Blake, *Milton*, Plate I [i], *The Complete Poetry and Prose of William Blake*, ed. David V. Erdman (Garden City, NY: Anchor Books, 1982), 95. All page numbers refer to this edition.

Preface to *Milton* which means, literally, "I shall struggle to restore our own lost British Jerusalem."[76]

Blake, of course, was perfectly aware of the political and military developments of the day. As David V. Erdman has pointed out in *Prophet Against Empire*, the great Victory song of Night I in *The Four Zoas* evidently celebrates the British defeat of Napoleon in the eastern Mediterranean, alluding to the Battle of the Nile and the siege of Acre.[77] Palestine, furthermore, appears in *Jerusalem* as one of the thirty-two nations that will "dwell in Jerusalems Gates"; it is tenth on the list, following Turkey and Arabia and preceding Persia and Hindostan (227). For Blake, Palestine is a nation, a portion of land located between Arabia and Persia. Jerusalem, sometimes represented by a figure of a woman, is essentially a spiritual concept signifying a perfect social order, to be established in England's green and pleasant land.

Turning away from the earthly city in the East, Blake's vision presented a bold geographical and imaginative movement which was a complete reversal of Brothers's colonial migration. Moreover, the similarities between Blake's work and Southcott's self-contained millenarian promise suggest that, rather than read her Jerusalem simply as a product of a limited geographical imagination – a "default" Jerusalem, as it were – we should perhaps approach it as a consciously inward-looking vision, shifting from the imperial to the indigenous; from the marvellous possessions overseas to social justice at home; from "there" to "here." Southcott, too, may have been a prophetess against empire.

The plebeian millenarian culture of the late 1790s, then, was an arena in which different visions of England and Englishness were juxtaposed. The same language which could generate an altogether broader imperial claim over parts of the East, was also the language employed to resist this imperial quest (and think, for example, of Gladstone's rhetoric during the Bulgarian Agitation in 1876, which presented Britain's Christian morality as the antithesis of its imperial interests in the Levant). Even today, Blake's dream of building Jerusalem in England's green and pleasant land is still associated with a utopian vision of a socialist England, fused with a nostalgic yearning towards a lost rural world. Paradoxically, it has also come to signify a much broader patriotic ethos, a relic of late Victorian imperialism (matched by the fading glamor of the Royal Albert Hall, where it is sung annually at

---

[76] A. L. Owen, *The Famous Druids: A Survey of Three Centuries of English Literature on the Druids* (Oxford: Clarendon Press, 1962), 233, 225, 235.

[77] David V. Erdman, *Prophet Against Empire: A Poet's Interpretation of the History of His Own Times* (1954; 2nd edn, Princeton University Press, 1969), 319–20.

the Last Night of the Proms). That these Jerusalems have very little to do with the actual city in the Middle East suggests that despite Brothers's zealous efforts, or the PEF's impressive commitment to imperial expansion, the notion that England itself was the Promised Land has eventually proved to be much more enduring for the "invisible Jews" than their actual inheritance in the Middle East.

CHAPTER 8

Protestant evangelicalism, British imperialism, and Crusonian identity

Hans Turley

Recent scholarship on Daniel Defoe and on *Robinson Crusoe* (1719) has been heavily influenced by postcolonial theory and the roles of sexuality, race, and gender. For example, Crusoe's relationship with Friday in the first volume has been the focus of a slew of essays over the past decade, often analyzed in tandem with the works of J. M Coetzee, South African author of *Foe*.[1] The paradigm of Crusoe's relationship to Friday offers a way to understand Coetzee's own critique of South African apartheid, as well as a way to understand postapartheid South Africa. Using Michel Tournier's *Friday*, several critics have interrogated *Crusoe* in order to understand the significance of gender (or lack thereof) in the novel, as well as how constructions of sexuality can shed new light on postmodern interpretations of the novel.[2] These rereadings all imagine the role of colonizing power in

---

[1] Lieve Spaas and Brian Stimpson, eds., *Robinson Crusoe: Myths and Metamorphoses* (New York: St. Martin's Press, 1996); Victoria Carchidi, "At Sea on a Desert Island: Defoe, Tournier, and Coetzee," in Christine Arkinstall, ed., *Literature and Quest* (Amsterdam: Rodopi, 1993), 75–88; Edith W. Clowes, "The Robinson Myth Reread in Postcolonial and Postcommunist Modes," *Critique*, 36, 2 (1995), 145–59; Derek Cohen, "The Woman and the Monster: *Foe*, Friday, and Caliban," in Ken L. Goodwin, ed., *Nationalism vs. Internationalism: (Inter)National Dimensions of Literatures in English* (Tubingen: Stauffenburg, 1996), 281–85; Steven Connor, "Rewriting Wrong: On the Ethics of Literary Reversion," in Theo D'haen and Hans Bertens, eds., *Liminal Postmodernisms: The Postmodern, the (Post-)Colonial, and the (Post-)Feminist* (Amsterdam: Rodopi, 1994), 79–97; Marta Sofia Lopez, "Historiographic Metafiction and Resistance Postmodernism," in Richard Todd and Luisa Flora, eds., *Theme Parks, Rainforests and Sprouting Wastelands: European Essays on Theory and Performance in Contemporary British Fiction* (Amsterdam: Rodopi, 2000), 215–26; Susan Naramore Maher, "Confronting Authority: J. M. Coetzee's *Foe* and the Remaking of *Robinson Crusoe*," *International Fiction Review*, 18, 1 (1991). 34–40; Mike Marais, "'One of Those Islands without an Owner': The Aesthetics of Space in *Robinson Crusoe* and J. M. Coetzee's *Life & Times of Michael K.*," *Current Writing* 8, 1 (1996), 19–32; Gayatri Chakravorty Spivak, "Theory in the Margin: Coetzee's *Foe* Reading Defoe's *Crusoe/Roxana*," in Jonathan Arac and Barbara Johnson, eds., *Consequences of Theory* (Baltimore: The Johns Hopkins University Press, 1991), 154–80; Hermann Wittenbert, "Spatial Systems in J. M. Coetzee's *Foe*," *Inter-Action*, 3 (1995), 142–51.

[2] Roger Celistin, "Can Robinson Crusoe Find True Happiness (Alone)? Beyond Genitals and History on the Island of Hope," in Paul Bennett and Vernon A. Rosario, eds., *Solitary Pleasures: The Historical, Literary, and Artistic Discourses of Autoeroticism* (New York: Routledge, 1995), 233–48; Margaret Anne Hutton, "Getting Away from It All: The Island as a Space of Transformation in Defoe's *Robinson*

what I call Crusonian identity, and how its link with three of the cultural studies Big Four – race, gender, and sexuality – can shed light on English and British imperialism.[3] And, of course, there has been, as always, some work on Defoe's dissenting Protestantism and its link to English mercantilism and the hegemony of British empire.[4] Oddly, however, Defoe's explicit attitudes toward empire *per se* have not been a prominent facet of Crusonian studies.

This chapter attempts to rectify that oversight. It differs from other analyses of *Crusoe* in two ways. Unlike most other critiques which focus only on volume one, it considers all three novels in the *Crusoe* trilogy in order to argue for the significance of the whole trilogy as a foundational and iconic work of the English novel. Secondly, and more important for this volume, unlike other literary studies that do touch on the trilogy, it argues for the importance of Protestant evangelism in the novels' constructions of sexuality, race, and gender. This emphasis will show that the trilogy is a singular seminal text for an understanding of how Protestant evangelism informs English identity that is also and equally shaped by imperialism and empire in eighteenth-century England.

Crusoe and Tournier's *Vendredi ou les limbes du Pacifique*," in Richard Maber, ed., *Nouveaux Mondes from the Twelfth to the Twentieth Century* (Durham: University of Durham Press, 1994), 121–33; Howard McNaughton, "The Semiotic Limbo of the Pacific," *Social Semiotics*, 7, 2 (1997), 189–200; and the articles by Anthony Purdy and Emma Wilson in Spaas and Stimpson, *Robinson Crusoe: Myths and Metamorphoses*, 182–98, 199–209.

[3] Other essays that examine the roles of race and gender through the lens of postcolonial theory include Markman Ellis, "Crusoe, Cannibalism, and Empire," in Spaas and Stimpson, *Robinson Crusoe: Myths and Metamorphoses*, 45–61; Jean Jacques Hamm, "Caliban, Friday, and their Masters," in ibid., 110–24; Minaz Jooma, "Robinson Crusoe Inc(corporates): Domestic Economy, Incest and the Trope of Cannibalism," *Lit*, 8, 1 (1997), 61–81; Mike Marais, "Colonialism and the Epistemological Underpinnings of the Early English Novel," *English in Africa*, 23, 1 (1996), 46–66; Peter E. Morgan, "*Foe's* Defoe and Le Jeune Nee: Establishing a Metaphorical Referent for the Elided Female Voice," *Critique*, 35, 2 (1994), 81–96; Maximillian E. Novak, "Friday: Or, The Power of Naming," in Albert J. Rivero, ed., *Augustan Subjects: Essays in Honor of Martin C. Battestin* (Newark, Delaware and London: University of Delaware Press, 1997), 110–22; Bill Overton, "Countering Crusoe: Two Colonial Narratives," *Critical Survey*, 4, 3 (1992), 302–10; Arnold Saxton, "Female Castaways," in Spaas and Stimpson, *Robinson Crusoe: Myths and Metamorphoses*, 141–7; Norman Simms, "On the Fringes: Translation and Pseudo-Translation in Intercultural Encounters," in Marilyn Gaddis Rose and Morman Toby Simms, eds., *What Price Glory – In Translation?* (Whitestone, NY: Council on National Literatures, 1987), 13–26; Lieve Spaas, "Narcissus and Friday: From Classical to Anthropological Myth," in Spaas and Stimpson, *Robinson Crusoe: Myths and Metamorphoses*, 98–109; John A. Stotesbury, "Constructions of Heroic Resistance: Crusoe, Mandela, and Their Desert Island," in Joi Nyman and John Stolesbury, eds., *Postcolonialism and Cultural Resistance* (University of Joensuu Press, 1999), 244–52; Roxanne Wheeler, "'My Savage,' 'My Man': Racial Multiplicity in *Robinson Crusoe*," *English Literary History*, 62, 4 (1995), 821–61.

[4] Most recently Andrew Fleck, "Crusoe's Shadow: Christianity, Colonization, and the Other," in John C. Hawley and Erick D. Langer, eds., *Christian Encounters with the Other* (New York University Press, 1998), 74–89; Gordon D. Fultor, "Dialogue with the Other as Potential and Period in *Robinson Crusoe*," *Language and Literature*, 3, 1 (1994), 1–20.

Tony Claydon and Ian McBride write that in scholarship on Britishness and Protestantism, "there is a preoccupation with 'the other'. As historians have tried to understand how collections of individuals came to imagine themselves as nations, they have borrowed the bi-polar approach of many anthropologists and literary critics, and have tended to concentrate on that which the national group has been defined against." This approach, Claydon and McBride argue, tends to see "the other" as completely alien and dangerous.[5] An examination of Crusoe and his relationship to Friday, however, shows how reductive this methodology can be. Crusoe's dissenting Protestantism, at times harsh, unyielding, and violent, is also a complication of the idea that the Englishman's "preoccupation with 'the other'" is simplistically dichotomous. Of course, Crusoe's evangelizing of Friday has to be seen in the context of his relationship to the world in general and his island in particular. That is, Crusoe's attitude toward empire and imperialism – the colonization of the island in volume one and his views on proselytizing the world in the following volumes – is a huge part of the Crusonian psychology. I don't want to suggest that Crusoe's Protestantism constitutes his entire identity. Claydon and McBride rightly point out that "national identities are always more complex and multifaceted" than that idea.[6] However, Protestantism and imperialism are invariably linked and foregrounded in Defoe's representation of Crusoe's world. And *Robinson Crusoe*, such an important literary text, is also a fascinating historical artifact. An analysis of the novel not only reaffirms other more historicist analyses of empire and Protestantism, but also complicates more monolithic historical readings such as Colin Kidd's recent *British Identities before Nationalism* (1999).

Kidd suggests that Protestant theology was so ingrained in British identity that early eighteenth-century Britons were unable to think in terms of ethnic difference or hatred. Kidd bases his argument on common genealogy accepted by pre-Enlightenment continental, English, and Scottish scholars: all of humankind is descended from Noah and his sons and grandsons; therefore all cultures, even pagan cultures, can be traced to a common father. Judaism was the universal faith; since the Tower of Babel only through generations of corruption did other heathen or pagan religions evolve. Thus since all peoples were seen as having common originary kin, Kidd argues, "Though guilty in practice of prejudice, exploitation and extirpation on grounds of religion and skin pigmentation, early modern Europeans were

[5] Tony Claydon and Ian McBride, eds., *Protestantism and National Identity: Britain and Ireland, c. 1650–1850* (Cambridge University Press, 1998), 7.
[6] Ibid., 9.

not intellectually programmed for ethnic hatred."[7] The problem with this argument is that it elides the very real consequences of European, and in this chapter, British imperialism in the eighteenth century: the systematic repression and subjugation of native American ethnic peoples that resulted in thousands if not millions of deaths. How can an entire group of people be "guilty in practice of prejudice" and not be racist? Because he gives little emphasis to the place of profit ingrained in Protestant theology, Kidd undermines his argument. Profit and Christian evangelism, I will argue, go hand in hand in understanding the ethnocide practiced by British colonialists, traders, and, here, marooned individuals. Early eighteenth-century men such as Crusoe literally *hate* heathens or non-Christians. These men believe heathens are thus potentially, if not in fact, evil; furthermore, heathens are not white and thus are racially different, "the other." Their differences, both theological and racial, cannot be untangled. To hate the religion, then, is to hate the race. This hatred is not "intellectual," but rather, as we shall see, faith based and economically based. This hatred is very real.

Indeed, Kidd does not really analyze the place of profit and capital in ethnic and religious historicism. As Linda Colley argues in *Britons* (1992), trade, Protestantism, and imperialism are completely linked in the British character.[8] I would argue that as the quintessential Englishman, Crusoe practices explicit ethnocide and even contemplates genocide in order to achieve his desires: more capital and more Christians over whom he can hold sway. He may not hate his man Friday (who after all accepts Jesus and becomes his "servant"), but his hatred for other ethnic people is based on both abhorrence toward their horrific heathenism and a desire to profit from their potential conversion, or ethnocide, and consequent subjugation and colonization.

French anthropologist Pierre Clastres makes clear the distinction between genocide and ethnocide. Genocide, he writes, "refers to the idea of 'race' and to the will to exterminate a racial minority." Ethnocide, on the other hand, "is the systematic destruction of ways of living and thinking of people different from those who lead this venture of destruction."[9] If practitioners of either genocide or ethnocide both see the Other in the same way, that is, as not only different, but embodying "wrong difference," those who practice genocide go one more step: they see difference as absolutely evil and

---

[7] Colin Kidd, *British Identities before Nationalism: Ethnicity and Nationhood in the Atlantic World, 1600–1800* (Cambridge University Press, 1999), 10.

[8] Linda Colley, *Britons: Forging the Nation, 1707–1837* (New Haven: Yale University Press, 1992), esp. ch. 2.

[9] Pierre Clastres, *The Archeology of Violence* [1980], trans. Jeanine Herman (New York: Semiotext(e), 1994), 45. Subsequent citations are noted in the text of the chapter.

therefore to be exterminated. Ethnocide is much more complex and demonstrates Claydon and McBride's correct discomfort with more monolithic historical and critical approaches. Unlike genocide, "Ethnocide," Clastres argues, " . . . admits the relativity of evil in difference: others are evil, but we can improve them by making them transform themselves until they are identical, preferably, to the model we propose and impose" (45).

All societies are ethnocentric, writes Clastres – that is, believe that their cultures are superior – but only the West practices ethnocide. And why? Because western states are capitalist states, and because capitalism means that everything must be used: "space, nature, seas, forests, subsoil . . . everything must be productive" (50), and that, of course, includes people. The West, then, sees the whole world as its platter, a world to colonize and subjugate in order to amass ever-increasing profit. One must historicize, however. The "West" that Clastres identifies has expanded by the twenty-first century. Other countries besides those in the West are capitalist states. None the less, I quote Clastres at length here because the distinction he makes between genocide and ethnocide, and between ethnocentrism and ethnocide, gives a context for this rereading of Defoe's *Crusoe* trilogy. This rereading, then, allows for an analysis of other eighteenth-century literary texts to show how Crusoe's dissenting Christian evangelism and always changing attitude toward race, together with an examination of gender and capital, all work to form a coherent psychology for Crusonian identity: the western capitalist par excellence, colonizer, and practitioner of ethnocide based on religious difference.

Crusoe manages to tame his land, to reproduce a European state – England – on a desert island. "The whole country was my own meer property," he proclaims toward the end of his stay (*RC* 240).[10] He uses the land, the flora, and the fauna in order to profit economically, and to accrue more and more stuff. Complicit with his colonization of the island is his own dissenting kind of Christianity, a belief in the direct route for salvation from the individual to God, and a belief that by reading the signs of providence he will be able to profit spiritually as well as economically. For Defoe – and for English imperialism in general – Christianity and capitalism are inseparable. Crusoe evangelizes in order to profit: Friday in the first volume; his settlers – pirates and their native mates – in the second volume, *The Farther Adventures of Robinson Crusoe* (1719).[11] The

[10] Daniel Defoe, *The Life and Adventures of Robinson Crusoe* [1719], ed. Angus Ross (London: Penguin, 1965). Subsequent citations are noted in the text of the chapter.
[11] Daniel Defoe, *The Farther Adventures of Robinson Crusoe* [1719] (New York: The Jenson Society, 1904). Subsequent citations are noted in the text of the chapter.

ethnocide that Crusoe practices is not on the grand scale of the English or French empire-builders; indeed, as he says, he allows "liberty of conscience throughout my dominion" (*RC* 241) for his islanders, his subjects. Further, he deplores the sixteenth-century Spanish genocide of the American natives "as a meer butchery, a bloody and unnatural piece of cruelty, unjustifiable either to God or man" (*RC* 178). The Spaniards practiced a genocide on native Americans that "however they were idolaters and barbarians, and had several bloody and barbarious rites in their customs, such as sacrificing human bodies to their idols, were yet, as to the Spaniards, very innocent people" (*RC* 178). Of course, Crusoe's views change in the two sequels and this change is but one cause for the dismissal of the two books as inferior to the original. Crusoe's character is inconsistent: his behavior on the island has little to do with his behavior throughout the rest of the much longer narrative. If we recognize the link between Crusoe's view on empire and his increasingly zealous Protestantism, we can see how "Protestantism secured to the English, and secondarily the British, the assuredness of their own entitlement, superiority, pulchritude and difference."[12] We can see, in other words, how the Crusoe trilogy reflects eighteenth-century attitudes toward empire and Christianity.

The first volume is hailed by critics as a progenitor of the modern novel. The "realism" of Crusoe's identity is indicative of a new kind of novel that stresses psychological believability as the standard for successful fiction.[13] The two sequels complicate this critical elevation of the first book. They demonstrate the importance of Protestant evangelism and its links with cultural and economic imperialism. In other words, Crusoe's "character" and conventional critical notions of what privileges realism are less important than the religious and economic points Defoe wants to make in his trilogy.

The Farther Adventures of Robinson Crusoe was published on the heels of the enormous success of the first volume. Critics argue that the sequel is an attempt to cash in on that success, while the third volume, *The Serious Reflections of Robinson Crusoe* (1720), is dismissed as nothing more than a

---

[12] Kathleen Wilson, "The Island Race: Captain Cook, Protestant Evangelicalism and Construction of National Identity, 1760–1800," in Claydon and McBride, *Protestantism and National Identity*, 290.

[13] For critical discussion, since Ian Watt's groundbreaking *The Rise of the Novel* (Berkeley: University of California Press, 1957), esp. ch. 2, of *Robinson Crusoe* as realist, see Hans Turley, *Rum, Sodomy, and the Lash: Piracy, Sexuality, and Masculine Identity* (New York University Press, 1999), esp. ch. 8; Lennard Davis, *Factual Fictions: The Origins of the English Novel* (New York: Columbia University Press, 1983); J. Paul Hunter, *Before Novels: The Cultural Contexts of Eighteenth-Century English Fiction* (New York: Norton, 1990); Michael McKeon, *The Origins of the English Novel* (Baltimore: The Johns Hopkins University Press, 1987).

collection of conventional homilies.[14] It does not reflect any sort of "character" for Crusoe because the Crusonian voice in the third volume does nothing more than ventriloquize Defoe's own beliefs.[15] This kind of critical thinking is short sighted, however. From Crusoe's travels around the world in the second volume we see a fundamental change in his character. Marooned he was a lone man who vacillated between a desire to wipe out the cannibals on his island – a genocide he rationalizes because the cannibals have been "entirely abandoned of Heaven and acted on by some hellish degeneracy" – and leaving that to God because he asks "How do I know what God Himself judges in this particular case" (*RC* 177)? Of course, he rescues Friday and teaches him the ways of God and Jesus Christ. By the second volume, appalled by the paganism he sees in Asia, he wants to perform an act of genocide without remembering his earlier ruminations. By the third volume, his views have changed yet again. Referring to his travels and what he has seen, he argues "would the Christian princes unite their powers and act in concert, they might destroy the Turkish Empire and the Persian Kingdom, and beat the very name of Mahomet out of the world" (*SR* 225), thus bringing the light of Jesus Christ to a goodly number of people of the world. Is this wishful thinking ethnocide or genocide? Regardless, his desire for a Christian world is implicitly a desire for western economic power as well. In conventional novelistic terms, then, the Crusoe of the three volumes is not a coherent, realistic character. However, if we assume that Defoe made no assumptions himself about "realism," then the books can be read as a complex meditation on early eighteenth-century attitudes toward ethnocentrism and ethnocide and their relationship toward imperialism. This meditation demonstrates a belief in the superiority of Christianity – religious ethnocentrism. This belief is justification for the subjugation and colonization of non-western societies – including great powers in the Muslim world – with the additional benefit of enormous economic profit.

   Robinson Crusoe is the original in a long line of books that are called Robinsonades. These novels use the Crusoe character and his situation as models for stories about marooned men and women but usually omit the

---

[14] *The Serious Reflections of Robinson Crusoe* [1720] (New York: The Jenson Society, 1904). Subsequent citations are noted in the text of the chapter.

[15] See, for example, J. Paul Hunter, *The Reluctant Pilgrim: Defoe's Emblematic Method and Quest for Form in* Robinson Crusoe (Baltimore: The Johns Hopkins University Press, 1966), esp. x, and Watt, *The Rise of the Novel*, 60–92, as well as most monographs that focus on the Crusoe character. Very few scholarly works focus on *The Serious Reflections*. Among the most recent are Jooma, "*Robinson Crusoe* Inc(corporates)," and Jeffrey Hopes, "Real and Imaginary Stories: *Robinson Crusoe* and the Serious Reflections," *Eighteenth Century Fiction*, 8, 3 (1996), 313–28.

complexity that Christianity and capital give to the trilogy.[16] I shall focus on one Robinsonade that is an exception, the extraordinary novel *The Female American* (1767).[17] I shall explore the complex nexus of religion, race, and gender that adds to the dialogue of imperialism and colonization surrounding the Crusonian character. By doing so I shall bring a semblance of cohesion that links the first volume to the two sequels as a singular important text for postcolonial literature and an understanding of how capitalism and eighteenth-century evangelism work to justify western colonization and imperialism.

"Unca Eliza Winkfield," the pseudonymous author and title character of *The Female American*, in many ways embodies the Crusonian character. She is resilient, intelligent, and domestic – all traits shared with Crusoe. She is a Christian, she is marooned on an island, and she is an articulate interpreter of Protestant theology. Written nearly fifty years after Defoe's trilogy, *The Female American* represents this character as a Christian who practices a kind of ethnocide similar to Cruoe's redemption of Friday in volume one. She and Crusoe both exercise what might be termed compassionate ethnocide. But more originally and more complexly, this Crusonian character is a woman who is half native American and half English. It could be argued that her racial heritage gives credibility to her efforts at religious ethnocide. Marooned on her desert island, she makes no attempt to profit economically. Instead, she successfully evangelizes a tribe of natives who (in a reflection of Crusoe's discovery of the cannibals and descriptions of pagans and heathens) use her island for their idolatry.

Crusoe's island is metaphorically a wild woman, a heathenish virgin whom he can tame and subjugate and from whom he can profit

[16] Coetzee's *Foe* and Tournier's *Friday* are the obvious exceptions from the late twentieth century. Coetzee uses Defoe's novel and *Roxana* in order to criticize apartheid and South African society. Tournier likewise uses the Crusoe and Friday characters to interrogate race and ethnocentrism in French culture. Robinsonades are too numerous to mention here, although some recent criticism includes Jeannine Blackwell, "An Island of Her Own: Heroines of the German Robinsonades from 1720 to 1800," *The German Quarterly*, 58, 1 (1985) 5–26; Patricia Harkins, "From Robinson Crusoe to Philip Quarll: The Transformation of the Robinsonade," *Publications of the Mississippi Philological Association*, 7 (1988), 64–74; Michael Harrawood, "The Child on the Desert Isle: The Robinsonade and the Family Formation," in Susan R. Gannon and Ruth Anne Thompson, eds., *The Child and the Family: Selected Pages from the 1988 International Conference of the Children's Literature Association* (New York: Pace University Press, 1989), 29–33; Susan Naramore Mahar, "Recasting Crusoe: Frederick Marryat, R. M. Ballantyne and the Nineteenth-Century Robinsonade," *Children's Literature Association Quarterly*, 13, 4 (1998), 169–75. J. M. Coetzee, *Foe* (New York: Penguin, 1988); Michel Tournier, *Friday* [1969], trans. Norman Denny (Baltimore: The Johns Hopkins University Press, 1997).

[17] Unca Eliza Winkfield (pseud.), *The Female American; or, The Adventures of Unca Eliza Winkfield* [1767], ed. Michelle Burnham (Ontario: Broadview Press, 2001). Subsequent citations are noted in the text of the chapter.

economically. In order to colonize it, he performs a metaphorical rape of the island. This rape suggests symbolic ethnocide as he recreates the island from a wild and alien paradise into a European colony. His success is a sign from God. Christianity, one can argue, justifies his colonization of the island because he is subduing it to procreate and thus to profit. On the other hand, Unca Eliza Winkfield discovers an island already colonized by a hermit: she finds a diary with helpful tips, discovers a ready-made castle constructed out of stone (an ancient temple built by ancient natives, she supposes) on top of which is an enormous effigy of a god, and comes across limitless gold and precious stones. Unlike Crusoe's "Island of Despair" Winkfield's island is an exotic place with wealth there for the taking. Her island is closer to Defoe's Africa where Captain Singleton treks across the continent and becomes rich merely picking up from the ground ivory and gold along the way.[18] "What wonders are here!" exclaims Winkfield (80). Searching the temple she says that she stumbles across "a variety of things, all of gold, of which I knew not the use, besides a great number of rings, bracelets, lamps and crowns. An immense treasure" (79). Crusoe must work for his "immense treasure," his profit from the island. Winkfield, rich before she is marooned, is impressed by the gold and jewels, but admits that their value is useless to her alone on a deserted island.

Crusoe is much more ambivalent toward found wealth, nowhere more than in an early scene. Shortly after his arrival on the island, he comes across some coins on the wrecked ship while salvaging things useful for his survival. "'Oh, drug!' said I aloud, 'what art thou good for? Thou art not worth to me, no, not the taking off of the ground; one of those knives is worth all this heap; I have no matter of use for thee, e'en remain where thou art, and go to the bottom as a creature whose life is not worth saving'" (75). But Crusoe reconsiders: "However, upon second thoughts, I took it away and wrapping all this in a piece of canvas, I began to thinking of making another raft . . ." (75). On the one hand, Crusoe recognizes that money is useless on his island given his situation. On the other hand, he keeps it because for Crusoe, profit is everything. He saves it for twenty-eight years, even though he rails against money as useless and possibly evil: an addictive drug. By keeping the money Crusoe demonstrates his own

---

[18] See Daniel Defoe, *Captain Singleton* [1720] ed., Shiv K. Kumar, introduction by Penelope Wilson (Oxford and New York: Oxford University Press, 1990), 94–7, for example. Laura Brown offers an especially good analysis of the African adventures in *Ends of Empire: Women and Identity in Early Eighteenth-Century Literature* (Ithaca: Cornell University Press, 1993). See also Turley, *Rum, Sodomy, and the Lash*, ch. 7.

capitalistic nature, that he is *homo economicus*, as Ian Watt among many others has pointed out.[19]

Winkfield's discovery of the treasure is useful to show the importance of capital in *Robinson Crusoe*. Crusoe's island is exotic, in its way, but not because of "wonders" over which Winkfield exclaims. Although he finds neither jewels, gold, nor other precious stuff, the island itself provides just about everything he needs: meat, corn, grapes, wood for shelter, and so on. It is a place where, to echo Clastres, "everything must be productive" and is indeed amazingly fertile. Exotic it may be, in a geographic sense, but the exoticism is tempered by the mundane detail of Crusoe's everyday life, his faith in God and providence, and his belief that he was put on the island as punishment for disobeying his father (105–6, for example). When he finds the footprint and walks away in fear and, as he says, "pensive and sad" (173), his concern is less to evangelize whoever might have made the print than to protect his possessions. As "king," as patriarch in an impossible position, Crusoe does not see the footprint as a salvation: at long last to have company, and perhaps more importantly, a person or people with whom he can trade and thus profit even more. Instead, he is terrified that he will lose everything he worked so hard to acquire. "Then terrible thoughts racked my imagination about their having found my board," he worries, ". . . and that if so, I should certainly have them come again in greater numbers, and devour me; that if it should happen so they should not find me, yet they would find my enclosure, destroy all my corn, carry away all my flock of tame goats, and I should perish at last for meer want" (163–4). He worries thusly even though he would not "perish . . . for meer want" because the island will always provide for him as he has demonstrated for fifteen years.

Winkfield, on the other hand, has no use for material goods of any sort such as gold and precious stones, what might be called found wealth in contrast to Crusoe's made wealth. The island and its riches are not there to be colonized. On the contrary, after discovering the wealth, Winkfield spends her time, as she says, with "little domestic concerns, my devotions, and reading the few books that I found in my chest" (82). She knows that the natives come to the island occasionally to worship at the enormous hollow statue, and she decides to hide deep in the bowels of the temple when that time comes. "I had no sooner made my fixed determination to retire to this place," she says, "but a very strange thought arose in my mind.

---

[19] Watt, *The Rise of the Novel*, 63.

It was nothing less than this, to ascend into the hollow idol, speak to the Indians from thence, and endeavour to convert them from their idolatry" (83). By climbing stairs into the idol's head, and speaking in a normal tone, she discovers that her voice is amplified: the statue "was so wonderfully constructed as to increase the sound of even a low voice to such a degree as to exceed that of the loudest speaker" (80).

Crusoe the patriarch and dissenting Christian turns his back in terror at the footprint. He imagines that cannibals might come and eat him and destroy all that he has built. He spends five years worrying about his discovery and fortifying what he calls his "castle, for so I think I called it ever after this" (162). This "castle" is reflective of the kinds of forts built to safeguard colonies or trading outposts by the Royal Africa and East India Companies in the seventeenth and eighteenth centuries. Winkfield, a woman of mixed race, has no such fears because she has nothing to lose except her life, and her faith gives her courage against the possibility of that event. She fearlessly ascends the statue in order to pretend that she is a messenger from God and will lead the natives toward salvation. She is proud of her native American heritage – the daughter of a princess – but equally comfortable with her English father's background. Her identity, then, is very complex. Is it ethnocide for her to evangelize when she has a native background? Or do these roots mitigate and authorize her Christian evangelizing? It seems so: the natives are willing almost immediately to give up their pagan worship and be taught the ways of Jesus Christ. Before their conversion, they are more like the natives of Surinam in Aphra Behn's *Oroonoko* (1680), a utopian society whose primitivism makes them metaphorically like the inhabitants of Eden in "the first state of innocence, before man knew how to sin."[20] In Behn's novel the natives live in "perfect amity" with the English colonizers willing to trade for the exotic stuff that Surinam gives to England. Unlike *Crusoe* or *The Female American*, there is no attempt to Christianize the natives. Indeed, Christianity itself is one of the targets of Behn's satire. However, precisely because Winkfield's natives live in a utopia their conversion to Christianity demonstrates their ethnocide by Winkfield. Her racial make-up may be complex but her psychology is not: she is a Christian born and raised with no sympathy for the natives' culture or religious identity. The natives' society changes from a heathen utopia to a Christian utopia, and their ethnocide is complete. But since English Protestantism cannot be separated from a desire for profit – spiritual or economic – the Christian

---

[20] Aphra Behn, *Oroonoko; or the Royal Slave* (1688) in Katharine M. Rogers and William McCarthy, eds., *The Meridian Anthology of Early Women Writers* (New York and Scarborough, Ontario: New American Library, 1987), 16.

utopia is a replication of Crusoe's island and cannot survive without trade and the eventual colonization and subjugation of the natives.

One could call *The Female American* a gendered rip-off of Defoe's seminal novel.[21] Winkfield says that if her writings "should be published in any country, I doubt not but they will soon be naturalized throughout Europe, and in different languages, and in succeeding ages by the delight of the ingenious and inquisitive; and that some future bold adventurer's imagination, lighted up by my torch, will form a fictitious story of one of his own sex, the solitary inhabitant of a desolate island" (105). The "editor," in a note, recognizes the similarities to Defoe's classic, and writes "Our authuress here seems to please herself with the thoughts of the immortality of her history, and to prophesy of that of Robinson Crusoe, which only is inferior to her own, as fiction is to truth" (105). Just as the "editor" of *Robinson Crusoe* insists on the truth of the narrative ("a just history of fact" [25]), so does the editor of Winkfield's narrative insist that *her* tale is true, and Defoe's is fiction. Conventional criticism of Defoe's novel privileges the truth within the fiction. That is, *Robinson Crusoe* – at least the first volume – works precisely because the narrative appears to be a history rather than a romance, and more importantly a history of an ordinary "private man" in extraordinary circumstances (25). Crusoe's character is realistic precisely because he is able to tame the island through hard work and demonstrates an interior exemplary Christian faith. *The Female American*, on the other hand, has been ignored not only because of the unbelievable aspects of its narrative, that it is but a poor and unconvincing example of a Robinsonade, but also because of the race and gender of the title character. It goes without saying that the best English imperialists were white and male.

Winkfield – given her exotic ancestry – is certainly not ordinary. Crusoe believes that because he disobeyed his father and ran away to sea, rather than be content with the middle state – "the best state in the world" (28) – he deserves his punishment: to be the lone survivor of a shipwreck and to be marooned on a desert island with plenty of time to ruminate about his fate. His growing Christian faith on the island is rewarded by his rescue and the discovery that he is rich: "I was now master, all of a sudden of above 5000*l*.

---

[21] Michelle Burnham, in her fine introduction to *The Female American*, writes that "although [*The Female American*] resembles *Robinson Crusoe* in outline and mimics some of its details, [it] is otherwise a different kind of story than Defoe's" (11). Outside of Burnham's introduction, no critical work has been published on this fascinating novel. Burnham's insights of course are influential for this chapter. She notes the ties to Behn's *Oroonoko*, the utopian aspects of the natives, and the importance of evangelizing, but does not discuss the economic imperatives of Defoe's work. However, I hope to move beyond her comparisons to complicate the relationship between the two works in order to provide a fresh rereading of the Crusoe novels.

sterling in money and had an estate . . . in the Brasils, of above a thousand pounds a year" (280). This reward, it would seem, should make Crusoe a pious man who has learned his lesson and stays home. Part of the problem that critics have with the ending of the novel and its sequel – that Crusoe's character becomes completely inconsistent and goes away on a long journey despite his great wealth and the lesson he ought to have learned – is the very thing that I believe makes the trilogy work as a whole. The books are a reflection on the complex relationship between Christianity, evangelism, and capital together with complicated notions of colonization and English imperialism. Crusoe ought to have learned his lessons and should stay at home in England counting his coins and thanking God for the generosity of his rewards. Instead, in the *Farther Adventures*, Crusoe leaves England once more and rambles the world in search of more wealth. In "realistic" terms, one wants to see the development of a character. It seems as if Crusoe has developed on the island, that he has learned that hard work can be rewarded by God; on the contrary, once he is rescued he forgets his faith: Crusoe's great wealth only results in his desire for more. He has not "grown" at all; in fact, the opposite. He is nothing more than a static – flat – character if the *Farther Adventures* is not considered part of the narrative.

But flatness of character relies on an analysis that privileges modern psychological interiority and identity. On the island, Crusoe can say "I was lord of the whole manor; or if I pleased, I might call my self king or emperor over the whole country which I had possession of" (139). The problem is that Crusoe is a capitalist and a capitalist always wants more. He needs others in order to put his capital into exchange and thus increase his wealth. He recognizes the dichotomy: "There were no rivals; I had no competitor, none to dispute sovereignty or command with me. I might have raised ship loadings of corn; but I had no use for it; so I let as little grow as I thought enough for my occasion" (139). His only subjects are his parrot, some cats, and an old senile dog. "In a word," he says, "the nature and experience of things dictated to me, upon just reflection, that all good things of this world are no farther good to us than they are for our use; and that whatever we may heap up indeed to give others, we enjoy just as much as we can use and no more" (140). These words seem to demonstrate that he is learning to be satisfied with what he has to fulfill his needs and no more. All of that changes, as we have seen, when Crusoe is finally rescued and returns home to discover he is rich beyond dreams. His increasing religious zeal – puzzling to critics who want to see a more coherent character – makes perfect sense if it is linked to his capitalist desires: the more he profits the more he wants, and to profit more requires the subjugation of those who are religiously – and racially – different to him. Evangelism is the justification for colonization and profit: the converted heathens will profit spiritually, and Crusoe will profit economically.

Winkfield has done nothing to disobey her father (who is dead in any case). In a reversal of Crusoe's own journey from England to foreign ports, she is put on her island by the captain of the ship that she hired for her return to England from America. He turns pirate with the rest of the crew and steals the estate she was taking with her. However, while this novel may have surface resemblances to *Robinson Crusoe*, the change of gender for the narrator exposes the reasons why I believe Crusoe has come to be one of the iconic figures within Western literature and indeed Western culture itself. After Friday appears, the novel acts as an implicit justification for the ethnocide practiced by Crusoe. It justifies his colonization of the island through Christian providence that rewards him through financial gain. Although he expresses affection for Friday, he needs Friday in order to help fulfill his desires: the exchange of capital and the power of being "lord" of his island. Friday, he says, has come "to be such a Christian, as I have known few equal to him in my life" (*RC* 223). Two paragraphs later, Crusoe says, "I described to him the country of Europe, and particularly England, which I came from; how we lived, how we worshipped God, how we behaved to one another; and how we traded ships to all parts of the world" (*RC* 223). Here God – evangelism – is the embedded rationalization of why trade and thus colonization can be warranted.

And Friday is the perfect pagan convert. He swears to Crusoe he will never leave him because he loves him and "'You do great deal much good ... you teach wild mans be good sober tame mans; you tell them know God, pray God, and live new life'" (227). He becomes complicit with Crusoe in the ethnocide of his own people. Afraid that Friday wanted to return to his home in order to come back with his tribe and destroy him and plunder his stuff, Crusoe discovers that he is wrong. He reasons Friday's "desire to go to his own country was laid in his ardent affection to the people, and his hopes of my doing them good" (228). In a vivid demonstration of ethnocide, Crusoe changes Friday's name (209), dresses Friday in his image (210–11), teaches Friday English (213), evangelizes Friday (218–21), and shows Friday how to make the island profit (215). The result: Friday wants his own people to follow in his footsteps (227). The natives will be brought to Jesus and like Friday will have an inferior though similar kind of identity to Crusoe's own, a perfect example of Clastres's exploration of the differences between genocide, ethnocide, and ethnocentrism. Crusoe does not follow through; however, in this scene can be found the inklings of the much more rigid Crusoe in the two sequels. This older Crusoe desires to force his own kind of dissenting Christianity on the whole heathen world because in "a circuit three times the diameter of the earth and every jot as far as the whole circumference, the name of God is not heard of . . . the Word of God is not known, or the Son of God spoken of" (*SR* 131). It is not a great leap, I would argue, that in Crusonian philosophy, evangelizing the world results in enormous economic profit for Britain. Furthermore, the iconic status of Robinson Crusoe can be traced to this justification of piety for profit. In other words, Crusoe *is* the iconographic model for the modern western capitalist.

Winkfield wants to bring the word of God on a smaller scale to the natives. Her ruse, to go into the statue and make the natives think she is a messenger from a new God, the true God, works almost immediately. However, she worries that she can't keep up the teachings by posing as an oracle in the statue. Instead, as the oracle, she tells the natives, "'A person shall come to you, like yourselves, and that you may be the less fearful or suspicious, that person shall be a woman who shall live among you as you do'" (111). She realizes that her ethnicity will work in her favor. She will not only be rescued from the island, but will be doing God's work. Oddly – because she is a woman and might not be respected by the patriarchal society of the natives – she makes the decision to show herself and says, "I might preserve a superiority over them, sufficient to keep them in awe, and to excite their obedience" (110). Perhaps her gender will prove less threatening to the priests and the people. On the one hand, she has no desire to profit from her evangelizing, as does Crusoe. On the other hand, she uses her race and indeed her gender to keep a semblance of power over them. The ethnocide she practices is not explicitly economic in motivation like Crusoe's. Rather the ethnocide is a real desire to show the natives "the knowledge of the true and only God . . . and of that happiness, which he will bestow upon all those who worship him according to his holy will" (110). This compassionate ethnocide makes clearer Crusoe's desire to evangelize Friday in order to profit even more from the colonization of the island.

Winkfield plans her entrance with the detail of a diva making a grand appearance on the stage. She dresses and bejewels herself in a spectacular way, not "from pride; but I thought the extraordinary appearance that they would give me, might procure me a more favorable reception" (113). And it works. But is Winkfield's evangelizing in truth the unselfish act she claims? As in the *Crusoe* novels there is some uncertainty. "When they were come near enough to hold a conversation," she says, "they halted and . . . prostrated themselves to the ground; I then arose and extending my golden rod to them said 'Arise'" (114). She says that she addresses them "with as much affability as I could; yet with an air of superiority" (114). Here is the stereotypical missionary in a nutshell – with a racial twist. Winkfield uses her ethnicity in order to make the natives friendlier to her. She also treats them with some condescension so that she can retain her power over them. She does not show a Crusonian desire for economic accumulation. Her only stated desire is to remain among the natives and bring them to Jesus.

Indeed, in a series of rather unbelievable events, her cousin Mr. Winkfield had been searching for Unca for two years, and eventually finds her one day when she has returned to the island for a day trip of prayer and meditation. After a courtship, they decide to marry and remain with the natives. He returns to England briefly in order to "settle half of his and my fortune upon his sisters," she says, "and leave the rest for charitable uses." Unlike Crusoe, Winkfield is perfectly happy to dispose of her wealth. It seems as if her decision is an altruistic desire to evangelize and allow the natives to keep their simple ways with no ulterior economic motives. However, next occurs a moment reminiscent of Crusoe's actions in the *Farther Adventures*, when he burns an idol worshiped by heathens on the Sino-Russian border (291–2). Winkfield says, "we first determined to go upon my island, to collect all the gold treasure there, to blow up the subterraneous passage, and the statue, that the Indians might never be tempted to their former idolatry. When all this was done, and the gold treasure put aboard [the ship], the captain and my husband set out upon their voyage" to England (154). The massive treasure of gold is a capital exchange in a way. The exchange is that the natives are now Christians and will not be tempted to their former idolatrous ways since there is no gold for them to desire. The natives seem to retain their simplicity, the utopian aspects of their self-sufficient world, their spiritual profit. England gains the gold, the economic profit, and a new Christian outpost in the Caribbean. The island may still be a utopia, but it is more significantly a Christian utopia. Or is it? As we have seen, the ethnocide practiced by Unca and her husband has implicit economic – and thus imperialistic – consequences.

By the end of the *Farther Adventures*, after Crusoe has over the past several decades been literally around the world, his faith has taken on a new zeal. He has, as I have mentioned, blown up some heathens' idol because the heathens have "sunk and degenerated to a degree so more than stupid as to prostrate itself to a frightful nothing, a mere imaginary object dressed up by themselves" (286). This is not the "pensive and sad" reaction he has at the discovery of the footprints and, indeed, in an earlier moment in the *Farther Adventures* when he is ashamed that his sailors committed genocide on a group of Madagascar natives (201–3). Instead he finds himself in a "rage" (286) and he paradoxically determines to commit this act of violent ethnocide that comes close to genocide. This adventure is the last in the trilogy. Finally rich enough even for his own desires, economic profit seems to drop out of the Crusoe narrative. As the *Farther Adventures* ends he says he has "learnt sufficiently to know the value of retirement" (322). For Crusoe, "profit" could stand in for value: he is a very old man and his "retirement" will allow him to reflect and meditate in the ease and comfort provided by his capitalist trade over the years. Indeed Defoe follows up the first two novels with the *Serious Reflections*. The "plot" is Crusoe's ruminations upon refashioning the world into his own kind of dissenting Christianity.

When all is said and done, both the *Crusoe* trilogy and *The Female American* use Christian evangelizing to legitimize ethnocide, and for Crusoe, to legitimize the colonization of not only his island but all of the world. *The Female American*, I argue, emphasizes the justification of this evangelizing for another group's cultural ethnocide through an almost ideal vision of Christian identity. With the minor exception of the movement of gold from the island to England, capital and economic colonization have little to do with the sentimental representation of the natives and their journey toward Christ. What *The Female American* demonstrates, I hope, is the complicity between evangelizing Christianity and economic colonization as a way to show the continuity of the *Crusoe* trilogy, and the Crusonian identity as a way to read all three of the books. By the *Serious Reflections* it seems as if Crusoe has made his peace with the world, and as a wealthy man, has no more desire to accrue economic profit. However, the final pages of the book vividly demonstrate the linkage between capital and evangelizing. Crusoe makes "a double argument for a war" against the "robbers" and "pirates" of Africa. By subduing the Africans' "rapine," Christians from Europe make "such a war not only just on a religious account, but both just and necessary upon a civil account" (242–3). These robbers and pirates worship "the worst of all imposters, Mahomet" (242). The ethnocide practiced by the Europeans will result in not only a Christian continent, but a new source for the economic empowerment of the West.

The ethnocide practiced by both Crusoe and Winkfield, finally, is justified by both Christian Protestant theology and, by Defoe particularly, enormous economic profit. It is *good* for these heathens to be brought to the One True God, and it is *good* for British economy to profit from this evangelism. It is impossible to overstate the importance of *Robinson Crusoe* to western culture. However, to focus only on volume one of Defoe's trilogy is to reduce Crusonian identity to a transparent character who represents hard work, strong faith, eighteenth-century racism, and not much else. Hard work and persistence pay off, literally, on Crusoe's island, and his example provides a conduct book for living the good Protestant life. His conversion of Friday is, as critics over the past ten years have noted, an example of western colonization and the demeaning of racial differ-ence. I hope I have demonstrated, however, that an analysis of Crusonian identity underscores the complicity of empire and Protestant evangelism in eighteenth-century popular culture and how Crusoe's racism works to uphold both tropes. Colin Kidd may argue that although there was prej-udice there was no ethnic hatred. That either-or dichotomy, however, is complicated by this analysis of the most important meditation on religion and empire in early modern fiction: Daniel Defoe's trilogy, *Robinson Crusoe*.

PART III

Time, identity, and Atlantic interculture

CHAPTER 9

Time and revolution in African America: temporality and the history of Atlantic slavery

Walter Johnson

I write in the cold, clear light that comes with the beginning of the fall. The World Trade Center has come down and the United States is bombing Afghanistan. Thousands are dead, and many thousands more, it appears, are destined to die. These events have changed the meaning of things, making planes overhead and sirens in the night into portents of terror, making symbols of loss into calls for war, making things that were once easy to say hard to think about.

To begin it is enough to say that on September 11 one version of history was punctured by another. Issues that most people in the United States had sealed off in the category of the "elsewhere" were suddenly made manifest in their relation to the daily lives of even the most complacent Americans: US troops in Saudi Arabia, fanatics in Afghanistan, suicide bombing and state-sponsored terror in Israel. It seems equally clear that simply to try to define the character of that collision of histories is to take a part in it. For Tony Blair, the present apparently began with the "atrocity" of September 11. For Osama Bin Laden, the present began eighty years ago, with the European partition of the Ottoman empire. For a man I heard on the radio last night, knowledge of the crusades, of the battles of Richard the Lionheart and Saladin (Salah-al-Din Yusef ibn-Ayyub), seemed usefully to illuminate the news on a day when the United States was using satellite-guided missiles to target the "air defense system" of Afghanistan. The parameters of these on-the-fly histories of the present define the horizons of the futures their tellers imagine.

My thanks to Mia Bay, Thomas Bender, Christopher Brown, Elizabeth Esch, Ada Ferrer, Robin D. G. Kelley, Maria Grazia Lolla, Molly Nolan, Ulfried Reichardt, Jeffrey T. Sammons, Nikhil Pal Singh, Stephanie Smallwood, Sinclair Thomson, Henry Yu, and participants in the 1997 and 1998 NYU/OAH conferences on "Internationalizing American History," the "New Perspectives on the Slave Trade" conference at Rutgers (November 21–22, 1997), and the Early American Seminar at Columbia University.

In light of this clash of history-tellings, it seems more important than ever to think hard about what we are saying when we use words like "empire" or "globalization," words that seem straightforward enough as accounts of history as presented by the metropolitan centers of the western world, but whose explanatory force begins to wane as they move outward and encounter other conflicting accounts of events – some of which are themselves imperial or global in outlook. This chapter represents an attempt to think about one element of the history of empire and global capital – the history of slavery – in relation to its own counter-histories. In relation, that is, to the alternative understandings and historical projects that were forcibly though never fully over-coded with the set of historical terms and definitions favored by European and American slaveholders.

Let me begin with a famous misunderstanding. As he later recounted it, when Olaudah Equiano first saw the white slave traders who eventually carried him to the West Indies, he thought they were "bad spirits" who were going to eat him. Awaiting shipment across an ocean he had never heard of, Equiano, like many of the slaves carried away by the traders, made sense of an absurd situation with a narrative of supernatural power.[1] When he sat down to write his narrative, of course, Equiano knew better than to believe that the white men on the coast were "spirits." By that time he called himself Gustavas Vassa, and, having spent ten years as a slave in the Americas and another twenty-three as a free man traveling throughout the world, Vassa could see what Equiano could not: that he was a descendant of the Lost Tribes of Israel, that his deliverance from heathenism marked him as a *particular favorite of heaven*," and that the events in his life were effects not of the evil intentions of African spirits but of the Christian God's "Providence."[2] Vassa resolved the collision of contending versions of cause and consequence in his own mind through a narrative of progressive enlightenment: he had learned that it was God's Providence to steal him

---

[1] Olaudah Equiano, *The Interesting Life of Olaudah Equiano, Written by Himself* (New York: St. Martin's Press, 1995), 53–4; see also narratives of Job Ben Solomon (p. 57) and Joseph Wright (p. 331) in Philip D. Curtin, ed., *Africa Remembered: Narratives by West Africans from the Era of the Slave Trade* (Madison: University of Wisconsin, 1967); "It was the Same as Pigs in a Sty: A Young African's Account of Life on a Slave Ship," in Robert Conrad, ed., *Children of God's Fire: A Documentary History of Black Slavery in Brazil* (Princeton University Press, 1984), 39; John Thornton, *Africa and Africans in the Making of the Atlantic World, 1400–1680* (Cambridge University Press, 1992), 161; Michael A. Gomez, *Exchanging Our Country Marks: The Transformation of African Identities in the Colonial and Antebellum South* (Chapel Hill: University of North Carolina Press, 1998), 160, where it is argued that fears of being made into oil and eaten were common among slaves in the trade; and Charles Piot, "Of Slaves and the Gift: Kabre Sale of Kin and the Era of the Slave Trade," *Journal of African History*, 37 (1996), 38.
[2] Equiano, *The Interesting Life of Olaudah Equiano*, 33, 44.

away from Africa and carry him to London where he could spread the gospel of anti-slavery.

Vassa's time travel reminds us that global historical processes are understood through locally and historically specific narratives of time and history. And yet by invoking God's Providence, Vassa did not so much resolve the contention of these temporal narratives as superimpose one upon the other. Equiano's initial understanding of the situation of the coast was incorporated into the story of Vassa's eventual enlightenment. His African history was reframed according to the conventions of his European one.

Recent work in the humanities and social sciences has emphasized the darker side of the temporal conventions that have framed many western histories of the rest of the world: their role in underwriting global and racial hierarchy. Concepts like primitiveness, backwardness, and underdevelopment rank areas and people of the world on a seemingly naturalized timeline – their "present" is our "past" – and reframe the grubby real-time politics of colonial domination and exploitation as part of an orderly natural process of evolution toward modernity. More than a fixed standard of measure by which the progress of other processes can be measured, time figures in these works as, in the words of Johannes Fabian, a culturally constructed "dimension of power."[3]

Seen in this light, Equiano's anachronistic account of the situation on the coast raises a host of questions about the history of Atlantic slavery. What were the historical and temporal narratives through which Africans and Europeans understood what was happening on the coast, in the slave ships, and in the slave markets of the Americas? How did these various understandings shape the historical process in which they were joined? In what cultural institutions were these ideas of time rooted and through what practices were they sustained? What was the fate of African time in the Americas? What were the practical processes of temporal domination and resistance?

Taking time seriously suggests, at the very least, that the slave trade was not the same thing for Olaudah Equiano that it was for his captors. Most simply, this difference might be thought of spatially: "the slave trade"

[3] Johannes Fabian, *Time and the Other: How Anthropology Makes its Object* (New York: Columbia University Press, 1983). See also Wai-Chee Dimock, *Empire for Liberty: Melville and the Poetics of Individualism* (Princeton University Press, 1989), 17–20; Dipesh Chakrabarty, "Postcoloniality and the Artifice of History: Who Speaks for the Indian Past?" *Representations*, 37 (1992), 1–26; Anne McClintock, *Imperial Leather: Race, Gender, and Sexuality in the Colonial Contest* (London: Routledge, 1995); Jonathan Crush, ed., *Power of Development* (London: Routledge, 1995); Reynaldo C. Ileto, "Outline of a Non-linear Emplotment in Philippine History," in Lisa Lowe and David Lloyd, eds., *The Politics of Culture in the Shadow of Capital* (Durham: Duke University Press, 1997), 98–131; Maria Josefina Saldana-Portillo, "Developmentalism's Irresistible Seduction – Rural Subjectivity under Sandinista Agricultural Policy," in ibid., 132–72.

did not begin or end in the same place for European traders, American buyers, and African slaves. The African slave trade, after all, had an eastern branch stretching to Asia as well as a western one which stretched to the Americas. Thus a historical account of the African experience of "the slave trade" necessarily has a different shape from an account of the European experience; indeed, properly speaking, "the slave trade" has not yet ended in some parts of Africa.[4] But even if we confine ourselves to the history of the Atlantic slave trade, the problem of boundaries persists. The journeys of the slaves who were shipped across the Atlantic Ocean often began in the interior of Africa, hundreds of miles from the coast where they eventually met the European slave traders, hundreds of miles away from where any European had ever been. Indeed, the First Passage was integral to the experience of those who eventually made the Middle Passage – to their understanding of what it was that was happening, their emotional condition going into the journey, and their ability to survive it.[5] And yet the First Passage is often elided from historians' accounts of "the slave trade," many of which focus solely on the Middle Passage, treating the trade as if it were something which began on the west coast of Africa with a sale to a European trader and ended in a port in the Americas with a sale to a colonial slaveholder. In so doing they have unwittingly embedded the historical perspective of a European slave trader – for it was only for the traders, not for the slaves or the buyers, that "the slave trade" happened only in the space between the coasts – in the way they have bounded their topics.[6]

The historical disjuncture marked by Equiano's version of the situation on the coast, however, was much deeper than a difference about beginnings

[4] Patrick Manning, *Slavery and African Life: Occidental, Oriental, and African Slave Trades* (Cambridge University Press, 1990). My thanks to Mia Bay for her pointed comments about contemporary slave trading.
[5] See Joseph C. Miller, *The Way of Death: Merchant Capitalism and the Angolan Slave Trade, 1730–1830* (Madison: University of Wisconsin, 1988). See also Stephanie Ellen Smallwood, "Salt-Water Slaves: African Enslavement, Forced Migration, and Settlement in the Anglo-American World, 1660–1700," unpublished Ph.D. dissertation, Duke University, 1999, 15–128.
[6] See, for instance, James A. Rawley, *The Transatlantic Slave Trade: A History* (New York: Norton, 1981), and David W. Galenson, *Traders, Planters, and Slaves: Market Behavior in Early English America* (Cambridge University Press, 1986). The unwitting prominence given to the traders' definition of the phenomenon in these and many other accounts has to do with the fact that they limit themselves to treating the trade as an economic and demographic phenomenon, and their sole reliance upon the records generated by the trade itself, an example of what the historian Michel-Rolph Trouillot has called "archival power," the material power that past actors have over their future through the records they create and keep. See Trouillot, *Silencing the Past: Power and the Production of History* (Boston: Beacon Press, 1995), 31–69.

and endings. It signals a fundamental difference between the versions of slavery which met in the Atlantic trade. To oversimplify: in Euro-America, slavery was, above all, a system of economic exploitation; in much of West Africa slavery was, above all, a system of political domination. In the Americas slaves were purchased in markets, held as legally alienable property, and put to work as laborers producing staple crops and some other goods which were generally shipped to Europe in exchange for money and more goods.[7] In much of precolonial West Africa, slavery began with capture: a warrior who would otherwise have been killed was allowed to live on as a socially dead slave. Though most slaves in West Africa were agricultural laborers, many were employed as soldiers, state ministers, and diplomats, and even as governing placeholders for princes and kings. Some slaves owned slaves.[8] As such, West African slavery has often been described as a system of "institutionalized marginality," one among a set of intertwined social relations – kinship, fealty, clientage, etc. – by which one group of people held "wealth in people" in another. Some slaves, over time and generation, through marriage and connection, were able to move out of slavery and into another status.[9]

Equiano's confusion on the coast reminds us that two versions of slavery – "aristocratic slavery" and "merchant slavery" in Claude Meillassoux's formulation – met in the African trade. Those who entered the slave trade had been extracted from histories of enslavement and slavery which sometimes had very little to do with the Atlantic slave trade in the first instance. Rather their story as they understood it was embedded in personal histories of isolation from protective kinship and patronage networks, in local histories

[7] Eric Williams, *Capitalism and Slavery* (Chapel Hill: University of North Carolina Press, 1944); Richard S. Dunn, *Sugar and Slaves: The Rise of the Planter Class in the English West Indies, 1624–1713* (Chapel Hill: University of North Carolina Press, 1972); Elizabeth Fox-Genovese and Eugene D. Genovese, *Fruits of Merchant Capital: Slavery and Bourgeois Property in the Rise and Expansion of Capitalism* (New York: Oxford University Press, 1983).

[8] Claude Meillassoux, *The Anthropology of Slavery: The Womb of Iron and Gold*, trans. Alide Dasnoism (University of Chicago Press, 1991). Meillassoux does not share the view of precolonial African slavery described in the following sentences.

[9] Suzanne Miers and Igor Kopytoff, "African 'Slavery' as an Institution of Marginality," in Miers and Kopytoff, eds., *Slavery in Africa: Historical and Anthropological Perspectives* (Madison: University of Wisconsin, 1977), 3–69; Jonathon Glassman, "The Bondsman's New Clothes: The Contradictory Consciousness of Slave Resistance on the Swahili Coast," *Journal of African History*, 32 (1991), 277–312; Jane I. Guyer, "Wealth in People and Self-Realization in Equatorial Africa," *Man*, 28 (1993), 243–65; Jane I. Guyer, "Wealth in People, Wealth in Things," *Journal of African History*, 36 (1995), 83–90; Jane I. Guyer and Samuel M. Eno Belinga, "Wealth in People as Wealth in Knowledge: Accumulation and Competition in Equatorial Africa," *Journal of African History*, 36 (1995), 91–120; Piot, "Of Slaves and the Gift," 31–49.

of slave-producing ethnic conflicts, in political struggles, and wars which occurred hundreds of miles from the coast.[10]

This is not, however, to say that all African slavery was aristocratic slavery. The jagged boundary between aristocratic and merchant slavery, after all, often lay hundreds of miles into the interior of the African continent – hundreds of miles beyond where any European had ever been. Many of the slaves who were eventually shipped across the Atlantic had been captured, transported to the coast, and sold by people who were themselves Africans. The frontier between the two types of slavery was patrolled by an African supervisory elite who presumably knew the difference between them and made their living by transmuting the one into the other. And just as the protocols of merchant slavery stretched well into the interior of Africa, those of aristocratic slavery could stretch well into the journey across the Atlantic. To describe the people they transported to the Americas, the ship captains and clerks of the French West India Company used the word "*captif*" rather than the more familiar "*esclave*," a designation which apparently referred to the aristocratic slavery origins of those in the trade rather than their merchant slavery destinations.[11]

Corresponding to the different versions of slavery which met in the Atlantic trade were different ways of measuring the extent of slavery and marking its progress through time. The (aristocratic) slaveholding kings of precolonial Dahomey, for instance, represented their history as a story of continuous growth through military expansion and enslavement. Their history was measured in a yearly census – taken, historian Robin Law argues, as a means of "political propaganda . . . advertising the kingdom's successful growth" – and in mythical bags of pebbles kept in the castle which tracked the kingdom's expansion – one pebble per person – over time.[12] Other systems of aristocratic slavery had other measures. In precolonial equatorial

---

[10] See David Ross, "The Dahomean Middleman System, 1727–*c.* 1818," *Journal of African History*, 28 (1987), 357–75; Robin Law, "Slave-raiders and Middlemen; Monopolists and Free Traders: the Supply of Slaves for the Atlantic Trade in Dahomey, *c.* 1715–1850," *Journal of African History*, 30 (1989), 45–68; Miller, *The Way of Death*, 40–9, 108–28; Meillassoux, *The Anthropology of Slavery*, 237–323; and Steve Feierman, "Africa in History: The End of Universal Narratives," in Gyan Prakash, ed., *After Colonialism: Imperial Histories and Postcolonial Displacements* (Princeton University Press, 1995), 40–65. From the other side of the Atlantic see Ira Berlin, "From Creole to African: Atlantic Creoles and the Origins of African American Society in Mainland North America," *William and Mary Quarterly*, 53 (1996), 251–88; Smallwood, "Salt-Water Slaves," 60–128.

[11] Gwendolyn Midlo Hall, *Africans in Colonial Louisiana: The Development of Afro-Creole Culture in the Eighteenth-Century* (Baton Rouge: Louisiana State University Press, 1992), *passim*; see also Smallwood, "Salt-Water Slaves," 127.

[12] Robin Law, "History and Legitimacy: Aspects of the Use of the Past in Precolonial Dahomey," *History in Africa*, 15 (1988), 431–65; see also Ivor Wilkes, "On Mentally Mapping Greater Asante: A Study of Time and Motion," *Journal of African History*, 33 (1992), 175–90.

Africa, Jane Guyer and Samuel M. Eno Belinga have argued, political power and historical progress were measured as wealth-in-knowledge rather than wealth-in-people. Rather than accumulating numbers of people, the leaders of kingdoms like that of the Kongo enhanced their power by acquiring, through capture or purchase, people with different types of knowledge.[13]

The African and European merchant slave traders with whom these kingdoms sometimes did business had still other ways of measuring the trade and imagining the history they were making: sacred time measured against an injunction to enslave non-Islamic outsiders or propelled by the "providence" of a Christian God; political history imagined as the conquest of monopoly rights along the African coast and market position in the Americas; market time imagined in macroeconomic cycles of depression and speculation; the microeconomic time of the slave trader, progress tracked across the pages of the ship's log, days defined by the weather and ship's speed, nights marked by the number of slaves who died in the hold – time reckoned in dead bodies and lost profits.[14]

For many of the slaves who were packed into the holds of the Atlantic slave ships we can imagine still another set of temporal frames: those derived from local political histories of war and slave raiding; a cultural cycle of social death and rebirth, the ethnic and political disorientation of capture and separation eventually giving way to new identifications with "shipmates" and "fictive kin"; a biographical culmination of lifetime fears of capture, kidnapping, or simply of falling through the cracks in the protections of patronage and kinship; the metaphysical horror of a "middle" passage that some must have thought would never end and others might only have recognized as a trip across the "*kalunga*," the body of water which separated the world of the living from that of the dead – a flight from time measured in the gradual physical deterioration of the worldly body.[15] And so on: as many journeys on a single ship as there were ways to imagine the journey.

[13] Guyer and Belinga, "Wealth in People as Wealth in Knowledge," 108–19.
[14] See Galenson, *Traders, Planters, and Slaves*; Miller, *The Way of Death*; Ross, "The Dahomean Middleman System"; Law, "Slave-raiders and Middlemen"; for Islam as a "merchant ideology" see Meillassoux, *The Anthropology of Slavery*, 243–8; for the slave trade as "providence" see Samuel Ajayi Crowther, *The Narrative of Samuel Ajayi Crowther* in Curtin, ed., *Africa Remembered*, 299.
[15] See Orlando Patterson, *Slavery and Social Death: A Comparative Study* (Cambridge University Press,1982); T. C. McCaskie, "Time and the Calendar in Nineteenth-Century Asante: An Exploratory Essay," *History in Africa*, 7 (1980), 179–200; Joseph K. Adjaye, "Time, the Calendar, and History among the Akan of Ghana," *Journal of Ethnic Studies*, 15 (1987), 71–100; Richard Price, *First-Time: The Historical Vision of an Afro-American People* (Baltimore: The Johns Hopkins University Press, 1983); Price, *Alabi's World* (Baltimore: The Johns Hopkins University Press, 1990); Smallwood, "Salt-water Slaves," 129–90; Gomez, *Exchanging Our Country Marks*, 147, 160.

Each of the narratives of slavery described above represents a dimension of that confrontation, a way of being in time – a temporality – according to which historical actors made sense of what it was that was happening (God's providence, the main chance, social death, etc.) and how they would respond at any given moment.[16] These temporalities were layered, intertwined, and mixed through the process of the slave trade, running sometimes concurrently, sometimes oppositionally, tangled together by a historical process that none of them alone sufficed to describe. None of this should be taken to suggest that societies are unified in their temporalities, still less that there was a simple division between a circular premodern African time and a linear modern European time.[17] Quite the contrary. Taking time seriously suggests that "the slave trade" was not a single thing that might be viewed from a European perspective and an African perspective (or a global perspective and a local perspective or a systemic perspective and an individual perspective) and then summed into a whole – the way one might walk around a physical object, measure every face, and create a three-dimensional diagram. Rather, like a web of unforeseen connections, the historical shape of the slave trade depended upon the point of entry. Time ran differently depending upon where you started the clock.

Lived history, I am suggesting, is produced out of the clash of contending temporalities. These temporalities, however, must be seen as being

---

[16] On temporality see Mikhail Bakhtin, "Forms of Time and Chronotopes in the Novel: Notes Toward a Historical Poetics," in Caryl Emerson and Michael Holquist, eds., *The Dialogic Imagination: Four Essays* (Austin: University of Texas Press, 1981), 84–258; Fernand Braudel, "Time, History, and the Social Sciences," in Fritz Stern, ed., *The Varieties of History, From Voltaire to the Present* (New York: Meriden Press, 1973), 403–29; the essays in John Bender and David E. Wellerby, *Chronotypes: The Construction of Time* (Stanford University Press, 1991), and Jonathan Boyarin, ed., *Remapping Memory: The Politics of Timespace* (Minneapolis: University of Minnesota, 1994). See also E. P. Thompson, "Time, Work-Discipline and Industrial Capitalism," *Past & Present*, 38 (1967), 56–97; Jacques LeGoff, "Merchant's Time and Church's Time in the Middle Ages" and "Labor Time in the 'Crisis' of the Fourteenth Century: From Medieval Time to Modern Time" in his *Time, Work, and Culture in the Middle Ages*, trans. Arthur Goldhammer (University of Chicago Press, 1980), 29–52; Michael O'Malley, *Keeping Watch: A History of American Time* (New York: Viking, 1990); Moishe Postone, *Time, Labor, and Social Domination: A Reinterpretation of Marx's Critical Theory* (Cambridge University Press, 1993); Mark M. Smith, *Mastered by the Clock: Time, Slavery, and Freedom in the American South* (Chapel Hill: University of North Carolina Press, 1997); and Michael Hanchard, "Afro-Modernity: Temporality, Politics, and the African Diaspora," *Public Culture*, 11 (1999), 245–68.
[17] For examples of cyclical time reckoning in Europe and linear time reckoning in Africa, see LeGoff, "Merchant's Time and Church's Time in the Middle Ages," 29–42; Akhil Gupta, "The Reincarnation of Souls and the Rebirth of Commodities: Representations of Time in 'East' and 'West,'" *Cultural Critique*, 22 (1992), 187–211; see also Gyan Prakash, "Writing Post-Orientalist Histories of the Third World: Indian Historiography is Good to Think," in Nicholas B. Dirks, ed., *Colonialism and Culture* (Ann Arbor: University of Michigan, 1992), 353–88. For the idea that "Christianization introduced Africans to a sense of history moving linearly" (with which I am disagreeing) see Mullin, *Africa in America*, 275.

themselves historical. Rather than marking the difference between timeless cultural essences – African time and European time – they reflect the politically and historically embedded circuits through which they were transmitted. And because they were historically shaped and politically situated, it is not enough simply to set these temporalities side by side and split the difference. The history of time is one of continual contest: a history of arguments about history; of efforts to control events by controlling the terms of their description; of situated and sometimes violent acts of synchronization; of forcible re-education, resistant appropriation, and everyday negotiation; of conflicts in which time itself was a dimension of contest.

As a way of illustrating the historical politics of time-making, I'd like to use the space I have left to consider briefly two aspects of the temporal politics of American slavery: the temporal dimension of slaveholders' domination and the way that slave rebels tried to make history by imagining themselves into time. As recent observers have noted, one of the many things slaveholders thought they owned was their slaves' time; indeed, to outline the temporal claims that slaveholders made upon their slaves is to draw a multidimensional portrait of slavery itself. Slaveholders, of course, defined the shape of the day. Whether it ran from sunup to sundown, was defined by the tasks that had to be done by its close, or was measured out into job-scaled clock time, slavery's daily time was delineated by the master and often enforced by violence. Those who turned out late, quit early, worked too slowly, came up short, or failed to wait deferentially while the master attended to other things were cajoled, beaten, or starved into matching the daily rhythms through which their owners measured progress.[18] As well as quotidian time, slaveholders claimed calendar time as their own. They decided which days would be work days and which days would be holidays (or holy days); they enforced a cycle of planting, growing, and harvesting timed around their crop cycles and commercial plans; they fractured their slaves' lives and communities with their own cycle of yearly hires and calendar-termed financial obligations.[19] And slaveholders thought they

[18] For time and "work-discipline" in American slavery see Smith, *Mastered by the Clock*, esp. 93–128, and Philip D. Morgan, *Slave Counterpoint: Black Culture in the Eighteenth-Century Chesapeake and Lowcountry* (Chapel Hill: University of North Carolina Press, 1998), 172–94.

[19] For crop and commercial calendars see Morgan, *Slave Counterpoint*, 147–72; Emilia Viotti da Costa, *Crowns of Glory, Tears of Blood: The Demerara Slave Rebellion of 1823* (New York: Columbia University Press, 1994), 171; and Winthrop D. Jordan, *Tumult and Silence at Second Creek: An Inquiry into a Civil War Slave Conspiracy* (Baton Rouge: Louisiana State University Press, 1993), 39–45, 213–14; for hiring see Charles B. Dew, *Bond of Iron: Master and Slave at Buffalo Forge* (New York: W. W. Norton, 1994), 67–70; for credit relations see Richard Holcombe Kilbourne, Jr., *Debt, Investment, and Slaves: Credit Relations in East Feliciana Parish, Louisiana, 1825–1885* (Tuscaloosa: University of Alabama Press, 1995), 49–74.

owned their slaves' biographical time: they recorded their slaves' birthdays in accounts books that only they could see; they determined at what age their slaves would be started into the fields or set to a trade, when their slaves would be cajoled into reproduction, how many years they would be allowed to nurse the children they had, and how old they would have to be before retiring; they reproduced their own family legacies over time out of the broken pieces of slave families and communities divided by sale and estate settlement.[20] They infused their slaves' lives with their own time – through the daily process of slave discipline, the foreign, the young, and the resistant were forcibly inculcated with the nested temporal rhythms of their enslavement.

As with any dimension of power, however, time could be turned back upon its master. By working slowly, delaying conception, shamming sickness, or slipping off, slaves short-circuited their master's algorithms of temporal progress. By using the time at the end of the day to cultivate their own plots, sell their produce, or visit their family members, slaves wedged their own concerns into the interstices of their enslavement.[21] By naming their children after the day of their birth (traditional among Gold Coast slaves) or giving them the names of ancestors, they reconstituted fractured links to their pasts and their families.[22] By adhering to the protocols of living with ancestors present in time and space, obeying the demands of moments that were themselves portentous of the success or failure of any action undertaken, and observing the injunctions and respecting the power of *obeah* men and conjurers, by finding time within the day to put down a rug, face Mecca, and pray, or by keeping the Sabbath for the Christian God, they bent themselves to systems of temporal discipline outside their slavery.[23]

The temporal conflicts between slaves and slaveholders were resolved in a series of unstable stalemates made at the scale of everyday life.

---

[20] See Herbert G. Gutman, *The Black Family in Slavery and Freedom, 1750–1925* (New York: Vintage Books, 1976); Deborah Gray White, *Ar'n't I a Woman? Female Slaves in the Plantation South* (New York: Norton, 1985) 91–118; da Costa, *Crowns of Glory, Tears of Blood*, 65–8, 117; Walter Johnson, *Soul by Soul: Life Inside the Antebellum Slave Market* (Cambridge University Press, 1999), 78–116.

[21] Mechal Sobel, *The World They Made Together: Black and White Values in Eighteenth-Century Virginia* (Princeton University Press, 1987), 15–67; White, *Ar'n't I a Woman?*, 104–10; Morgan, *Slave Counterpoint*, 48–50, 153–5, 183–4, 191–3, 359–76; and da Costa, *Crowns of Glory, Tears of Blood*, 75–85, 115–18.

[22] Adjaye, "Time, the Calendar, and History among the Akan of Ghana," 71–95; Smallwood, "Salt-water Slaves", 317–19; Gutman, *The Black Family in Slavery and Freedom*, 185–201.

[23] Sobel, *The World They Made Together*, 171–229; Mullin, *Africa in America*, 175–84, 201–2; Gomez, *Exchanging Our Country Marks*, 2–3, 55–6, 59, 249, 283–90; da Costa, *Crowns of Glory, Tears of Blood*, 176–7, 271.

Through acts of passive resistance like slowing down and of active defiance like running away, slaves were able to gain acceptance – sometimes explicit, sometimes tacit – of their right to use a portion of the day for visiting, worshiping, provisioning, or simply resting.[24] The boundaries of the possible, however, were hedged by slaveholders' willingness to enforce their own ideas of time through force. In fact, by attributing their slaves' failure to work as hard, as eagerly, or as long as they wanted to savagery, primitivism, and biological lassitude, slaveholders invested their own everyday politics of labor discipline with the force of natural history.[25] On the surface, at least, enslaved Africans were being dragged into their masters' history, forced into temporal frames of reference defined by slavery and race.

Occasionally, however, these everyday conflicts gave way to the broader, historical acts of resistance that historians have called slave revolts. These events have generally been explained according to one of two grand narratives of African-American history: the story of how black slavery was superseded by "freedom" or the story of how Africans became African-Americans. The first narrative has emphasized the commonality of the oppressions visited upon enslaved people over the differences between them and treated events disparate in time and space – the maroon wars in Jamaica (1690–1740, 1795–6) and Nat Turner's rebellion in Virginia (1831), for example – as similar phenomena, part, at bottom, of the same broad history of the attempt of enslaved people to gain their freedom.[26] The second narrative has framed the history of these events as part of a broader story of acculturation – the transformation of Africans into African-Americans – and used the cultural content of New World slave revolts to measure the progress of this ongoing transformation at a series of stops along the way.[27]

---

[24] Ira Berlin, *Many Thousand Gone: The First Two Centuries of Slavery in North America* (Cambridge University Press, 1998), 2–6; da Costa, *Crowns of Glory, Tears of Blood*, 61–80.

[25] See, for instance, Samuel Cartwright, "Diseases and Peculiarities of the Negro Race," *DeBow's Review*, 11 (1851), 64–9, 212–13, 331–7; "Philosophy of the Negro Constitution," *New Orleans Medical and Surgical Journal*, 9 (1852), 195–208; and "Ethnology of the Negro of Prognathous Race," *New Orleans Medical and Surgical Journal*, 15 (1858), 149–63. For the idea that ideas of historical alterity can develop out of everyday conflicts over time discipline see Frederick Cooper, "Colonizing Time: Work Rhythms and Labor Conflict in Colonial Mombasa," in Dirks, ed., *Colonialism and Culture*, 209–45, and Keletso E. Atkins, *The Moon is Dead! Give Us Our Money! The Cultural Origins of an African Work Ethic, Natal, South Africa, 1843–1900* (London: Heineman Currey, 1993); Smith, *Mastered by the Clock*, 132.

[26] See, for instance, Herbert Aptheker, *American Negro Slave Revolts*, 6th edn (New York: International Publications, 1969); Eugene D. Genovese, *From Rebellion to Revolution: Afro-American Slave Revolts in the Making of the New World* (Baton Rouge: Louisiana State University Press, 1979); and Michael Craton, *Testing the Chains: Resistance to Slavery in the British West Indies* (Ithaca: Cornell University Press, 1982).

[27] See, for instance, Mullin, *Africa in America*, and Douglas Egerton, *Gabriel's Rebellion: The Virginia Slave Conspiracies of 1800 and 1802* (Chapel Hill: University of North Carolina Press, 1993).

There is no doubt that both of these explanatory paradigms are instructive: there were, as I have argued above, certain material and ideological features common to merchant slavery that were shared by all of the Atlantic slave societies; and African populations in the New World *did* become African-American, a change that *was* reflected in their collective lives and their revolts.

And yet neither of these stories fully exhausts the historical content of the events they seek to explain. The set of explanations which emphasizes the similarities between slave rebels and their sequential struggle toward "freedom" has glossed over very real differences (over space and time) in the ideologies which defined the purposes of collective revolt, leaving a host of questions: if the Jamaican maroon chieftain Cudjoe had met the Christian millenarian Nat Turner, what would they have said to one another? Would Cudjoe have tried to capture Turner and return him to his owner in order to protect his own community from slaveholders' reprisals? Would Turner have tried to convert Cudjoe or struck him down with all of the force of the Christian millennium? Nor, however, can the other set of (culturalist) accounts fully contain the complex history of these events. They cannot, for instance, explain why New World slave rebels were almost exclusively male nor why those conspirators were so often betrayed by their fellow slaves. They cannot, that is, explain why women or non-conspirators, who were presumably as African or African-American as their rebellious counterparts at any given moment in time, were not visible on the leading edge of what historians have taken to be their history.[28]

In fact, scarcely concealed in the contrasting outlines of these separate sets of explanations is a single story of progress: the metanarrative of racial liberalism – the story of black freedom and racial acculturation, of how black slaves became American citizens.[29] In treating slave revolts as a way to take the temperature of a historical process with a foreordained outcome, historians have often overlooked the way that the slaves themselves imagined the history that they were making – the arguments and politics, the historical process, through which they imagined themselves into time.[30]

[28] For these points see James Sidbury, *Ploughshares into Swords: Race, Rebellion, and Identity in Gabriel's Virginia, 1730–1810* (Cambridge University Press, 1997), 87–116.
[29] For "liberal developmentalism" as a historical metanarrative immanent in the work of Marxist and other scholars see Chakrabarty, "Postcoloniality and the Artifice of History."
[30] The best account of a slave revolt as a process of political organization remain C. L. R. James, *The Black Jacobins: Toussaint Louverture and the San Domingo Revolution*, 2nd edn (New York: Vintage, 1963). Notable recent examples, to my way of thinking, are Jordan, *Tumult and Silence at Second Creek*, da Costa, *Crowns of Glory, Tears of Blood*, and Sidbury, *Ploughshares into Swords*. For the argument that I'm making – that the realm of "politics" is where historical subjectivities are argued

Historians, that is, have reworked the history of the rebels who were willing to risk their lives to escape from American history into a part of that history.

Excavating the internal politics of slave conspiracies from an archival record produced by slaveholders requires careful reading. The most detailed accounts we have of the way that slaves talked to one another about conspiracy and rebellion come from the records of the trials that followed the discovery of their plans: they are accounts shaped by slaveholders' fevered projections of their slaves' unfathomed purposes, by the terror of slaves whose lives depended upon the extent to which their confessions matched the expectations of their inquisitors, and by the torture riven so deeply into the archival record of Southern "justice." And yet, as anyone who has ever told a lie can tell you, the best way to make a story seem true is to build it out of pieces of the truth. Read against the grain, the conspiracy probes provide a sense of what slaves knew of the nature of slave conspiracies – where they happened, who was involved and what their plans were, and, most importantly for our purposes here, what kinds of reasons slaves gave to one another as they argued about what they should do, to whom, and when. If we wish to understand the practical complexity and political philosophy of New World slave conspiracies, the trial records are our best source.[31]

The most elementary point that emerges from those records is that talk about subversive ideas and rebellious plans had to occur off the grid of everyday life: at the margins of a landscape defined by slavery and in the interstices of weeks, days, and even hours structured by slaveholders' demands. Plans for Gabriel's revolt (1800) in Virginia, for example, were apparently discussed at riverside taverns on the James and at revival meetings and picnics in the countryside beyond the eyes of white Richmond, and spread by mobile skilled slaves, men with abroad marriages that gave them an excuse to travel between plantations, and a network of enslaved rivermen. The Demerara revolt (1823) in British Guyana was plotted at slave-led Sunday school meetings sponsored by the London Missionary Society,

---

over and articulated – see Stuart Hall, "The Toad in the Garden: Thatcherism among the Theorists," in Cary Nelson and Lawrence Grossberg, ed., *Marxism and the Interpretation of Culture* (Urbana: University of Illinois Press, 1988), 35–57.

[31] For the inability of slaveholders (and subsequent historians) to imagine their slaves' motivations see Trouillot, *Silencing the Past*, 70–107; for torture and testimony see Elaine Scarry, *The Body in Pain: The Making and Unmaking of the World* (New York: Oxford University Press, 1985), and Saidiya V. Hartman, *Scenes of Subjection: Terror, Slavery, and Self-Making in Nineteenth-Century America* (New York: Oxford University Press, 1997); for examples of historians' efforts to read terror-shaped sources against the grain see Carlo Ginzburg, *The Cheese and the Worms: The Cosmos of a Sixteenth-Century Miller*, trans. John and Anne Tedeschi (Baltimore: The Johns Hopkins University Press, 1980), and Jordan, *Tumult and Silence at Second Creek*.

hushed encounters between slaves whose work took them to town, and in the large uncultivated spaces between plantations; news was spread through an interlocking set of connections between kin networks, mobile skilled and hired slaves, churchgoing slaves, and, apparently, the colony's large population of Coramantee slaves.[32]

The discussions that traveled this hybrid circuitry reflect the difficulty of the organizational task facing slave conspirators. Activating the existing circuitry of everyday life – family, community, and ethnicity – with the historical current of revolt was dangerous, and conspirators took a great deal of care to do it safely. In relating the shape of a conversation between two of the conspirators in Gabriel's Revolt, Douglas Egerton captures the tentative exchange of signs of dissatisfaction which could turn commiseration about the quotidian rigors of slavery into conspiracy. Egerton relates that the conversation in which Ben Woolfolk recruited King began with what must have been a commonplace discussion of King's dissatisfaction with the harsh discipline imposed by a new master. Woolfolk responded to King's comments with a series of non-sequiturs that must have put King on the alert that something important was about to happen – "Are you a true man?" and "Can you keep an important secret?" – and when King didn't shirk from the direction conversation was taking, Woolfolk escalated it to the point of conspiracy: "the Negroes are about to rise and fight the white people for our freedom."[33] In Denmark Vesey's Charleston (1822), the signal that subversive speech was about to begin seems to have been a question about "the news." Over and over again in the Vesey trial transcripts, the phrase "he asked me the news" is followed by accounts of the type of back-and-forth escalation which characterized the conversation between Ben Woolfolk and King. Other times, however, the ostensibly innocuous inquiry was shortly followed by answers which were not so much direct responses as attempts to end the conversation entirely: "I replied I don't know" or "I said I could not answer" or "I begged him to stop it" or "I told him I did not understand such talk and stopped the conversation."[34] The signs that conspiratorial speech was beginning were apparently well known among Charleston slaves and viewed as being so explosive that some slaves wouldn't listen any further.

[32] Egerton, *Gabriel's Rebellion*, 29, 53–65, 119–123; Sidbury, *Ploughshares into Swords*, 61–70; da Costa, *Crowns of Glory, Tears of Blood*, 190–6.
[33] Egerton, *Gabriel's Rebellion*, 56–7. For more on the conversational protocol of plotting a conspiracy see Johnson, *Soul by Soul*, 71–6.
[34] Lionel Kennedy and Thomas Parker, eds., *An Official Report of the Trials of Sundry Negroes Charged with an Attempt to Raise an Insurrection in the State of South Carolina* (Charleston, 1822), 45, 50, 62, 68.

Indeed, the records of the trials which followed New World slave conspiracies are full of objections, of the arguments of slaves who tried to get the conspirators to slow down, leave off, or just leave them alone – of slaves who took a different view of the moment in time. Some were simply afraid to die: "I said I did not want death to take me yet and I quit him," remembered Patrick of a conversation with a man who tried to recruit him on the street. Some framed their objections in strictly pragmatic terms, saying they would join once it was apparent that the rebellion was going to succeed, but not before. Some felt bound by family obligations; asked if he would join Vesey's army, Bram responded, "I was so bound to my father that I could not go without his leave." Others clung to notions of justice and moral conduct that were a familiar feature of their everyday lives but were out of step with the plans of the conspirators. Acts that were axiomatic if you accepted Vesey's definition of the relation between master and slave as a state of "war," for instance, were murder if you did not. Many of those present at a meeting where Vesey outlined his plans remembered that, in the words of Jesse, "some said they thought that it was cruel to kill the ministers and the women and the children."[35] Still others remained divided from the rebels by local, historical, or traditional antagonisms: the Demerara revolt was apparently shot through with the suspicion that field slaves had of their enslaved drivers, that Creoles had of Africans, that the members of one chapel had of the members of another, and that many of those who revolted had of Muslims.

And, finally, there were those who were certain that the time just was not right. In Demerara, Daniel advised conspirators who approached him for help that they should wait for freedom rather than trying to seize it: if it was "a thing ordained by the Almighty," it would come in time. In the aftermath of Gabriel's rebellion, Ben Woolfolk reported that he had advised his fellows to postpone their plans because "I had heard that in the days of old, when the Israelites were in Servitude to King Pharoah, they were taken from him by the Power of God – and were carried away by Moses – God blessed them with an angel to go with him, but that I could see nothing of the kind in these days."[36] Framed as a matter of political organization, and viewed in light of the objections of reluctant slaves, the magnitude of the achievement of slave rebels in the New World is brought into sharper relief. Their task was nothing less than to compress the various scales of

[35] Edward A. Pearson, ed., *Designs against Charleston: The Trial Record of the Denmark Vesey Slave Conspiracy of 1822* (Chapel Hill: University of North Carolina Press, 1999), 172, 195; Kennedy and Parker, eds., *An Official Report*, 59, 68, 90.
[36] Da Costa, *Crowns of Glory, Tears of Blood*, 195, 186; Sidbury, *Ploughshares into Swords*, 76–7.

time running through the everyday life of slavery – the biographical, tribal, metaphysical, and other definitions of self and situation evident in the objections of these reluctant conspirators – into the focused immediacy of a single shared imperative.

Given the extraordinary complexity of the layered temporalities evident in the objections of non-conspirators, it took feats of extraordinary imagination (and sometimes intimidation) to synchronize slaves into a shared account of what was happening and what was to be done about it. Indeed, the shared accounts of time and history for which enslaved conspirators risked their lives and by which subsequent historians have measured their progress along the path from African to American were as much effects as they were causes of the process of revolt. When the Bambara leaders of the Natchez uprising (1731) or the Kongolese warriors at Stono (1739) or the Coramantee rebels in Jamaica (1760), for example, prepared themselves for war through the sacred practices of their homelands, they were making an argument rather than proceeding according to a timeless cultural script known and readily accepted by all of their fellow slaves. As they drummed, danced, swore oaths, assigned ranks, and made plans to enslave rival groups, they were, through ritual practice at the scale of everyday life, giving a moment in time an identifiable historical shape: that of a war.[37] Not only that, they were doing so in a specifically male ritual idiom which underwrote the authority of male warriors to tell everybody else what to do. They were making a politically situated claim on the right to determine the proper correct collective response: this is a war and we are in charge.[38] New World slave rebels were making history by re-making time.

The history slave conspirators tried to make changed shape over time. In Haiti (1791–1804) Toussaint L'Ouverture joined his black followers to the revolution in the rights of man that was re-making the Atlantic world.[39] Gabriel in Virginia and Denmark Vesey in South Carolina imagined their own histories as continuation of the revolution begun in Haiti. Vesey, in fact, courted uncertain slaves by reading to them from the newspapers about the freedoms of Haitian blacks, advertising that he had written to the leaders of the black republic requesting military support, and promising

[37] Hall, *Africans in Colonial Louisiana*, 97–118; John K. Thornton, "African Dimensions of the Stono Rebellion," *The American Historical Review*, 96 (October 1991), 1101–13; Mullin, *Africa in America*, 40–2. See also Sidbury, *Ploughshares into Swords*, 11.
[38] On sex-specific societies see Francesca Declich, "'Gendered Narratives,' History, and Identity: Two Centuries along the Juba River among the Zigula and Shamabra," *History in Africa*, 22 (1995), 93–122, and Gomez, *Exchanging Our Country Marks*, 94–102.
[39] See James, *The Black Jacobins*. James interestingly and continually (see pages 108, 117, 125, 146, and 394) downplays evidence of "African" definitions of the rebellion in Haiti.

that, in the words of two of the conspirators, "Santo Domingo and Africa will help us to get our liberty" by sending ships to carry them to Haiti where "they would receive and protect them."[40] Effectively, Vesey was inviting his co-conspirators to join him in fighting their way out of the history of slavery and into that of a new Black Atlantic, or, as he put it, the "war" between the "blacks" and the "whites." In Southampton County, Virginia, Nat Turner followed a series of signs – marks on his own head and breast from the time of his birth, the voice of the Holy Spirit, drops of blood on the corn in the fields and hieroglyphs on the leaves in the woods, a crashing thunder in the sky in April 1828, and a total eclipse of the sun in February 1831 – to the millennial recognition that "the time was fast approaching when the first should be last and the last should be first."[41] Rather than tracing out points along a foreordained path of historical development, these rebels were investing their everyday lives with temporal purpose – cracking moments open and giving them the shape of imperatives.[42]

In practice, none of these versions of cause and consequence had the simplicity of a pure form; the most successful of the nineteenth-century conspirators, at least, were those who could loosely gather a number of alternative accounts of what exactly it was that was happening into the common purpose of making whatever it was happen. Gabriel, whom the historian Douglas Egerton has identified as a "black Jacobin" seeking to pull Virginia into the history of black liberation that had begun in Haiti, was able to abide, if not himself articulate, other versions of the struggle. When challenged about his choice of the day upon which the slaves were to rise in arms, Gabriel turned to his brother, Martin, who settled the question in terms that were at once prophetic, pragmatic, and deeply personal: "There was this expression in the Bible – delay breeds danger . . . the soldiers were discharged, and the Arms all put away – there was no patrolling . . . and before he would any longer bear what he had borne he would turn out and fight with a stick." And when challenged again: "I read in my Bible where God says, if we will worship him, we should have peace in all our

[40] Genovese, *From Rebellion to Revolution*, 95; Sidbury, *Ploughshares into Swords*, 257–66; Kennedy and Parker, eds., *An Official Report*, 28, 42, 59, 68 (quotations on 42 and 59). See also Julius S. Scott, "Afro-American Sailors and the International Communication Network: The Case of Newport Bowers," in Colin Howell and Richard Twomey, eds., *Jack Tar in History: Essays in Maritime History* (Fredericton, New Brunswick: Acadiensis Press, 1991), 11–36.

[41] Kenneth S. Greenberg, ed., *The Confessions of Nat Turner* (Boston: Bedford Books, 1996), 46–8.

[42] Walter Benjamin puts it this way: "To articulate the past historically does not mean to recognize it 'the way it really was.' It means to seize hold of a memory as it flashes up at a moment of danger. Historical materialism wishes to retain the image of the past which unexpectedly appears to a man singled out by history at a moment of danger." Walter Benjamin, "Theses on the Philosophy of History," in *Illuminations* (New York: Schocken Books, 1968), 255.

Lands, five of you shall conquer a hundred, and a hundred, a thousand of our enemies."[43]

Vesey, whose own ideology apparently synthesized the divided tribal legacies of South Carolina slaves into a revolutionary call for the liberation of a new historical subject, "the blacks," nevertheless organized some of his men into an "Ebo company" and a "Gullah company," the latter led by the conjurer "Gullah" Jack Pritchard.[44] Indeed, Vesey seems to have been remarkable for the number of temporal scales he could invoke in making the argument that the time for armed rising had come – or, even, in answering a single question. Among those who were present when Vesey was asked whether ministers, women, and children should be killed, there were slaves who recalled at least three versions of temporal scale of his response. "He then read in the Bible where God commanded, that all should be cut off, both men, women, and children, and said, he believed, it was no sin for us to do so, for the lord had commanded us to do it," remembered Rolla. "He thought it was for our safety not to spare one white skin alive, for this was the plan they pursued in St. Domingo," remembered Jesse. "Smart asked him if you were going to kill the women and children – Denmark answered what was the use of killing the louse and leaving the nit – Smart said, my God, what a sin – Vesey told Smart he had not a man's heart, told Smart that he was a friend to Buckra," read Smart Anderson's account of the meeting.[45]

Even Nat Turner was not above relying on the intricate complexities of psychological domination which characterized the daily life of slavery to help him clear the path for God's unfolding Providence – "Jack, I knew, was only a tool in the hands of Hark," he said of one of the slaves whom he entrusted with his plans.[46] Working their way up and down scales of time – metaphysical, political, local, psychological – the theorists of New World slave conspiracies were able to urge any number of historical agents – a tribal warrior, a Christian soldier, a liberal individual, a black man – to anneal themselves to the gathered strength of a single struggle.

When, in the aftermath of events, slaveholders tried to figure out what had caused the uprisings that had convulsed their societies, slaveholders restaged them as effects of their own agency rather than that of their slaves: *they* had allowed their slaves too much liberty (or not enough); *they* had

---

[43] Sidbury, 76–7. Sidbury identifies the source for Martin's second statement as Leviticus 26:6–8.
[44] For the racial ideology and tribal organization of the Vesey conspiracy see Gomez, *Exchanging Our Country Marks*, 1–3.
[45] Kennedy and Parker, eds., *An Official Report*, 46, 59, 90.
[46] Greenberg, ed., *The Confessions of Nat Turner*, 48.

given their slaves too much access to Christianity (or not enough); *they* had provided for too few patrols or allowed too many black seamen or poor whites or Frenchmen or missionaries or steam doctors or Yankee peddlers to come into contact with their slaves. They told themselves stories about what happened that emphasized their own agency and reworked the unfathomed aspirations of their slaves, whether they were African, Jacobin, or millenarian, into a part of history as they recognized it – the ongoing history of New World slavery.[47]

As I have argued, historians have often taken the slaveholders at their word and written these events into the history of American slavery as accounts of a labor force in arms. But look again and these conspiracies look like battle plans in a war for control of the New World, efforts to force Euro-Americans into another place in time: into the well-grooved tribal histories of African wars to determine who would be slave and who would be master; the history of the Black Atlantic that had begun in Haiti with the idea that freedom (rather than mastery) was the opposite of slavery; or the history of the Christian millennium when the first would be last and the last would be first. The seemingly neutral phrase "slave revolt" provides less a description of these events than it does an account of one side (the winning side) of a bloody conflict which was itself characterized by the clash of alternative understandings of time and history – of exactly what it was that was at stake in the Americas.

---

[47] See Trouillot, *Silencing the Past*, 70–107.

CHAPTER 10

The Green Atlantic: radical reciprocities between Ireland and America in the long eighteenth century

Kevin Whelan

A neglected topic in standard treatment of the Enlightenment is its engage-ment with minority cultures. A focus on the Enlightenment's excluded others – Catholics, Gaelic, Indian, Afro-American, indigenous peoples – offers a rich theoretical and historical topic. It also exposes counter-currents within the Enlightenment that sought to bring these cultures into moder-nity on their own terms, rather than within the protocols of progress, civility, and inevitable cultural obsolescence. These strands made space for a bottom-up process of engagement, a vernacular enlightenment. Ireland, Europe's major internal colony, offers an appropriate terrain for consider-ing these complex issues. This chapter opens up the Irish experience of the Enlightenment and its others, viewed through the optic of Ireland's relation-ship with the Atlantic world in the long eighteenth century. It also explores the cultural and political reciprocities between Ireland, America, and the Caribbean in the late eighteenth century at the level of both elite and radi-cal politics. Inspired by, but following a different trajectory to, recent work on the Atlantic world, this chapter inserts the Irish example into the wider literature, expanding the insular horizons of Irish historiography. To the top-down and Anglocentric Atlantic Revolution discovered in the 1960s, we might now want to add red (bottom-up) and green (Irish) Atlantic tinges.[1] Renewed study of the Irish impact of the American Revolution is first required: it has been neglected in favor of the French one.[2] This accentuates an artificially sharp divide between the 1780s and the 1790s in Irish historiography.

[1] R. Palmer, *The Age of the Democratic Revolution: A Political History of Europe and America 1760–1800* (2 vols., Princeton University Press, 1959–64); Peter Linebaugh and Marcus Rediker, *The Many-Headed Hydra: The Hidden History of the Revolutionary Atlantic* (London: Polity, 2000); Nini Rodgers, "Ireland and the Black Atlantic in the Eighteenth Century," *Irish Historical Studies*, 76 (2000), 174–92.
[2] Maurice O'Connell, *Irish Politics and Social Conflict in the Age of the American Revolution* (Philadelphia: University of Pennsylvania Press, 1965).

IRELAND AND THE AMERICAN REVOLUTION

The Seven Years War (1754–61) redefined the nature of the relationship between the imperial center and its peripheries. Not least, it required a Pitt-prompted London to relinquish centralized, coercive military discipline, to abandon a fiscal policy of forced contributions, and to embrace the Americans as allies and partners in empire. The spectacular success of this novel policy enabled the British to crush the French challenge.[3] However, this constitutional modus vivendi was not continued after the cessation of war. Halifax and Grenville pursued instead an aggressive policy of an "incorporating" rather than a "federal" empire, with a new centralized administrative architecture, radiating authority from a controlling metropolitan center. These new policies (on taxation, restriction of settlement, smuggling, military discipline) alienated and embittered the Americans, as the 1760s became a decade of destabilization. Increased imperial expenditure and indebtedness led to increased taxation – and resentment. Rather than partners in empire as free-born Britons, the Americans felt slighted, diminished to the level of mere imperial subjects, with duties not rights. American exceptionalism then solidified as a hurt defense against this newly aggressive, exclusive British nationalism – metropolitan, militant, imperial, xenophobic.[4] This loss of status as free-born Britons particularly galvanized the Anglo-American elite, inflaming their sense of occupying a precarious, marginalized, and exposed constitutional position. Their response was to develop a more explicit sense of their distinctive destiny. From this perspective, the American Revolution revolved around not the birth of a nation but a messy divorce.

These American developments resonated in Ireland. Since the seventeenth century, Ireland had been increasingly absorbed into the Atlantic world as a result of its conquest by the emerging British state: the Atlantic world was increasingly a British world too, and Ireland's participation in it was always regulated through this distinctive British filter.[5] In both Ireland and America, the Anglo-colonial elite shared growing ideological reciprocities, as was demonstrated in the immense Irish interest in the American war. In Ireland as in America, the 1760s had been a decade of destabilization:

[3] Fred Anderson, *Crucible of War: The Seven Years War and the Fate of Empire in British North America 1754–1766* (New York: Knopf, 2000).
[4] T. H. Breen, "Ideology and Nationalism on the Eve of the American Revolution: Revisions Once More in Need of Revising," *Journal of American History*, 84 (1997), 13–39.
[5] Kevin Whelan, "Ireland in the world system 1600–1800" in H. J. Nitz, ed., *The Early Modern World System in Geographical Perspective* (Stuttgart: F. Steiner, 1993), 204–18.

explosive but episodic economic development; rampant population growth; increased emigration flows at the end of the war; a broadening social base of political participation (the *Freeman's Journal* was established in 1764) and the emergence of an identifiable public opinion; the explosion of potent social protest, notably the agrarian redresser Whiteboy movement; the explicit political organization of the hitherto cowed Catholics and increased discontent amidst the Ulster Presbyterians against the Erastian Williamite settlement. These new energies received additional inputs during the American crisis, crystallizing in the Volunteer movement.[6] A direct response to the removal of regular British army troops to the American sphere, the Volunteers quickly evolved from a paramilitary into a patriot political body. The American war allowed Irish patriot politicians to take advantage of the imperial crisis to readjust the external constitutional relationship between Ireland and Britain, and to contemplate readjusting the internal relationship between the Irish parliament and the Irish people.[7] The patriots had three essential ingredients for success: articulate political leadership from Henry Grattan; a national political pressure group (the Volunteers) with paramilitary capabilities; and a weak, internally fissured English cabinet. Selfish English policies were blamed in the 1770s for accentuating a wartime depression by their embargo on Irish provisions export to the colonies – a classic demonstration of the cavalier way in which Ireland's commercial interests were high-handedly sacrificed as a result of its constitutional subordination. The patriots could now fuse the potent combination of constitutional and commercial grievance, to which the American precedent gave the oxygen of publicity. Issues of sovereignty, imperial rights, mutual obligations were all aired incessantly in both countries, and an emerging sense of a shared grievance and a shared destiny developed. Benjamin Franklin argued that America's struggle was Ireland's struggle and he was rapturously received by the radicals on his Dublin visit in 1771, with James Napper Tandy to the fore.[8] If America was spurned constitutionally and then taxed without representation by a rapacious imperial center, Ireland inevitably would be next. The American struggle transfixed Ireland. George

---

[6] Breandan Mac Suibhne, "Whiskey, Potatoes and True-Born Patriot Paddies: Volunteering and the Construction of the Irish Nation in North-West Ulster 1770–1789" in Peter Jupp and Eoin Magennis, eds., *Crowds in Ireland, 1720–1920* (Basingstoke: Macmillan, 2000), 45–82.

[7] Maurice Bric, "Ireland, America and the Reassessment of a Special Relationship 1760–83," *Eighteenth Century Ireland*, 11 (1996), 88–119.

[8] Franklin later claimed in 1778 that "the Irish patriots were disposed to be friends to America": *Hibernian Journal*, November 4, 1778. He had visited Ireland on two occasions in 1769 and 1771: see J. Bennet Nolan, *Benjamin Franklin in Scotland and Ireland* (Philadelphia: University of Pennsylvania Press, 1938).

Washington became a fashionable icon. Louisa Connolly placed his bust on the mantlepiece of Ireland's finest mansion, Castletown House. The great man corresponded with Irish patriots like Edward Newenham and congratulated the country on its constitutional achievement in 1782: "I would felicitate the Kingdom of Ireland on their emancipation from British controul . . . enjoying a freedom of legislation, and an unconfined extension of trade."[9] The patriot politician Henry Flood waxed lyrical: "A voice from America [had] shouted to liberty, the echo of it caught your people as it passed along the Atlantic, and they re-echoed the voice till it reverberated here."[10] The Charitable Irish Society in Boston, meeting again in 1784 after a gap of ten years, congratulated themselves that the Americans had "conquered one of the greatest and most potent nations on the globe so as to have peace and independency." They then pointed the moral: "May our friends, countrymen in Ireland, behave like the brave Americans till they recover their liberties."[11]

The American Revolution eased the transition of republicanism from outmoded classical theory to modern reality. By the 1790s republicanism had become an accepted political framework for conceptualizing modern commercial society.[12] As William Sampson phrased it, "The American Revolution had reduced the theories of the great philosophers of England, France and other countries into practice."[13] The influence of Paineite language was also important in establishing a "new republican" agenda. Paineite republicanism was a self-consciously international language, which fused radical and Christian principles into a radical vernacular vocabulary. The "old republicanism" of the civil humanist variety had proved signally bankrupt in grappling with the realities of dynamic, complex, modern societies, as opposed to idealized veneration of antique agrarian democracies. The American Revolution dramatically closed the gap between the abstract and idealized ancient world and the realities of modern commercial society. It renovated the concept of virtue. America occupied a pivotal position in the emergence of this new republicanism – an ambitious attempt to ground

[9] Letter of August 10, 1783 in Jared Sparkes, ed., *The Writings of George Washington* (12 vols., Boston: American Stationers Company, 1834–7), VII, 90–1.
[10] Cited in Denis Gwynn, *The Struggle for Catholic Emancipation 1750–1829* (New York: Longman, 1928), 29.
[11] James Bernard Cullen, *The Story of the Irish in Boston* (Boston: J. B. Cullen, 1893), 34.
[12] For work that has revised the older model of republicanism drawn by Caroline Robbins and J. G. A. Pocock, see Judith Shklar, "Montesquieu and the New Republicanism," in G. Bock, Q. Skinner and M. Viroli, eds., *Machiavelli and Republicanism* (Cambridge University Press, 1990), 265–79; James Livesey, "Happiness Universal? Commercial Republicanism in the 1790s," ch. 2 of his *Making Democracy in the French Revolution* (Cambridge, MA: Harvard University Press, 2001), 48–87.
[13] William Sampson, *Memoirs* (New York, 1807), 311.

antiquated classical republicanism in a modern context of trade, commerce, social stratification, consumerism, and mobile identities. The success of the novel American experiment confirmed its symbolic and practical role as "the land of liberty." Jeffersonian political economy, developed out of Locke, Smith, and especially Paine, espoused a liberal democracy in which cohesion would be maintained under a common adherence to republican rubrics, under the aegis of the law, rather than by a coercive, centralized "big" government. America then could weld economic progress to social harmony, rooted in republican principles of "compact and equality," under a regime of consent rather than coercion.[14] It could diminish the clash of class interest by favoring agrarian independence over credit and trade, avoiding the federalist obsession with the mercantilist, militarist, and imperial destiny of America.

THE DISSENT OF DISSENT: IRISH PRESBYTERIANS

The American experiment had two unintended side-effects. The departure from the British system of what had been thirteen heterogeneous colonies with a mish-mash of constitutional arrangements exposed Ireland more nakedly as a remaining anomaly in the redefined imperial system. There was also the problem of absorbing Ireland's dominant Catholicism within a definition of Britishness.[15] In England as in America, Catholics represented less than one per cent (two in Scotland) of the population; in Ireland, the figure was close to 80 percent. But the threat of Canada seceding to the French encouraged British toleration of Roman Catholicism in the Quebec Act of 1774: its passing threw into ever more glaring relief the anomalous issue of the Irish Catholics.

In Burke's famous phrase, the American Revolution had represented "the dissent of dissent" – with the additional complication that American dissent was largely an offshoot of Ulster.[16] In the first half of the eighteenth century, a thousand Presbyterians left Ireland annually (an emigration rate of four in every thousand), with peaks in the 1720s and again in the 1770s

---

[14] Peter Onuf, *Jefferson's Empire: The Language of American Nationhood* (Charlottesville: University of Virginia, 2000); Joyce Appleby, *Inheriting the Revolution: The First Generation of Americans* (Cambridge, MA: Harvard University Press, 2000); Joanne Freeman, *Affairs of Honor: National Politics in the New Republic* (New Haven: Yale University Press, 2001).

[15] Kevin Whelan, "The Other Within: Ireland, Britain and the Act of Union," in Daire Keogh and Kevin Whelan, eds., *Acts of Union: The Causes, Contexts and Consequences of the Act of Union* (Dublin: Four Courts Press, 2001), 13–33.

[16] Elizabeth Nybakken, "New Light on the Old Side: Irish Influences on Colonial Presbyterianism," *Journal of American History*, 68 (1982), 13–32.

when it reached ten in every thousand in response to the opening of the American frontier and a linen recession in Ulster.[17] The earlier emigration had been driven by the ministers and it frequently involved the migration of entire congregations, fleeing Anglican oppression in Ireland.[18] A stark Ireland/America opposition now came into play in the dissenting imagination.

The American experience – reported in detail to a highly literate population – fueled the Ulster-Presbyterian culture of grievance, potent in a covenanted community, tightly knit by kinship, geographically concentrated, and with a sharp spur to maintain a distinct sectarian and ethnic identity through their juxtaposition with English Anglican and Irish Catholic communities. The Test Act of 1704 excluded from public office all those who refused to take communion according to the rites of the established church and, despite indemnity acts, inflicted second-class citizenship status on dissenters. Between 1704 and 1780, they were excluded from local government; their meeting houses were confined to the disreputable fringes of the towns; their restless spread south from their Ulster plantation heartland was vigorously resisted by the Anglican elite, who viewed them with distaste as "the most irritable and the most implacable men in the world."[19]

These early anti-establishment sentiments were to create a crucial bridge to the political radicalism of the 1790s. Implacable differences between an Anglican elite and a Presbyterian "middling sort" ensured that in eighteenth-century Ireland there was no whole Protestant community.[20] They also exposed the weakness of the Irish Erastian state, precariously founded on 5 percent of the population. The theoretical possibility always existed of a political alliance between dissenters and papists against this narrow Anglican elite. The American war increased the possibility. The Ulster colonists settled mostly in the American backcountry: they were frontiersmen in America as in Ireland, as they fanned out from Philadelphia and Charleston. By 1790, they comprised 10 percent of the American population (with a high of 20 percent in South Carolina, and 15 percent in

---

[17] L. M. Cullen, "The Irish Diaspora of the Seventeenth and Eighteenth Centuries," in Nicholas Canny, ed., *Europeans on the Move: Studies on European Emigration 1500–1800* (Oxford: Clarendon Press, 1994), 113–49; Marianne Wokeck, "Irish Immigration to the Delaware Valley," in Wokeck, *Trade in Strangers: The Beginnings of Mass Migration to North America* (University Park: Pennsylvania State University Press, 1999), 167–220.

[18] Ian McBride, "Presbyterians in the Penal Era," *Bullan*, 1, 2 (1994), 73–86.

[19] Charles Woodmason, "The Carolina Backcountry on the Eve of the Revolution: The Journal and Other Writings of Charles Woodmason," edited by Richard J. Hooker (Chapel Hill: University of North Carolina Press, 1953), 60.

[20] Terence Brown, *The Whole Protestant Community: The Making of an Historical Myth* (Derry: Field Day Theatre Co., 1985).

Pennsylvania).[21] They carried with them to America their democratic congregational spirit; their resentment and aggression; their anti-establishment, anti-deferential ethos. In America, this took the form of an anti-urban, anti-Quaker, anti-Anglican bias. It also embraced the radical egalitarianism of the frontier (notable for its response to the Great Awakening).[22] When the American war broke out, they were initially cautious, skeptical of its urban, East Coast origins. They joined it from a calculated fear of an Indian-British alliance against them (a reprise of 1763); they quickly gave the American cause military muscle and indomitable determination. One Hessian mercenary in 1778 was moved to call it "not an American Rebellion: it is nothing more or less than an Irish-Scotch Presbyterian Rebellion."[23]

Backcountry support for the patriot cause also led to the demand for and granting of an egalitarian expansion of the electorate and a dilution of aristocratic privilege. Above all, the great victory of American dissent was the separation of church and state in the new constitution, a crushing defeat for the Anglican church.[24] This victory over their Anglican enemies enthralled Irish Presbyterians. Rev. William Steel Dickson (later a prominent United Irishman) opposed "the unnatural, impolitic and unprincipled war in America"[25] while the lord-lieutenant in 1775 described Irish Presbyterians as "Americans in their hearts."[26] Close commercial and kin connections deepened their interest in the American experiment, and emboldened the Volunteers. The American experience was constantly in the air, as in 1780 when "an elastic uncontrollable spirit . . . pervaded the six northern counties."[27] Anglicans were seen in much the same light as American loyalists, and Irish Anglican fears escalated in the excited aftermath of the French Revolution. In Derry in 1796, it was said: "The Presbyterians of every different sect are a stiff, proud, discontented people. They wish to have no king but a republican government. They were all on the

[21] Thomas Purvis, "The European Ancestry of the United States Population 1790," *William and Mary Quarterly*, 41 (1984), 85–135.

[22] Nathan Hatch, *The Democratization of American Christianity* (New Haven: Yale University Press, 1989).

[23] Cited in David Doyle, *Ireland, Irishmen and Revolutionary America 1760–1820* (Dublin: Mercier Press, 1981), 110.

[24] Howard Miller, "The Grammar of Liberty: American Presbyterians and the American Revolution," *Journal of Presbyterian History*, 54 (1976), 19–29.

[25] William Steel Dickson, *A Narrative of the Confinement and Exile of William Steel Dickson* (Dublin, 1812), 7.

[26] Harcourt to North, October 11, 1775, in William Harcourt and Lewis Harcourt, 1st Viscount Harcourt, *Harcourt Papers* (14 vols., Oxford: J. Parker and Co., 1880), IX, 363.

[27] Frederick Augustus Hervey [Bishop of Derry] to John Foster, MP, Dublin, April 17, 1780, Royal Irish Academy, MS G 39/2.

Americans' side during the American War. Now they are all on the French side."[28]

The fall of the Bastille ushered in the possibility of a novel alliance between Presbyterian and Catholic radicals.[29] The Volunteer project and its enthusiastic Presbyterian backing had acrimoniously disintegrated over the old bugbear of popery. Parliamentary reform was chimerical without including the majority Catholics, but many patriots (including talismanic figures like Charlemont and Flood) balked at this formidable hurdle. This was one area of the Irish experience with no obvious American resonance. Catholics comprised less than one percent of the population there in 1776 and no serious thought was required about their relationship to a reformed constitutional and parliamentary system. The French Revolution regenerated the stalled American momentum here. A democratic republican experiment in the paradigmatic papal country broke through the sectarian boom that immobilized political radicalism, and a wave of radical energy coursed through the stagnant channels of Irish politics. The United Irishmen, established in 1791, represented a novel Irish attempt to breach the sectarian limits of the Glorious Revolution by extending full citizenship rights to Catholics.[30] Their movement for the first time united in a single political organization a coalition of Presbyterian and Catholic radicals, inspired by the cumulative impact of the American and French revolutions.

When the radical Volunteers marched in Dublin on Bastille Day 1790, they carried a transparency of a large illuminated globe, in which the New World (America) was represented as shedding a blaze of light on the Old World (Europe). They also carried a bust of Franklin with the motto: "Where liberty is, there is my country."[31] The principal cohort of United Irish leaders (Theobald Wolfe Tone, Lord Edward FitzGerald, Thomas Addis Emmet, Arthur O'Connor, Samuel Neilson, Oliver Bond, William James MacNevin, James Hope, William Sampson, Bagenal Harvey) were all born between 1761 and 1764 and were teenagers during the American War of Independence. Archibald Hamilton Rowan was later to say about

---

[28] Letter from Derry area to James Lenderick (Shane's Castle, Co. Antrim) [late 1796], National Archives of Ireland, Rebellion Papers, 620/53/23.

[29] Kevin Whelan, *The Tree of Liberty: Radicalism, Catholicism and the Construction of Irish Identity* (Cork University Press, 1996).

[30] Kevin Whelan, *Fellowship of Freedom: The United Irishmen and 1798* (Cork University Press, 1998).

[31] John Binns, *Recollections of the Life of John Binns* (Philadelphia, 1854), 26.

this period: "I regretted not being an American but I made up my mind that if I ever could, I would play the same role in Ireland."[32] The American precedent was always present in the self-image of the United Irishmen. Their newspaper, the *Northern Star*, looked back on the gloomy political outlook of the 1770s and noted that "A sudden light from America shone through our prison."[33] A favorite toast was: "A fourth and fourteenth July to Ireland: we will die to achieve them."[34] America had long occupied an evocative rhetorical space as "the land of liberty," being used in advertisements for emigrant ships from the 1780s. John Dunlap (printer of the American Declaration of Independence) wrote back from Philadelphia to his native Strabane in 1785: "The young men of Ireland who wish to be free and happy should leave it and come here as quick as possible. There is no place in the world where a man meets so rich a reward for good conduct and industry as in America."[35] As repression mounted in the 1790s, the attraction of America increased. Bridget Brannon, fearful for her Catholic sons in a Protestant-dominated Tyrone militia, advised them: "I desire you and Henry to save as much as will take you to America for no poor man can live here."[36] From Wexford in the spring of 1798, the United Irishman Walter Devereux wrote to his brother in Utica that he was ready to "leave this land of tyranny and seek a land of liberty."[37]

THE UNITED IRISHMEN AND JEFFERSONIAN REPUBLICANISM

So many Irish left in the 1790s – as many as 60,000 – as to alter the complexion of American political life.[38] Over 3,000 flooded into Philadelphia, the capital of the new republic (1790–1800), augmenting its population by 20 percent. This emigration had two novel characteristics. Many were ideological immigrants, drawn to America by its republican character; these immigrants did not pursue assimilation, but retained a strong sense of

---

[32] A. H. Rowan, Memorial to the Committee of Public Safety, March 18, Correspondance politique Angleterre, 1794, Paris, vol. 588, f. 271.
[33] *Northern Star*, October 3, 1796.
[34] Cited in Joseph Shulim, "John Daly Burk: Irish Revolutionist and American Patriot," *Transactions of the American Philosophical Society*, n.s., 54 (1964), 3–60, at 25.
[35] John Dunlap (Philadelphia) to Robert Rutherford (Strabane, Co. Tyrone), May 12, 1785, Public Record Office of Northern Ireland, Dunlap MS., T 1336/1/27.
[36] Bridget Brannon (Strabane, Co. Tyrone) to Pat Kerr, Lord Abercorn's Company, Dublin, August 14, 1796, National Archives of Ireland, Rebellion Papers, 620/24/131.
[37] Walter Devereux (The Leap, Co. Wexford) to John Devereux (Utica, New York), April 1, 1798, in possession of John Devereux Kernan, New Haven, CT.
[38] The figure is derived from Hans Jurgen Grabbe, "European Immigration to the United States in the Early National Period 1783–1820," *Proceedings of the American Philosophical Society*, 134 (1989), 194.

ethnic allegiance (this "nationalist" sensibility was not in evidence prior to the impact of the Volunteers in the 1780s). In the 1790s, Hibernian societies sprang up in American cities. Irish immigrants were immediately immersed in the Federalist /Republican struggle.[39] The Federalists tended to be Anglophile, Francophobe, nativist, and opposed to a party political system. The Republicans promoted a liberal democratic agenda of pluralist politics, and welcomed political refugees. The Federalists were seen as favoring a hierarchical, aristocratic society, based on high taxation and a centralized executive. For the Irish, it was easy to transpose the existing Irish "aristocrat/democrat" divide into this American context. The Irish vote became important in Baltimore, New York, and especially Philadelphia with its permissive voting laws (55 percent of naturalizations there between 1789 and 1806 were Irish).[40] The Irish were influential in developing the language of the first party political system and were also a driving force in the creation of the Republican party cohering around Thomas Jefferson.[41] The United Irish émigrés, in particular, through their pivotal role in print culture, were especially important in generating a national profile for what became Jeffersonian republicanism. From vantage points in journalism, law, and politics, the United Irishmen added sophisticated propaganda, organizational know-how, class-muscle, and ethnic solidarity, weapons sharply honed in an Irish context of adversarial and aggressive political division. In 1795, the newly exiled Archibald Hamilton Rowan "amused himself with the politics of America and is as busy, as sincere and as zealous as he was in Kilmainham jail."[42]

These skills were crucial to seeing off the Federalist challenge, with its incipient nativism, notably in the Alien and Sedition Acts, themselves an explicit response to the 1798 Rebellion in Ireland, with the consequent fear of a deluge of disgruntled United Irish rebels pouring into the United States.[43] The Federalists represented the insecurity of early American state-formation, with their intense fear of destabilization, social ferment, internal shredding. Hence the Federalist insistence on immigrants shedding their

---

[39] Maurice Bric, "The Irish and the Evolution of the New Politics in America," in P. J. Drudy, ed., *The Irish in America: Emigration, Assimilation and Impact* (Cambridge University Press, 1985), 143–68.

[40] Rex Syndergaard, "Wild Irishmen and the Alien and Sedition Act," *Eire-Ireland*, 9 (1974), 14–24.

[41] Maurice Bric, "Ireland, Irishmen and the Broadening of the Late Eighteenth-Century Philadelphia Polity," Ph.D. thesis, The John Hopkins University, 1990.

[42] *Gazette of the United States*, July 27, 1795.

[43] J. M. Smith, *Freedom's Fetters: The Alien and Sedition Laws and America's Civil Liberties* (Ithaca: Cornell University Press, 1966); J. Miller, *Crisis in Freedom: The Alien and Sedition Acts* (Boston: Little, Brown, 1952).

cultural identity in the American public sphere of politics: as this happened, the Irish shifted their allegiance from Washington to Jefferson.

The United Irishmen espoused Jefferson, described by them as "the first man for purity of character, talents and amiable manners in the Republican world."[44] His victory in 1800 was a second American Revolution that saw off the Federalist, Anglophile, and loyalist challenge. It also clarified the American debate on national character. The Federalist "One America" position and its dislike of "the multifarious heterogeneous compound"[45] had to yield to a more pluralist conception of America as a composite mosaic of cultures unified by equality under republican law rather than culturally homogeneous and socially conservative. The Irish espousal of ethno-particularism was crucial to this development of a multicultural, cosmopolitan society and to the emergence of a bipolar party system.[46] Thus, the republicans ended the 1790s with an increasingly national as opposed to a local voice. Print culture was essential to this achievement, and here the émigrés were a key component. Ten of the United Irish group – John Binns, John Daly Burk, James Carey, Mathew Carey, Watty Cox, Denis Driscol, William Duane, Edward Gillespy, Samuel Neilson, Thomas O'Connor – became editors of newspapers – some of them highly influential at a national level, like Duane's *Aurora* in Philadelphia.[47] Their opponents, notably William Cobbett,[48] recognized the importance of these republican editors, especially Duane, Binns, and the two Careys.

The émigré printers – Mathew Carey, John Chambers, Thomas Stephens, Patrick Byrne, Bernard Dornin – were also highly influential in both the original and the reprint trade. Many Dublin printers flocked to America, under the twin pressures of political repression and the implementation of copyright restrictions after the Act of Union of 1800.[49] By

[44] Watty Cox, *Advice to Emigrants* (Dublin, 1802), 11. See also John Daly Burk's panegyric: *An oration delivered on 4 March 1803 at the courthouse in Petersburg to celebrate the election of Thomas Jefferson and the triumph of republicanism* (Petersburg, VA, 1803): Binns, *Recollections*, 239.

[45] *People's Friend* [New York], May 2, 1807.

[46] Walter Walsh, "Religion, Ethnicity, and History: Clues to the Cultural Construction of Law," in Ronald Bayor and Timothy Meagher, eds., *The New York Irish* (Baltimore: The Johns Hopkins University Press, 1995), 48–69.

[47] Kim Philips, "William Duane, Revolutionary Editor," Ph.D. thesis, University of California, Berkeley, 1968: J. M. Smith, "William Duane and the *Aurora,*" *Pennsylvania Magazine of History and Biography* 77 (1953), 123–55: James Greene, *Mathew Carey: Publisher and Patriot* (Philadelphia: University of Pennsylvania Press, 1985); Michael Durey, "Irish Deism and Jefferson's Republic: Denis Driscol in Ireland and America 1793–1810," *Eire-Ireland*, 25 (1990), 56–76; Shulim, "John Daly Burk."

[48] See David Wilson, *United Irishmen, United States: Immigrant Radicals in the Early Republic* (Ithaca: Cornell University Press, 1998).

[49] Mary Pollard, "John Chambers, Printer and United Irishman," *Irish Book Lore*, 3 (1964), 1–22; Pollard, *Dublin's Trade in Books, 1550–1800* (Oxford: Clarendon Press, 1989): Pollard, *A Dictionary of Members of the Dublin Book Trade 1550–1800* (London, 2000).

1796, it was noted of the Philadelphia, New York, and Baltimore book trade that "the whole trade centres among foreigners."[50] These republican publishers and printers consolidated public opinion around the Jeffersonian project and also broadened the parameters of the imagined political nation to include the 1790s flood of immigrants. In the aftermath of 1798, America became a magnet for radicals. John Daly Burk in 1796 observed that "the moment a stranger puts his foot on the soil of America, he is a free man and is virtually a citizen."[51] The Hibernian Society of Charleston offered the toast "The United States of America – the abode of liberty and the persecuted patriot's secure asylum" on St Patrick's Day in 1811.[52] To the earlier arrivals (Wolfe Tone, Tandy, Rowan, Daly Burk, Reynolds) were added well-known figures like Henry Jackson, Thomas Addis Emmet, William Sampson, and William James MacNevin. At least thirteen Presbyterian ministers and probationers arrived, including the soon-to-be-influential David Bailie Warden. The *Salem Gazette* colorfully reported in 1798 that "every ship vomited United Irishmen on the American shore."[53] In 1800, a shipload of four hundred '98 men landed at Norfolk, Virginia, whence they quickly dispersed into the surrounding countryside.[54]

THE UNITED IRISH ORGANIZATION IN AMERICA

In these circumstances, it is not surprising to find the United Irish organization establishing itself in America. The United men had always prided themselves on belonging to a cosmopolitan project with a common republican ideology and shared political objectives. They had forged close links with the French Directory and with their sister organizations in England (United Britons) and Scotland (United Scotsmen).[55] It was therefore entirely natural for them to establish the American Society of United Irishmen on August 8, 1797, initially in Philadelphia. Their printed constitution[56] emphasized Ireland's "colonial subserviency," which induced internal "division" and subjected them to "a foreign tyranny, more odious than Asiatic despotism." But "this is the time to act": as "Irishmen are united at home, we will not be disunited abroad." Membership of the American

[50] *Recorder* [Richmond, VA] April 3, 1802.
[51] *Boston Polar Star*, October 6, 1796. Binns described America as "the sure and certain refuge of every friend of freedom and every honest man": Binns, *Narrative*, 28.
[52] *Irish Magazine*, June 1811, 260.   [53] *Salem Gazette*, September 18, 1798.
[54] Carl Wittke, *The Irish in America* (Baton Rouge: Louisiana State University Press, 1959), 76.
[55] E. W. McFarland, *Ireland and Scotland in the Age of Revolution: Planting the Green Bough* (Edinburgh University Press, 1994).
[56] *Declaration and Constitution of the American Society of United Irishmen* (Philadelphia, 1797).

Society would be open to three categories – "those who suffered in the cause of freedom," those who exhibited "zeal for the rights of mankind," and those of "moral character and civism." The political test introduced the following questions: "Do you think Great Britain ought of right to govern Ireland?" and "Are you willing to do all that in you lies to promote the emancipation of Ireland and the establishment of a republican form of government?" The "Secret Test," sworn in the presence of the supreme being, pledged the oath-taker to pursue "the attainment of liberty and equality to mankind in whatever nation I may reside." The "General Executive Committee" would be based on at least two state committees; a state committee would comprise at least two sections (with a maximum number of eighty members). The general committee would "possess the direction of the great interests of the whole society" and there would also be committees of secrecy and correspondence. The recognition words were the Irish-language versions of fraternity (*codramacht*) and liberty (*saoirseacht*). United Irish societies are subsequently known to have existed in Philadelphia, Wilmington, and Montgomery County (Pennsylvania), Delaware, Baltimore (Maryland), Charleston (South Carolina), Albany (New York), and Ohio. The Philadelphia Society – including Congressman Matthew Lyons, the Carey brothers, James Reynolds, John Daly Burk, and William Duane – had by far the highest profile and attracted the ire of the Federalists. Some believed it to contain an assassination committee and described the United Irishmen as "the dagger men of Philadelphia." William Cobbett described them as "a reckless and rebellious tribe of Jacobins," "factious villains which Great Britain and Ireland have vomited from their shores."[57] A Federalist politician described Irish republicans in 1800 as "United Irishmen, freemasons and the most God-provoking democrats on this side of hell."[58] In Congress in 1797, Congressman Harrison Gray Otis of Boston said that he did "not wish to invite hordes of wild Irishmen nor the turbulent and disorderly of all parts of the world to come here with a view to disturb our tranquility."[59] The United Irishmen were targeted alongside French republicans – notably Constantin de Volney, himself a leading influence on United Irish thought.[60]

The upshot was the three Alien and Sedition Acts of June and July 1798, some of the most repressive legislation ever passed in the United States. The first act – seen as a direct attack on the Irish – lengthened the naturalization

---

[57] William Cobbett, *Detection of a conspiracy formed by the United Irishmen with the evident intention of aiding the tyrant of France in subverting the government of the United States* (Philadelphia, 1798), 22.
[58] Uriah Tracy of Connecticut, cited in Miller, *Freedom's Fetters*, 24.
[59] Quoted in Miller, *Freedom's Fetters*, 24.   [60] See Whelan, *Tree of Liberty*, 78–9.

process from five to fourteen years. The United Irishmen, notably in Philadelphia, organized to oppose it. James Reynolds and William Duane were arrested when challenged by Federalists while collecting signatures for a petition against it outside the gates of the Presbyterian and Catholic churches in Philadelphia on July 8, 1799 – an incident dubbed "the Irish riot" by their Federalist opponents.[61] The Alien Enemies Act of July 6, 1798 conferred a presidential power of internment for nationals of countries against whom America was at war. The Sedition Act of July 1798 expanded this power to cover internal enemies, extending to publications seen as hostile. The act was interpreted as targeted against the republican press, and as a serious assault on the freedom of the press. The United Irishmen were to the fore in protesting against these acts.

The issue dominated the 1799 Pennsylvanian gubernatorial election, won by the republican Thomas McKean, a former president of the Hibernian Society, and described by his opponents as a Presbyterian "Paddy."[62] A second massive row brewed over the proposed immigration of the high-profile United Irish "state prisoners" to the USA in 1799 – successfully blocked by Rufus King, the American minister to Great Britain, after a vigorously prosecuted campaign. King urged John Adams that United Irish "principles and habits would be pernicious to the order and industry of our people and I can't persuade myself that the malcontents of any country will ever become useful citizens of another."[63] However, the republican momentum of 1799 carried into 1800 and the election of Jefferson marked the death-knell of the Federalist party.[64] Jefferson viewed the United Irishmen as kindred spirits (some of them worked with him on the design of Monticello) and he repealed the Alien and Sedition Acts in 1804. The United Irishman John Nevin, who had fled Ireland in 1798, hailed this moment: "We are now in this country under a real republickan government and the best in the world. Here I enjoy equal rights and privileges as the governor and I am an equal companion of our first rank while you must pour out your

---

[61] William Duane, *A report of the extraordinary transactions which took place at Philadelphia in February 1799 in consequence of a memorial from certain natives of Ireland to Congress praying repeal of the Alien Bill containing an account of the proceedings which produced the memorial, the assault on the committee at St Mary's church, and the proceeedings at the Mayor's office . . .* (Philadelphia, 1799).

[62] *Gazette of the United States*, November 22, 1799.

[63] Charles King, ed., *The life and correspondence of Rufus King, comprising his letters, private and official, his public documents and his speeches* (6 vols., New York, 1895), II, 637.

[64] Bernard Weisberger, *America Afire: Jefferson, Adams and the First Contested Election* (New York: William Morrow, 2000).

purse to landlord and whipper-ins and your hat in your hand at the same time."[65]

ZERO-SUM: THE RETREAT OF REPUBLICANISM IN IRELAND

The Irish had therefore contributed handsomely to the formation of American political parties. Ironically, these gains to the American political system were at the expense of Irish politics. An entire generation of radical political leadership was removed from Ireland in the 1790s – by exile, hanging, and transportation. The United Irishmen were scattered to America, to the Irish legion of Napoleon's army, to Botany Bay, to the Silesian coalmines, to the fleets, to the West Indies.[66] With this cull came a collapse of radical politics. Richard Lalor Shiel famously described political activists in the first two decades of the nineteenth century: "We sat down like galley-slaves in a calm. A general stagnation diffused itself over the national feelings. The public pulse had stopped, the circulation of all generous sentiment had been arrested and the country was palsied to the heart."[67] This leadership vacuum created the space for Daniel O'Connell – himself carefully covering his United Irish tracks – to dominate Irish politics for three decades with his new brand of politics which merged Catholic confessional solidarity with conventional Whig ideology. He thereby narrowed the global scope of United Irish ambition, abandoning their principled non-sectarianism for a Catholic stance.

The American context helps provide an answer to another puzzle of Irish politics after 1798: the seemingly rapid subsidence of Presbyterian radicalism.[68] In 1797, faced with an inability to prosecute Ulster radicals

---

[65] John Nevin (Knoxville, Tennessee) to James Nevin (Kilmoyle, Co. Derry), April 10, 1804, letter in possession of Ruth Ann Harris, Boston. The war of 1812 against Great Britain marked the point at which the United Irishmen were absorbed into the American mainstream: "Republican Greens," officered and recruited by veteran United Irishmen, joined up in droves. As on many other occasions (the Indian wars, the 1770s, the Civil War, the First World War), the Irish were integrated into civic life not only by becoming white, but by becoming soldiers.

[66] Michael Durey, "The Fate of the Rebels after 1798," *History Today*, 48 (1998), 21–7: Durey, "The United Irishmen and the Politics of Banishment 1798–1807," in Michal T. Davis, *Radicalism and Revolution in Britain, 1775–1848* (Basingstoke: Macmillan, 2000), 96–109; Durey, "Marquess Cornwallis and the Fate of Irish Rebel Prisoners in the Aftermath of the 1798 Rebellion," in James Smyth, ed., *Revolution, Counter-Revolution and Union: Ireland in the 1790s* (Cambridge University Press, 2000), 128–45.

[67] Cited in Thomas Bartlett, *The Fall and Rise of the Catholic Nation* (Dublin: Gill and Macmillan, 1992).

[68] Finlay Holmes, "From Rebels to Unionists: The Political Transformation of Ulster's Presbyterians," in R. Hanna, ed., *The Union: Essays on Ireland and the British Connection* (Newtownards: Colorpoint, 2001), 34–47; D. Thompson, "Seceding from the Seceders: The Decline of the Jacobin Tradition in Ireland 1790–1850," in Thompson, *Outsiders: Clan, Gender and Nation* (London: Verso, 1993) 134–63.

successfully because of jury resistance, local magnates like John Knox in Tyrone and George Hill in Derry implemented an informal policy of releasing United Irishmen if they entered into recognizances to voluntarily banish themselves to America for the duration of the French war. Presbyterian United Irishmen were treated more leniently after 1798 than their Catholic counterparts. The canny Castlereagh, himself from a family with a very recent dissenting background, lanced the Presbyterian boil by forcing radicals out, thereby fundamentally altering the political complexion of Ulster. The Presbyterian share of the population in Ulster, especially in the linen triangle of north and mid-Armagh, west Down, and east Tyrone, dropped after 1798, as judged by figures from 1766 and 1831.[69] This area was the epicenter of Anglican loyalism and Orangeism in the 1790s; the subsequent drop in its Presbyterian component reflects the triumph and consolidation of loyalist conservatism. Rather than Ulster Presbyterians shedding their ephemeral republicanism as mere "sunshine patriots" or "summer soldiers," its radicals were disproportionately siphoned off to America, where they were readily assimilated, given the extent of prior emigration from within their communities. This elegant explanation would also explain the otherwise puzzling subsequent lack of a vibrant memory of the rebellion in Presbyterian Ulster – the memory had been transferred to America. The most significant Ulster accounts of 1798 appear in America – Thomas Ledlie Birch, Rev. Patrick Sterling, William Grimshaw.

ANTI-SLAVERY

So far, this account of the "Green Atlantic" bears the imprint of elite politics but it also had profound radical strands. Both trajectories of this transatlantic community depended upon the "wooden world" of the ship, the pivotal technology of eighteenth-century trade.[70] Here the "motley crew" comprised a shipboard mingling of a multinational proletariat. By the end of the Napoleonic Wars, one-third of the British navy was Irish, one-quarter was black. The jig and the fandango became a common body language in this Babelian world. But this sea world was never that of the isolated heroic/nomadic individual – the solitude and alienation of a Robinson Crusoe or the Ancient Mariner – but rather of necessity a cooperative collective. In this young man's world (twenty-seven was their average age),

[69] I owe these observations to recent work by Kerby Miller, based on comparisons of the 1766 religious census with the returns furnished to the Commission on Public Instruction in 1831 (and published in 1834).

[70] Marcus Rediker, *Between the Devil and the Deep Blue Sea: Merchant Seamen, Pirates and the Anglo-American Maritime World 1700–1750* (Cambridge University Press, 1993).

the sailor occupied a mobile, fluid, dispersed social field, held together by dense rituals of sociability and bonding. The information flow was diffuse, a world of rumor, superstition, the song, the yarn, and the networks broad and amorphous. The points on this network – ships, docks, brothels, pubs, boarding houses, pawnshops, chapels, coffee shops – tingled at the nerve ends of this Atlantic system – the ports. The constant motion of the ships tied and untied connections across and between disparate worlds and a commonality emerged in these Atlantic port cities. Here was the most complex blending of peoples and cultures, where the "green" and "black" merged into an incipiently "red" Atlantic of a newly internationalized proletariat.[71]

These minglings could be seen, for example, in the Irish engagement with anti-slavery and the importance of its vocabulary to the radical movement. Olaudah Equiano visited Ireland in 1790 to promote his *Interesting Narrative*, whose ninth edition was published in Dublin in that year.[72] He spent nine months there, hosted by the Quakers and by the United Irishmen – Simon Maguire, Oliver Bond, and especially James Napper Tandy in Dublin, Samuel Neilson in Belfast. Equiano sold 1,900 copies of his *Narrative*, and was particularly welcomed in Belfast. The proposed direct involvement of Belfast in the slave trade – in 1786, its wealthiest merchant, Waddell Cunningham, had promoted the formation of a Belfast slave-ship company – had been stopped in its tracks when Thomas McCabe (later a prominent United Irishman) wrote on the subscription document "May God wither the hand and assign the name to eternal infamy of the man who will sign that document." McCabe rejoiced in his nickname "the Irish slave," and Belfast prided itself on its cosmopolitanism. In the Belfast Academy were "to be seen young lads of colour, sent by their fathers for education, both from the East and the West Indies, intermingled with the sons of the proudest gentry and nobility in the land."[73] At the celebrated Belfast Bastille Day procession in 1790, two Volunteers carried a portrait of Mirabeau, with the motto drawn from his oration on the rights of man: "Can the African slave trade though morally wrong be politically right?" That same year, in the procession in favor of the popular candidates in the

---

[71] Linebaugh and Rediker, *Many-Headed Hydra*, passim.
[72] Nini Rodgers, "Equiano in Belfast: A Study of the Anti-Slavery Ethos in a Northern Town," *Slavery & Abolition*, 18 (1997), 73–89: Rodgers, "Ireland and the Black Atlantic in the Eighteenth Century," *Irish Historical Studies*, 126 (2000), 174–92: Rodgers, *Equiano and Anti-Slavery in Belfast* (Belfast: Ulster Historical Foundation, 2000).
[73] William Grimshaw, *Incidents recalled or sketches from memory of the establishment of the cotton manufacture in Ireland, the Irish Volunteers, the rebellion of 1798, the Irish parliament, the Union with Great Britain, Emmet's insurrection, distinguished political and professional characters, remarkable duels: also anecdotes of fashionable life and robbers who infested the country* (Philadelphia, 1848), 17.

Dublin election, one of the participants was "a Negro boy well dressed and holding on high the cap of liberty."[74] This was presumably Tony Small, the friend and servant of Lord Edward FitzGerald.[75]

The language of slavery had repeatedly been applied in eighteenth-century Ireland to link the common experience of the Irish Catholic poor and of the African-American slave. In 1721, the Irish poor were described as "being as very slaves as any in America."[76] George Berkeley in 1735 quoted a plantation negro proverb: "If negro was not negro, Irishman would be negro."[77] Lord Chesterfield in 1746 commented that "the poor people of Ireland are used worse than negroes by their lords and masters."[78] Most tellingly of all, the Irish cottiers used the word *schlabhái* (slave) to describe themselves. The imaginative identification between the poor Irish and the African-American slave is vividly present in Thomas Russell's letter of 1796:

Are the Irish nation aware that this contest involves the question of the slave trade, the one now of the greatest consequence on the face of the earth? Are they willing to employ their treasure and their blood in support of that system, because England has 70 or 7000 millions engaged in it, the only argument that can be adduced in its favour, *monstrous* as it may appear? Do they know that that horrid traffic spreads its influence over the globe; that it creates and perpetuates barbarism and misery, and prevents the spreading of civilization and religion, in which we profess to believe? Do they know that by it thousands and hundreds of thousands of these miserable Africans are dragged from their innocent families like the miserable Defenders, transported to various places, and there treated with such a system of cruelty, torment, wickedness and infamy, that it is impossible for language adequately to express its horror and guilt, and which would appear rather to be the work of wicked demons than of men.[79]

His Cork United Irish colleague John Swiney made the same point: "the poor wretches of this country are reduced to a state of degradation below that of the negroes of the West-Indies."[80] The ancillary point could also be made – that the Irish gentry were simply a pack of slave owners. James Coigly pointedly asked them: "Why have you rejected the glorious title

[74] D. A. Chart, ed., *The Drennan Letters* (Belfast: HMSO, 1931), I, 349.

[75] Stella Tillyard, *Citizen Lord: Edward FitzGerald 1763–1798* (London: Chatto and Windus, 1998).

[76] *Mist's Weekly Journal*, September 30, 1721.

[77] George Berkeley, *A word to the wise: address by the Bishop of Cloyne to the Roman Catholics of Ireland* (Dublin, 1735).

[78] Chesterfield to Bishop of Waterford, October 1, 1746 in Philip Mahon, *History of England from the Peace of Utrecht to the Peace of Versailles* (7 vols., London, 1858), v, 123.

[79] Thomas Russell, *A letter to the people of Ireland on the present situation of the country* (Belfast, 1796), 22–3.

[80] In 1808, Swiney named one of his sons Toussaint.

of United Irishmen to accept that of West Indian bloodhounds?"[81] The English Whig visitor George Cooper made the same comparison about the lives of the Irish poor: "The condition of the West Indian negro is a paradise to it. The slave in our colonies has meat to eat and distilled spirits to drink, whilst the life of the Irish peasant is that of a savage who feeds upon milk and roots [potatoes]."[82]

These reciprocities and fluxes across the Green Atlantic were also in evidence in the Irish reaction to Toussaint L'Ouverture. Many exiled United Irishmen had joined maroon colonies in Jamaica in 1799, where they were "incautiously drafted into the regiments" and promptly fled to the mountains to fight with maroons and French against the British.[83] The veteran United Irishman James Napper Tandy, although based in France, disapproved of the ruthless French suppression of the Toussaint insurrection: "We are all of the same family, black and white, the work of the same creator." Toussaint's struggle engaged the attention of the Irish "rhyming weaver" and United Irishman, James Orr (1770–1816) of Ballycarry, County Antrim. His "Toussaint's Farewell to St Domingo" is full of Irish resonance (it was originally published in September 1805):

> Can ye look, without grief, on your land's devastation?
> Can ye think, without rage, on your foe's usurpation?
> Are ye men? Are ye soldiers? and shall the great nation
> Enslave this, our small one? – No! curs'd be her chain![84]

The apostacy of the English radical generation led to their being at once fascinated, repelled, and tortured by Despard, Emmet, L'Ouverture – emblems of a fate they had personally shrunk from and therefore accusing ghosts of the failure of the English romantics of the 1790s.

Orr had also written in praise of Francisco de Miranda (1750–1816), the Venezuelan republican, who fought in the American and French revolutions, before launching an abortive expedition to his native country in 1806. He returned with Simon Bolivar in 1810 (after Napoleon had attacked Spain) and in 1811 the first Republic of South America was declared at

[81] Daire Keogh, ed., *A Patriot Priest: The Life of Father James Coigly, 1761–1798* (Cork University Press, 1998), 68.

[82] George Cooper, *Letters on the Irish nation written during a visit to that kingdom in the Autumn of the year 1799* (London, 1800), 72–3. The best-documented example of this imaginative sympathy is the relationship between Lord Edward FitzGerald and the African-American slave, Tony Small: see Kevin Whelan, "New Light on Lord Edward FitzGerald," *History Ireland*, 7, 4 (1999), 40–4.

[83] Alexander Marsden to Castlereagh, October 10, 1799 in Charles Vane, ed., *Memoirs and Correspondence of Viscount Castlereagh* (12 vols., London, 1850), II, 417.

[84] James Orr, *The posthumous works of James Orr of Ballycarry with a sketch of his life* (Belfast, 1817), 31–3.

Caracas.[85] Orr's poem "Miranda's Address to his Army," published in Belfast in 1806,[86] indicates the broad political awareness of this self-educated rural weaver, who had also spent time in the United States and who wrote poems about Washington, Locke, Fox, and Grattan. He also published two poems concerning slavery – "The Dying African" (1806) and "The Persecuted Negro" (1809).

UNITED IRISHMEN, UNITED INDIANS

While Lord Edward FitzGerald's warm engagement with Native American culture is well known, a similarly positive version of that culture came from other United Irishmen. Indeed, the United Irishmen continued to repudiate the (divisive) colonial past and promote their own place within liberationist narratives of Ireland and the Atlantic world. They defended cultural autonomy, and sought in culture as in religion to escape the baleful binary of native and newcomer. Archibald Hamilton Rowan, when contemplating the choice of settling in either urban or backwoods America, asserted: "I will do neither; I will go to the woods; but I will not kill Indians, nor keep slaves. Good God! If you heard some of the Georgians, or the Kentucky people, talk of killing the natives! Cortes, and all that followed him, were not more sanguinary in the South, than they would be in North America."[87] On a more philosophical level John Dunn (1752–1827) published an essay in 1803 in the *Transactions of the Royal Irish Academy*, which offered a cogent defense of Native American culture.[88] The poet and former United Irishman William Hamilton Drummond, editor of Archibald Hamilton Rowan's life,[89] describes Dunn's American journey, including his wish to conform "to the manners and customs of an Indian tribe": he was

fully gratified by the friendship of a Miami chief, who adopted him, (according to their custom, in the place of a deceased friend by whose name he was distinguished) and who entered warmly into his views and gave him his confidence. The chief who thus honoured him was the celebrated Tchikanakoa who commanded the united Indians at the defeat of General St Clair.[90]

[85] Robert Harvey, *Liberators: Latin America's Struggle for Independence 1810–1830* (New York: Overlook Press, 2000).

[86] *Belfast Commercial Chronicle*, Aug. 11, 1806.

[87] W. H. Drummond, ed., *The Autobiography of Archibald Hamilton Rowan* (Dublin, 1840), 291.

[88] John Dunn, "Notices Relating to Some of the Native Tribes of North America," *Transactions of the Royal Irish Academy*, 9 (1803), 101–37.

[89] Philip Orr, "Doing History: A Re-interpretation of the Life of the United Irishman Archibald Hamilton Rowan 1751–1834" in Myrtle Hill, Brian Turner, and Kenneth Dawson, eds., *1798 Rebellion in County Down* (Newtownards, 1998), 211–30.

[90] Drummond, *Rowan*, 136–8.

Like Lord Edward, Dunn had quickly formed friendships with leading
Native Americans, including FitzGerald's old friend Joseph Brant, and "the
celebrated Tchikanakoa." His interpreter was the famous "white Indian"
William Wells. Dunn was interested in the "gradual degenerating and wast-
ing away"[91] of the Native Americans but was not, unlike Jefferson and other
leading republicans, convinced of the inevitability and desirability of their
obsolescence.[92] He cites Little Turtle on the dark side of the heroic narrative
of American expansion: "The dark cloud from the east dashing against our
coast, bursting on the shores, and of length drifting its rack in broken but
still spreading and advancing masses over our land, has not only destroyed
whole nations of Indians but has cankered and withered and blasted whatever is left that bears the Indian name."[93] Highly aware of the politics of
representation (the United Irishmen had actively sought to bring Gaelic
culture in from the Enlightenment cold), Dunn notes that "it is part of
the destiny of an unlettered people to write their memorials with the pen
of a stranger. They have no alternative – imperfect representation or blank
oblivion."[94] He is also aware that the Native American "is a man, a real
man," not the hideous barbarian of the prevalent stereotype.[95] Dunn also
knew that the Native American was fully aware of what lay ahead, not just
some passive victim of an impersonal and progressive historical process:
"He sees his approaching ruin, he sees it appalled, it haunts him in his solitude; it fills him with bitterness, when he beholds his devoted children."[96]
He thus offered a powerful intellectual defense of the indigenous people of
the American Great Lakes, at precisely the moment when other republican
thinkers, like Jefferson, offered them nothing but an America cleansed of
their stain, a white republic free "of either blot or mixture on that surface."
On February 18, 1803, Jefferson wrote to his principal Indian superinten-
dent, Benjamin Harrisson, urging him that "the natural progress of things,"
would be that the native Americans would be assimilated as quickly as possible, ceasing to exist as "a separate people," and concluding that Harrison's
"reflections must have led you to view the various ways in which their
history may terminate."[97]

[91] Dunn, "Notices," 103.
[92] Anthony Wallace, *Jefferson and the Indians: The Tragic Fate of the First Americans* (Cambridge, MA:
Harvard University Press, 1999).
[93] Dunn, "Notices," 104.   [94] Ibid., 106.
[95] Ibid., 107. See also Peter Linebaugh, "The Red-Crested Bird and Black Duck, a Story of 1802:
Historical Materialism, Indigenous People and the Failed Republic," *The Republic*, 2 (2001),
104–25.
[96] Dunn, "Notices," 106.
[97] Antony Wallace, *Jefferson and the Indians: The Tragic Fate of the First Americans* (Harvard University
Press, 1999), 223.

CONCLUSION

Looking at the 1790s as a whole, a republican triangle linked America, France, and Ireland. Many activists visited all three countries. Serious United Irish-related incidents broke out in Jamaica, Newfoundland, Guernsey, South Africa, Botany Bay, and the United States. The international horizons of the United Irishmen and their sense of participation in a cosmopolitan political project to transform the entire global order comprise a crucial dimension in a full understanding of them. Thus we need a wide-angle lens to encompass the world of the United Irishmen, which should include in one frame of vision Hesse and Haiti, Bantry Bay and Botany Bay, Fort George and Fort MacHenry. Among the absorbing issues of the day for Atlantic citizens of the radical enlightenment were slavery and the fate of indigenous peoples. The slavery issue had been a conspicuous motif in the early United movement and remained an abiding concern for many of them when they had to grapple with the reality as opposed to the theory of the issue in the United States.[98] A flaw in Enlightenment thought generally and in republicanism specifically was an inability to safeguard cultural as opposed to individual rights. Republican thought was unable to break out of the prison of gender: there was little concern for the rights of women alongside the rights of (a carefully abstract) man. It was generally accepted that the specifity of local cultures had to yield to the superior forms of a wider, rational cosmopolitanism. Thus while there could be sympathetic ethnographic and imaginative engagement with "savage" or regional cultures, European Enlightenment judged that these cultures could have no legitimate claim on the modern public sphere and were accordingly doomed to necessary obsolescence in the name of progress.

Clearly, Irish republicans were vitally engaged with these issues. They were better equipped to do so, given the longstanding issues of colonialism and the treatment of the majority Irish-speaking population. Thomas Russell, Lord Edward FitzGerald, Edward Marcus Despard, John Dunn, John Nevin, and William Sampson all grappled with the issue. These men met such Native American leaders as Joseph Brant (Thayendanega) of the

---

[98] On the United Irishmen and slavery, see Rodgers, "Equiano in Belfast," 73–89; Rodgers, "Two Quakers and a Utilitarian: The Reactions of Three Irish Women Writers [Maria Edgeworth, Mary Leadbetter, Mary Birkett] to the Problem of Slavery 1789–1807," *Proceedings of the Royal Irish Academy*, C, (2000), 137–57; Richard Twomey, *Jacobins and Jeffersonians: Anglo-American Radicalism in the United States 1790–1820* (Dekalb: s.n, 1989); Michael Durey, ed., *Andrew Bryson's Ordeal: An Epilogue to the 1798 Rebellion* (Cork University Press, 1998).

Mohawks, David Hill of the Iroquois, and Little Turtle of the Miami, all of whom were engaged in a united Native American policy that resonated with the United Irishmen.[99] Russell, FitzGerald, Dunn, and Despard are examples of an incipient Irish enlightened thinking which could navigate the Jeffersonian cul-de-sac. Their defeat in the revolutionary period was to close down this appealing vista.

[99] Ian Kelsay, *Joseph Brant 1743–1807: Man of Two Worlds* (Syracuse University Press, 1984). See also Richard White, *The Middle Ground: Indians, Empires and Republics in the Great Lakes Region 1650–1815* (Cambridge University Press, 1991); Daniel Richter, *Facing East from Indian Country: A Native History of Early America* (Cambridge, MA: Harvard University Press, 2002).

CHAPTER II

Brave Wolfe: the making of a hero

Nicholas Rogers

How he fell
I need not tell
The British Annals know it well[1]

We all know Wolfe. At least we all know Benjamin West's Wolfe, the painting that was exhibited at the Royal Academy in 1771 and caused such a stir. Although George III and others "thought [it] very ridiculous to exhibit heroes in coats, breeches, and cock'd hats,"[2] hundreds flocked to see it. Alongside his *Death of Nelson*, West's painting of Wolfe's final moments on the Plains of Abraham became one of the most memorable military scenarios of the Georgian era. That it became so should remind us that much of what we know of Wolfe the hero is encased in representation. Among Wolfe's projectors, among those who sought to inscribe his exploits within larger national and imperial narratives, the representational fashioning is quite self-conscious. By noting this I do not wish to suggest that there was nothing intrinsically heroic about Wolfe's actions; only that people like Wolfe are seldom in control of their "heroism," which is constructed by others out of the filaments of their lives and refashioned into different narratives over the course of time. In adopting such a perspective on heroism I do not wish to imply that anything goes, or that the meanings of heroism are irrevocably deferred as some deconstructionists might claim. But there is some play between the constructions of heroism and the deeds they purport to describe that is important to explore. This is what is investigated here. Rather than adopt a myth-and-reality perspective that one often finds in conventional histories of empire, where matters of colonial policy, its implementation and response, remain paramount, I am interested in how heroes like Wolfe embodied imperial hopes and aspirations,

---

[1] *Gazetteer and New Daily Advertiser*, September 18, 1772.
[2] John Galt, *Life, Studies, and Works of Benjamin West, Esquire* (2 vols., Gainesville: Scholars' Facsimiles, 1960), II, 46–50.

achieved metonymic status within imperial discourses. I am also interested in how the communicative practices of the eighteenth century affected perceptions of Wolfe and worked themselves out within the contested terrain of popular politics. Put somewhat differently, how did Wolfe's contemporaries construct and understand his heroism? What was emphasized, what was known about his exploits, what was glossed? What was the discursive context, the political conjuncture, in which Wolfe's feats were situated and elaborated?

Wolfe's victory at Quebec in September 1759 came in the wake of a series of successful engagements against the French in Europe and America. Horace Walpole recalled that the celebratory bells were "worn threadbare with ringing for victories" in this "glorious and ever-memorable year."[3] Yet the success of British arms threw into high relief the failures of the previous years. The Seven Years War began badly for Britain with the capture of Minorca by the French in 1756 and an unsuccessful British expedition to Rochefort the following year. Both of these failures had prompted courts martial and squalid recriminations among politicians and senior officers over what had happened. In the case of Minorca, where the government doctored some of the official dispatches to exculpate itself from any responsibility for the loss of the island, it even involved the execution of Admiral John Byng for failing to engage the French fleet in a forceful manner.

In fact, public morale in Britain in the opening years of the war was only buoyed up by the victories of its Prussian ally on the continent. Frederick's victories at Rossbach and Crevelt gave the British something to celebrate against the disappointments of their own forces. In January 1758, the Prussian king's birthday was commemorated in many towns and villages throughout Britain. The Newcastle newspapers mentioned festivities in more than twenty towns in the north of England for "the best Friend and Ally ever Great Britain had" with bonfires, bells, *feux de joie*, and military parades.[4] Yet while the bumpers of beer and festive roasts went some way towards satiating the public thirst for victory, they did not altogether dispel the abiding concern for some news of a genuine British victory.

Indeed, Frederick's successes underscored the patent failure of British engagements and the deepening concern that British commanders lacked the necessary mettle to score hard-won victories against the French. Frederick was openly praised for his professionalism.[5] By contrast, British officers, and the British upper class generally, seemed too besotted with "unmanly

[3] Helen Wrigley Toynbee, *Letters of Horace Walpole* (16 vols., Oxford: Clarendon Press, 1905), IV, 314.
[4] *Newcastle Journal*, January 21–28, 1758; *Newcastle Courant*, January 28, 1758.
[5] *Bath Journal*, September 25, 1758.

Luxury" and "selfish Effeminacy" to generate the necessary martial spirit for victory on the field of battle.[6] Moreover, because high military commands appeared to be distributed according to political influence rather than tried experience, the wrong people were sometimes assigned important roles in the conduct of a war on which Britain's imperial destiny rested. As the *Gazetteer* ruefully remarked, if politicians chose men of true abilities "instead of having recourse to those Toast and Butter Captains who spend their times at Tea Tables, china shops, masquerades and brothels, the British would now, as heretofore, be the terror of all enemies."[7]

British military failures were thus attributed to the inadequacy of aristocratic leadership and the deepening profligacy of the ruling class.[8] The charges had been tellingly made at Minorca against Admiral Byng, the son of a viscount whose cosmopolitan manners and love of polite society were thought to have enervated his fighting prowess.[9] Similar accusations were also leveled against Lord George Sackville, the commander of the British forces at Minden, whose failure to advance his cavalry regiment during the heat of the battle earned him the scorn of his officers.[10] Like Byng, Sackville was a scion of the aristocracy, something of a fop, and suspected of winning promotion only by virtue of his social rank. One print portrayed him as a "Pompadour General" more familiar with perfumes than gunpowder, with court repartee than battlefield orders. Another depicted him both literally and metaphorically from the rear, a commentary on his cowardice and alleged homosexuality.[11] Although Lord George protested that he had been given contradictory orders from Prince Ferdinand, many people believed his craven attitude at Minden underscored the parlous state of a British command enervated by luxury and insulated from real accountability by political interest. Indeed, it was widely believed that it was only because he was the third son of one of the most eminent Whig noblemen in the land, the Duke of Dorset, that he escaped Byng's fate.[12]

Subsequent victories had helped to dispel public anxiety about the deleterious effects of upper-class luxury and the alleged effeminacy of the British high command. And if one person served as a singular antidote to those anxieties it was James Wolfe, whose triumph at Quebec occurred only

---

[6] Ibid., January 23, 1758.   [7] *Gazetteer*, August 24, 1756.
[8] Kathleen Wilson, *The Sense of the People: Politics, Culture and Imperialism in England, 1715–1785* (Cambridge University Press, 1995), 178–205.
[9] *Monitor*, March 12, 1757.
[10] Alan Valentine, *Lord George Germain* (Oxford: Clarendon Press, 1962), 58.
[11] *British Museum Catalogue* (*BMC*) 3682, 3680.
[12] Piers Mackesy, *The Coward of Minden* (London: Allen Lane, 1979), chs. 9 and 10. For the later rumor that Sackville's father had successfully pleaded for a merciful verdict, see Valentine, *Germain*, 67.

weeks after Minden. Born in a Kentish parsonage to a military officer and the daughter of a squire, Wolfe was never identified with the aristocracy, who at the time made up almost a quarter of the officer class.[13] Rather he represented the professional soldier, a subaltern who had risen through the ranks by perseverance and application at a time when the army required efficient officers quickly.[14] Wolfe's promotion was not as meteoric as that of Napoleon fifty years later, but it was impressive: adjunct at sixteen; brigade-major a year later; lieutenant-colonel by twenty-three; brigadier-general by thirty-one; general by thirty-two. It was self-evidently based on merit rather than privilege; as Burke remarked, "un-indebted to family or connection, unsupported by intrigue or faction."[15]

Moreover, Wolfe appeared to have avoided the usual pitfalls of a military career in the eighteenth century. He was a man whose "Virtues were *numerous*," remarked the *London Evening Post*, "undiminished by enormous *Vices*."[16] Wolfe did not play the rake or spend his off-duty hours at the cockpit or gambling table. Apart from one brief relapse into gentlemanly dissipation, he led an upright, disciplined life. In Paris he was said to have spent his time improving his French rather than his dalliance. His first biographer, John Pringle, portrayed him as a paragon of bourgeois rectitude: a Christian soldier; a devoted son; an officer who looked forward to the delights of domestic felicity with his fiancée, Miss Katherine Lowther, even though his engagement to her appears to have been a rather hurried pre-embarkation affair that had little of the passion associated with an earlier flame, Miss Elizabeth Lawson.[17] "Recreation and Pleasure never so prevailed over him," intoned Pringle, "as to make him forget what he owed to himself and his Country."[18] Playwrights like George Cockings would dramatize this choice in a classical idiom, stressing the heroic but necessary primacy of civic over domestic virtue.[19] Here, as elsewhere, Wolfe emerged as an upright figure ready to do battle for his country.

If Wolfe seemed a fitting counterpoint to the salon officers who filled the army, he was not identified with any of the setbacks that had plagued British forces during the war. Although he had been on active service at

---

[13] P. J. Razzell, "Social Origins of Officers in the Indian and British Home Army 1758–1962," *British Journal of Sociology*, 14 (1963), 248–60.

[14] Stuart Reid, *Wolfe* (Staplehurst, Kent: Spellmount, 2000), 15. During the course of the Seven Years War, the army establishment rose from 450 cavalry and nearly 1,650 infantry officers to 600 and 4,000 respectively.

[15] Cited in John Clarence Webster, ed., *Wolfiana* (n.p.; privately printed, 1927), 14.

[16] *London Evening Post*, October 27–30, 1759.   [17] Reid, *Wolfe*, 128, 166.

[18] John Pringle, *The Life of General James Wolfe, the Conqueror of Canada* (London: G. Kearsly, 1760), 5–7, 17.

[19] George Cockings, *The Conquest of Canada, or, The Siege of Quebec* (London: J. Cooke, 1766).

Rochefort, he was too junior an officer to be associated with its failure. In fact, as the quartermaster-general in that expedition, he was frustrated by the indecision of his superiors. "Admirals and Generals consult one another," he remarked to his uncle, "and resolve upon nothing."[20] Some of this frustration must have filtered through the inquiry, for the press depicted Wolfe as a subaltern officer who had always been ready to engage the French.[21]

Wolfe emerged from Rochefort with an untarnished reputation. In the train of victories that Britain achieved in 1758 and 1759, he indelibly stood out. At the capture of Louisbourg, Wolfe consolidated a difficult landing in high winds and seas, capturing the lighthouse battery and cannon. For this action he was warmly commended in General Amherst's official dispatches and hailed as a hero at home and in America.[22] At Minden, Wolfe was indirectly associated with the stalwart stand of the British infantry against the French, for it was publicly remarked that it was his training of the troops that enhanced their performance.[23] Yet it was Quebec that consolidated Wolfe's reputation as the consummate patriot. To the British and American public, the sheer intrepidity of his ascent at Foulon, the brief but dramatic battle on the Plains, the manner of his dying, all redounded to his honor and fame. Amid the addresses and celebrations that greeted the 1759 victories, it was Quebec and its victor that were prominent. Although the British public had inklings that the struggle for New France was incomplete after the battle of Abraham, it chose to represent it as a definitive victory that would irrevocably compromise French territorial ambitions in North America. The subsequent battle of St. Foy in the spring of 1760, in which the French forced the British forces to retreat within the fortress of Quebec and await relief from Britain, did little to undermine this perspective

The battle of Abraham was also viewed as a victory in the most adverse of circumstances. The *Ipswich Journal* remarked: "Our Soldiers have traversed inhospitable Plains, been exposed to all Extremities of Weather, and scaled almost inaccessible Mountains to find those Foes," who "vainly looked upon themselves as invincible, because their Posts were inaccessible."[24] Such a victory was a great fillip to patriotic endeavor comparable to the epic battles

---

[20] Beckles Willson, *The Life and Letters of James Wolfe* (London: W. Heinemann, 1909), 336.
[21] *Newcastle Courant*, October 27, 1759.
[22] *London Evening Post*, 17–19 August 1758; see also 22/24 August 1758, for brief descriptions of the celebrations at Winchester and Chatham, and A. E. Wolfe-Aylward, *The Pictorial Life of Wolfe* (Plymouth: W. Brendond, 1933), 12. For celebrations and appraisals of Wolfe's actions in America, see *Boston Gazette*, 3, 10 July, 21 August 1758.
[23] *Ipswich Journal*, October 27, 1759.   [24] Ibid., November 3, 1759.

of old. "In Wolfe was revived the Courage of our Edwards and Henries," declared the *Monitor*, "and that military skill and Discipline which enabled those puny Armies at Poitiers, Cressy and Agincourt, to defeat the vast Armies of France."[25]

Poets ransacked the classics for appropriate analogies. As a triumph over difficult terrain, Wolfe's victory was compared to Hannibal's.[26] Others compared Wolfe to Leonidas of Thermopylae or to Epaminondas, the Theban general fatally wounded at the battle of Manitea. Some fused classical with contemporary comparisons. "Rome has beheld her much lov'd Cato bleed," ran one popular poem addressed to his mother:

> An aged Priam mourn'd his Hector dead:
> Grieve not, thou honour'd Parent, WOLFE shall live
> While grateful Britain can just praises give;
> In list of Fame, her Hero great shall stand,
> His compeers, Fred'rick, Minden Ferdinand.
> Not least, O WOLFE, of the illustrious Three
> QUEBEC gives Immortality to Thee.[27]

As this much-cited verse implied, the British public found in Wolfe a genuinely British hero, not some German surrogate, around whom the taint of careerism, profiteering, and huge subsidies still lingered.[28] This was of some relevance to the emerging debate on the huge expenses of the war and to the question of when an honorable peace with France might be secured.[29] Wolfe's valor and death reinforced the hawkish claims of Pitt's allies that hard-won victories on the field of battle should not be casually abandoned in any peace negotiations. As one Londoner reminded his readers, British victories had not been simply "attained by an Expense of *Money,* but at the *Expense of Men,* which is infinitely of greater value." Lives given in battle were the "indelible *Proofs* of BRITISH FORTITUDE, and of that MAGNANIMITY which is the true *Characteristick* of a FREE PEOPLE. It remains that we make a *right use* of *them,* for the Attainment of what we ought sincerely to *wish,* a *solid, lasting,* and *honourable*

---

[25] *Monitor*, October 27, 1759; reprinted in the *Ipswich Journal*, November 10, 1759.

[26] *London Evening Post*, November 8–10, 1759.

[27] *London Chronicle*, October 25–27, 1759. Also published in the *Bath Advertiser*, November 3, 1759 and the *Bath Journal*, November 5, 1759.

[28] See *BMC* 3737, a 1760 print, where there is a call for "no more Mercinary Foreign Generals, nor no more War than is Nessesary."

[29] Nicholas Rogers, *Whigs and Cities: Popular Politics in the Age of Walpole and Pitt* (Oxford: Clarendon Press, 1989), 114–29.

PEACE."[30] As another bluntly put it: "If Quebec be restored, Wolfe fell in vain."[31]

The reference in the poem to Cato also had a special resonance. Well established as an icon of liberty in the British political lexicon, this signifier epitomized the fusion of libertarian and imperial goals that were the hallmark of British national aggrandizement in this period, a coupling that elaborated the emergent British empire of the Atlantic as Protestant, commercial, maritime, and free.[32] In effect, Wolfe, by capturing the headquarters of New France, had helped liberate North America from French religious bigotry and absolutist rule, and paved the way for a new era of commercial expansion under British auspices. Such a construction had a particular resonance for the American colonists, who had been particularly troubled by the potential expansion of French influence from Canada to Louisiana. With Wolfe's victory, settler expansion westwards was now secure. In a sermon before the Massachusetts House of Representatives, Samuel Cooper celebrated Wolfe's victory in the language of Protestant providentialism and commercial optimism. God had not only secured the "reformed religion" and the liberties associated with it at Quebec; through Wolfe he had assured the colonists "peace, prosperity and unhindered commercial expansion."[33] As far as many Americans were concerned, Wolfe required no monument in his honor. For them, his apotheosis was telling enough[34]

In pondering the meaning of the conquest of Quebec and in reconstructing narratives of that victory, there was much that was embroidered and glossed. In the context of the war there was a strong disposition to make Wolfe an exemplary hero; in the words of the City of Bath's address to the king, to recognize his "noble Example of Bravery and Virtue, for the Excitement and Imitation of his Fellow-Subjects."[35] This meant that Wolfe's conduct was almost invariably placed in a positive light. The inclination to do this was facilitated by the fact that little was actually known of the problems that Wolfe and his officers encountered at Quebec, or of the disagreements they engendered. Some of these quarrels filtered through

---

[30] *London Evening Post*, November 1–3, 1759.   [31] Ibid., November 3–6, 1759.
[32] For the emergence of this conception of empire see Wilson, *Sense of the People*, ch. 3; David Armitage, *The Ideological Origins of the British Empire* (Cambridge University Press, 2000), ch. 7.
[33] Cited in Alan McNairn, *Behold the Hero. General Wolfe and the Arts in the Eighteenth Century* (Montreal and Kingston: McGill-Queen's University Press, 1999), 13–14. See also *London Chronicle*, March 18–20, 1760.
[34] *Boston Gazette*, October 15, 1759; *Pennsylvania Gazette*, October 25, 1759; *Maryland Gazette*, November 1, 1759.
[35] *Bath Journal*, November 12, 1759.

to the British public, as references in the *Monitor* make clear.[36] Yet the public dispatches that addressed the difficulties of forcing the surrender of this well-fortified city as the Canadian winter approached arrived only two days before the news of the victory.[37] In his last report before the battle of Abraham, Wolfe told Pitt that he might "be assured that the small part of the campaign which remains shall be employed (as far as I am able) for the honour of his Majesty and the interest of the Nation."[38] In some newspapers, this rather pessimistic message, which anticipated that the siege of Quebec would be significant only in diversionary terms, was published in the same issue as news of the town's eventual surrender.[39] In others, the dispatches were printed days or, in the case of the provincial papers, a week apart. Inevitably, the elation that greeted the news of the surrender of Quebec subsumed any further inquiry into the expedition beyond seeing the victory on the Plains of Abraham as a great victory over adversity.

For Wolfe's posthumous reputation this was fortuitous. The early months of the expedition to the St. Lawrence had not gone well for the commander-in-chief. Little was actually known of the fortress of Quebec. The British were reliant upon an outdated map and a report from an engineer who had been imprisoned there in 1756.[40] Wolfe soon discovered that while it was possible to bombard Quebec from the boats and British batteries across the river at Point aux Peres, it was much harder to force a surrender. Wolfe also found the French defenses to the north at Beauport virtually impenetrable. After lengthy deliberations about where the British troops should engage the French forces, Wolfe's decision to attack from the tidal flats of the Beauport bank ended in miserable failure. It simply exposed his grenadiers to the withering fire of the French from their well-fortified entrenchments. After three months in the St. Lawrence, Wolfe's efforts to capture Quebec had come to naught. With the Canadian winter impending and the St. Lawrence soon to be ice-bound, time was running out.

To complicate matters further, Wolfe's relations with his more aristocratic brigadiers were deteriorating. His relations with James Murray were frosty, perhaps because they had been adversaries during the Rochefort inquiry. And he was never on good terms with George Townshend, a nephew of the Duke of Newcastle and Pitt's closest ally in piloting a militia bill through Parliament. A former officer in the Foot Guards, Townshend called in

[36] *Monitor*, October 27, 1759.   [37] Wolfe mentioned his ill health in his own dispatch.
[38] *London Chronicle*, October 16–18, 1759; *Derby Mercury*, October 12–19, 1759.
[39] *London Chronicle*, October 16–18, 1758; *Ipswich Journal*, October 20, 1759.
[40] Reid, *Wolfe*, 164.

old favors and foisted himself upon Wolfe at the last minute. Wolfe took this with a bad grace while Townshend resented his superior's fame and condescension. He worked off his spleen by drawing cruel caricatures of Wolfe and by generally being argumentative, threatening his superior on one occasion with a parliamentary inquiry.

What aggravated the differences between the general and his brigadiers was Wolfe's own moodiness, irascibility, pedantry, and self-absorption. Some of this off-putting behavior may be attributed to his ill health: rheumatism, a "racked" bladder, gravel, and very likely consumption. But Wolfe's own indecision and aloofness hardly helped. Townshend was probably not alone in thinking that while Wolfe's health was "very bad," his generalship was "not a bit better."[41]

As Wolfe despaired of success, he was prevailed upon by Admiral Saunders and his brigadiers to sail further up river and engage the French from the west. Strategically this was an astute move, because a successful landing would cut off the French supply lines from Montreal. Characteristically, Wolfe withheld the precise point of disembarkation from his officers until the last hour. He tartly told Moncton that it was "not a usual thing to point out in the publick orders the direct spot of an attack, nor for any inferior not charg'd with a particular duty to ask instructions upon that point."[42] In fact, Wolfe planned to land at Foulon, far closer to Quebec than his subalterns anticipated. The choice of landing was a little reckless. The 175-foot ascent to the Plains of Abraham from the Anse au Foulon was very steep, for soldiers and supplies. The first transports actually overshot the Foulon road, forcing the troops to scale the shale slope using tree roots and branches. Had the French been alert, both in detecting the flat-bottomed boats as they floated down the river and in locating the point of disembarkation, the difficult maneuvers of the British forces might have been easily frustrated.

The British force would have faced a more formidable foe had Montcalm been able to persuade Vaudreuil, the Governor-General of the French colony, to loan him some field cannon from the fortress. Since the British had been able to hoist only two small field pieces up the cliff, they were extremely vulnerable to a heavy cannonade. But in his haste to engage the enemy, Montcalm lost this potential advantage. In fact he ultimately played to Wolfe's best suit. Once the battle commenced, Wolfe's skills came to the fore. Personally fearless, he commanded his troops with aplomb, telling

[41] A. G. Doughty, *The Siege of Quebec and the Battle of the Plains of Abraham* (6 vols., Quebec, 1901), v, 195.
[42] Reid, *Wolfe*, 185.

his men to hold their fire until the advancing French regiments were well within range. Although they were outnumbered, the discipline and training of the British troops ensured a quick victory.[43]

The British and American public knew little of the disagreements within the British command or of Wolfe's dubious qualities as a strategist. Its attention was transfixed by the daring venture on the Plains of Abraham, Wolfe's personal bravery, and his ultimate sacrifice. Even pamphleteers who were disposed to play down the victory in order to focus public attention upon the need for peace talks recognized this to be the case. One openly speculated as to whether the Quebec expedition might not have been regarded as a "wrong-headed Enterprise, favouring of Quixotism" had victory not been secured, but conceded it was a "favourite object of Triumph."[44] Such fervor also disposed Brigadier-General Townshend to muzzle his own thoughts of the expedition. Whatever misgivings Townshend had held about Wolfe's qualities as a leader were discreetly kept within his own circle: to have circulated them further would only have invited hostility from a public that saw criticism of its hero as a reproach upon itself.[45] In fact, Townshend found himself under attack for his lukewarm references to Wolfe's achievement in his official dispatch on the battle of Abraham. It was also alleged that during the battle he had retained "a safe and honourable Distance from the Scene of Action."[46] This was patently untrue and unfair, because Townshend's task during the battle was to protect the main line from the cross-fire of the Canadian militia and their indigenous allies near the St. Foy road. Even so, these allegations, and the more serious charge that Townshend sailed back to England too precipitously, leaving the British army at Quebec under-resourced, kept the nobleman on the defensive. Indeed, Townshend became so tetchy about the slurs on his military reputation and honor that he threatened one newspaper with a libel and challenged the Duke of Albemarle to a duel for his alleged complicity in venting some of the rumors.[47] His only public commentary on Wolfe's reputation was a caustic riposte to the desire to erect a monument in his memory. Entitled "A Living Dog is Better than a Dead Lion," this anonymous print depicted a less than flattering portrait of Wolfe on a monument, beneath which a "Minden" dog is urinating on a disconsolate

---

[43] On the battle and its prelude, and on Wolfe's mixed qualities as a general, see C. P. Stacey, *Quebec, 1759* (Toronto: MacMillan, 1959).

[44] *A Letter to the People of England, on the Necessity of putting an Immediate End to the War; and the Means of obtaining an Advantageous Peace* (London: R. Griffiths, 1760), 5.

[45] See Israel Mauduit, *An Apology for the Life and Actions of General Wolfe* (London, 1765), 6.

[46] *A Letter to an Honourable Brigadier General, Commander of His Majesty's Forces in Canada* (London: J. Burd, 1760), 8–9, 21.

[47] Ibid., 29–30; McNairn, *Behold the Hero*, 21–2.

British lion.[48] It was a cynical observation on how the public traduced some military commanders and lionized others.

Townshend's print did, however, point to one of the difficulties that Wolfe's admirers had to confront. That was embodying him in a heroic form. Physically, Wolfe was not the stuff of heroes. He was no Achilles or Roman general. Joseph Wilton attempted to dress him up as one, complete with wolf-head epaulettes. Shiavonetti even produced a classically inspired engraving of Wolfe with a rippling torso that stood in ironic contrast to actuality.[49] At six foot, he was tall by eighteenth-century standards, but he looked like a gangly weakling, with a loping gait, sloping shoulders, a receding chin, and turned-up nose. One French contemporary thought him "very skinny" and "very ugly."[50] To some engravers this did not matter. In their haste to visualize Wolfe for a curious public, some illustrators confronted their ignorance of the general's physiognomy by drawing archetypical military gentlemen; or in one case, by reworking an old engraving of Bonnie Prince Charlie.[51] It was not until the mid-1760s, in fact, that there were any engravings of Wolfe that approached his likeness. These were based on drawings by Wolfe's military personnel, most notably by Henry Smythe, Wolfe's aide-de-camp, and by George Townshend, who produced a more sympathetic portrait of his superior officer for Isaac Barre. It was from these sources, together with Joseph Highmore's earlier painting, that Benjamin West constructed his visage of the dying Wolfe, and then from a three-quarter view to minimize the general's unflattering profile.[52]

For those who hankered after a modicum of authenticity, Wolfe's physical features posed something of an impediment to translation in a heroic idiom unless one went totally classical. In more naturalistic settings, the heroic effect could be achieved only by placing Wolfe in a tragic ensemble of admirers, by turning the head, or, as in the case of George Romney's portrait, by accentuating the cleft in the general's chin. Yet it was possible to take advantage of Wolfe's physical infirmity, to emphasize his perseverance and diligence to duty in spite of his own state of health, to remind readers of the "excruciating Pain" brought on by the stone and gravel that led him to

[48] BMC 3696. There is some doubt as to whether Townshend was the author of this print, but the similarity between this portrait of Wolfe and the private caricatures is compelling evidence that he was responsible for it.
[49] McNairn, Behold the Hero, 64; Ann Uhry Abrams, The Valiant Hero (Washington, D.C.: Smithsonian Institute, 1985), 181 fig. 113.
[50] Nicolas Renaud d'Avenue Des Meloizes, Journal militaire 1756–1759 (Quebec: n.p., 1930), 51.
[51] McNairn, Behold the Hero, 191–3.
[52] Abrams, The Valiant Hero, 179. One of Wolfe's engineers, Captain John Montresor, also sketched him in profile on September 1, 1759, at Montmorency. This drawing was subsequently mezzotinted and published July 30, 1783. See G. D. Scull, ed., "The Montresor Journals," Collections of the New York Historical Society, 10 (1881), 5.

consider resigning from the service after the Quebec expedition.[53] As the *London Chronicle* remarked, Wolfe "was himself sensible of the weakness of his constitution, and determined to croud into a few years, actions that would have adorned a length of life."[54] This was not stressed as much by eighteenth-century writers as it would be by later biographers, for whom Wolfe's triumph over physical adversity accentuated his Christian fortitude. But it was a minor theme in the early narratives that were constructed around Wolfe's body.

More important to eighteenth-century commentators was his physical courage, his willingness to lead his men into battle whatever the risk. Modern commentators have sometimes seen Wolfe's actions on the Plains of Abraham as those of a melancholic dying man, ready to fulfill the message of Thomas Gray's *Elegy* that "the paths of glory lead but to the grave."[55] There is some recognition of these sentiments in the contemporary record. The *Ipswich Journal*, for example, speculated that "the brave General Wolfe's Death, tho' most unfortunate for his Country, was, with respect to himself, not more glorious as to the Manner than happy as to the Time of it."[56] Yet most of his contemporaries saw his valor in more unqualified terms, as the epitome of self-sacrifice for king and country. They depicted Wolfe unconcerned by the wounds he had sustained, reserving his energies to learn of the French retreat, issuing final orders, and purportedly murmuring with his dying breath, "thank God, I die contented."[57] There were thirteen versions of what he actually said,[58] and in all likelihood no one knew for sure. What mattered was the manner of his dying, his resolution to the last. "He rushes forward and disdains the Gaul," imagined one poet from Wiltshire:

> His brave Example ev'ry Soldier fires,
> And ev'ry Corps, with his own Flame inspires;
> Shot after Shot the British Leader feels,
> Each Wound his Valour fires, and Courage steels:
> At length he greatly falls; the Purple Tide
> Spouts from his Breast, and trickles down his Side:
> But Conquest gain'd, he pleas'd resign's his Breath,
> Rejoic'd in Agonies, and smil'd in Death.[59]

[53] *Ipswich Journal*, November 17, 1759; *Bath Journal*, December 10, 1759.
[54] *London Chronicle*, November 10–13, 1759.
[55] Simon Schama, *Dead Certainties* (New York: Knopf, 1991), 13–20; Fred Anderson, *Crucible of War: The Seven Years' War and the Fate of Empire in British North America 1754–1766* (New York: Knopf, 2000), 353–4.
[56] *Ipswich Journal*, November 17, 1759.   [57] As reported by Pringle, *Life of Wolfe*, 15.
[58] Webster, *Wolfiana*, 38.   [59] *Bath Journal*, November 26, 1759.

Wolfe's legendary death on the Plains of Abraham deflected attention from his unprepossessing physique. Yet there were aspects of Townshend's criticism of him that might have tarnished his reputation, had they been known. In a letter to his wife, written in early September 1759, Townshend complained that British operations in the St. Lawrence had degenerated into "a Scene of Skirmishing, Cruelty and Devastation. It is War of the worst Shape."[60] He was referring to the activities of the British as an army of occupation, to the dirty war of controlling the civilian population and rooting out French sympathizers.[61] Upon his initial landing on the Île d'Orléans in June, Wolfe had issued a manifesto to the French-Canadian population promising not to molest them if they refrained from taking up arms against the British. But the persistent attacks upon British outposts by Canadians and their Amerindian allies, and Wolfe's frustrations about his own military progress, prompted him to embark upon a series of punitive reprisals. As one of Wolfe's officers put it: "If we can't beat them, we shall ruin their country."[62] On both shores of the St. Lawrence over 1,400 farms and barns were burnt to the ground and their inhabitants taken into custody.[63] Those who resisted were put to the sword and threatened with scalping if they were Amerindians, or Canadians disguised as such. Among those so punished were the curé of Sainte Anne de Beaupré and his band of resisters. Although they had attempted to negotiate with the British, thirty of them were "surrounded, killed, and scalped" by soldiers of the 43rd regiment under Captain Alexander Montgomery, a commander who the following year harshly punished the Cherokee for resisting settler expansion in South Carolina.[64] In the "marchlands" of North America, to use a phrase of Bernard Bailyn, brutal reprisals like this were commonplace.[65]

In the British press Wolfe was portrayed as a man who would have deplored this irregular violence. He was depicted as an opponent of scalping and as an officer who punished soldiers for committing atrocities upon

[60] Doughty, *Siege of Quebec*, V, 195.
[61] On this, see Guy Fregault, *Canada: The War of Conquest*, trans. Margaret M. Cannon (Toronto: Oxford University Press, 1969), 256.
[62] "Extract of a Letter from an Officer in Major Genl Wolfe's Army," August 10, 1759, in Stanley Pargellis, ed., *Military Affairs in North America 1748–1765* (New York and London: D. Appleton–Century, 1936), 434.
[63] Stacey, *Quebec, 1759*, 90–1; Fregault, *Canada*, 244–5. According to the *Ipswich Journal*, December 8, 1759, the number of buildings burnt by November 1759 was around three thousand.
[64] Stacey, *Quebec*, 89–92; Ian K. Steele, *Warpaths* (New York: Oxford University Press, 1994), 230–1; Hal T. Shelton, *General Richard Montgomery and the American Revolution* (New York University Press, 1994), 27.
[65] Bernard Bailyn, *The Peopling of British North America: An Introduction* (New York: Knopf, 1986), 112–21; on scalping see James Axtell, *The European and the Indian: Essays in the Ethnohistory of Colonial America* (New York: Oxford University Press, 1981), chs. 2 and 8.

the civilian population. In one anecdote, he reportedly hanged a private for needlessly killing an infant in a Canadian village, so consoling the "weeping mother" that she gave the army "several very important pieces of intelligence" in return.[66] Yet the fact was that Wolfe was not a compassionate paternalist. He was a hard-headed commander schooled in the tactics of occupying armies. He had served under Cumberland after Culloden and had approved of his methods of dealing with rebel Highlanders and their families, notwithstanding rumors to the contrary.[67] Like his former commander, General Amherst, he had a particularly low tolerance of irregular troops and Amerindian war parties, especially after the "massacre" of Fort William Henry in 1757. "Tho' I am neither inhuman nor rapacious," he wrote to Lord George Sackville of the incident, "yet I own it would give me pleasure to see the Canadian vermin sacked and pillaged and justly repaid [for] their unheard cruelty."[68] His tough attitude towards the *habitants* of the St. Lawrence and the Amerindian allies of the French was influenced by such resentments. As he wrote to Sackville in July 1759 of his indigenous enemies such as the Abenaki: "I take them to be the most contemptible *canaille* upon earth . . . a dastardly set of bloody rascals. We cut them in pieces whenever we found them, in return for a thousand acts of cruelty and barbarity."[69]

   Within this context it is worth considering how Benjamin West configured the painting that so captivated the eighteenth-century imagination. Casting it within an epic frame, West had no intention of replicating historical verisimilitude, even if he could have found it. As he himself admitted, he could not allow Wolfe to die "like a common soldier under a bush."[70] In order to capture the sublimity of the event, he portrayed the dying Wolfe in the manner of Van Dyck's portrait of Christ taken from the cross, transforming Wolfe's wounds into modern stigmata.[71] From this perspective, Wolfe died to redeem British liberty and empire. The gravitas of Wolfe's death is further accentuated by the ensemble of figures that surround him, including the surgeon who is attempting to stanch the flow of the blood from the fatal wound. Although we know that only a handful of people attended Wolfe in his dying moments, the company in the painting was expanded to thirteen. Unlike West's later painting of Nelson's death

[66] *Bath Journal*, January 11, 1773; *Bath Advertiser*, November 3, 1759.
[67] W. A. Speck, *The Butcher: The Duke of Cumberland and the Suppression of the 45* (Oxford: Blackwell, 1987), 148, 157.
[68] Willson, *Life and Letters of Wolfe*, 389.   [69] Ibid., 385.
[70] Schama, *Dead Certainties*, 28; McNairn, *Behold the Hero*, 138–9.
[71] McNairn, *Behold the Hero*, 165–6.

aboard the *Victory*, it included relatively few common men: a volunteer, a grenadier, an American ranger, and a crouching, pensive Amerindian. The majority of the men are of the officer class. They include the surgeon, an engineer, his friend, Major Isaac Barré, his aide-de-camp, Captain Hervey Smyth, an officer from the artillery, a Scotsman, Lieutenant-Colonel Simon Fraser, who is partially obscured by the only brigadier-general in the picture, Robert Monckton.

Monckton, like Barré and Smyth, had been wounded in battle, and was not present on the Plains of Abraham when Wolfe fell. In fact, only one of the soldiers identified in the painting was likely present at Wolfe's death. This in itself is not very important since West made no pretension to historical accuracy. But it is interesting to speculate on the symbolic meaning of his entourage. The preponderance of elite figures was not out of keeping with classical tradition, but one cannot resist the conclusion that West was anxious to show that Wolfe was popular with both officers and men and to erase from the record any suggestion that there were any serious divisions within the expeditionary force. In this respect, the exclusion of Brigadier-General Townshend is noteworthy, because his veiled criticism of Wolfe's command was sufficiently public to have excited comment, had he been included in the painting.

The relative obscurity of the Highland officer is also worth noting. The Highlanders played a critical role in the battle on the Plains of Abraham. James Colcraft reported from Quebec that they "drove every Thing before them that came their way, and Walls could not resist their Fury. Those breechless brave Fellows are an Honour to their Country."[72] In these circumstances, and in view of Joseph Wilton's willingness to foreground their contribution in his Westminster monument to Wolfe, West's marginalization of the Highlanders is instructive. It is doubtful that this was out of deference to Wolfe, who had little regard for soldiers in general – he once called them the "Geneva and piss" of the country[73] – and for Highlanders in particular. It is more likely that West was acutely aware of anti-Scottish sentiment in the wake of Lord Bute's ascension to power and of the lingering suspicion, as late as 1771, that he was still an important political player "behind the curtain."[74] Certainly West was ambitious enough to avoid being embroiled in political controversies that might sully his reputation.

Of the figures in West's painting, the Amerindian is clearly the most allegorical and enigmatic. At one level it is surprising that West should

[72] *Derby Mercury*, October 19–26, 1759.   [73] Willson, *Life and Letters of Wolfe*, 274.
[74] John Brewer, "The Misfortunes of Lord Bute: A Case Study in Eighteenth-Century Political Argument and Public Opinion," *Historical Journal*, 16 (March 1973), 7–43.

have featured him in the painting at all. There were relatively few indigenous scouts in Wolfe's army, and given his known antipathy to Amerindian
raiders and the hostile publicity that swelled around the practice of scalping, his inclusion might be considered a cruel joke. Yet the British public
had become more familiar with the exotic Amerindian in the course of the
1760s. Cherokee chiefs had visited London and contracted treaties with
the British. George Stevens's popular *Lecture on Heads* opened with the
exhibition of the head of a Cherokee chief, "Sachem Swampum-Scalpo-
Tomahawk," a man described as a "great hero" and "warrior."[75] The fascination with exotic savages, as imperial trophies, but also as people whose
simplicity, incorruptibility, and basic egalitarianism was something to be
admired, grew apace in this decade. The horror of scalping was even mitigated by a dose of cultural relativism. George Lyttelton's *Dialogues of the
Dead* publicly wondered whether the European practice of dueling was any
less "savage" than the Amerindian rituals of reprisal, particularly when it
was conducted on the slimmest of pretexts and involved unnecessary violence against people from one's own social circle.[76] Seen in this context,
the athletic, tattooed, figure of the Amerindian, cast in the classical mode
of poetic contemplation, takes on new meanings. He represents "the raw
vigour of the New World"[77] which the British would now have to mold,
accommodate, and civilize. The aboriginal warrior's devotion to his band,
his intrepidity, his respect for leaders of proven experience and ability, is
also a fitting counterpoint to European war promotions, where social privilege and political interest too often determined command. It is also, by
extension, a compliment to Wolfe's skill and bravery. The Amerindian is
not placed in a subservient pose to Wolfe. He is seen transcending cultural
differences in recognizing the qualities of leadership that made Wolfe a
genuine hero of his day.

By foregrounding the Amerindian and the American ranger in the painting, West also emphasized that the battle for Quebec was a joint British-
American venture, one that might even lead to a new era of metropolitan–
colonial relations. This expectation was in keeping with colonial sentiment during the war and its immediate aftermath. Yet by the time the
Philadelphian came to paint *The Death of Wolfe* in 1770, it was one that was
a good deal more problematic. British colonial policy after 1763 was largely
predicated on the notion that the American colonists should make a larger

[75] See the excellent discussion of the Amerindian in West's painting in McNairn, *Behold the Hero*,
167–75.
[76] George Lyttelton, *Dialogues of the Dead* (London: W. Sandby, 1760).
[77] The phrase is Schama's: *Dead Certainties*, 31.

financial contribution to the maintenance of the empire, and that imperial security could best be achieved through the exercise of a sovereign British authority than through relying on the uncertainties of American militias and self-governing institutions. This led Britain on a collision course with her colonists over internal taxes, the policing of maritime trade, and the billeting of soldiers, inaugurating a new era of confrontation with colonial governors and metropolitan ministries.

None of this political uncertainty was even hinted at in West's painting, even though it must have been completed around the time of the Boston massacre of March 1770.[78] West was fortunate that his painting of Wolfe was exhibited at the Royal Academy during a hiatus in Anglo-American confrontations, when the prospect of an enduring reconciliation between Britain and her Atlantic colonies still seemed a real possibility. And yet the following year, when a group of gentlemen at Almack's club invited the public to submit model obituaries to accompany Joseph Wilton's monument of Wolfe at Westminster Abbey, the contention over America leaked into assessments of Wolfe's heroism. Most of the obituaries were unexceptional, with Britannia or Victory mourning a soldier noted for his valor, virtue, honor, his fortitude in battle and in ill health.[79] But some were troubled by what his legacy might be in the new political conjuncture. One obituary ended with the couplet, "In ev'ry age may Britons find/Gen'rals as brave, and Kings as kind,"[80] an open criticism of George III's policy towards America in contrast to that of his grandfather. Another in the Wilkesite *Middlesex Journal* submitted a politically loaded obituary which hinted that Wolfe's conquest of Quebec might be a forerunner of British military rule in America.[81]

The meaning of Wolfe's victory became the focus of further debate three years later, when the Americans besieged Quebec at the outset of the war with Britain. On this occasion the contest pitched two of Wolfe's former subalterns against one another: Guy Carleton, the governor of Quebec, to whom Wolfe had bequeathed one thousand pounds and all his books and papers, and General Richard Montgomery, a former captain who had participated in the siege of Louisbourg in 1758 alongside Wolfe. The third son of an Irish gentleman – the eldest was "Black" Alex the "scalper" – Richard

[78] John Shy, *Toward Lexington* (Princeton University Press, 1981), 303–20; Robert C. Alberts, *Benjamin West: A Biography* (Boston: Houghton Mifflin, 1978), 106.
[79] *London Chronicle*, September 3–5, October 6–8, 1772.
[80] Published in the *London Evening Post*, September 12–15, 1772 and the *London Chronicle*, 12–15 September 1772.
[81] *Middlesex Journal*, September 15, 1772.

Montgomery was frustrated by his inability to rise in the ranks of the army without the right political patronage. He was an opposition Whig in the era of Lords Bute and North. "As a man with little money cuts but a bad figure in this country among peers, nabobs," he declared, "I have cast my eye on America."[82] There he married into the influential Livingston family of New York and planned to spend his days as a gentleman-farmer. As Anglo-American relations deteriorated, he acted for the New York Provincial Congress and eventually agreed to take up the sword on America's behalf, hoping that armed resistance would bring the British to their senses. In the winter of 1775 he led a motley company of New England volunteers and Green Mountain Boys into Canada, pushing Guy Carleton back to Quebec. As winter set in and smallpox spread amongst his troops, Montgomery ventured an assault upon the fortress. It was a risky decision that cost him his life at Près de Ville in Quebec's Lower Town.

In America Montgomery became the nation's first military martyr, a Cincinnatus whose love of liberty brought him into conflict with his native country.[83] In the eyes of one writer in the *Boston Gazette*, Montgomery "generously bled to save his country and nobly fell agonizing in the cause of liberty."[84] In recognition of his services, Congress voted a monument in his honor, praising his patriotism, enterprise, perseverance, and "contempt of danger and death." Inevitably comparisons were made between Montgomery and Wolfe. In the eyes of Provost William Smith, who delivered the oration in Montgomery's honor, both achieved apotheosis as patriots whose private and public conduct were unimpeachable. Although Montgomery was not an advocate of American independence, Smith reminded his audience, he was none the less a "Proto-martyr to your rights."[85]

To some Britons Carleton rather than Montgomery was the more appropriate comparison to Wolfe. "Dying, heroic Wolfe this conquest gain'd," ran one poem in the *St. James's Chronicle*, "Which Carleton living, sav'd and fame obtained."[86] This was pre-eminently the loyalist point of view, one that cast Montgomery as a traitor who fell in "foul Rebellion's cause" or mocked his death as the triumph of false valor over discretion. But to pro-Americans in Britain, Montgomery died for liberty. In the Commons, Charles James Fox, Edmund Burke, and Isaac Barré all delivered panegyrics

[82] Shelton, *Montgomery and the American Revolution*, 35.
[83] *Pennsylvania Gazette*, January 24, 1776.   [84] *Boston Gazette*, February 26, 1776.
[85] See William Smith, *An Oration in Memory of General Montgomery and of the Officers and Soldiers who fell with him, December 31, 1775, before Quebec* (Philadelphia, 1776), 14, 23, 28.
[86] *St. James's Chronicle*, July 16, 1776, cited in McNairn, *Behold the Hero*, 210.

on their friend Montgomery to underscore the disastrous, civil war to which Britain was now committed. In Newcastle-upon-Tyne, where pro-Americanism was rife, Montgomery was represented as a genuine patriot, a "most respectable character" who "united with it . . . an enthusiastic love of liberty and justice, which made him determine never blindly to draw his sword in a national quarrel his judgment did not approve." In another paper Montgomery was described as the "empire's pride" who "living dar'd be free/ And dyed contending for *your* liberty."[87]

In radical Newcastle no comparison between Wolfe and Montgomery was made, perhaps because Geordies remembered Wolfe's reputation as a Jacobite hunter, or perhaps because the seeming inevitability of American independence made the comparison inapt. But in London, Montgomery and Wolfe were both placed in the pantheon of libertarian heroes, alongside people like John Hampden.[88] This identification of Wolfe with the course of liberty was also made by Tom Paine, another ex-patriot committed to the American cause. In a fictitious dialogue between Generals Wolfe and Gage, published in the *Pennsylvania Journal* in 1775, Paine has Wolfe berate the commander-in-chief of the British forces for taking up arms against the Americans who were only protesting the impolitic policies of British ministers.[89] Similar sentiments surfaced the following year, when the ghosts of Wolfe and Montgomery appeared before Admiral Shuldham and the British navy, warning them how "Vainly now you stand to ruin/That Empire which we died to raise."[90] Two years later, the ghost of Wolfe visits another British officer, this time General Richard Howe, to dissuade him from attacking the American colonists.[91] In these cases Wolfe is cast as the radical conscience of the anglophone world, reminding British admirals and generals of their country's long-standing commitment to liberty. Such an argument had a strong following in America, where Wolfe was toasted alongside radical revolutionaries and esteemed as a patriot general whose disinterested, virtuous conduct and critical victory over the French spurred Americans in their struggle for liberty.

The radical appropriation of Wolfe did not go unchallenged. For some Britons the American revolt was a shameful repudiation of Wolfe's legacy. In *Dialogues in the Shades*, Wolfe accuses Montgomery of being a

[87] *Newcastle Chronicle*, March 30, 1776; *Newcastle Journal*, February 3, 1776.
[88] *London Evening Post*, March 9–12 and 23–26, 1776; *London Chronicle*, March 28–30, 1776.
[89] *Pennsylvania Journal and Weekly Advertiser*, January 4, 1775, cited in McNairn, *Behold the Hero*, 215–16.
[90] *Boston Gazette*, April 15, 1776.
[91] M—P—, *Peace, A Poem* (London: Bew, 1778), cited in McNairn, *Behold the Hero*, 216.

sedition-monger, a man infatuated by liberty, a concept "prophaned in every age by turbulent designing men."[92] In Wolfe's view some of the measures against which the Americans protested, such as the Quebec Act, were honorable, equitable, and perfectly justifiable.[93] As for the others, Wolfe held out the hope they could be negotiated. Unlike one of the other interlocutors in the *Dialogues*, George Grenville, who demands that the Americans submit to the "yoke of subordination, without which there can neither be liberty nor safety,"[94] Wolfe is positioned as a Chathamite, as a man in favor of reconciliation in the name of imperial unity. This is how the poet William Cowper ultimately saw Wolfe, although by 1782, both Wolfe and Chatham are viewed as tragic figures, as irreproachable patriots whose devotion to empire ultimately ended in failure.[95]

In the American war, then, Wolfe's memory was associated with the spectrum of political opinion. The hero of Quebec is posthumously cast as a loyalist, a Chathamite, and an American sympathizer. To loyalists Wolfe was the architect of imperial grandeur, a man of unquestioned loyalty to king and country. To Chathamites, he inaugurated an era of Anglo-American cooperation that might have invigorated Britain's Atlantic empire rather than destroyed it. To British pro-Americans he represented the martial arm of liberty that British ministerialists had foolishly undermined, although those who acknowledged the inevitability of American independence might not have pressed the point very far. To the Americans, Wolfe was cast as one of the catalysts of national consciousness, a man whose victory over the French prompted colonists to reappraise their own destiny. In Hugh Henry Brakenbridge's play *The Death of General Montgomery*, published in Philadelphia in 1777, the ghost of Wolfe appears in the final scenes to ponder whether his own life laid the foundation of the gallant general's death. He declares that he had not shed his own blood to allow a "False-council'd king and venal parliament" to trample over American liberties. And he trusts that Montgomery's heroism will inspire America to gain independence from Britain and in due course generate "golden commerce and literature."[96] Such a teleological view of American history, linking Wolfe to that nation's manifest destiny, had a long-standing appeal. At the centenary of Wolfe's death, Lorenzo Sabine argued that the fall of Quebec "hastened the freedom of the Anglo-Saxon colonies" and

---

[92] Anon., *Dialogues in the Shades* (London: G. Kearsley, 1777), 9–10.
[93] Ibid., 48.   [94] Ibid., 67.   [95] McNairn, *Behold the Hero*, 224.
[96] Hugh Henry Brakenbridge, *The Death of General Montgomery in Storming the City of Quebec* (Philadelphia: Robert Bell, 1777), 39–40, cited in McNairn, *Behold the Hero*, 220–1.

gave ascendancy to "English civilization and the Protestant religion" in America.[97]

This Anglocentric view of Wolfe's achievement would eventually provoke a more critical, jaundiced view of his generalship, most notably from the French Canadians. At the tercentenary of Champlain's founding of Quebec City in 1908, French nationalists feared that Wolfe and the battle of the Plains would upstage French-Canadian achievements in the re-enactment of Canada's early history. In order to offset this criticism, the battle of Ste. Foy was judiciously paired with the Plains, General Lévis's victory with Wolfe's. In an effort to create a consensual, bi-cultural finale to the pageant, spectators were also reminded that the French-Canadian militia helped Guy Carleton defend Quebec from Montgomery and the Americans in 1775.[98] None of these gestures did much to abate French nationalist sentiments. Increasingly they viewed the events of 1759 as a disaster, conducted by a general whose attitude towards the civilian population was harsh and ruthless. But in the eighteenth century no public criticisms tarnished Wolfe the hero, at least in the anglophone world. Coming at a critical point in the Seven Years War, when Britons despaired of their aristocratic leaders, Wolfe's victory on the Plains of Abraham was the tonic that British and American expansionists desired. Whatever reservations British officers in the field had of Wolfe's command were shelved; whatever misgivings his occupational policy provoked among those on the St. Lawrence were off limits. By the time Benjamin West commemorated Wolfe's apotheosis, little could dispel the "odour of sanctity" that surrounded his name.[99] All that remained, in the contentious politics of American independence, was a battle over his legacy.

[97] Lorenzo Sabine, *An Address before the New England Historical and Genealogical Society* (Boston: A Williams, 1859), 5, 12.
[98] H. V. Nelles, *The Art of Nation Building: Pageantry and Spectacle at Quebec's Tercentenary* (University of Toronto Press: 1999), 126, 190–2, 309.
[99] See Schama, *Dead Certainties*, 37.

CHAPTER 12

Ethnicity in the British Atlantic world, 1688–1830

Colin Kidd

Traditionally, historians of empire, with certain distinguished exceptions,[1] tended to treat the topic of ethnicity in a brisk, cavalier fashion, in terms of the binary relationship between two unproblematic givens, Britons and indigenous peoples. In certain respects this was understandable, for, historiographically, imperial history was treated quite separately from domestic "British" history,[2] and the latter was itself largely Anglocentric and indifferent to issues of state and identity formation within the British archipelago, if indeed British history proper could be said to have existed at all. More recently, historians have begun to respond to John Pocock's agenda for a new British history, a pluralistic approach to the interactions of the various communities of the British Isles, not forgetting the history of the exportation of these "British" peoples across the globe.[3] As a result, historians have become more sensitive to the domestic tensions which underlay a British imperial identity,[4] and to the fact that certain groups enjoyed not only multiple identities, but also an uncertain status. Highland Scots, for example, held identities as both Scots and Britons, while being subalterns at home, yet white oppressors abroad. In addition, as Irish historians have known for some time, the English learnt to conceptualize the ethnic "Other" first of all through encounters with the white Celtic peoples on the fringes of the

---

[1] Most notably, P. J. Marshall, ed., *The British Discovery of Hinduism in the Eighteenth Century* (Cambridge University Press, 1970); Marshall and G. Williams, *The Great Map of Mankind: British Perceptions of the World in the Age of Enlightenment* (London: Dent, 1982).

[2] D. Armitage, *The Ideological Origins of the British Empire* (Cambridge University Press, 2000), 3.

[3] J. G. A. Pocock, "British History: A Plea for a New Subject," *Journal of Modern History*, 47 (1975), 601–21.

[4] B. Bailyn and P. Morgan, eds., *Strangers within the Realm: The Cultural Margins of the First British Empire* (Chapel Hill: University of North Carolina Press, 1991); Kathleen Wilson, *The Sense of the People: Politics, Culture and Imperialism in England, 1715–1785* (Cambridge University Press, 1995); Martin Daunton and Rick Halpern, eds., *Empire and Others: British Encounters with Indigenous Peoples, 1600–1850* (London: UCL Press, 1999).

British Isles.[5] Much as there is to be learnt, as we shall see, about the particular identities of Britons and indigenous peoples by considering ethnicity
holistically in a British Atlantic context, there also exists a much deeper
historiographical problem which historians of the first British empire have
barely noticed, far less confronted. Ethnicity itself, one of the foundational
analytic categories of imperial history, turns out to be very slippery, indeed
to have an unexpected history of its own.

Although the "ethnic" was part of the stock furniture of British thought
during the long eighteenth century, its meaning differed, in an important
way, from current usage. Dr. Johnson's *Dictionary* (1755) defined "Ethnick"
as "heathen; pagan; not Jewish; not Christian." Other dictionaries of this
period reiterate the same broad definition of "heathenish."[6] One can also
find examples of this older usage from every corner of the early modern
British world. Sir Robert Gordon of Lochinvar's proposal of 1625 for the
establishment of a Scots colony on Cape Breton had as its principal declared
aim the propagation of Christian truth and the enlightenment of "those
that are captivate in ethnicke darknesse."[7] The eighteenth-century Irish
Catholic antiquary Sylvester O'Halloran described the pagan rites of the
ancient pre-Christian Gaels as "our national ethnic worship."[8] The shift in
the meaning of "ethnic" over the past couple of centuries, from an original
association with religious otherness towards a more secular description of
racial, national, or cultural distinctiveness, should dent any complacency
among imperial historians that a category such as ethnicity or race can
be applied without substantial qualification to past societies. Any serious
attempt to capture eighteenth-century attitudes to the ethnic "Other" has
to confront a further kind of alterity, the historical otherness of a bygone
mentality. In particular, the historian must recreate the place of ethnicity in an eighteenth-century world which – the march of Enlightenment
notwithstanding – was still far from secularized. Despite the undoubted
reality of racism, slavery, and xenophobia, anti-Catholicism was a more
pronounced feature of eighteenth-century British discourse than hostility
to blacks. Eighteenth-century British culture was, moreover, drenched in
the humanistic values associated with the early modern recovery of classical

[5] E.g., N. Canny, "The Ideology of English Colonization: From England to America," *William and Mary Quarterly*, 3rd ser, 30 (1973), 575–98.
[6] Colin Kidd, *British Identities before Nationalism: Ethnicity and Nationhood in the Atlantic World, 1600–1800* (Cambridge University Press, 1999), 34.
[7] Robert Gordon, "Encouragements for New Galloway in America," in D. Laing, ed., *Royal Letters, Charters and Tracts, relating to the colonization of New Scotland* (Edinburgh: Bannatyne Club, 1867).
[8] Sylvester O'Halloran, *A General History of Ireland* (2 vols., London, 1778), II, 113.

antiquity. Significantly, the focus of classical political thought – despite an acceptance of non-racial slavery as a social practice – was on the institutions of the polis, not upon ethnic or national identities.[9]

Early modern Europeans and colonial Americans were not intellectually programmed for ethnic hatred, however much they engaged in practice in racial enslavement, mouthed prejudices, or demonized "otherness." Differences between peoples and races were conceived in terms of degrees of consanguinity among a world of nations descended from Noah. Amerindians and blacks were, of course, routinely depicted as inferior, savage, and primitive; but, ultimately, they presented a theological problem. Our modern obsessions with issues of identity and with relations of power tend to obscure the extent to which the expansion of Europe not only paved the way for the rise of the white West, but also presented major challenges to Christendom. Certainly, ethnicity was first and foremost a theological issue throughout the early modern period. Questions of racial superiority, however important in an era when Europe was expanding overseas and expropriating the lands and labor of non-white peoples, were trumped by religious anxieties about how the dramatic ethnic differences revealed by global exploration appeared to undermine the authority of the Bible. Throughout much of the early modern period theologians were concerned to reconcile the ethnological diversity of the world – whether in terms of color and other physical differences, language and religion – with the common origins of humanity set out in Scripture and agreed to belong to a timespan of around six thousand years. For example, if Native American racial and linguistic difference could not be reconciled with the Genesis story of humankind's unitary origins, then the authority of the Bible as a reliable historical source was undermined. From the mid-seventeenth century heterodox thinkers had begun to exploit this Achilles heel, and during the Enlightenment assaults on the status of Scripture were linked inextricably with skepticism about the unitary origins of the human race and the possibility of multiple, possibly pre-Adamic, centers of creation. Ideas of polygenesis – the plural origins of the races of humankind – undermined assumptions of the universal genetic transmission of Adam's original sin, thus subverting the whole sacred drama of Fall and Redemption.[10] From the late seventeenth to the mid-nineteenth century a phalanx of British

[9] Cf. I. Hannaford, *Race: The History of an Idea in the West* (Baltimore: The Johns Hopkins University Press, 1996).
[10] R. H. Popkin, *Isaac La Peyrere (1596–1676)* (Leiden: Brill, 1987); Popkin, "The Philosophical Basis of Eighteenth-Century Racism," in H. Pagliaro, ed., *Studies in Eighteenth-Century Culture III: Racism in the Eighteenth Century* (Cleveland: Ohio State University Press, 1973).

writers on ethnological topics from Edward Stillingfleet to James Cowles Prichard kept guard against this devastating error.[11]

Throughout the period of the – so-called – Enlightenment, to vent racialist doctrine was to court accusations of religious deviance. It is, perhaps, more than a coincidence that David Hume, who used his skeptical metaphysics to launch several penetrating assaults on the central tenets of Christianity, was "apt to suspect the negroes to be naturally inferior to the whites," wondering whether "nature had not made an original distinction between these breeds of men."[12] In the case of another Lowland Scot, the strident late Enlightenment Celtophobe John Pinkerton, a direct connection between religious heterodoxy and racism is quite explicit. Pinkerton directly challenged the authority of the Bible as a guide to the the science of ethnology. Liberated from the shackles of the deceptive "Judaic legends" of the Old Testament, and thus from biblical monogenesis, Pinkerton had recourse to nature, which seemed to produce variety in every class of animal. Just as there were forty or fifty types of dog, he argued, "so, by analogy and actual observation, we know that, so far from being descended of one man, there are many races of men of quite different forms and attributes."[13]

Doctrinal racism – as opposed to unthinking prejudice and xenophobia – appears to have developed as a by-product of the Enlightened critique of Christianity. The subversion of Scripture was not in most cases a strategy designed consciously to provide new polygenetic supports for white domination of non-European peoples; rather Enlightened critics used the fact of racial diversity as a weapon to undermine the authority of Scripture. As a result of these heretical associations, polygenesis remained the preserve of a daring minority. Racism derived little ideological sustenance from the orthodox Protestant mainstream of political and intellectual culture. Indeed, there was a marked reticence – imposed by theological orthodoxy – to say what seemed obvious to many commentators, namely that different races had distinct biological origins in the mists of antiquity.[14] Even in the high Enlightenment Lord Kames drew back – albeit somewhat unconvincingly – from Co-Adamitism – the notion that every race had its own Adam

---

[11] Kidd, *British Identities*, 39–58; G. Stocking, *Victorian Anthropology* (London: Free Press, 1987), ch. 2; H. F. Augstein, *James Cowles Prichard's Anthropology* (Amsterdam: Rodopi, 1999).

[12] David Hume, "Of National Characters," in Hume, *Essays*, ed. E. F. Miller (Indianapolis: Liberty Classics, 1987), 208n.

[13] John Pinkerton, "An Essay on the Origin of Scottish Poetry," in Pinkerton, ed., *Ancient Scotish Poems* (2 vols., London, 1786), I, xxiv–xxvi. For Pinkerton as anti-Gaelic racialist, see C. Kidd, "Teutonist Ethnology and Scottish Nationalist Inhibition, 1780–1880," *Scottish Historical Review*, 74 (1995), 45–68, esp. 51–4.

[14] D. N. Livingstone, "The Preadamite Theory and the Marriage of Science and Religion," *Transactions of the American Philosophical Society*, 82, 3 (1992), 9–10.

and Eve – for this was an "opinion . . . we are not permitted to adopt; being taught a different lesson by revelation." Instead, he argued that a miracle at the Tower of Babel must have wrought "an immediate change of bodily constitution" which fitted the dispersing peoples of the world for the various climes they were destined to inhabit.[15] Theological doctrine did not, of course, prevent the emergence of racist attitudes and practices – whether at elite or popular levels of society in the British Atlantic world.[16] Nevertheless, the fear of lapsing into heterodoxy did serve to inhibit a fuller articulation of white Christian racialism.

The orthodox Christian majority was concerned not so much with racial difference as with the details of racial filiation. The overall picture was clear. Given that the biblical flood had been universal in its effects, all humanity must have sprung from the loins of Noah. Thus the genealogical descent of Noah's sons – Ham, Shem, and Japhet – offered the orthodox point of departure for students of ethnic filiation. Thereafter the filiation of ancient peoples began to become obscure. Antiquaries tried to fill in gaps in the story of the descent of the Noachids between their last mention in Scripture and the appearance of ethnic and racial groups in the historical record: for early modern anthropology this was the "missing link." There was until the 1770s a scholarly consensus that the Celts and Germans were closely related within the Noachic family tree. Most antiquaries believed the Celts to be the descendants of Gomer, the son of Japhet, while they identified the Germans as the offspring of Gomer's son Ashkenaz.[17] However, there were quite clearly gaps in human history between Genesis and the historical emergence of distinct races and nations. Although a crude biblical literalism in the ethnological sphere was marginalized during the Enlightenment, monogenesis and filiation remained central features of the British Protestant Enlightenment.[18]

Much of the early literature on Native Americans, for example, was written to answer the question of where these people came from, how they got to the Americas, and whether their distinctiveness somehow challenged the basic tenets of monogenesis. The Scots Presbyterian clergyman David Malcolme used perceived similarities in the languages of Scottish Gaels, Amerindians of the Darien Isthmus, and the Chinese to refute the arguments of those Deists who "pretend that the languages of America

[15] Kames, *Sketches of the History of Man* (1774: 2nd edn., 4 vols., 1778) I, 22–8, 64, 73–80.
[16] W. D. Jordan, *White over Black: American Attitudes towards the Negro, 1550–1812* (Chapel Hill: University of North Carolina Press, 1968); Marshall and Williams, *Great Map of Mankind*, 246.
[17] Kidd, *British Identities*, chs. 3, 8.
[18] See, e.g, William Robertson, *History of America* (1777) in Robertson, *Works* (London, 1831), 784.

have no affinity to any of the languages in Europe, Asia or Africa; and then infer, that therefore they must be a quite distinct race of mortals, and not sprung from Adam and Eve."[19] In his *History of the American Indians* (1775) James Adair explicitly challenged the Co-Adamite suggestions advanced by Kames, claiming instead that the Native Americans were "lineally descended from Adam" who was "the first, and the great parent of all the human species." Adair married the techniques of comparative ethnography to his orthodox apologetic. He contended on the basis of their division into tribes, laws of purity, abstinence from unclean food, and the nature of their languages that American Indians came from Israelite stock. Native Americans, in the words of Adair, were "copper colour American Hebrews."[20] Others disagreed. Andrew Turnbull, a Charleston physician, contended that American Indians were descended from seafaring Carthaginians who had made it across the Atlantic to the Americas,[21] while another minority tradition posited the Welsh colonization of America under the leadership of Prince Madoc.[22] However, most commentators argued for the Asiatic origins of the Amerindians who had crossed into the continent of America from Siberia, possibly via a landbridge.[23] The theological implications of Native American origins would remain a burning issue after the winning of American independence.[24]

The most important example of filiation was in the sphere of religion itself. Curiously, theologians were more interested in tackling pagan otherness than they were bothered by physical difference. Idolatry mattered more than color; hence, of course, the original definition of ethnic as "heathen," by contrast with its current – vague – associations with cultural, national, tribal, and racial groups. To eighteenth-century commentators ethnicity was a matter not just of accounting for racial and linguistic differences but also – most importantly – of explaining why so many apparently non-Judaeo-Christian religions could be found throughout the world. Surely these religions were not the products of authentic divine revelation? One

---

[19] David Malcolme, *Letters, essays and other tracts illustrating the antiquities of Great Britain and Ireland* (1738: London, 1744), "Collection of Papers," ix, 22.

[20] James Adair, *The History of the American Indians* (London, 1775), esp. 3, 11–12, 15, 18–19, 34, 37, 96, 119, 118, 124, 132–4, 218.

[21] A. F. C. Wallace, *Jefferson and the Indians* (Cambridge, MA: Harvard University Press, 1999), 137.

[22] G. A. Williams, *Madoc: The Legend of the Welsh Discovery of America* (Oxford: Clarendon Press, 1987); Wallace, *Jefferson and the Indians*, 130.

[23] B. W. Sheehan, *Seeds of Extinction: Jeffersonian Philanthropy and the American Indian* (Chapel Hill: University of North Carolina Press, 1973), 61–3.

[24] D. Boorstin, *The Lost World of Thomas Jefferson* (Boston: Beacon Press, 1960), 77–9; Sheehan, *Seeds of Extinction*, 46, 48, 52, 54, 59–60; S. Williams, *Fantastic Archaeology: The Wild Side of North American Prehistory* (Philadelphia: University of Pennsylvania Press, 1991), 39–42.

common strategy was to explain these heathen religions as corruptions of the ancient patriarchal religion of Noah. As the descendants of the Noachids spread throughout the world and moved into remote geographical locations, it was argued, they developed their own cultures. The passage of time obliterated any clear memory of the original religion of Noah; thereafter, with the posthumous deification of local heroes, warriors, and kings, the legacy of monotheism itself was eclipsed, and pagan polytheism flourished atop an unrecognizable core of Ur-Christianity. Indeed, John Pocock has argued that in the eighteenth century anti-Hamitic prejudice did not constitute "a racism based on colour." While the curse of Ham was indeed deployed to justify the enslavement of black Africans, Pocock notes that "the distinguishing characteristic of the descendants of Ham [was] not pigmentation but idolatry." The Hamites were held particularly responsible for the degeneration of the ancient monotheistic religion of the Noachic era into idolatrous polytheism.[25]

During the eighteenth-century Enlightenment new scientific explanations appeared to account for racial, linguistic, and cultural differences. Some of these were biological, environmentalist, and sociological. Not only did this pose little threat to monogenesis – indeed the science of man was generally predicated upon a uniform human nature – but biblical exegesis also continued to flourish alongside the discourses of Enlightenment, sometimes in the same work. For most of the long eighteenth century the authority of the Pentateuch remained central to the Christian mainstream of the Enlightenment. In 1697 the clerical scientist John Harris produced both a Hamitic interpretation of the origins of the black African peoples, and an environmentalist argument that the "colour of the Negroes is not ingenite; but proceeds from accidental natural causes, and such as are peculiar to the countries they inhabit."[26] Over half a century later James Boswell recounted that on Saturday June 25, 1763

Johnson and an Irish gentleman got into a dispute concerning the cause of some part of mankind being black. "Why, Sir, (said Johnson,) it has been accounted for in three ways: either by supposing that they are the posterity of Ham, who was cursed; or that God at first created two kinds of men, one black and another white; or that by the heat of the sun the skin is scorched, and so acquires a sooty hue. This matter has been much canvassed among naturalists, but has never been brought to any certain issue."[27]

[25] J. G. A. Pocock, *Barbarism and Religion, Vol. II: Narratives of Civil Government* (Cambridge University Press, 1999), 358.
[26] John Harris, *Remarks on some late papers, relating to the Universal Deluge* (1697), 66.
[27] James Boswell, *Life of Johnson* (1791: Oxford World's Classics, 1980 edn.), 284.

Scientific and specifically scriptural solutions still seemed equally plausible.

Contemporary Afro-British commentary on race was characterized by this hybrid strain of Christian Enlightenment. Both Olaudah Equiano and Ignatius Sancho subscribed to the orthodox canons of sacred history and to the importance of divine providence in the civil history of humankind (Sancho having been an enthusiastic reader of Bossuet's providentialist account of universal history); yet each black Briton was also in touch with new enlightened approaches to racial questions. In his autobiography Equiano displays a mixture of ethnic theology and stadialism when discussing his own ethnic origins. Not only did Equiano cite the central text of orthodox monogenesis Acts 17:26, he also wondered if the West African tribe in which he had grown up before his enslavement and transportation had been a branch of the Old Testament Jewish nation. Equiano's people had believed in "one Creator of all things," engaged in male circumcision, and practiced various ritual "purifications and washings." Supporting his comparative ethnography with contemporary theological opinion, Equiano was struck by the similarity between the manners of his own people and the Jewish "patriarchs while they were yet in that pastoral state which is described in Genesis." Note here Equiano's awareness of the stadialist account of progress – pioneered most famously in the Scottish Enlightenment – which explained humankind's rise from the primitive hunter-gatherer state to commercial society via pastoral and agrarian phases. Science was also allied to theology in Equiano's account of his ethnic background. Acknowledging the problematic "difference of colour between the Eboan Africans and the modern Jews," Equiano had confidence that the environmentalist explanations of modern scientists could account for such variations.[28]

Ethnic theology also crops up in Sancho's letters. He wondered in jest to a correspondent whether there were "any blackamoors in the Ark," a question which challenged European complacency about an original whiteness. Peppered throughout Sancho's correspondence are references to "the race of Adam," his preferred formulation to describe humanity as a whole. Nor was this a mere idle expression; Sancho, like Equiano, used Scripture as a weapon against racism and against the inhumanity of the slave trade. However, it is important not to privilege the racial import of such remarks above

---

[28] Olaudah Equiano, *The Interesting Narrative*, ed. Vincent Carretta (Harmondsworth: Penguin, 1995), 40–5, 246–7; A. Potkay, "Olaudah Equiano and the Art of Spiritual Autobiography," *Eighteenth-Century Studies*, 27 (1994), 677–92; Ignatius Sancho, *Letters*, ed. Vincent Carretta (Harmondsworth: Penguin, 1998), 54–5.

their immediate theological significance. It was not race or slavery, but the "improbability of eternal damnation" which provoked Sancho's outpouring on the "blessed expiation of the Son of the Most High God – who died for the sins of all – all – Jew, Turk, Infidel, and Heretic; – fair – sallow – brown – tawney – black – and you – and I and every son and daughter of Adam." A follower of the vogue towards sensibility and sentiment in mid-eighteenth-century culture (which also fueled contemporary revulsion against the slave trade), Sancho had no more truck with corruptions of the benevolent message of Christianity than he did with race slavery itself.[29]

Yet an obvious sense of racial otherness and awareness of the horrors of slavery did little, it seems, to preclude a strong dose of Afro-British imperial patriotism. Sancho, the only known black voter in eighteenth-century parliamentary elections, was a proud and conscientious member of the British political nation. In November 1779, during the crisis of the first British empire, Sancho wondered if the election of some fresh faces to the House of Commons might "save Old England": "This looks dark – whilst Ireland treats us rather laconic – Scotland not too friendly – America speaks, but too plainly." The Catholic question also cut across racial boundaries. Although a number of blacks appear to have been involved in the anti-Catholic Gordon Riots, Sancho was not among them. Instead he stands representative of a new strain of enlightened Protestantism in eighteenth-century Britain which appreciated the diminution of the Counter Reformation threat under the moderate papal regimes of Benedict XIV, Clement XIII, and Clement XIV. Sancho was, for example, a keen admirer of the purported *Letters of Pope Clement XIV*, the liberal pope, Lorenzo Ganganelli, who established his enlightened credentials in Protestant Europe with his suppression of the Jesuit order in 1773.[30]

Unsurprisingly, theological concerns also shaped British attitudes towards the Jews, but sometimes in surprising ways. Judaeophobia, the traditional antipathy towards the Jews as Christ-killers and usurers, was an undoubted feature of British life. The outraged reactions to the Jewish Naturalization measure of 1753 indicate a deep reservoir of anti-Semitic sentiment.[31] Nevertheless, the Plantation Act of 1740, which enabled Jews resident in the colonies for seven years to qualify for naturalization, had

---

[29] Sancho, *Letters*, 83, 86, 88, 93, 109, 111, 131, 138, 143, 151–2, 170, 180, 308.
[30] Ibid., xiv, 113–14, 150, 187, 216, 220, 229, 306, 318, 322.
[31] T. W. Perry, *Public Opinion, Propaganda and Politics in Eighteenth-Century England: A Study of the Jew Bill of 1753* (Cambridge, MA: Harvard University Press, 1962); M. Duffy, *The Englishman and the Foreigner* (Cambridge: Chadwyck-Healey, 1986), 17–18, 164–7; F. Felsenstein, *Anti-Semitic Stereotypes: A Paradigm of Otherness in English Popular Culture, 1660–1830* (Baltimore: The Johns Hopkins University Press, 1995).

not provoked controversy.[32] Furthermore, antipathy towards the Jews was somewhat counterbalanced by a large measure of philo-Semitism within British Protestantism, which was present from the radical biblically inspired culture of the Commonwealth, but became even more pronounced from the 1790s onwards.

In 1656 the Jews had been readmitted to England *de facto*, amidst an outpouring of radical millenarianism. Towards the end of 1655 a special commission authorized by Oliver Cromwell, himself a millenarian, had sympathetically considered the plight of the Jews, though without reaching a formal conclusion. Expectations that the "last days" were at hand had been raised by the Puritan revolution, and there was a widespread assumption among millenarian commentators that the reign of Christ on earth would be preceded by the conversion of the Jews.[33] Some British Puritans cultivated a distinctively Judaic religiosity. The millenarian goldsmith Thomas Tany, an early proto-Zionist, who believed that the restoration of the Jews to Palestine was another precondition of the Second Coming, went as far as to circumcise himself in the cause.[34] Despite the disappointment of the Restoration, Messianism survived in various corners of British culture into the age of Enlightenment. In his *Enquiry into the Time of the Coming of the Messiah* (London, 1751) Robert Clayton, a Church of Ireland bishop controversial for his Arian Christology, anticipated the Second Coming when "Jews and Gentiles shall be united into one People under Messiah, the Shepherd and King."[35] From the seventeenth century, Welsh Hebraists championed the notion that Welsh was a sister language of Hebrew.[36] The heterodox Irish-born radical John Toland, in his *Reasons for Naturalizing the Jews in Great Britain and Ireland, On the same foot with all other nations* (1714), even claimed that "a considerable part of the British inhabitants are the undoubted offspring of the Jews."[37] On the other hand, there were anti-rabbinical tendencies within British Hebraic scholarship.[38]

[32] D. Katz, *The Jews in the History of England 1485–1850* (Oxford: Clarendon Press, 1994), 242.
[33] D. Katz, *Philosemitism and the Readmission of the Jews to England 1603–1655* (Oxford: Clarendon Press, 1982).
[34] D. Katz, "The Restoration of the Jews: Thomas Tany to World Jewry (1653)," in J. van den Berg and E. van der Wall, eds., *Jewish-Christian Relations in the Seventeenth Century* (Dordrecht: Kluwer Academic Publishers, 1988), 187.
[35] Quoted in Katz, *Jews in the History of England*, 237.
[36] G. H. Jenkins, *The Foundations of Modern Wales 1642–1780* (Oxford: Clarendon Press, 1987), 221, 223.
[37] Quoted in Katz, *Jews in the History of England*, 235.
[38] W. McKane, *Selected Christian Hebraists* (Cambridge University Press, 1989), "Alexander Geddes," 168–9.

Philo-Semitism re-emerged in the 1790s as a more central – though controversial – component of British culture. The dramatic revolutionary events of the 1790s seemed to be harbingers of the millennium. The restoration of the Jews to their homeland became once more an urgent concern. Richard Brothers proclaimed a mission to lead the Jews back to Palestine. Evangelicals became obsessed with the conversion of "God's ancient people," and the London Society for Promoting Christianity amongst the Jews was established in 1809. During the feverish decades of the revolutionary and Napoleonic wars philo-Semitism became tinged with francophobia. Which nation had been charged with the divine mission of restoring the Jews to their homeland: Christian England or atheistic France? While conservative loyalists such as Thomas Witherby and Samuel Horsley, Bishop of Rochester, rubbished the claims of France, the radical philo-Semite James Bicheno combined a francophobia directed against the *ancien régime* – identifying Louis XIV as the Second Beast of The Book of Revelation – with the view that Revolutionary France might indeed be the instrument of providence for the restoration of the Jews. On the other hand, Edmund Burke seized upon the radical, regicidal associations of English philo-Semitism. Had not Lord George Gordon, the notorious fomenter of the Gordon Riots, converted to Judaism? Nevertheless, Michael Ragussis has shown how other influential commentators wove the plight of the Jews into the fabric of England's Protestant destiny. Charles Simeon, a prominent Anglican evangelical, promoted the notion that the English were a chosen people, among whose responsibilities was the protection and conversion of the Jews. However, philo-Semitism was not confined to the English. It is clear from the work of Ruth Bloch on American millenarians of the 1790s that the same philo-Semitic themes also reverberated among Protestants stationed outside the formal boundaries of the British empire.[39]

Of course, as Frank Felsenstein points out, philo-Semitism involved a deliberate Christian failure to appreciate the authenticity of Judaism as a religion in its own right: "No less than the purveyor of traditional anti-Semitism, though perhaps with greater subtlety, the theological philo-Semite ultimately seeks to undermine the very existence of Jews as Jews."

[39] Thomas Witherby, *An Attempt to Remove National Prejudices concerning the Jewish Nation* (London, 1804), 157, 161–2, 170, 296–7; Samuel Horsley, *Critical Disquisitions on the Eighteenth Chapter of Isaiah* (London, 1799), 16–17; James Bicheno, *The Signs of the Times, or the Overthrow of the Papal Tyranny in France, The Prelude to the Destruction of Popery and Despotism*, 4th edn. (London and Edinburgh, 1794), 21–9, 32–5; James Bicheno, *The Restoration of the Jews, The Crisis of all Nations* (London, 1800), 18, 59, 65, 113–14; M. Ragussis, *Figures of Conversion: "The Jewish Question" and English National Identity* (Durham: Duke University Press, 1995); M. Ragussis, "Writing Nationalist History: England, the Conversion of the Jews and Ivanhoe," *English Literary History*, 60 (1993), 181–215; R. Bloch, *Visionary Republic: Millennial Themes in American Thought, 1756–1800* (Cambridge University Press, 1985), 146–7.

However, in this regard at least, the Jews were, although singled out as a special remnant, not treated very differently from other forms of non-Christian religion encountered by early modern British Protestants. Orthodox critics portrayed all other creeds with reference to a Christian benchmark: while they depicted most communities of pagans as the degenerate offspring of primeval monotheists, they viewed Muslims as unitarians and interpreted the Karaites as anti-rabbinical "Protestant" Jews.[40]

Where other ethnic groups were concerned, eighteenth-century Britons throughout the Atlantic world found conversion much more problematic than in the case of the Jews. The possibility of religious conversion created particularly knotty dilemmas for white anglophone Protestants, who were committed to the priesthood of all believers and the concomitant ideal of spreading the word of the Bible in the vernacular. Examples drawn from various parts of the British empire demonstrate how hypocrisy and vested interests worked to undermine the universalist ideals of Christianity. Nowhere was the quandary greater than among white Christians in slaveholding colonies. Before the late seventeenth century slavery in the English colonies of North America was justified by "ethnicity" – in its early modern meaning of heathenism – not by race as such. Blacks were enslaved not because of color but because they were non-Christians. Most scholars agree that racism was a consequence rather than a cause of slavery. Only in the aftermath of Bacon's rebellion (1676) had Virginia's rulers encouraged slave – rather than servant – labor and racial differentiation between black and white as a means of dividing and ruling the colony's insubordinate lower orders.[41] From the mid-seventeenth century slaveowners expressed concern that the conversion and baptism of slaves compromised rights of ownership. To calm these worries various measures were passed in colonial

[40] Felsenstein, *Anti-Semitic Stereotypes*, 11; P. Harrison, *"Religion" and the Religions in the English Enlightenment* (Cambridge University Press, 1990); J. Champion, *The Pillars of Priestcraft Shaken: The Church of England and its Enemies 1660–1730* (Cambridge University Press, 1992), 99–132; J. van den Berg, "Proto-Protestants? The Image of the Karaites as a Mirror of the Catholic–Protestant Controversy in the Seventeenth Century," in van den Berg and van der Wall, *Jewish-Christian Relations*, 33–49.
[41] See, e.g, W. Billings, "The Cases of Fernando and Elisabeth Key," *William and Mary Quarterly*, 3rd ser, 30 (1973), 467–74; W. Wiecek, "The Statutory Law of Slavery and Race in the Thirteen Mainland Colonies of British America," *William & Mary Quarterly*, 3rd ser, 34 (1977), esp. 263–4; E. Morgan, *American Slavery, American Freedom* (New York: Norton, 1975). The place of race in slavery can perhaps be illuminated by way of a comparison with another part of the Atlantic world: in Scotland the servitude of white colliers was only fully abolished in 1799, two decades after the case of "Knight v. Wedderburn" had liberated any black slave who set foot on Scottish soil. See C. Whatley, "The Dark Side of the Enlightenment? Sorting Out Serfdom," in T. M. Devine and J. R. Young, eds., *Eighteenth-Century Scotland: New Perspectives* (East Linton: Tuckwell Press, 1999); D. Walker, *A Legal History of Scotland, Vol. V: The Eighteenth Century* (Edinburgh: Green, 1998), 313, 651–3.

legislatures, such as the Virginia law of 1667, which explicitly rejected the notion that the baptism of a slave necessitated his manumission. Despite the trend towards an explicitly racial definition of slavery in colonial slave codes, anxieties about the consequences of conversion would continue to be aired throughout the eighteenth century. The stubbornly persistent notion that it was wrong to hold one's fellow Christian – of whatever color – in bondage hampered efforts to win souls for Christ among the slave population, much to the disappointment of pro-conversionist clergy.[42]

An analogous dilemma arose in eighteenth-century Ireland, where an Anglocentric language policy dented the declared Protestant ideal of making the Scriptures available as widely as possible in the vernacular. In 1711 the Reverend John Richardson launched proposals for an Irish New Testament, catechism, and prayer book (alongside a parallel proposal for charter schools in every parish offering education in the English language). Even this two-pronged strategy failed to win wide support, and Richardson's project failed to come to fruition. The major objection, among several, mooted against Richardson's scheme was that it would give sustenance to the barbaric Gaelic language of the indigenous natives. Contemporary supporters of Richardson's conversionist scheme were forced to justify not only its utility, but even its legality. In 1713 there appeared an anonymous pamphlet entitled *Preaching the gospel in Irish, not contrary to law*.[43] Moreover, commentators saw clear disincentives to proselytizing among the subordinate ethnic population. In 1719 Edward Synge, Archbishop of Tuam, wondered whether there were not "too many amongst us who had rather keep the Papists as they are, in an almost slavish subjection, than have them made Protestants, and thereby entitled to the same liberties and privileges, with the rest of their fellow subjects."[44]

Parallels can also be found in Scotland where Lowland hostility to the Gaelic language – often characterized as Erse, or Irish – dominated the educational policies of its Society for Propagating Christian Knowledge (SPCK), a missionary body established in 1709. Only in the 1760s, when it

---

[42] Jordan, *White over Black*, 92–3, 180–7; J. Butler, *Awash in a Sea of Faith: Christianizing the American People* (Cambridge. MA: Harvard University Press 1990), 132–3.

[43] T. Barnard, "Protestants and the Irish Language, c. 1675–1725," *Journal of Ecclesiastical History*, 44 (1993), 243–72; S. Connolly, *Religion, Law and Power: The Making of Protestant Ireland 1660–1760* (Oxford: Clarendon Press, 1992), 294–307; S. Mandelbrote, "The Bible and National Identity in the British Isles, c. 1650–c. 1750," in T. Claydon and I. McBride, eds., *Protestantism and National Identity: Britain and Ireland, c. 1650–c. 1850* (Cambridge University Press, 1998); J. Leerssen, *Mere Irish and Fíor-Ghael* (University of Cork Press, 1996), 285–6; R. Eccleshall, "Anglican Political Thought in the Century after the Revolution of 1688," in D. G. Boyce, R. Eccleshall, and V. Geoghegan, eds., *Political Thought in Ireland since the Seventeenth Century* (London: Routledge, 1993), 45.

[44] Quoted in Connolly, *Religion, Law and Power*, 306.

introduced a Gaelic New Testament, did the Scottish SPCK come to realize the absurdity of excluding the language of the natives. Was it not better to teach in the despised native tongue, if only to accomplish more effectively the aims of one's mission? Although the Scottish SPCK and other agencies of "improvement" remained committed to the extirpation of the Gaelic language and culture, the argument of Allan Macinnes that mainstream mid-eighteenth-century British attitudes to the Highlanders "verged on ethnic cleansing" or had "genocidal intent" involves a considerable measure of exaggeration.[45] Contemporary Englishmen and Lowland Scots considered Highlanders to be backward, barbaric, and alien, but also deemed them to be capable of improvement. Curiously, ethnicity as such scarcely features in the papers of contemporary policymakers dealing with the Highland question, never mind "ethnic cleansing." In fact, these memoranda are awash with a universalist language of philanthropy and improvement. The declared aim of policy was to detach clansmen from their chiefs, to free ordinary Highlanders from feudal vassalage and slavish subjection to their chiefs. The Gael was to be liberated from his oppressive culture; and in gratitude he would become a loyal Hanoverian Briton. Although improvement was closely linked to cultural extinction, the intended goal, as in the case of late eighteenth-century attitudes to the Native American, was the absorption of the ethnic other into civilization. It followed logically from the orthodox unity of humankind and the notion of a universal moral sense that the unfortunate circumstances of the Highlanders and the Amerindians did not affect their "moral potentiality." Barbarity was not innate, for all human beings were endowed, in the words of Bernard Sheehan, with "a faculty for further accomplishment." Policies of removal and clearance were only formulated later in the more overtly racialist climate of the early nineteenth century.[46]

The constraints imposed by religion on British assumptions about ethnic difference received considerable reinforcement from another influential quarter of eighteenth-century cultural life: the profane legacy of classical antiquity. Civic humanism or classical republicanism constituted one of the

[45] A. Macinnes, *Clanship, Commerce and the House of Stuart, 1603–1788* (East Linton: Tuckwell Press, 1996), 211–12, 215.

[46] See, e.g., "Some Hints to his Royal Highness the Duke of Cumberland concerning the Highlanders of Scotland," Edinburgh University Library MS. Dc.6.70 (2); various memoranda in National Archives of Scotland, esp. RH 2/4/360, ff. 24–31; 100–4; RH 2/4/368, ff. 313–14; *Remarks on the People and Government of Scotland, particularly the Highlanders* (Edinburgh, 1747); *A Second Letter to A Noble Lord with a plan for effectually uniting and sincerely attaching the Highlanders to the British Constitution* (London, 1748); C. Kidd, *Subverting Scotland's Past* (Cambridge University Press, 1993), 155–60. Cf. Sheehan, *Seeds of Extinction*, 28, 30, 44.

liveliest and most influential traditions of British political thought during the long eighteenth century. Not only did it shape the British response to the rise of commerce and the fiscal-military state, it also proved decisive in shaping provincial political cultures throughout the Atlantic world, not least in the thirteen colonies, where it provided the ideological underpinnings of the American Revolution.[47] The civic humanist agenda focused, in the words of Walter Moyle, upon "the natural transmigrations of dominion, from one form of government to another [which] make the common circle in the generation and corruption of all states."[48] Here character and its deformations were central issues, yet cast largely in moral and political rather than in ethnic terms. For the gaze of civic humanists – largely indifferent to ethnic factors – was fixed predominantly on the potential for destabilizing *internal* transformations of political communities. Although there was some acknowledgment that foreign importations might well accelerate the decline of political virtue – with French effeminacy the modern counterpart of the Oriental luxury which had enervated the moral fiber of republican Rome – corruption itself was ultimately a domestic process. Otherness, or at least the causes of a people's corrupting transformation from virtuous liberty through torpid and luxurious self-indulgence to political enslavement, lurked within one's own polis.[49]

Civic humanists busied themselves over the size of state most appropriate for republican self-government, and obsessed over the threat posed to small states by the aspirations of conquering despots to universal monarchy. Nevertheless, they expressed little or no concern for the fate of distinct ethnicities. The real issue was how to maintain an enduring system of constitutional self-government. In his utopian vision of Europe Andrew Fletcher of Saltoun cavalierly carved up a whole continent into various confederations of city-states, paying very little regard to ethnic constituencies and established nations or conventional boundaries. Even his beloved Scotland was split into two regional city-states cenetred on Inverness and Stirling.[50]

The political ideals of the civic humanist tradition embodied universal – rather than particular – goods. Classical republicans did not celebrate the liberties of the ancient Roman republic as peculiarly appropriate to the

---

[47] See, e.g., B. Bailyn, *The Ideological Origins of the American Revolution* (Cambridge MA: Harvard University Press, 1967); J. G. A. Pocock, *The Machiavellian Moment* (Princeton University Press, 1975).

[48] C. Robbins, ed., *Two English Republican Tracts* (Cambridge, 1969), 231.

[49] See J. Sekora, *Luxury: The Concept in Western Thought from Eden to Smollett* (Baltimore: The Johns Hopkins University Press, 1977).

[50] Andrew Fletcher, *Account of a Conversation concerning a right regulation of governments for the common good of mankind* (1704), in J. Robertson, ed., *Fletcher: Political Works* (Cambridge University Press, 1997).

Roman *Volksgeist*. After all, according to Thomas Gordon the nature of its government and laws determined the "character" of a people. In their declension from a virtuous political golden age, wrote Gordon, the Athenians and Spartans "seemed afterward another race of men, though their blood and climate were still the same." Civic humanists eschewed rigid ethnocentric categories in favor of a cyclical interpretation of history which traced the vicissitudes of political communities. Like all things sublunary, the character of a people was mutable rather than fixed and innate. "Between the Roman people under the commonwealth, and the Roman people under the dominion of the emperors," claimed Gordon, "the difference was as great as between different nations, and they only resembled each other in language and dress. They were indeed as different, or rather as opposite, as men uncorrupted and free are to debauched slaves."[51] In civic humanist thinking the gulf between freedom and slavery provided the key distinction, not the superficial ethnic differences to be found among ancient Romans, Athenians, and Spartans, or indeed among eighteenth-century Britons, Frenchmen, and Spaniards.

In so far as an ethnocentric analysis surfaced in the discourse of civic humanism, it related to the recent fate of Europe's Gothic mixed governments, a subject upon which patriotic humanists across the British Atlantic world were fixated. Gothicism gave an ethnocentric inflection to the dominant universalist values of the civic humanist tradition. In particular, the *Germania* of Tacitus, with its contrast between corrupt Romans and virtuous Germans, operated both as a universal point of comparison and also as a portrait of the vigorous, liberty-loving character of the biological ancestors of the English – and, as contemporaries noted, of many other modern European nations.[52] Despite the aggressive francophobia which, as Linda Colley has pointed out, was such an important feature of eighteenth-century British integration,[53] there was in fact very little sense of a huge *ethnic* gulf between the fortunate peoples of the English-speaking world and benighted continental Europeans. Historians agreed that most of the political nations of Europe shared common ethnic origins. The peoples of Europe, they argued, were largely the descendants of the libertarian Gothic peoples who had erected limited governments on the ruins of the Roman empire: the Saxons in England, the Franks in France, the Visigoths in Spain.[54] Early modern factors alone explained the divergence of the

---

[51] Thomas Gordon, "Discourses upon Tacitus," Discourse IX, "Of the People," in Gordon, ed., *The Works of Tacitus, Vol II, part I* (Dublin, 1732), 159–66.
[52] S. Kliger, *The Goths in England* (Cambridge, MA: Harvard University Press, 1952), 112–13.
[53] Linda Colley, *Britons: Forging the Nation, 1707–1837* (New Haven: Yale University Press, 1992).
[54] Kidd, *British Identities*, ch. 9.

continental experience from the British: the Counter Reformation and the rise of absolutism on the ruins of medieval Europe's mixed monarchies. Eighteenth-century British commentators felt very little ethnic triumphalism; rather they experienced a keen anxiety that if Britain's Gothic cousins on the continent had fallen prey to the rise of modern despotism, then the Goths of Britain might be the next to fall.[55] Protestantism in itself provided ineffective inoculation against these trends: this was the depressing message of Molesworth's notorious discussion of how Lutheran Denmark had succumbed to despotism.[56]

Just as the identification with the Goths was as much institutional as ethnocentric, so Englishness itself for most of the long eighteenth century was associated not only with an ethnic descent but also with a set of universal political and legal values. This malleability facilitated the easy Anglicization of the eighteenth-century British Atlantic world.[57] When Protestant Irishmen, North Britons, and colonial Americans described themselves as English, more often than not they were asserting their claim to enjoy the rights and liberties of Englishmen, including government by consent and full protections for liberty and property such as jury trial and the need for parliamentary approval of taxation. By the mid-eighteenth century an emulative patriotism prevailed throughout the British Atlantic as the keynote of provincial identities. Everywhere provincial Britons invoked their stake in these concrete English liberties, whether on the basis of ethnic descent as the colonial offspring of English ancestors or through non-ethnic incorporation within the English political community. However, there was a narrow line between imperial, integrationist identifications with Englishness and a rejection of English rule itself. Throughout the eighteenth century provincial Britons – in Scotland, Ireland, and, most spectacularly, the American colonies – complained about their exclusion from the full enjoyment of English liberties, which were, as patriotic Americans noticed, akin to the natural rights of humankind.[58]

Curiously, the winning of independence did not dent a strong sense of American identification with the English motherland. Indeed, this discourse became more overtly ethnocentric in the century *after* independence. As in Britain, an institutionally orientated Gothicism gave way to a more overtly racialist Teutonism in the early nineteenth century. Indeed,

---

[55] Ibid., 225–7.
[56] Robert Molesworth, *An account of Denmark as it was in the year 1692* (London, 1694).
[57] C. Kidd, "North Britishness and the Nature of Eighteenth-Century British Patriotisms," *Historical Journal*, 39 (1996), 361–82.
[58] T. H. Breen, "Ideology and Nationalism on the Eve of the American Revolution," *Journal of American History*, 84 (1997), 38.

nineteenth-century white Anglo-America shared a common ethnic identity which transcended national frontiers.[59] Over the course of the long eighteenth century the parallel decline of ethnic theology and patriotic humanism as central elements of British social thought had paved the way for the emergence of racialist doctrine and a more familiar set of attitudes to ethnicity. Whereas once blacks and Amerindians were pitied as heathens, now they were despised – explicitly – on account of racial differences. Not only did racialism directed at people of color become more pronounced in the nineteenth century, so too did a Teutonist consciousness of distinctiveness from the peripheral white Celtic peoples of the British Isles.[60]

The eighteenth century had probably been just as prejudiced in practice as the nineteenth century was to become racist in dogma. Yet prejudices are themselves subject to historical change, and need to be carefully parsed. In the eighteenth century white-on-white antipathies – such as Protestant demonizing of the Catholic "Other" or the "lava-flow of abuse"[61] directed at the Scots in the era of Bute and Wilkes – were pitched at a much higher level of intensity than racial animosities. Racial and sectarian prejudices may indeed have been inversely related. The very insistence on religious orthodoxy which set limits to the ideological elaboration of racist instincts also incited a more zealous and uninhibited expression of confessional hatreds. The first British empire was acquired, ironically, during a period when the racist imagination was severely circumscribed. Respect for the ethnically undifferentiated polities of classical antiquity pushed ethnic factors to the margins of political culture, while sacred history reminded Britons of the aboriginal interconnectedness of "Self" and "Other."[62] Nor, of course, was the English "Self" defined strictly in terms of ethnicity. That Englishness was conceptualized in terms of Protestantism, Hanoverian allegiance, and a parcel of historic privileges scarcely distinct from the natural rights of humankind made it ripe for appropriation by other ethnic groups: colonial Americans, Scots, even – on occasions – loyal Protestant Afro-Britons.

[59] R. Horsman, *Race and Manifest Destiny: The Origins of American Racial Anglo-Saxonism* (Cambridge, MA: Harvard University Press, 1981); E. Kaufmann, "American Exceptionalism Reconsidered: Anglo-Saxon Ethnogenesis in the 'Universal Nation', 1776–1850," *Journal of American Studies*, 33 (1999), 437–57.
[60] R. Horsman, "The Origins of Racial Anglo-Saxonism in Great Britain before 1850," *Journal of the History of Ideas*, 37 (1976), 387–410; Kidd, "Teutonist Ethnology," 45–68.
[61] Duffy, *Englishman and the Foreigner*, 20.
[62] Cf. B. Braude, "The Sons of Noah and the Construction of Ethnic and Geographical Identities in the Medieval and Early Modern Periods," *William & Mary Quarterly*, 3rd ser, 54 (1997), 104–5.

PART IV

Englishness, gender, and the arts of discovery

CHAPTER 13

Writing home and crossing cultures: George Bogle in Bengal and Tibet, 1770–1775

Kate Teltscher

The Pacquet came up last night, and was this morning opened at the Governor's, I went and Breakfasted there, and wached with the greatest Impatience, – about fifty Gentlemen surrounded the Table and one took out the Letters and called over the names, – I squeezed in amongst them and was all Attention, – Not a George was named but I expected to find a Bogle after it, however the Box emptied apace not a word, when at last just at the Bottom, where it had hid itself, appeared my good Freind Mr. Brown's hand writting – You never tore upon a Letter in your Life with half the Impatience, that I did – I waited half a minute, till they were finished, and not a single Scrape for me besides. I immediately elbowed myself out of the Croud which was then very great, and retiring to a Corner of the Room broke open the Seal with a heart half affraid, and half hopeful – I had not heard a Syllable abut any of my freinds for eight Months.

George Bogle in Calcutta, November 1, 1770 to his sister, Mrs Brown[1]

The arrival of the mail was a moment of talismanic significance for East India Company servants in 1770s Calcutta, as it was for colonial functionaries, immigrants, and refugees the world over. Here the anxiety of the recipient testifies to the emotion invested in correspondence. The eighteenth-century familiar letter, written to friends and family, was part of the wider culture of sensibility. It provided the occasion for the expression of feeling; indeed much of sentimental literature, famously Richardson's *Pamela* (1741) and Rousseau's *Julie, ou la Nouvelle Héloïse* (1761), took epistolary form. The receipt of letters from home reaffirmed domestic identity and renewed familial bonds. Such scenes of eager anticipation functioned partly as a means to elicit future correspondence. The exchange between home and abroad, between the family and the individual, was an ongoing dialogue (in the case of Calcutta, a dialogue with lengthy silences: the time lapse between sending a letter and receiving an answer could be as much

[1] Bogle Collection, Mitchell Library, Glasgow.

as sixteen months). Mediating between the periphery and the metropolis, the exotic and the domestic, the spheres of work and home, the familiar letter was central to the construction of colonial identity.

Imperial historians do not always make full use of the potential of familiar correspondence. Letters offer much more than mere registers of information; they supply new ways to read the colonial archive. If sufficient attention is paid to epistolary language, style, and form, letters can provide a fresh approach to the relationship between the colony and the metropolis. Indeed, familiar letters offer as valuable a resource to historians of empire as official correspondence, state papers, or government proceedings. In this chapter I want to consider how the colonial self is narrated in letters home. In what ways are personal and national affiliations reasserted in the presence of alterity? Is a sense of national identity compromised by the state of being "in-between," ambiguously situated between places and cultures? How is the distance between locations negotiated? Read aloud to family and friends, letters brought the colony into the heart of the home. Empire becomes a surprisingly intimate affair when placed in this domestic context; the conversational and often nostalgic tone of these letters only adds to this sense of proximity. The circle of listeners turns the familiar letter into a form of performance where the letter-writer stages the encounter between cultures, locations, and peoples. Many of the set-piece descriptions included in letters home are notably theatrical or self-conscious, with the writer alternating between the parts of actor and cross-cultural interpreter. And as a vehicle for the expression of sentiment, the familiar letter provides an ideal space where cross-cultural intimacies can – unusually – be acknowledged.

My discussion will focus on the letters of an individual East India Company servant, George Bogle (1746–81). In many ways, Bogle is a far from representative figure. A talented and engaging writer, Bogle corresponded regularly with his father, four sisters, and two brothers during the 1770s. This period saw him rise quickly through the ranks of East India Company service, finding particular favor with Warren Hastings, Governor-General of Bengal. Bogle started his career in Calcutta as Writer to the Select Committee (the committee in charge of political matters), then as Assistant Secretary to the Board of Revenue, followed by appointments as Registrar of the Court of Appeals and Secretary to the Select Committee. But Bogle's main claim to our attention is as Hastings's envoy to Bhutan and Tibet in 1774–5, the first British traveler in the region. During this mission, Bogle spent five months with the Third Panchen Lama of Tibet, and the two men appear to have established relations of remarkable openness, even friendship. I want to argue that the qualities which Bogle developed in his familiar correspondence are also apparent in his account of diplomatic negotiation; that both letter-writer and envoy practice the arts of conversation, self-dramatization, and cultural mediation. Bogle's letters will be discussed in conjunction with his mission in an attempt to come to a fuller understanding of Bogle's capacity for crossing cultural boundaries and of his role as emissary of the evolving colonial state.

George Bogle was the youngest child of a prominent Glasgow merchant, one of the trading elite who came to be known as the "Tobacco Lords." During the second half of the eighteenth century, Glasgow grew hugely in size and prosperity. The city's wealth was based on its location which ensured a quick sailing route to the American colonies. Glasgow developed into a major commercial entrepôt, storing and processing American products, particularly tobacco and sugar, for resale in the rest of Britain and Europe. The tobacco trade was controlled by a small number of companies, run by an interrelated network of around twenty families. The Bogles played a central role in this group, as in Glasgow's commercial and civic affairs, with members of the family serving on the town council and as Dean of Guild in the Merchants' House.[2] The Bogle family papers, deposited in the Mitchell Library, Glasgow, provide a rich archive of correspondence, account books, and diaries over successive generations of this trading dynasty. Among the collection are to be found George Bogle's letters to his family from India, Bhutan, and Tibet covering the years 1770–81. Further correspondence, journals, and official reports relating to Bogle's mission are housed in the British Library, in the Oriental and India Office Collections, and among the Anderson and Hastings Papers.

Bogle was writing home at a time when the letter enjoyed unprecedented popularity as a literary form. Collections of letters – actual, fictitious, and model – flooded the market. Advice on epistolary style abounded. The familiar letter was often compared to a kind of written conversation. In his *Lectures on Rhetoric and Belles Lettres* (1783), Hugh Blair defined the familiar letter as "a conversation carried on upon paper, between two friends at a distance."[3] The punctuation of a letter was even a matter of convention: the dash and exclamation mark were generally used to approximate the

---

[2] See T. M. Devine, *The Tobacco Lords: A Study of the Tobacco Merchants of Glasgow and their Trading Activites, 1740–90* (Edinburgh: John Donald, 1975; repr., Edinburgh University Press, 1990); Carolyn Marie Peters, "Glasgow's Tobacco Lords: An Examination of Wealth Creators in the Eighteenth Century," Ph.D. thesis, Glasgow University, 1990.

[3] Cited in Keith Stewart, "Towards Defining an Aesthetic for the Familiar Letter in Eighteenth-Century England," *Prose Studies*, 5 (1982), 179.

immediacy and informality of speech.[4] Bogle thus draws on a common trope when he imagines his correspondence with his siblings as conversation. Writing to his eldest brother, Robert, from the ship *Vansittart*, en route to Calcutta, he announces his intention "to sit down now & then for half an Hour of Crack with you".[5] Of his sister Anne's letters, Bogle teasingly observes: "they are just as if you was chattering with this advantage that they cannot give one a Headake and I can stop them if I chused which you know is not always an easy Matter with your Ladyship – they want however the snap of the Fingers, and the hearty Laugh."[6] Here the types of conversation are interestingly gendered: with his brother, Bogle engages in manly, companionable "Crack"; while an unending torrent of inconsequential chatter issues from his sister. In thus differentiating between his siblings on the basis of gender and family status, Bogle is following another common epistolary precept: that the letter should be crafted to suit the individual recipient.[7]

Although apparently dismissive of his sister's letters, it was in fact to Anne (also known by the pet name of Chuffes) that Bogle wrote most extensively and imaginatively. Indeed in the same letter, Bogle describes the pleasure which her correspondence brings: "Your letters my Dear Chuffes are the very Nutmeg of Delight so long so particular about every thing that my Freinds are doing and so droll."[8] The image of Anne's correspondence as a nutmeg – spicy, valuable, and eastern – is particularly arresting. Nutmeg was a much desired product in seventeenth-century Europe and featured prominently in the early rivalry between the English and the Dutch East India Companies. In 1616, the tiny, nutmeg-growing island of Pulo Run in the Banda Islands became the first overseas territory acquired for the British crown by the English East India Company. Nutmeg could thus be regarded as one of the founding goods of empire. The nutmeg trope both commodifies and orientalizes Anne's correspondence, a move typical of Bogle's letters which slip easily between the domestic, the exotic, and the colonial.

Writing home, Bogle attempts to diminish both the geographical distance between India and Scotland, and the imagined difference between

---

[4] Cynthia Lowenthal, *Lady Mary Wortley Montagu and the Eighteenth-Century Letter* (Athens, GA: University of Georgia Press, 1994), 29.

[5] Bogle to Robin, March 27, 1770, Bogle Collection, Mitchell Library [ML], Glasgow.

[6] Bogle to Annie, January 15, 1773, Bogle Collection, ML.

[7] For an extended discussion of Bogle's various epistolary personae, see my "The Sentimental Ambassador: The Letters of George Bogle from Bengal, Bhutan and Tibet, 1770–1781," in Rebecca Earle, ed., *Epistolary Selves: Letters and Letter-Writers, 1600–1945* (Aldershot: Ashgate, 1999), 79–94.

[8] Bogle to Annie, January 15, 1773, Bogle Collection, ML.

Orient and Occident. In a long, digressive paragraph of a letter from Calcutta to Anne of March 1771, Bogle enacts a conversation between writer and recipient which encompasses past and present, East and West, fantasy and reality. Located initially at the family estate of Daldowie, the scene shifts first to an imaginary Orient, then returns to a Scottish boyhood, refocuses on colonial Bengal, and concludes with the beloved landscape of home:

You begin to tell me that Daldowie is looking Charming and then you stop because you think how many Places I have seen, and that I am perhaps siting [*sic*] in an Orange Grove, and serenaded with the most melodious Birds – I am almost sorry, but I must break this Enchantment otherwise you will write me nothing at all because I have seen so many things Preferable – I must first make a little address to Fancy – How often hast thou transported me from one Corner of this Globe to another, on the Backs of Genii, or with Fortunatus Cap on my Head – Sometimes you have alighted at a Palace of Chrystal, and the Rooms of Pearl, Rubies Diamonds – Cascades of Rose Water, and most Heavenly musick, while every Zephir came from Arabia, and every Ray of the Sun was enlivening & Delightful – then the Shade of Orange, and Citron Groves, with Collations of Pomegrenates, Pineapples, Guavas, and a thousand other exquisite fruit, whole Choires of the most melodious Birds serenaded us at the Repast – and pray George, if it is not interrupting you, where was all this, and what Part of the world were you in – why I was sitting at Mrs. Young's just recovering from a fever, and Bob Graham and I were reading the Arabian Nights, and the Doctor would not give us anything to eat so that we used to steal the Cheese the woman that attended us had for her own Supper – But it is all nonsense for an Orange Grove is really a very ugly Clump of Trees, and for Pomegranates they are the worst fruit I know, next to a Sloe but the Asiatics give us fine Descriptions from fancy and we beleive that they are copying Nature, – I have said too much Chuffes; for really I dont know anything of the Country of Asia, which I dare say possesses some of the most Charming Spots upon Earth, and that Persia, or Arabia deserve everything that can be said in their Praise – but this country of which I have hardly seen anything has little to recommend it besides its verdure, and Fertility, the Ganges is a muddy River, & the flatness of the Country affords no Prospects, so you may write me as much about Daldowie as you Please, you know I am naturally Prejudiced in its favor, and at any rate I have seen no place equal to it since I left England.[9]

Bogle attributes to his sister and his own boyhood self a version of the Orient derived from folktales, both eastern and western. Under the combined influence of genii from the *Arabian Nights' Entertainments* and a wishing hat from European folklore, the Orient is transformed in an extravagant vision of sensuous excess. But as Fortunatus' cap suggests, the East becomes

[9] Bogle to Ann, March 7, 1771, Bogle Collection, ML.

a place of wish-fulfillment: the hungry child dreams of exotic banquets, and the naive reader mistakes fanciful descriptions for realist texts. The vision of the Orient shades into delusion through its association with childhood illness and hyperbolic Asiatic fancy. The letter both indulges and denies the lure of the exotic. The fanciful digression is long but relentlessly undercut: fabulous repasts are juxtaposed with stolen hunks of cheese, orange groves become ugly clumps of trees. The letter continually shifts between the locations of writer and recipient, between their shared past and separated present, but importantly concludes with an affirmation of the primacy of home.

This split focus is characteristic of many of Bogle's letters and is suggestive too of the ambivalence of colonial identity, divided between "here" and "there," between past and present, suspended between cultures and places. Nowhere is this sense of a divided self more vividly conveyed than in a variation on a familiar epistolary device, the description of the scene of writing. In a letter to his sister Bess of March 1774, Bogle first evokes Daldowie domesticity, then recreates the evening in Calcutta:

I dont know how it is but there is a vast Satisfaction in Letters from our friends at a Distance to know what they were employed about at any particular Time. Your telling me that you are sitting in the Nursery, that my Father & Sisters are at Cribbage, or reading some light Summer – better Winter – Reading – and all the domestick economy of the Family, brings to my Mind stronger the Idea of former Days, transports me in a moment to Daldowie, and fills me with Emotions, half pleasant & half melancholy. Now Bess though I dont imagine I can have the same success in my Descriptions, because (for I wont give you any humble Reasons) you have, I believe, little knowledge of Bengal, and were I out of it, as little Interest in it yet I will attempt the same Thing and give you an Account of myself at this present time of writing Friday the 25 March, half past Nine at night.

Having finished all that odd hurry Scury Business in which I am every day engaged, and got all my Business Letters into the Pacquets, Mr Elliot (whom I'll make you acquainted with) and I resolved to come out to Mr Stewarts Gardens – a Country House about three Miles from Calcutta we got into our Palankins – look at some Glossary – and arrived just at Tea Time where we found Mr Stewart, and a young Man who is his Clerk, and after some hearty laughing in those high Spirits which one has when meer Business is finished, and each of us having told a good Story, among which mine was not the worst for I told the story of Woodhall and Aunt Peggy about the Mistake of living in such Suspense, and at such Expence – which I learnt from Mrs. Brown with all her little Embellishments – we agreed to retire to our Rooms & attack our Europe Letters, and here I am in a Room with a Ceiling (almost) as high as my Father's Barn, with your Letters before me in my wais-coat with Sleeves, & two Shirts to keep me cool. The Garden in the middle of which the House stands, is (if it were Daylight – or indeed whether it is daylight or no) laid out very prettily Plenty of Trees and Shrubs, and not one of them except two Peach Trees which are dying, that you ever saw, there are plenty of Deer in a Paddock adjoining in the Garden, among the rest Antelopes which are the most beautiful Creatures in the world – and two Tigers confined in a Cage long much to have the pawing of them.[10]

In a gesture indebted to Samuel Richardson, Bogle advocates writing "to the moment," insisting that the act of writing is contemporaneous with the scene described. But as Janet Altman has shown, one of the defining characteristics of epistolary discourse is "temporal polyvalence"; that is, there is always a time-lag between the event described and the moments of writing, posting, receipt, reading, and rereading a letter.[11] Descriptions of the scene of writing which emphasize the very moment of inscription thus attempt to defy what is one of the essential elements of the genre. The time lapse in epistolary discourse is of course an effect of the distance between writer and addressee. To give the impression of immediacy might therefore be understood as a denial of the separation of writer and recipient. It is this illusion of proximity that accounts for the "vast Satisfaction" which Bogle describes initially. A precisely dated and timed account of the family's activities, Bogle observes, "transports me in a moment to Daldowie." Interestingly, Bogle uses the same idea of being "transported . . . from one Corner of this Globe to another" in his address to Fancy, quoted previously. Although here it is quotidian detail, rather than genii, that transport Bogle, there remains a trace of enchantment in the notion of instantaneous travel. The verb also seems to carry its figurative sense of being "carried away" by the strength of feeling: Bogle is filled with "Emotions, half pleasant, half melancholy." This is the longed-for return home, the desired reunification of the divided colonial self. But the colonial condition remains haunted by a third meaning of transportation: the sense of being banished from home. Split into two paragraphs, the extract clearly contrasts the two locations. Shared family lore ("the story of Woodhall and Aunt Peggy") and specific domestic analogy ("a Ceiling (almost) as high as my Father's Barn") are set against deliberately unfamiliar vocabulary ("we got into our Palankins – look at some Glossary"), unnamed flora, and exotic fauna (antelopes and tigers). The passage at once asserts a nostalgic longing for home and emphasizes, even flaunts, the distance and difference of the colony. The state of being in-between places and cultures inevitably destabilizes the sense of personal and national identity.

[10] Bogle to Bess, March 24, 1774, Bogle Collection, ML.
[11] Janet Gurkin Altman, *Epistolarity: Approaches to a Form* (Columbus: Ohio State University Press, 1982), 118.

This ambivalent positioning between locations is evident throughout Bogle's familiar letters. The correspondence is studded with fond recollections of childhood which counterpoint or provide parallels with accounts of the colony. Writing, for instance, to Anne in September 1770, shortly after his arrival in Calcutta, Bogle compares learning to read with his current lessons in Persian (the official language of the East India Company):

You remember I dare say My Dear Annie, when you and I learnt to read, and were bribed to make out one of the Esop's fables by Sugar & Water, in a vial, made by Bess, & dealt out in three Teaspoonfull at a time, which was an amazing Incitement, in those days – I doubt not but you coud say, for you have a most excellent Memory, when it was, & at what Particular fable, that I got no Sugar, for not having my Lesson – Now you must know that I am returned, to the same Situation, and am learning to read again, – At this moment there is a man standing behind me, dressed something like a woman, but with large Mustachos & a Turban, who only waites till I have finished my Letter to you, when he will step up and make me repeat my A.B.C. in Persian. Tho to be sure he is not so generous as my Sisters were, who not only taught us for nothing, but gave us the Syrop for a Reward, nor as Aunt Peggy, who gave me a Gold, or rather Tinsell, laced Hat for geting the Economy of Human Life by heart, whereas Mounchi must be paid so much a month and never gave me anything at all.[12]

The Daldowie past is rehearsed in the presence of alterity (quite literally, the *munshi*, or Persian scholar, is at Bogle's back). The nursery parallel at once infantilizes Bogle and feminizes the teacher: the *munshi* is placed in the position of Bogle's older sisters or aunt and is "dressed something like a woman." The childhood reminiscence brings the colony and home into surprisingly intimate relation. Indeed the connection between Scotland and India is forged even in the nursery. The text which the young Bogle learnt by heart, Robert Dodsley's *The Oeconomy of Human Life* (1751), was supposed, according to its subtitle, to have been "translated from an Indian Manuscript, written by an ancient Bramin." But the passage also differentiates between the familial and the colonial: the first is motivated by affection, the second driven by economics. Indeed Bogle demonstrates his power as employer and colonial master by continuing to write in the *munshi*'s presence. In a move typical of Bogle's correspondence (as we have already seen) the passage suggests both the similarity and difference of the two locations.

The letter continues with an account of the Persian lesson. Without a common language, *munshi* and pupil struggle to comprehend each other:

---

[12] Bogle to Annie, September 23, 1770, Bogle Collection, ML.

When nobody is in the way to interpret between us, which very often happens, we are sadly puzzled, what to do – and sounds and signs are all we have for it – If the Persian word means, a Head, a Foot, a Book, or that sort of thing, it is very easy, and only having recourse to the thing itself; as for Instance, Sīr, signifies a head – upon which Mounchi taking off his Turban, clasping his neck with one Hand, so as to seperate it from the Rest of his body, points, with the other hand to his bare pash, and so makes me understand what he means – The fingers and thumbs are of prodigious use in expressing Numbers – The Motions of the body, such as running, or walking, or Jumping, or Hoping [*sic*] are also to be made out tho with some little difficulty to Mounchy, for the weather is rather too hot for these Excersises. But we can make nothing of the Affections of the mind, unless now and then when there happens to be a great deal of Passion in it – Fear is expressed by Starting, & Staring, and His large black Eyes roll about sometimes with Rage and Fury, – and once to make him self understood, he was obliged to kiss my Hand, and make Love to me.[13]

The language lesson turns into pantomimic performance, a kind of charade depicting the colonial relationship. Running the gamut of emotions from rage to love, the *munshi* enacts the resistance and collusion of the colonized, the violence and intimacy of the colonial encounter. As language student, Bogle is in the position of participant and spectator, but as letter-writer, he also plays the role of impresario, restaging the spectacle for his audience at home.

The theatricality of the cross-cultural encounter and the attempt to converse with other peoples, here comically rendered, preoccupy Bogle later in his career. As an envoy of the East India Company, Bogle was concerned as much with diplomatic show and court ceremonial as with formal negotiation and behind-the-scenes conversation. In outlining the object of Bogle's embassy to Bhutan and Tibet in 1774, Warren Hastings emphasized the importance of communication – both commercial and verbal: "The design of your mission is to open a mutual and equal communication of trade between the inhabitants of Bhutan and Bengal, and you will be guided by your own judgement in using such means of negotiation as may be most likely to effect this purpose."[14] The mission was conceived as a means of reviving the trans-Himalayan trade route, disrupted by recent war with Nepal. It was hoped that Tibet might provide the East India Company with an opening to the Chinese market bypassing the restrictions operating at Canton. The financial losses sustained by the Company during the Bengal famine of 1770 made it imperative to find new sources of income.

---

[13] Ibid.
[14] Hastings to Bogle, May 13, 1774 quoted in Clements R. Markham, *Narratives of the Mission of George Bogle to Tibet and of the Journey of Thomas Manning to Lhasa* (London: Trübner, 1876), 6.

But the embassy was also a fact-finding mission: Bogle was briefed to make detailed notes on the politics, history, geography, and culture of the region, recording everything that he encountered: "the people, the country, the climate, or the road, their manners, customs, buildings, cookery &c."[15]

The opportunity to expand British influence in the Himalayan region was offered by a succession struggle in Cooch Behar, a small state bordering on Bengal. In 1772 the Bhutanese Desi or ruler, Zhidar, invaded Cooch Behar and installed his own candidate on the throne. The ousted Raja of Cooch Behar appealed to the East India Company for help. With British military aid, the Bhutanese forces were defeated and the Raja reinstalled – on condition that the British gain control of the state. Zhidar, a ruler renowned as much for the harshness of his regime as for his military adventures, returned home to find that his subjects had risen against him. Fleeing the rebellion, Zhidar sought refuge with the Panchen Lama, who made peace overtures to the British on behalf of the Bhutanese. Hastings responded positively to the Lama's initiative, and in the wake of these negotiations, Bogle was appointed envoy to Tibet.

The Third Panchen Lama (or abbot of Tashilhunpo Monastery), Lobsang Palden Yeshé, had risen to a position of religious and political pre-eminence in Tibet and the neighboring states during the childhood of the Eighth Dalai Lama. Although a regent nominally headed the Tibetan government during this period, the Lama's talents as a statesman and mediator made him a respected figure throughout the Himalayan region. In matters of external affairs, however, the Lama was subject to China. Although acknowledging the spiritual authority of the Panchen Lama, the Manchu emperor stationed Chinese residents or *ambans* at Lhasa to monitor Tibetan policy. By entertaining Bogle, the Lama was thus asserting Tibetan independence from Chinese control. In fact, the Lama cultivated diplomatic relations with many of the neighboring powers. In the case of India – the sacred land of Buddhism – the Lama may also have had religious objectives. He sent monks on Indian pilgrimages and negotiated with Bogle for the establishment of a Tibetan Buddhist monastery near Calcutta.

Before the 1774 embassy, the British knew little about the region or the Lama. One of the few Europeans to have entered Tibet, Samuel van de Putte, an early eighteenth-century Dutch explorer, had ordered his papers be burnt on his death. The handful of Jesuit and Capuchin missionaries operating in the area left accounts that Bogle regarded with derision. In

---

[15] Private Commissions to Mr Bogle, MSS Eur E 226/6, Oriental and India Office Collections [OIOC], British Library.

one of the rare letters to survive from a female member of the Bogle family, Mary Bogle described the limited information available in Britain about Tibet:

With how much Spirit My Dear George do you give an account of the Customs of the People to whom the Europians are so great Strangers, that Part of the World has been little heard off in Britain, and you even clear up some Notions which those who Pretend to any knowledge of it had adopted and Published, one thing in Particular was believed that the Lama of Thibet was not allowed to open his mouth but sat like a Statue, and his approbation was only found out by the moving of his Hand, or by a Nod of his Head, but you have set his Character in a Proper Point of View, and done him that justice to a Man (who is from your account of him much to be esteemed) that he deserves.[16]

That Mary Bogle should focus on the mistaken notion of the Lama's silence and impassive demeanor suggests the emphasis placed by her brother on the Lama's conversational skills. The Lama spoke Hindustani (Urdu) so he and Bogle were able to communicate without an interpreter and they moved quickly from official discussion to private conversation. In the journals that made up part of the report on his embassy, Bogle recorded the many exchanges between the two of them on trade, politics, culture, and religion. For indeed the relationship with the Lama and the information gathered constituted Bogle's major diplomatic triumph. The regent continued to oppose all contact between Tibet and Britain, and Bogle failed in his aim of opening Tibet up to East India Company servants. His only concrete achievement was to secure the Panchen Lama's recommendation to Tibetan traders to develop links with Bengal. So for the British, the mission could be judged productive only in terms of improved relations with the Lama (whom Bogle regarded as a possible future intermediary between the Company and the Manchu emperor) and in the increase in general intelligence. In this light, personal conversation and cross-cultural contact carry a wider political significance.

In his journal Bogle recorded his first exchange with the Lama in detail. Encountering an initial difficulty in understanding each other, Bogle attempted to "imitate the phraseology" of the Lama's Hindustani, and they began to converse with ease:

He enquired what office I held under the Company – He asked if the Company was "King" – I told him they were not but protected by him. He asked the name of my Country which he said he heard was an Island – He enquired if it was near the country of the Cannibals. In answer I told him that I had read and heard much

---

[16] Mary Bogle to Bogle, November 4, 1775, Bogle Collection, ML.

of that people, but as none of my nation, who sailed in ships to most parts of the World, had ever met with them, I could give him no particular information about them. He than asked if my country was near Sunderdeep – I replied that Sunderdeep was an Island at no great distance from Bengal, but England was four or five months voyage from it – He made me repeat *England* two or three times. He desired me to put on my Hat – I declined it in his presence – he said that the Chinese wore their Hats before him, and insisted that I should – I just put it on and took it off again.[17]

The Lama, as host and hierarch, takes the conversational initiative, plying Bogle with questions. For the European reader (and writer), these queries have a oddly alienating effect, relegating Britain to the periphery of the known world. Home becomes as strange and potentially threatening as the cannibal islands so frequently encountered in European travelogues. It is perhaps Britain's status as an island which renders it exotic to those who live on a great continent. In this interview, it is Bogle who is the curiosity, Bogle who performs for the benefit of the Lama, taking off and replacing his hat (in a manner reminiscent of the *munshi* in the language lesson letter). Through this moment of self-estrangement, the European is briefly granted the perspective of another culture. But at the same time, the Lama's questions sound comically naive and only serve to emphasize his own remoteness. The passage positions reader and writer between cultures and locations, destabilizing a secure sense of national identity, in a move familiar from our earlier analysis of the tropes of Bogle's letters.

After the Lama had received Bogle a few times, all ceremony was dispensed with. The two men began to meet regularly to discuss the politics, history, customs, and religion of their respective countries. For both parties, the embassy was an opportunity to gather intelligence. The Lama requested that Bogle write an account of Europe, and at the same time supplied Bogle with materials for a history of Tibet. Indeed it was as a raconteur that the Lama figured in Bogle's journal. Briefly sketching his host's character, Bogle wrote: "His disposition is open, candid, and generous. He is extremely merry and entertaining in Conversation, and tells a pleasant Story with a great deal of Humour and Action."[18] In praising the Lama's candor, Bogle allies himself with the Scottish philosopher Adam Ferguson, who valued the "real sentiments of humanity and candour" as a sign of a vigorous and cultivated spirit.[19] Interestingly, candor itself was a trait which was often

[17] MSS Eur D 532, f. 32, OIOC.   [18] MSS Eur E 226/18, OIOC.
[19] Adam Ferguson, *An Essay on the History of Civil Society*, ed. Fania Oz-Salberger (Cambridge University Press, 1995), 42–3.

attributed to the British.[20] As a nation, the British were supposed to be frank, open, sincere, free from malice, and impartial. Etymologically, the word "candor" derives from the Latin "candidus" meaning "white." In the eighteenth century, "candid" still retained its original meaning of "white," so a submerged racial association may have been at work in the British claim of this quality. By terming the Lama candid, Bogle thus blurs the boundaries of national identity. In the intimate space of conversational exchange, the distance between cultures and races is diminished. We may detect a racial element here for Bogle remarks that the Lama's "Complexion is fairer than that of most of the Thibetians, and his arms are as white as those of a European."[21]

Although distinguished from his fellow countrymen in terms of skin color, the Lama shares his unaffected good humor with Tibetans in general. Bogle writes at length of their conviviality and honesty in his familiar letters. To his sister Elizabeth, he describes Tibetan manners as:

plain and downright – free from the fawning Servility of the Bengalee, and equally free from Pride or Affectation. I am sensible that a man more flegmatick than myself might write a very different Character [of] them. He would tell you that they are dirty in their Persons; that they know nothing of the Bon Ton; that they are ignorant of all those Arts which adorn and embellish Life; but I cannot help being pleased with People who seem to wish to please me, and value an Ounce of good humour and Honesty above a Pound of Politeness and Refinement.[22]

Bogle contrasts the Tibetan character both with the stereotype of Bengali insincerity and with the affectation of polite society at home (the French "Bon Ton"). The unmanly colonial subject is here linked to the over-refined master. True manliness and sincerity are to be found in the mountainous retreat, beyond the reach of colonial power or, indeed, beyond the reach of commerce. For the Scottish philosopher David Hume, the spread of politeness and refinement was determined by the growth of commerce.[23] Bogle seems to glance fleetingly at Hume in his reference to "those Arts which adorn and embellish Life," but to ignore Hume's connection between refinement and commerce. There is no sense that in seeking to open Tibet up to East India Company trade, Bogle might be responsible for initiating

---

[20] Paul Langford, *Englishness Identified: Manners and Character 1650–1850* (Oxford University Press, 2000), 87–135; Katherine S. H. Turner, "At the Boundaries of Fiction: Samuel Paterson's *Another Traveller!*" in A. Ribeiro and J. G. Basker, *Tradition in Transition: Women Writers, Marginal Texts and the Eighteenth-Century Canon* (Oxford University Press, 1996), 153–4.

[21] MSS Eur E 226/18, OIOC.

[22] Bogle to Bess, December 30, 1774, MSS Eur E226/80, OIOC.

[23] See for instance "On the Rise of the Arts and Sciences," in David Hume, *Selected Essays*, ed. Stephen Copley and Andrew Edgar (Oxford University Press, 1993), 56–77.

a change in taste among the Tibetans. Effectively effacing his own role as trade emissary, Bogle represents the relationship between the Tibetans and himself simply as one of reciprocal affection: "I cannot help being pleased with People who seem to wish to please me." Rejecting European notions of refinement, Bogle aligns himself with the Tibetans. I have argued elsewhere that Bogle's familiar letters tend to rewrite the trade mission in terms of sentiment, but that the notion of commerce, although repressed, keeps surfacing.[24] Here the Tibetans "value an Ounce of good humour and Honesty above a Pound of Politeness and Refinement"; the different qualities associated with rude and polished societies are commodified, weighed, and valued, much as the trading goods which it is Bogle's mission to seek out.

Writing in his official capacity, Bogle reported on Bhutanese and Tibetan products which might be of interest to Britain. Indeed much of diplomatic ritual was structured around symbolic gift-giving, those theatrical exchanges which, for the British at least, represented amity and the possibility of future commercial relations. The Tibetans, however, may have construed the offering of gifts somewhat differently: it was customary for devotees to donate goods to the Panchen Lama as a sign of their reverence.[25] In private, conversation between the Lama and Bogle at times centered on the material traces of cross-cultural contact. The Lama showed Bogle his collection of European artifacts: a French compass (from the Chinese emperor who, in his turn, may have received it from the Jesuits at Peking), six Dutch or German watches (all stopped except one), a broken-down hand organ, and a camera obscura with views of London. Unexpectedly encountered in a Tibetan monastery, the objects testify to the long reach of European commerce, but their dilapidated state suggests an unsettling dislocation. Particularly arresting is the camera obscura: Bogle journeys into an unfamiliar land only to encounter a vision of the metropolis. As we have already noted of Bogle's writing, travel unsettles a secure sense of national identity: the familiar is rendered strange (and the strange familiar).

Bogle's journal repeatedly disturbs European cultural coordinates. He writes of his easy adaptation to Tibetan ways and eager adoption of Tibetan dress:

The Lama used to send a Priest to me, early every morning with some Bread and Tea, or some boiled Rice and chopped Mutton; of which last, as I always like to do at Rome as they do at Rome, I used to eat very heartily . . . Some days

---

[24] See Teltscher, "The Sentimental Ambassador."

[25] Compare the discussion of the different constructions of gift-giving by the Tibetans, Chinese, and British in James L. Hevia, *Cherishing Men from Afar: Qing Guest Ritual and the Macartney Embassy of 1793* (Durham, NC: Duke University Press, 1995), 47, 81.

after my arrival the Lama had given me a Thibetian dress, consisting of a purple
sattin Tunick lined with Siberian Fox Skins; a yellow Sattin Cap, faced round with
Sable and crowned with a Red Silk Tassel, and a pair of red Bulgar Hide Boots.
In this I equipped myself, glad to abandon my European Habit, which was both
uncomfortable and exposed me to abundance of that troublesome Curiosity which
the Thibetians possess in a Degree inferior to no other people.[26]

The allusion to the proverbial "When in Rome . . ." indicates a temporary
accommodation to foreign custom. But Bogle's rejection of his "European Habit" as uncomfortable suggests a more profound dissatisfaction
with European ways (a sense reinforced by a pun on "habit" as custom).
The lingering description of his splendid Tibetan dress serves to heighten
the idea of enthusiastic assimilation. No longer an object of curiosity to
Tibetan onlookers, Bogle turns himself into a spectacle for his British audience instead. Attired in Tibetan costume, Bogle becomes a cultural hybrid,
suspended between peoples and locations. But the transgressive potential of
cultural cross-dressing is kept in check by Bogle's claims for the practicality
of the outfit. As in his familiar correspondence, Bogle remains ambivalently
situated between cultures.

Throughout this chapter, I have stressed Bogle's capacity for crossing
cultural boundaries rather than crossing over, for moving between rather
than transgressing, but as with many East India Company servants, there is
a hidden history of sexual liaison. Hugh Richardson has argued that Bogle
may have started an affair with one of the Lama's female relatives during
his mission.[27] There is evidence that Bogle had two daughters, Mary and
Martha, who were sent home to be raised at Daldowie, after Bogle's death.
The two girls grew up in the care of Bogle's sisters, and later married Scotsmen. According to family tradition, their mother was a Tibetan "princess"
called Tichan or Dechen, a "sister" of the Lama. Mary and Martha were
not Bogle's only children, however. Another daughter, also called Mary, was
dispatched to London during Bogle's lifetime, and at least one son died in
infancy in Calcutta. It appears that Bogle maintained two (or more) separate families. One of the mothers of these establishments was probably
the "Bebee Bogle" to whom Bogle's executors paid a life-long pension of
20 rupees a month. Scarcely any trace of these children or their mothers survives in the Bogle family papers preserved at the Mitchell Library,
Glasgow. The "going native" narrative remains hidden, probably obscured
by the hands of the family friend who "judiciously sorted and arranged"

---

[26] MSS Eur E 226/18, OIOC.
[27] H. E. Richardson, "George Bogle and his Children," *Scottish Genealogist*, 29 (1982), 73–83.

the collection, before it was consulted by Clements Markham (first Honorary Secretary, later President, of the Royal Geographical Society) who published an edition of Bogle's journal in 1876.[28] The censorship of the papers suggests the increasingly strict policing of British sexual conduct in nineteenth-century India and the growing fear of miscegenation. But it seems unlikely that Bogle would have directly informed his family, particularly his devout Presbyterian father, of his unorthodox (though by no means uncommon) domestic arrangements.[29]

The familiar letter may not disclose the full extent of interracial contact, but it is to this genre that historians of empire should look for expressions of cross-cultural intimacy. Bogle's warmest declarations of affection for the Lama occur in letters to his family. Writing home in November 1774, for instance, Bogle describes the Lama as "a short fat Man, and as merry as a Criquet."[30] The studied informality of the familiar letter, its conversational and often nostalgic tone constitute a textual performance of affection. The genre thus provides the perfect discursive space for the topic of friendship. Facing Janus-like in two directions, letters address both the home and the periphery. Mediating between the two, the familiar letter furnishes an ideal vehicle for narratives of contact between cultures. Indeed, in the imperial context, letters act much like colonial functionaries themselves: crossing cultural boundaries, disrupting fixed notions of national and personal identity. In this chapter I have attempted to demonstrate how a new approach to the colonial letter may open up the vast imperial archive to alternative readings, and to emphasize the ambiguities of cross-cultural encounters. In the familiar letter, we may find fresh ways to construct colonial identity, assess the impact of empire on metropolitan culture, and understand the hybrid construction of Englishness itself.

[28] Richardson, "George Bogle," 74.
[29] See, for instance, *Memoirs of William Hickey 1749–1775*, ed. Alfred Spencer (4 vols., London: Hurst & Blackett, 1913–25), III, 276–7, 284–5, 327; IV, 140–1.
[30] Bogle to the family at Daldowie, November 27, 1774, MSS Eur E 226/77 (g), OIOC.

CHAPTER 14

Decoding the nameless: gender, subjectivity, and historical methodologies in reading the archives of colonial India

Durba Ghosh

I

This chapter interrogates the links between naming practices, methodologies of historical research, and writing about subaltern women who appear as nameless in historical archives. In spite of over two decades of scholarship in South Asian women's history and subaltern history,[1] a central obstacle to incorporating women into South Asian and imperial historiographies is the anonymity of native women in archives. While we know very well that women who were on the bottom of the social scale or marginal altogether have been generally excluded from historical projects, relatively few scholars have attempted to address the ways in which naming conventions in colonial archives reinforced this anonymity and continue to be an obstacle in pursuing historical research on subaltern subjects.

Perhaps the most widely known study of this period is Lata Mani's article and book, *Contentious Traditions*, which have both proved hugely influential in gender and colonial history, but do not directly discuss women's lives or historical agency and subjectivity, instead focusing on women as the site of discourses about tradition.[2] As Janaki Nair asks about Mani's arguments about sati, "Thus, even a source which purports to speak about women remains silent about them: how then may the feminist historian read such material?"[3]

The author would like to thank Amrita Basu, Rosanna Hertz, Tabitha Kanogo, Tom Laqueur, Tom Metcalf, Robert Travers, and audiences at the Women and Gender Studies seminar at Amherst College, the Wellesley College Feminist Inquiry Group, and fellow panelists at the Berkeley Conference on South Asia (1999).
[1] Kumkum Sangari and Sudesh Vaid, *Recasting Women: Essays in Indian Colonial History* (New Brunswick, NJ: Rutgers University Press, 1989); Ranajit Guha and Gayatri Chakravorty Spivak, eds., *Selected Subaltern Studies* (New York: Oxford University Press, 1988).
[2] Lata Mani, *Contentious Traditions: The Debate on Sati in Colonial India* (Berkeley and Los Angeles: University of California Press, 1998) and her essay in Sangari and Vaid, *Recasting Women*.
[3] Janaki Nair, "On the Question of Agency in Indian Feminist Historiography," *Gender and History*, 6 (1994), 86.

Writing histories of non-western worlds has been the focus of intense theoretical scrutiny, particularly since history as an academic discipline relies so heavily on scholarly practices originating in Europe and the "West." As Dipesh Chakrabarty, a founder of the Subaltern Studies collective, has noted, "European thought is at once both indispensable and inadequate" in the practice of subaltern history.[4] To this, one might add that European colonial archives are both "indispensable and inadequate" to writing new imperial and South Asian histories.[5] Historians of subaltern groups have looked to different types of archives, although many remain indebted to colonial archives on the Indian subcontinent and in Britain. The subject of personal names has not been directly addressed by Subaltern Studies scholars, but essays in the series have implicitly demonstrated that the named historical actor is necessary for historical analysis, particularly if he or she is identifiable as a subaltern agent.[6] Hence by interrogating the connections between naming, historical methodology, and subjectivity, I want to examine the unspoken assumption that historical actors have names that enable them to be easily found and followed through historical records and archives.

Relying on names to do historical research may be obvious to anyone who has spent hours looking through indexes, catalogues, and other archival aids. Yet names are so institutionalized to the practices of historical research that the problem of researching subjects without proper names is rarely addressed, even among historians of the dispossessed and the marginal. In the records of a modern state, naming is constitutive of various gender, class, racial, and religious hierarchies, making the state's subjects legible along various axes of political and social power.[7] In the modern archive, governmental records and the naming practices embedded within them have reproduced these multiple hierarchies.[8] An early essay by Gayatri Spivak has shown how colonial records maintained and archives preserved particular forms of legibility as parts of a continuing collective discursive effort to produce and reproduce certain types of imperial subject-formation.

[4] Dipesh Chakrabarty, *Provincializing Europe: Postcolonial Thought and Historical Difference* (Princeton University Press, 2000), 6, 16.
[5] Nicholas B. Dirks, "The Crimes of Colonialism," in Peter Pels and Oscar Salemink, eds., *Colonial Subjects* (Ann Arbor: University of Michigan Press, 1999), 173–7.
[6] For instance, Gautam Bhadra, "Four Rebels of 1857," *Subaltern Studies IV* (New Delhi: Oxford University Press, 1985), 229–75; Ranajit Guha, "Chandra's Death," *Subaltern Studies V* (New Delhi: Oxford University Press, 1987), 135–65.
[7] James Scott et al., "The Production of Legal Identities Proper to States: The Case of the Permanent Family Surname," *Comparative Studies in Society and History*, 44 (2002), 4–44.
[8] Dirks, "Crimes of Colonialism."

As she has observed about a list of misspelled and mistranscribed native women's names, "Against the olympian violations of women's names, we have the meticulously preserved baptismal records of each and every cadet in the Company's service."[9] In "Can the Subaltern Speak?" Spivak went further, arguing that the absence of female subaltern subjectivity in colonial records poses an insurmountable obstacle to writing the histories of subaltern women.[10] Yet, Spivak's provocative critique offered little insight into how to compensate for these kinds of archival shortcomings and foreclosed the ways in which historians might consider how the exclusion of women's names from colonial records and archives can be historically informative about native women's encounters with various parts of the colonial enterprise.

While namelessness seems like a very basic problem – a problem that philosophers, anthropologists, and literary critics have considered – in the discipline of history, naming or namelessness has not been analyzed as a methodological obstacle.[11] This chapter argues that historians need to be more critical of the ways in which naming practices operate within various historical moments and social formations, particularly if we are to better account for the subjectivities and historical agency of groups and individuals whose names have been incompletely recorded and remain anonymous in archives.

This chapter draws from a larger study on interracial domestic relationships between native women on the Indian subcontinent and European soldiers, officials, and merchants during the early phase of Anglo-Indian colonial contact (*c.* 1760–*c.* 1840). Because female historical subjects were rarely identified by complete names, it was difficult to determine which native women were the conjugal companions and wives of European men. This problem gives rise to a series of general and broad-ranging questions. How can historians decipher women from the archives when they are unnamed or renamed? How can scholars recuperate women's subjectivity, their own means of self-identification and self-naming when it seems that others more often were responsible for the names by which they were called? Finally, can historians gauge or follow the narratives of women's agency in the daily histories of the Anglo-Indian encounter when they go unnamed in colonial documents? If one is examining women who were not

---

[9] Gayatri Chakravorty Spivak, "The Rani of Sirmur: An Essay in Reading the Archive," *History and Theory*, 38 (1985), 267.
[10] Gayatri Chakravorty Spivak, "Can the Subaltern Speak?" in Cary Nelson and Lawrence Grossberg, eds., *Marxism and the Interpretation of Culture* (Urbana: University of Illinois Press, 1988), 271–313.
[11] Saul Kripke, *Naming and Necessity* (Cambridge, MA: Harvard University Press, 1980).

elite, who were largely lower class and lower caste, and decidedly marginal in colonial and in indigenous society, how can one not let their anonymity in history be reinforced by their namelessness?

Interrogating the conditions that produced the exclusion of women and their names from most colonial records and archives is critical if we are to understand better how the question of naming structures historical subjectivity and agency. While Spivak's analysis of colonial discursive practices has been central to understanding the terms under which "historical facts" were recorded, we still need to unravel the multiple ways in which the production of records affected and effected native women's subjectivities, as constructed by themselves and others in early colonial India. In the case of native conjugal partners of Europeans, archival exclusions were representative of the partial social and civil death that was crucial to specific efforts to dispossess native women of financial and parental claims that they might otherwise have made of the East India Company. Keeping the names of native women out of official documents had material, political, and social consequences in terms of how women became attached or removed, either by themselves or by others, from familial and other social units.

In a general sense, naming practices are crucial to the topographies of any society; they make subjects legible not only to the state, but to their communities.[12] Naming is a social practice that brings people into a particular community, while making distinctions between individuals of different names. Naming often reflects one's kinship group, however that group is structured or located among other groups. At the level of an individual, a name is a common way of identifying and understanding a person's subjectivity. Names often refer to a reasonably fixed notion of one person within a given community. Naming provides contexts for an individual subject and suggests ways in which a subject becomes socialized and incorporated into a given society. In various ways, naming provides cues for one's gender, status, religion, ethnicity, and nationality. If one is a namesake, it provides a history and perhaps even a template for behavior. For example, names such as "Red" for someone who is red-haired, "Sunny" for someone of a cheerful disposition draw attention to traits that a person might exhibit. When a woman changes her last name to her husband's last name, or reverts to her maiden name after a divorce, it marks a shift in marital status, lifestyle, and location in terms of kin status. When a woman marries and takes on her husband's last name, she symbolically dissolves her ties

---

[12] Richard D. Alford, *Naming and Identity: A Cross-Cultural Study of Personal Naming Practices* (New Haven: HRAF Press, 1988).

as the daughter of one man and becomes the husband of another in what is a standard pattern of sexual and social traffic signifying the exchange of women between men.[13] The power to name, rename, or change one's name is crucial to illuminating the ways in which social relationships work between name-givers and name-takers.[14] Renamings, such as the renaming that occurred when African-American slaves were given their master's last name, or when immigrants changed their names on arriving at Ellis Island, are ways in which a person's past identity is erased in order to give way to a new identity and cultural location. Following Orlando Patterson, changing one's name is a way of marking one's social death in one context, while creating a new social being in another.[15]

In conducting my study, I located women in the archives who were the sexual companions, domestic servants, and conjugal partners of European men by doing the opposite of what most historians do: I looked for subjects with incomplete or partial names because the lack of a complete name signaled the presence of a native female. Naming in this colonial context was a gendered practice that was structured by racial or ethnic identifications: while men, native, European, and mixed-race, were easily traceable by their names, native women only became visible in these archives because they lacked surnames or were listed only as "native woman." So, for instance, in baptismal records of the late eighteenth century, when baptized children of European mothers and fathers were listed, the full names of both parents appeared in the church register. In cases where the child was born to a prominent member of the East India Company's establishment, the godparents were also listed so that the baptismal record read like a social register that linked high-ranking members of colonial society with each other. Yet in cases where the child was born to a European father and a native mother, only the father's name was listed and in the column listing the mother, the entry read "native woman." In these cases, the practice of recording the name of the European father while erasing the identity of the native mother worked to mark the illegitimate and relatively lower social and racial status of the child.

As Luce Irigaray suggests more generally of the practice of naming children after their fathers, overriding the mother's name suggests a way in

13 Gayle Rubin, "The Traffic in Women: Notes on the 'Political Economy' of Sex," in Rayna R. Reiter, ed., *Towards an Anthropology of Women* (New York: Monthly Review Press, 1975); Carole Pateman, *The Sexual Contract* (Stanford University Press, 1988), 121.
14 Rubie S. Watson, "The Named and the Nameless: Gender and Person in Chinese Society," *American Ethnologist*, 13 (1986), 619–31.
15 Orlando Patterson, *Slavery and Social Death* (Cambridge, MA: Harvard University Press, 1982), 54–8.

which men reclaimed their fatherhood and guaranteed, at least in the
record books, their patrimony.[16] By giving mixed-race children born of
Indian mothers and European fathers English-sounding names, most, but
not all, men staked their sole patrimony through the practice of naming and
marked the first stage in making these children "English," masking their
racial origins, and dispossessing the maternal claims of the native mother.

By erasing the names of native women who threatened the whiteness of
this colonial community, these church records contributed to a historical
archive that presented a colonial society in which native women did not
exist, although as the numbers of "natural children" in the records attest,
native mistresses were a commonplace feature of early colonial society.[17]
Colonial societies were deeply anxious about maintaining racial boundaries
and hierarchies of colonizing groups; managing sexual behavior and policing racial transgression were critical aspects of this colonial disciplinary
regime.[18] Colonial records, such as those produced by the church, were
crucial to maintaining racial and societal distance between Europeans and
non-Europeans, colonizers and colonized. This kind of social stratification
was expressed very clearly in the lists of names that form the church's baptismal and marriage registers and was reinforced by the anonymity of native
mothers. Excluding women's names was representative of colonial anxieties
about interracial sex: keeping written track of who belonged in this colonial
community enabled the archival fiction of a colonial society without racial
contamination or interracial sex.

Other documents also demonstrated the ways in which community
boundaries and hierarchies were repeatedly maintained. In directories and
calendars of the East India Company's servants birth registers indicated
whether the child had been born in wedlock. For instance, when an officer
was married to a European or half-European woman, notice of the birth

---

[16] Luce Irigaray, *Speculum of the Other Woman*, trans. Gillian C. Gill (Ithaca: Cornell University Press,
1974), 23; Anne McClintock, *Imperial Leather: Race, Gender and Sexuality in the Colonial Context*
(New York: Routledge, 1995), 29–30; Gauri Viswanathan, "Yale College and the Culture of British
Imperialism," *Yale Journal of Criticism*, 7 (1994), 1–30.

[17] For precise figures, see C. J. Hawes, *Poor Relations* (London: Curzon Books, 1996), 4, 17; S. C.
Ghosh, *The Social Condition of the British Community in Bengal, 1757–1800* (Leiden: Brill, 1970),
60–1.

[18] Kenneth Ballhatchet, *Race, Sex, and Class under the Raj* (New York: St. Martin's Press, 1980); Ann L.
Stoler, *Race and the Education of Desire* (Durham, NC: Duke University Press, 1994); Ann L Stoler,
Carnal Knowledge and Imperial Power: Race and the Intimate in Colonial Rule (Berkeley and Los
Angeles: University of California Press, 2002); Roxann Wheeler, *The Complexion of Race: Categories
of Difference in Eighteenth-Century British Culture* (Philadelphia: University of Pennsylvania Press,
2000).

was listed as "Born on the 15th instant, a son to Col. and Mrs. Monson." In cases where a marriage was not acknowledged, the notice read, "Born on the 15th instant, a son to the lady of Col. Monson at Berhampore."[19] By marking the first example as "legitimate" (because it was a child born to a married couple) and the second as "illegitimate" (because it did not involve a married couple and was likely an interracial couple), publications that circulated among the East India Company's employees drew distinctions between and consolidated a hierarchy of legitimate and illegitimate children, and by implication, of European and mixed-race children born to Company employees. At the turn of the nineteenth century, it was a fairly common practice to claim responsibility for illegitimate or, as the records say, "natural," mixed-race children as British, but native women were neatly cordoned off from inclusion in this community by being left unnamed in the historical record.

By their very absence, it was apparent that local women were the grounds on which boundaries of colonial communities were formed. When native women were recorded without names, they were stripped of their positions as mothers of elite mixed-race men and women who were considered subjects worth recording. Indeed, in their attempts to be considered British subjects, mixed-race elites moved up the social scale by erasing any trace of an indigenous past and suppressing their maternal lineage. Most prominent mixed-race men of British India were known by name through their European fathers, not their indigenous mothers.[20]

Using the archives of the East India Company, we could start to recognize such children, enumerate interracial liaisons, and show which Europeans were involved in them, but we would still know very little of the subjectivity of native women or of the effects this type of erasure had on their lives.

II

For the modern-day researcher, at the heart of archival erasure is the question of how we find native women and understand their historical circumstances if they lacked complete names. This lack, however prohibitive it may seem for mining the archives, was indicative of social and material

---

[19] In the case of the death of an infant, directories often listed "Died on the 15th instant, the son of Col. and Mrs. Monson," or in the case of the illegitimate child "Died on the 15th instant, the son of Col. Monson."
[20] See Herbert Stark and E. Walter Madge, *East Indian Worthies, being memoirs of Distinguished Indo-Europeans* (Calcutta, 1892).

impact that native women experienced at the hands of various institutions of the early colonial state. Colonial records and archives often constructed native women into particular types of subjects – conjugal, maternal, married, converted – by naming and renaming them in particular ways. In doing so, the names that native women were given related to the multiple ways in which they were situated in colonial society and what kinds of benefits they might receive as different types of subjects.

Although historical sources concealed the names of native women, traces of these women's existence entered into the colonial archive in other ways. From indexes of colonial historical records, I found clues and then followed these in the records themselves. In church registers, native women were either unnamed or named in quotation marks. In court records, such as wills written by men who had some sort of a conjugal domestic arrangement with native women, I was alerted to native women based on the terms that the men used for them. The term "companion" was one that British men most often used in their wills and diaries to describe their relationships with local women.[21] Other terms that were often used were "my housekeeper," "my girl," "a woman under my protection."

Church documents, particularly baptismal and marriage records, proved to be especially revealing. Although there was a long-established Catholic church establishment in India, as well as a Baptist missionary church in Serampore, the records from St. John's (an Anglican church intended to serve the needs of the East India Company's servants) are the only church registers from Bengal housed with the official records collection at the India Office Collections at the British Library in London.[22] Examples from 1810 illustrate the ways in which names were crucial in categorizing native women into ethnic and racial categories while erasing their origins.

In 1810, a total of 278 people were baptized in the Company's dominions in the Bengal Presidency. Of the baptized infants, there were twenty-six "natural children," or children who were born out of wedlock. In these cases, the record listed the name and rank of the European father, and in the column listing the mother, it read "native woman," thereby making the native mother anonymous and suppressing a way of identifying her further in the records.

---

[21] For instance, George Arrow, major in the native infantry, wrote, "to Emaumee Khanum, a native woman formerly my companion," High Court (Calcutta) Original Side [HCOS], 1825, 1–3; John Williams, a lieutenant-colonel in the Company's army, wrote, "to my female companion Minoo," HCOS, 1815–16, 277. Although "companion" leaves the impression of a companionate marriage, various inequalities structured the terms on which these relationships were based.

[22] These records are available at St. John's Church in Calcutta, or in the Oriental and India Office Collections at the British Library in London, in the N-series (Bengal).

There were also three non-European named women in the records for 1810: a "native" woman named Elizabeth, aged 25 years; a woman named Christiana, described as a "hindoo woman"; and Lucia, "a Malay girl, aged 21 years." With a specificity that foreshadowed the late nineteenth-century census and its designations for ethnicity, religion, and caste, these records omitted last names but included a Christian first name and added a racial, religious, or ethnic description: native, hindoo, and Malay.[23] Since these women were baptized, their Christian names signified their detachment from their natal communities and suggested closer ties to the community of the East India Company's European employees and their families.

Why, however, did three women with first and Christian names appear in the Company's official church record? In the marriage records, an entry noted that Elizabeth was baptized on February 4, 1810, and married John Cox, "Sergeant of the 9th European Regiment at Dinapore, widower," a week later. Lucia married John Cashman, "Gunner in the Invalid Artillery" stationed at Chunar, on June 19, 1810, and converted a few weeks later on July 8. Lucia, once married, became Lucia Cashman and became, as a named subject, a little easier to track through these records. Lucia Cashman became a widow soon after her marriage, and a little over a year later, she married Thomas Deacon, "Sergeant of the 1st Company, Artillery."

In the entry for her second marriage, Lucia gave way to a more British name, Lucy, and she is listed as "Lucy Cashman, widow." In documenting the transformation of her name from "Lucia, a Malay girl, aged 21 years" to "Lucy Cashman, widow," her new first and last names and marital designation masked her racial and ethnic origins. Notably, Lucy Cashman was no longer identified by her ethnicity. One might speculate that her marriage and subsequent name change enabled Lucy Cashman to improve her racial and social status in this colonial society, but without more historical evidence, it is difficult to elaborate further.

As Gauri Viswanathan has argued, from the middle of the nineteenth century onward, native Christian converts were considered "civilly dead" under the law and had no legal status within the bifurcated colonial judicial system that maintained separate courts for the British and for Hindus and Muslims.[24] Yet even before the 1860s, native converts with European names, particularly native women who converted to marry British men, posed a

---

[23] Bernard S. Cohn, *An Anthropologist among the Historians and Other Essays* (Delhi: Oxford University Press, 1987); Nicholas Dirks, *Castes of Mind: Colonialism and the Making of Modern India* (Princeton University Press, 2001).

[24] Gauri Viswanathan, *Outside the Fold: Conversion, Modernity, and Belief* (Princeton University Press, 1998).

dilemma for colonial officials at various levels in that their Christian names
did not correspond to their racial and ethnic status under colonial rule. In
the years between 1760 and 1840, often considered the early phase of British
expansion on to the Indian subcontinent, the administrators of the East
India Company were faced with various unexpected problems in ruling a
population of which it had little experience. In judicial and administrative
cases, in which a European name often masked the identity of a native
woman, colonial officials were repeatedly at pains to rationalize why native
Christian converts with European names could not be considered rights-
bearing European subjects.

Native women married to European men encountered various obstacles when they attempted to claim their husbands' estates, receive financial
allowances from the military, and avail themselves of the right to return to
England with their husbands.[25] Policies of the East India Company's charitable organizations for widows and orphans demonstrated how entrenched
was the assumption that European names reflected European parentage.
Under the regulations of widows' pension fund and the military orphan
society, British subjects were eligible to receive financial support as a result of
their familial affiliation with a European soldier in service of the Company.

When the plan for granting pensions to European soldiers' widows was
initially approved in the 1770s, colonial officials in London assumed that
soldiers' wives were British. Upon finding out that British wives were rare
and Indian wives more commonplace, the charitable plan was revised by
British officials in India to supply pensions to wives who were born of
European parents on both sides.[26] These regulations became a means for
the nascent colonial state to distinguish pure European wives from native
wives, to enforce appropriate marriages as those between Europeans and to
guarantee that only uniracial families would receive the financial support of
the East India Company's administration. Because the widows in these cases
were Indian or half-Indian but had European names, and the children were
mixed-race, determining who was eligible for benefits and to what degree
family relationships were modified by race became central subjects of debate
and subject to the regulations of the Company's charities.

---

[25] *Morley's Digest*, 181: Sir Edward Hyde East's Notes, Oriental and India Office Collections, the British
Library [OIOC], F/4/1115, no. 29907, "Country-born Widows of Soldiers now Admitted to Clive's
Fund; Half Castes to be called Indo-Britons." See also Indrani Chatterjee, "Colouring Subalternity:
Slaves, Concubines and Social Orphans in Early Colonial India," *Subaltern Studies X* (New Delhi:
Oxford University Press, 1999), 70.
[26] For more detail, see Durba Ghosh, "Making and un-making Loyal Subjects: Pensioning Widows
and Educating Orphans in Early Colonial India," *Journal of Imperial and Commonwealth History*, 31
(January 2003), 1–28.

Names were crucial to deciding who should be supported by the Company's benevolence and charity: starting in 1792, the East India Company's Board in London required that annual rolls of names of the widows and orphans who received charity from the pension fund or the military society be sent to London.[27] By making such a demand, the Board hoped to make legible those subjects who were unworthy recipients of the Company's charity: specifically, the Board intended to spot native wives and mixed-race children who, in the Board's imagination, were likely to have foreign names. In this way, names were envisioned as an effective tool of the colonial regime's efforts to delineate who could receive financial help from the Company. Yet this effort was effectively a failure since so many native wives and mixed-race children had English names; none the less, schemes to cleanse these early welfare rolls continued apace and in the years after 1800, various other measures were taken to deny native women married to European soldiers the right to collect a pension when their husbands died.

Although Indian women were often written out of the Company's archives and excluded from receiving the Company's charity, their children were treated marginally better. Mixed-race children were sent to the military orphan schools that educated (or re-educated) the children of European rank-and-file soldiers who had died or gone home. The goal was to remove children from their native mothers' homes and place them under the supervision of the Managers of the Military Orphanage Society for a more appropriate education.[28] Beyond the 1790s, when mixed-race individuals were widely considered a threat to the colonial enterprise in India and prohibited from holding covenanted civil or military positions with the Company, these measures were a means through which children born of European fathers and native mothers could be made useful to the British in India, even when Company policies worked against such incorporation.

Parallel to record-keeping practices that constructed a history in which native women's names were absent, various colonial policies, such as the administrative practices of the pension fund and the orphan society, attempted to cordon the existence of native women out of European domestic life while appropriating their children as future subjects who might be loyal to British aims. Through these material and social practices, naming, unnaming, and renaming were constitutive parts of the Company's efforts to create a colonial society appropriate to British India.

---

[27] National Archives of India (NAI), Military Proceedings February 22, 1793, no. 30, Military Dept. order, June 29, 1791.
[28] OIOC, L/AG/23/7/5, "Rules and Regulations of the Bengal Military Society . . ." (London, 1827).

I have suggested some ways in which one might reckon with the presence
of women who were left unnamed in the archives and explain the effects
of subject erasure in terms of this colonial society and its racial and family
policies. I want to turn now to naming practices that were beyond the
institutions of colonial governance and consider the ways in which practices
of naming oneself and one's "family" members were crucial ways through
which subjectivity was negotiated. How did familial and domestic practices
of self-naming shape the lives of native women and children? How did native
women express their location in colonial society through their names?

Wills stored in the High Court in Calcutta partially describe the
family biographies of mixed-race families, and they also include self-
representations of native women who cohabited with or married European
men. These wills begin in 1727 and continue, with gaps, until 1857. After
1857, the record becomes much more consistent. Some, but not all, of
these wills were sent back to England to be kept with the India Office
Records because most of the wills were by British subjects. Between 1770
and 1840, over 600 wills mentioned bequests to natural children or native
companions. Many of the wills are repetitive and reiterate that Englishmen
had sexual relationships with local women. Read carefully, these wills
also show how men identified the women with whom they had conjugal
relationships.

Men commonly referred to their female companions by partial names.
One dying man asked that "my girl Munnah" should receive Sicca Rs.
500.[29] Another left Sicca Rs. 2,400 to "my girl Flora, a native woman."[30]
Another wrote, "I bequeath to my female companion, commonly called
Nancy . . ."[31] English names such as Ann, Elizabeth, Mary, or Maria seem
to have been commonly used, or native names such as Peerun, Golaub, and
Bunnoo.[32] Many men described these women very clearly as "natives" of the
Indian subcontinent regardless of what their names were. While one might
imagine that Englishmen renamed their mistresses with European names
in order to pronounce their names more easily, renaming had the effect
of detaching women from their prior communities by erasing a crucial
identifier of their social and cultural background.

[29] OIOC, P/154/22 (1772), 23–4.   [30] OIOC, L/AG/34/29/4 (1782), no. 17.
[31] OIOC, L/AG/34/29/4 (1782), no. 32.
[32] Peter Robb, "The Clash of Cultures?" Inaugural Lecture, School of Oriental and African Studies,
University of London, March 12, 1998, 40.

The large majority of children born of these liaisons were given their father's last name and an English first name.[33] Some of the children were given nicknames and rechristened, as in the case of John Fairfax, major in the Bengal Army, whose son was named "Soldier" – no doubt from living on a cantonment – and was to be renamed Harry after his father's death.[34] Many of the boys were named after their fathers or after another family namesake. By naming a mixed-race child with an Anglican name, a father could (even after his death) undo the fact of an illegitimate birth and remake the child as legitimate even if the Company's policies against hiring mixed-race subjects worked against such a plan. More important, claiming the children as British separated them from their native mothers.

Many European men, particularly high-ranking employees of the East India Company, cohabited with native women, had children with them, and returned to England to more respectable, socially approved marriages. Occasionally, illegitimate offspring of upper-class men were sent to England to be educated and later were nominally assimilated into an English household and lifestyle.[35] This practice reflected the ways in which class position might mitigate (although never completely) the stigma of a mixed-race background. The circulation of these mixed-race children from the Indian subcontinent to England shows how names and the social status attached to particular names resonated between the metropole and the colony. Most famously, the father of the novelist William Makepeace Thackeray had an illegitimate daughter named Amelia while he was stationed as a collector in the District of Sylhet in Bengal. Amelia grew up alongside William in the Thackeray household. When William wrote his famous novel *Vanity Fair* in 1837, the name Amelia received top billing as the simple and unsophisticated heroine whose fortunes were supported by the profits of the East India Company (via the income of her nabob brother, Jos Sedley, District Collector of Bogleywallah).

Another famous example is that of Kitty, the daughter of high-ranking military official James Achilles Kirkpatrick and Khair-un-nissa, an elite noblewoman who lived in the ruling household of Hyderabad.[36] When Kirkpatrick died, he asked that the children be sent to England and christened.[37] The children were renamed James George and Catherine Aurora

---

[33] See also Chatterjee, "Colouring Subalternity," 69–71, 78.
[34] OIOC, L/AG/34/29/5 (1785), 84.
[35] Among 627 wills, 58 asked that children be sent to England. This was common in various parts of the British empire, including North America.
[36] William Dalrymple, *The White Mughals* (London: HarperCollins, 2002).
[37] HCOS (Calcutta), Will Register, 1805–6, 125–33.

and were sent to England in September 1805. Although Catherine's native mother was still alive and continued to live in Hyderabad, Catherine was sent, at age four, to her aunts and uncle in England. Thomas Carlyle later described the adult Catherine as "a strangely-complexioned young lady, with soft brown eyes and floods of bronze-red hair, really a pretty-looking, smiling and amiable, though most foreign bit of magnificence and kindly splendour; . . . half-begum in short; an interesting specimen of the Semi-oriental Englishwoman."[38] Although Catherine had been renamed, sent to England, grown up in an English household, and had become Anglican, Carlyle's account showed that her name never completely concealed her racial background.

The examples of Catherine Kirkpatrick and Amelia Thackeray show the ways in which naming practices were by no means limited to the cultural and social terrain of the Indian subcontinent. For the mixed-race children of European men and native women, naming acted as a way of highlighting one set of racial identifications over another; indeed, naming may have been a way of climbing the social/racial ladder of the British imperial world. But as the example of Catherine Kirkpatrick suggests, in spite of an appropriately English name, her appearance and comportment did not conceal her mixed-race parentage.

While court and church records speak to the ways in which native women were represented by others, a brief examination of women's wills demonstrates how women identified and named themselves. A final famous example suggests how one woman managed her names as a way of fashioning political and religious subjectivities in late eighteenth- and early nineteenth-century British India.

Although women who left wills were fairly uncommon, their wills and multiple names within these documents reflected a complex picture of their cultural identities and locations. Unlike other archival records in which women were named by others, wills called on native women with property and large estates to designate heirs, and define their families and their communities, thereby demonstrating a kind of historical agency and subjectivity that is hard to find for incompletely named subaltern subjects. Their practices of self-naming became a way in which they made use of the names and categories of social identification available to them.

One of the earliest wills dates from 1800, by a woman who identified herself as "Elizabeth, a Native Woman." Her children and her former

---

[38] T. Carlyle, *Reminiscences* (London, 1823), 247. A "begum" is defined in *Hobson-Jobson: A Glossary of Anglo-Indian Colloquial Words and Phrases* (London, 1886) as "a princess, a mistress, a lady of rank; applied to Mahommedan [Muslim] ladies." Also spelled "begam" or "beegum".

partners were more fully named, which enables us to gain a sense of how she situated herself and her children. She began, "In the Name of God, Amen, I, Elizabeth a Native Woman, formerly companion of the late Conductor Ferrier, now living with Serjeant [*sic*] F. Fitzpatrick, finding myself weak in Body thro Sickness but sound in mind and memory do make this my last will and testament . . ."[39]

The names recorded in her will are indicative of Elizabeth's sexual and reproductive history: she cohabited with a series of European men and bore each of them children. Isabella Ferrier, her only daughter, was about nine years old (a note in the margin indicated that she was born in December 1793). William Butler Fitzpatrick, her elder son, was likely younger than Isabella since Elizabeth took up with Fitzpatrick after Ferrier died. Since the father of Elizabeth's other son, William Hume, was never mentioned, we can guess he was another of Elizabeth's partners. Although Elizabeth went only by a first name, other native women went by several names and specified surnames.

For instance, "I, Beebee Nancy commonly called Beebee Willoughby of Calcutta" left her son, James Willoughby, her entire estate.[40] Another woman identified herself as "Bebee Munnoo, or Jane Mitchell, native of Hindostan."[41] Bibee Peary Khanum was "well known by the name of Bibi Reed." In these cases, from Elizabeth to Beebee Nancy, these women self-identified as "native women," whose last names suggested they were conjugal partners to British men. That their names were multiple suggests that the women situated themselves both as native women and as members of European families. One woman, not a bibi or native wife, but the daughter of a native woman, identified herself as "I, Moosummat Isabella Rawstone, daughter of General Rawstone . . ."[42] signaling that she was both a Rawstone and of Muslim descent. Multiple aliases suggest that these women had several cultural contexts that they inhabited simultaneously and they relied on names as a way to mark the different contexts in their lives.

Although these wills appear in the records in English, notes in the margin suggest that there were several contexts of translation. Names did not completely identify one's cultural identity, religious affiliation, or even the language one spoke. Names could be a highly unstable way of locating one-self: a European name did not necessarily mean that one lived a European

---

[39] OIOC, L/AG/34/29/14, 10–11.

[40] HCOS, 1829, 49. "Bibi," also spelled "bibee" and "beebee," is a transliteration of the Hindustani word for wife. In the eighteenth century, it was commonly used by Englishmen to refer to their native conjugal partners.

[41] HCOS, 1838, 416–18.   [42] HCOS, 1819, 223–4.

lifestyle or even among a community of Europeans. In the postscript to
the will of one woman, identified as Anne Elizabeth Smith, the mother
of four children named Catherine Lantour, Lydia Swaine, Thomas Smith,
and Charlotte Smith, the translator's note read: "Explained to me by Mrs.
Anne Elizabeth Smith in the common Hindustanee language."[43]

Another female companion's will was translated from Urdu. In it, without
invoking any Christian preamble, this woman wrote, "I, Hinda Husunah
Khadejah Begum do constitute my Master Stephen Davis Reilly to be
administrator . . ."[44] She asked that her estate of Sicca Rs. 10,000 (which
was equivalent to about £1,000) be divided between the two children she
had with Reilly. Her will bears her signature in Perso-Arabic script. Beebee
Lucy of Taultollah asked that her house and grounds be given to her son,
Charles Phillips, and signed her will in Nagiri.[45] Punna Purree Pearse's will
was signed in Persian and witnessed by Thomas Christie, William Bell, and
Madam Ghosh, who signed in Bengali.[46] Another woman began, "In the
name of God Amen I Beebee Mehtaub of Bengal in the East Indies Mother
of Mrs. Colonel Maria Ann Doveton by my late Lord and Master Major
General John Arnold Knight Companion of Bath do make this my last
will and Testament I resign my soul to Almighty God its creator my body
to be buried."[47] She stated that she had been under John Arnold's "protection" for fifty-eight years. Her will had been transcribed from "spoken
Hindustani into written by Goluck Chunder Sircar," and then translated
into English.

Even in the names that native women used to identify themselves, there
were no easily defined boundaries between British and Indian, Christian
and non-Christian, or English- and non-English-speaking. Nor were there
any uniform characteristics or behaviors that applied to any of these categories of names. Roza Hickey, "alias Bebee Rozie," asked to be buried by
Catholic rites. According to the text of the will, she had inherited her money
from a European who had long since returned to England. In the postscript
to her will, the translator wrote, "read and explained [to the testator] in
Bengali."[48]

While many colonial documents contained unnamed native women
within particular categories such as concubine, mistress, single mother,
Hindu, Christian convert, etc., women who were in the position to write
legal wills strained against these categories as they situated themselves within
the multiple contexts that were relevant to their lives.

[43] HCOS, 1834–5, 146–7.   [44] HCOS, 1820–1, 200–3.   [45] HCOS, 1822, 137–8.
[46] HCOS, 1819–20, 277–9.   [47] HCOS, 1838, 520–1.   [48] HCOS, 1833–4, 335–7.

Although it is tempting to see these acts of naming and renaming as a way in which native women could exercise agency in how they were represented, these examples also show the ways in which naming was rarely ever a complete form of historical identification. Renamed and self-named female subjects did not take on names only as a way of expressing cultural, religious, or linguistic affiliations; rather, renaming was also often deeply implicated within structures of political and social power and was indicative of how names could be used strategically in the service of one's political and military ambitions.

One final example shows how one woman negotiated and managed her names and titles to advance her political career. For Begum Samru, changing names served strategic ends at the critical moment of political transition between the Mughal empire and the British empire. As the Comaroffs have noted in a parallel study on the transition to colonial rule in Africa, naming "introduced a vehicle by means of which persons could make, and remake, their subjective identities on a changing social stage."[49]

The story of Begum Samru (1751?–1836) has been narrated in numerous biographies that emphasize her exceptional skills and political savvy in transforming herself from a dancing girl/slave to a *jagirdar* (landholder) in northern India. But more attention should be focused on the multiple (re)namings and religious conversion of the woman who was most famously known as Begum Samru. Through her names and conversion, Begum Samru fashioned herself alternatively as a Muslim noblewoman, as a Catholic, and as a European noblewoman, and attached herself in various ways to these different ethnic, cultural, and religious communities.

Begum Samru began her life as Farzana, a Muslim dancing girl from Delhi. In 1765, Farzana was "discovered" by Walter Reinhardt, an Austrian mercenary soldier who was himself renamed and known among Indians as Samru. From then until Reinhardt's death thirteen years later, she was, by all accounts, his constant companion.

Through her relationship with General Samru, Farzana became known as Begum Samru although whether they were legally married is unclear.[50] In standard local practice, "begum" was used to describe a woman of noble descent and was often paired with her given name; begum was rarely used

[49] John and Jean Comaroff, *Of Revelation and Revolution* (Chicago: University of Chicago Press, 1991), 219–20.
[50] William Sleeman, *Rambles and Recollections of an Indian Official* (2 vols., Westminster, 1893), I, 285; James Skinner, *Military Memoir of Lt. Col. James Skinner, CB*, edited by J. Baillie Fraser (2 vols., London, 1851), I, 285; See also Indrani Chatterjee, *Gender, Slavery and the Law in Colonial India* (Oxford University Press, 1999), 85–9.

as a prefix like Mrs. as Begum Samru's name might indicate.[51] By retaining
the name Begum Samru, Farzana did two things simultaneously: one was
to affirm herself as a Muslim noblewoman (undoing the traces of her past as
a slave and dancing girl), the second was to solidify her spousal connection
to Samru, who was by the late 1760s a formidable officer who commanded
four battalions and about 2,000 soldiers.

When Samru died, the Begum became his military and political suc-
cessor. She was granted authority over Samru's armies and his lands. Her
elevation from a slave dancing girl to primary spouse was not uncommon,
nor was it uncommon for a woman to hold a high political position.[52]
Indeed, in precolonial and early colonial India, changing names and titles
marked the upward shifts in status that occurred when one became a valued
member of the ruling family's court.

In 1781, three years after the death of Reinhardt, Begum Samru was
baptized by a Carmelite monk and christened Joanna.[53] By converting to
Catholicism, like many other native women, Begum Samru exchanged one
name for another name. In 1787, Begum Samru was given the name Zeb-
un-nissa by the Mughal emperor and given ceremonial robes (*khilat*) for
her service in the Rohilla attacks against Delhi in that year.[54] The title
brought the Begum into the circle of trusted nobility upon whom the
Mughal emperor relied. She also received an additional land grant south of
Delhi.

In 1790, a French nobleman, Le Vassoult, exiled during the French Revolution the year before, joined the Begum's military cadre. By the time
that the Begum and Le Vassoult were married in 1793, Begum Samru had
added Nobilis to her name and adopted a seal that proclaimed her as Joanna
Nobilis Somer. The seal-added "Nobilis," inscribed in English, enabled her
to fashion herself as a member of European nobility while she maintained
her attachment to General Samru. Her seal also included an inscription in
Persian which confirmed her status as a noblewoman in the Mughal court;
the Persian reads, "Under the reign of Shah Alam, in the year Hijrah 1200
[*c.* 1785/86], Zeb-un-nissa." By invoking her noble status in her seal, she

---

[51] "Begum" was the feminine of the Turkish term "beg," which signified prince or nobleman. See
Ghulam Hussain Khan, *Seir Mutaqherin*, transl. by Nota Manus (Calcutta, 1902; orig. 1780), I, 274,
fn 253. See also footnote 38.
[52] Chatterjee, *Gender, Slavery and the Law*, ch. 3.
[53] Sleeman, *Rambles*, II, 273; Brajendranath Banerji, *Begam Samru* (Calcutta: M. C. Sarkar and Sons,
1925), 18.
[54] Banerji, *Begam Samru*, 28; M. N. Sharma, *The Life and Times of Begam Samru of Sardhana* (Sahibabad:
Vibhu Prakashan, 1985), 75–8; John Lall, *Begum Samru: Fading Portrait in a Gilded Frame* (New Delhi:
Roli Books, 1997), 75.

doubly affirmed her aristocratic standing within India both among Indian nobility and also among the growing influence of the British.

The Begum's multiple names were constitutive of her shifts in status from a dancing girl to a local ruler; changing names was also part of a strategic process through which she expressed political allegiances crucial to gaining the power to rule over her lands outside Delhi. When the British replaced the Marathas as the dominant power in north India in 1803, the Begum left the Marathas' service and became an ally of the British, who then promised to protect her lands until she died.[55]

IV

Doing research on partially named and renamed subaltern women has been a methodological challenge. But rather than seeing the lack of names as an insurmountable obstacle, this chapter has suggested that naming practices as they were preserved in archives were constitutive of multiple subjectivities in a colonial society that was keen to maintain particular kinds of racial, social, and gender hierarchies.

In contrast to Spivak and Mani, who have represented colonial archives as totalitarian and as precluding any understanding of subaltern and female subjectivity, I have argued that official colonial archives were uneven in their erasures and that these erasures are highly instructive for historians today. These moments of partial erasure are an opportunity for the archival researcher, but these opportunities are not without pitfalls. As Kamala Visweswaran has said, "the point of retrieval marks the subaltern's silencing in history, and it is at the point of erasure where the emergence of the subaltern is possible . . ."[56] While the practice of incomplete naming, such as in church records or men's wills, enables the writing of the history of colonial female companions, this history cannot fully write the history or reclaim subjectivities that existed beyond these historical records. Without a complete name, the archival trail goes cold.

In the case of native colonial companions mentioned in wills and church registers, the absence of indigenous names makes it difficult to know the communities from which these women came. Renaming a local woman with a European or Christian name was a kind of archival death that for the modern-day researcher obscures the history of who she was, where she

---

[55] NAI, Foreign Dept. Proceedings, August 2–25, 1807, Vol. 306, cons. 23–4.
[56] Kamala Visweswaran, "Small Speeches, Subaltern Gender: Nationalist Ideology and its Historiography," *Subaltern Studies IX* (New Delhi: Oxford University Press, 1996), 124.

came from, what kind of status she enjoyed in local society, and how her status changed when she cohabited with or married a European man. The renaming that a native woman experienced at the hands of the man she cohabited with or in the church involved *un*naming her, perhaps severing some of her attachments from the community in which she originated or erasing a prior set of identifications. For women who named themselves, taking names representative of different cultural, social, and religious affiliations was a way of marking overlapping cultural locations and multiple, shifting subjectivities, but these acts of self-naming were often also shaped by demands placed by community and governmental structures. Naming practices were a crucial mechanism through which questions of subjectivity were being constantly constructed, negotiated, and managed by native women and by colonial institutions that made subjects legible, or illegible, as was the case here.

By paying careful attention to the ways in which historians rely on names as a way of doing archival research, we can start to break apart the unspoken continuities between goals and priorities of the institutions that recorded archival "facts" at the turn of the nineteenth century and historians who use these archives for their research two centuries later. Historians working in archives have long relied on a sense that historically relevant subjects have names, these names are written down in documents, and documents create the textual records that are later indexed, catalogued, and made legible for the researcher in historical archives. In urging historians to be more critical of naming practices in the production of the archival documents and the ways we do historical research, this chapter suggests that incompletely named and renamed subjects have histories that are waiting to be told.

CHAPTER 15

Ornament and use: Mai and Cook in London

Harriet Guest

On July 14, 1774, Mai (or Omai) arrived in London having traveled half way round the world on HMS *Adventure*, one of the two ships involved in James Cook's second voyage to the Pacific. *The Westminster Magazine* for that month commented that the European voyagers:

have dived so deep into foreign parts, that they are absolutely Crusoes. But with all their penetration, I do not find that any good hath accrued to the Community. Numbers of our hardy subjects have died on the passage – many have been roasted and eaten by Cannibals – numbers have been drowned – and a great expence the nation hath been put to; and only to bring home a few seeds – some shells – stuffed fish – dried birds – voracious animals – pressed plants – and an Indian – in short, as many rare things as would set up a Necromancer or a Country Apothecary.

The journalist contrasts Cook's two circumnavigations with the expeditions of earlier "Heroes," whose successes could be measured by the quantity of "territories and islands . . . annexed" by their countries. Compared with the acquisitive feats of Columbus or Raleigh, he suggests, Cook's voyages have merely shopped for fashionable knick-knackery: "the present mode of exploring only appears to be an expedition to pick up shells and preserve butterflies for the Fair Sex. The Isles of Otaheite and New Zeland are not to be visited or inhabited, and therefore these jaunts to the southern latitudes are only to amuse the Court, and encrease our collections of trifles." The trifles listed by the journalist are reminiscent of the exotic and enigmatic "encyclopaedia of show-pieces" displayed on the walls of the quack doctor in the third engraving of Hogarth's *Marriage A-la-Mode* series (fig. 4), which a visitor to England in the 1770s thought were designed to afford some "preliminary entertainment" to soften up the minds of patients in readiness for the meaningless "jibber-jabber" of the French doctor, and which he regarded as "a perfect general satire upon certain collectors of all the rubbish of Nature and Art."

Figure 4   William Hogarth, *Marriage A-la-Mode*, Plate 3, 1743–5
(National Gallery, London).

In the essay the commodity that most clearly indicates the meaningless-
ness and superfluous expense of British "jaunts to the southern latitudes"
is the so-called Indian, Mai himself: "all the world are running to see this
exotic Black. The King is to see him – the Queen is to see him, and his
velvet skin is to be touched by the Maids of Honour; and all this is the
wondrous production of a voyage of two years to the *South Seas!*" Here
the imaginary and tantalizing body of the islander, whose exotic blackness
must be seen, and whose "velvet skin" must be touched, is the measure of
the hollowness of the achievement of the voyages, the excess of an imperialism that drains the wealth and wastes the manpower of the nation not
to produce any expansion of territory but merely in order to gratify the
"extravagant . . . curiosity" of women and courtiers.[1] The satirist's contempt for collectors and their curiosities focuses on the contrast between

[1] Momus: or The Laughing Philosopher, *The Westminster Magazine; or The Pantheon of Taste*, July
1774, 348, 346. This chapter is deeply indebted to E. H. McCormick, *Omai: Pacific Envoy* (Auckland:
Auckland University Press, 1977).

the expense of the voyages and the implied uselessness of Mai as an acquisition, to suggest that the desire to see and touch the islander is a sign of the misplaced, frivolous, or licentious ambitions of the court. Mai is drained of any profitable significance beyond that created by the desires of the court, but the satirist's disappointed expectations suggest that he is more than a curiosity. They indicate that he may be more reminiscent of the objects of desire discussed by Adam Smith in his account of "the Effect of Utility upon the Sentiment of Approbation," in his *Theory of Moral Sentiments*. Smith writes that men "have entirely changed the whole face of the globe, have . . . made the trackless and barren ocean a new fund of subsistence, and the great high road of communication to the different nations of the earth"; and he argues that men have effected these changes because nature deceives them into laborious pursuit of "the idea of a certain artificial and elegant repose which [they] may never arrive at" – a repose that does not in itself offer any "real satisfaction."

Smith explains the allure of this pursuit in an extended meditation on the appeal of gadgets:

How many people ruin themselves by laying out money on trinkets of frivolous utility? What pleases these lovers of toys is not so much the utility, as the aptness of the machines which are fitted to promote it. All their pockets are stuffed with little conveniences. They contrive new pockets, unknown in the clothes of other people, in order to carry a greater number. They walk about loaded with baubles . . . some of which may sometimes be of some little use, but all of which might at all times be very well spared, and of which the whole utility is certainly not worth the fatigue of bearing the burden.

The collector admires the fitness or convenience of the object, the complexity of its design, and accepts or even welcomes the inventiveness he has to develop – the new pockets he has to contrive – in order to have the thing to hand; but the possibility that the object might at some point come in handy is at most an incidental or remote contingency. Both the function of the gadget and the repose it might help to secure are endlessly deferred, but they are also central to its present attraction, imbuing the ingenious design of the object with an almost magical charm. The gadgets Smith has in mind – he mentions "the curiosity of a tooth-pick, of an ear-picker, of a machine for cutting the nails" as well as the perhaps more obvious hi-tech attractions of watches – do not conceal or deny the labor that has gone into their production; indeed, the evidence of skilled workmanship is part of their appeal. But they do veil the labor and inconvenience entailed on their consumer behind the pleasing confirmation of his preferential position, his relative proximity to the ideal repose that is nature's deceptive reward.[2]

Mai is not an ingenious contrivance, and he no doubt understood his sojourn in London in quite different terms – so, for example, he often spoke of his "desire to kill his enemy the King of Bolabola," and is reported to have believed the trip would furnish him with "men & guns in a Ship" to enable him to achieve this end.[3] But most of the accounts written about him show no sign of any interest in his point of view. To the satirist of the *Westminster Magazine* at least, he is the trinket of frivolous utility which indicates that the labor and contrivance invested in circumnavigating the globe have resulted only in trivial or fantastic gratifications, because he is the representative of a part of the world that seems to offer no profit, no advantage to commerce or trade, and which the British do not intend to improve, colonize, or even plunder. In the issue of the *Westminster Magazine* for August 1774, only a month after the publication which had suggested that Mai was a suitable article to be included in the exotic stock of a country apothecary's "needy shop," a fuller and more serious-minded account of "Authentic Particulars relating to OMIAH" was published, offering what was to become a much more familiar but perhaps no more sympathetic account of him.

Omiah is so far from shewing . . . marks of simplicity and ignorance . . . that his deportment is genteel, and resembles so much that of the well-bred people here, as to make it appear very extraordinary to those who know how little a time it is since he left the South-Sea islands, where the manners, by no means savage, are yet so totally different from those of polished people in Europe.[4]

The persistence with which commentators dwell on the natural gentility of Mai is usually glossed as an allusion to the theme of the noble savage. But Smith's account of the value of objects of frivolous utility provides a means to unpack that familiar theme, for Smith, in contrast to the satirist of the *Westminster*, sees the inutility of gadgets as the indirect means to more worthwhile and complex ends: their ingenious contrivance demonstrates in synecdoche the allure of the complex economy of modern society. I want to look again at some accounts of Mai in London and on his return to the South Pacific, to consider what they tell us about how that society thinks

[2] Adam Smith, *The Theory of Moral Sentiments*, edited by D. D. Raphael and A. L. Macfie (Oxford: Clarendon Press, 1976), IV. I. 8, 6.
[3] Letter from Rev. Michael Tyson to Rev. Sir John Cullum, January 4, 1775, and Sarah S. Banks, "Memorandums," pp [15]–[17], cited in McCormick, *Omai*, 130, 113.
[4] "Authentic Particulars relating to OMIAH," *The Westminster Magazine; or, The Pantheon of Taste*, August 1774, 427.

of itself, how it conceives of its own structuring heirarchies and differences, and their ability to accommodate the increasing demands of empire. Smith argues that when we are "charmed with the beauty of that accommodation which reigns in the palaces and oeconomy of the great," our imagination confounds the appearance with "the system, the machine or oeconomy by means of which it is produced."[5] The accommodation, the fixtures and fittings of the stately edifice are in themselves "contemptible and trifling"; but they charm because of the art and ingenuity that have produced them, and because they remind us of the aesthetically pleasing order of the economy which has made them the means of imaginary ease. Mai appears charming and indeed beautiful most immediately because he is exotic – because of the oceans that have been traversed to fetch him. Smith's argument suggests that polite London society take pleasure in Mai because their imaginations confound him with the skill and ingenuity necessary to Cook's voyages, and with the effortless increase of riches which the expansion of empire implies but does not always deliver; in praising his gentility, they displace on to Mai, who is in a sense the most immediate product of the second voyage,[6] their admiration for the extraordinary proficiency in navigation and naval healthcare that the voyage involved; they celebrate him because he is the sign of their culture's progress in technology, in manners, in civilization, and because he seems to herald the success of imperial ambition.

One of the most familiar tropes, in accounts of meetings with Mai during his visit to England, is that which contrasts his natural civility with the barely equal or even inferior charms of a European man. Samuel Johnson, for example, claimed that he could not distinguish between the manners of Mai and Constantine Phipps, Lord Mulgrave, because "there was so little of the savage in Omai." Hester Thrale praised "the savage's good breeding" at the expense of the "impatient spirit" of Baretti (the critic and journalist), claiming that the European could be taken for the savage of the pair. Frances Burney compared Mai's manners favorably with those of Philip Stanhope, Lord Chesterfield's nephew, commenting that the islander "appears in a *new world* like a man who had all his life studied *the Graces*, and attended with unremitting application and diligence to form his manners, and to render his appearance and behaviour *politely easy*, and thoroughly *well bred!*" Where Burney sees nature exceeding the polish of art, Johnson sees Mai's graces as the effect of the company he has kept, as a result of which "all that

[5] Smith, *Theory of Moral Sentiments*, IV. 1. 9, 183.
[6] See Nigel Leask, *Curiosity and the Aesthetics of Travel Writing, 1770–1840: "From an Antique Land"* (Oxford University Press, 2002), 22.

[Mai] has acquired of our manners was genteel"; though Mai's gentility has a puzzling tendency to exceed that of the aristocratic examples he imitates.[7]

The sense in which these commentators perceive Mai's superabundant and perhaps superfluous social polish as evidence of their own cultural superiority and gentility may be confirmed by their reluctance to see Cook in the same terms. Neither Johnson nor Thrale met Cook, though it does not sound as if it would have been difficult to manage: Boswell dined and talked with Cook on several occasions, and visited him at Mile End, where he was staying. Burney did meet Cook when he called on her father in 1773. Her account of him is respectful, but suggests none of the pleasure she took in the society of Mai. She wrote that Cook was "well-mannered and perfectly unpretending; but studiously wrapped up in his own purposes and pursuits; and apparently under a pressure of mental fatigue when called upon to speak, or stimulated to deliberate, upon any other."[8] She seems more oppressed by the narrowness of Cook's conversational range than by Mai's, and more doubtful of his claim to politeness. Burney's curiosity about the South Pacific (except as the theatre for her brother's professional career) does not extend far. When she meets Mai again in 1775, a year after the encounter I have mentioned, she finds that "He has learnt a great deal of English . . . and can with the assistance of signs and action, make himself tolerably well understood." But despite this new fluency, she explains that: "As we are totally unacquainted with his country, connections, and affairs, our conversation . . . consisted wholly in questions of what he had seen here."[9] For these polite commentators, meeting Mai seems to be an experience that allows them quite thoroughly to conceal any interest they may have had in learning more about the South Pacific, or about the voyages there, or about Cook's skills as a navigator and hygienist. Where, for Burney at least, Cook himself seems too purposive, perhaps too functional, too professional and pragmatic, Mai suggests a more familiar and acceptable idea of the exotic.

The representation of Mai in these encounters seems to offer his audience no improvement or instruction, and indeed to present them with little that is unfamiliar – he seems to present them only with an improved version

[7] James Boswell, *Life of Johnson*, edited by R. W. Chapman, introduction by Pat Rogers (Oxford University Press, 1980), Wed. April 3, 1776, 723. McCormick, *Omai*, 169. Annie Raine Ellis, ed., *The Early Diary of Frances Burney, 1768–1778* (2 vols., London: Bell, 1907), Letter to Mr. Crisp, December 1, 1774, I, 337.
[8] Burney, *Memoirs of Doctor Burney* (1832), I, 270–1, quoted in J. C. Beaglehole, *The Life of Captain James Cook* (London: Hakluyt, 1974), 289.
[9] Burney, *Early Diary*, December 14, 1775, II, 130–1.

of aristocratic or cosmopolitan civility. The indirect and concealed implications his presence bears – the sense that he is evidence of the ambition
and technical accomplishment of Cook's voyages – and the possibility that
his presence may have a deferred function, in furthering British imperial
expansion, are eclipsed by his more ornamental or frivolous utility, the
confirmation his presence offers through comparison and contrast of the
advanced state of British civilization. Adam Ferguson, in his *Essay on the His-*
tory of Civil Society (1767), writes an account of the "Corruption Incident to
Polished Nations" which is strongly reminiscent of Smith's discussion of the
charms of ingenious contrivances, and which illuminates the association of
ornament and aristocracy that frequently occurs in discussions of Mai. But
the displacement of ambition into trinkets of frivolous utility and fantasies
of deferred ease which for Smith is the motor of civilized progress is for
Ferguson the sign of incipient corruption, of distraction from the supreme
ambition of serving the public good. Ferguson argues that "Nations are
most exposed to corruption . . . when the mechanical arts, being greatly
advanced, furnish numberless articles, to be applied in ornament to the
person, in furniture, entertainment, or equipage; when such articles as the
rich alone can procure are admired; and when consideration, precedence,
and rank, are accordingly made to depend on fortune." Ferguson claims
that as nations advance in commercial civilization, they are also progressively corrupted by the amoral instability of commercial notions of value.
The worth or distinction which had been attached to moral characteristics
such as "the reputation of courage, courtly manners, and a certain elevation
of mind," as well as to "birth and titles" and "superior fortune," becomes
attached exclusively to the "sumptuous retinue which money alone may
procure." He suggests that "the idea of perfection" is transferred "from the
character to the equipage," to the frivolous trinkets in which the wealthy
display their status. This corruption erodes all sense of relative value, and
introduces a "fatal dissolution of manners, under which men of every condition, although they are eager to acquire, or to display their wealth, have
no remains of real ambition."[10]

Ferguson's discussion of the corruptions attendant on commercial
progress argues that the transfer of status on to equipage displaces moral
value from people to their possessions, to the "productions of a few mechanical arts," so that, he writes, "excellence itself" becomes "a mere pageant."
In Smith's argument, ornamental gadgets provide indirect evidence of the

---

[10] Adam Ferguson, *An Essay on the History of Civil Society*, introduction by Louis Schneider (New
Brunswick: Transaction, 1980), 251, 253.

progress in complexity and sophistication of the social economy, but in Ferguson's account their pettiness indicates cultural impoverishment. Mai in London is the sign, the polished ornament of those with whom he associates, and, as many commentators pointed out with varying degrees of amusement or disapprobation, his associates seem to have been anxious to impress him principally with the polish and grandeur of English civilization, rather than with any more improving information. The extent to which Mai was imagined to have been civilized by his stay in England, many commentators thought, was measured by his success in reflecting his associates' admiration for the trivial pageant of civilized excellence. The author of "An Heroic Epistle from OMIAH to the QUEEN of OTAHEITE; being his REMARKS on the ENGLISH NATION," which was published in the *London Chronicle* for June 1775, has Mai respond to enquiries about "how farther I my hours employ,/ What learning gather, and what sports enjoy?" with an account of guided visits to "plays, museums, conjurers, and shows."[11] His English acquaintances often seem most interested, most gratified, by measuring his responses to the conjurers and shows, the spectacle of European civilization – as Burney was. At Leicester, for example, what was claimed to be "the greatest number of musicians hitherto assembled in England" performed Handel's *Jeptha*, with the Earl of Sandwich, First Lord of the Admiralty, on the kettle drums, all apparently in order to record Mai's "wild amazement at what was going on."[12] Sandwich had been at pains to impress Mai during his stay in England. He entertained Mai with a tour of the dockyard at Chatham, where Mai was taken on board HMS *Victory*, and the newspapers offered the gratifying report that "his joy was amazing at seeing so large a ship."[13] Mai also visited Sandwich's country house, Hinchingbrooke, in Huntingdonshire, where the islander was reported to have been "entertained in the most magnificent manner, and where the neighbouring gentlemen vied with each other in varying his diversions, in order to raise his ideas of the splendor and gaiety of this country."[14]

Where Mai is offered a voice, in the numerous satires spoken from his imagined subject position which reflect on similarities between British high society and a fantasy of Tahitian life, his comments are close to those of observers writing about him, and while it is unsurprising that no independent voice should emerge, it also indicates the ease with which his perceived

[11] *London Chronicle*, June 22–24, 1775.
[12] William Gardiner, *Music and Friends; or Pleasant Recollections of a Dilettante* (2 vols., London, 1838), I, 4–5, cited in McCormick, *Omai*, 114.
[13] *General Evening Post (London)*, June 10–13, 1775.
[14] *Gentleman's Magazine*, Historical Chronicle for September 1, 1774.

Figure 5   Joshua Reynolds, *Omai*, 1775 (Yale University Art Gallery).

exotic characteristics could be Anglicized, could be masked or adequately expressed in the idea of his social rank – the rank attributed to him as a result of his association with high society. In Joshua Reynolds's oil sketch of the *Head of Omai* (fig. 5) (probably painted in 1775) he has acquired at least a suggestion of the cavalier, and a sort of Van Dyck costume. Reynolds argued in his seventh Discourse, delivered at the Royal Academy in December 1776, that representations of "fantastick dress" reminiscent of Van Dyck could make portraits appear to be "better . . . than they really were", by which he seems to mean that their subjects appear more socially exalted. He suggests that this dress appeals to a prejudice in favor of the age of Van Dyck that is second nature to the educated viewer, and could lend the sitter something like the elevation above mundane circumstance that classical drapery effected in statuary.

Van Dyck costume does not, in Reynolds's account, have the timeless simplicity of classical drapery, however, and his account of it as a fantastic fashion, and his increasing preference for using it in portraits of children, point to the extent of its share in (what he calls) "those whimsical capricious forms by which all other dresses are embarrassed." In comparison with the portrait head of Mai which William Hodges painted for John Hunter, the surgeon and physiognomist, at around the same time (fig. 6), the suggestion, in Reynolds's sketch, of Mai as a young cavalier becomes more prominent, thrown into relief by the contrast between the vigor of Hodges's painting, which suggests mobility and transient expression, and the decorative passivity of the face Reynolds portrays, with its fine features and more elegant locks. Reynolds's sketch seems to poise the islander between an ideal moment above time and change, and a curiously incongruous and anachronistic role in seventeenth-century European history.[15]

George Forster, who served with his father as naturalist on Cook's second voyage, was disappointed by the cultural education Mai received among the English aristocracy, which he thought offered polish at the expense of improvement. He noted that from the outset of his stay, Mai was "led to the most splendid entertainments of this great and luxurious metropolis, and presented at court amidst a brilliant circle of the first nobility." The naturalist suggested that proximity to high life led Mai rapidly to absorb its habits: "He naturally imitated that easy and elegant politeness which is so prevalent in all those places, and which is one of the ornaments of civilized society; he adopted the manners, the occupations, and amusements of his companions."[16] David Samwell (surgeon on the third voyage) was also concerned. He wrote of Mai that "he was a goodnatured sensible young fellow, of a careless Disposition, too inattentive to his own Interest," and he observed that though Mai initially seemed willing and able to learn useful lessons from his stay in England, his aristocratic guardians "have made him more of the fine Gentlemen than anything else," and taught him "nothing . . . but to play at cards, at which he is very expert."[17] William Bligh (master of the *Resolution* on the third voyage) regretted that Mai had "been led into Idleness and Dissipation as soon as he arrived in

---

[15] Sir Joshua Reynolds, *Discourses on Art*, edited by Robert R. Wark (New Haven: Yale University Press, 1975), 138–9.

[16] George Forster, *A Voyage Round the World*, edited by Nicholas Thomas and Oliver Berghof with Jennifer Newell (2 vols., Honolulu: Hawaii University Press, 2000), I, 11.

[17] J. C. Beaglehole, ed., *The Journals of Captain James Cook on his Voyages of Discovery* (3 vols., Cambridge, 1957–61), III, 1514–5. Samwell was first appointed as surgeon's mate on the *Resolution*, but was promoted to surgeon on the *Discovery* following the death of Anderson.

Figure 6 *Omai, a Polynesian*, by William Hodges, RA (1744–97). Reproduced by kind
permission of the Royal College of Surgeons.

Europe,"[18] and James King (then second lieutenant on the *Resolution*) commented that if, after his experiences, "Omai remains unhappy it arises from
his want of some useful Knowledge that might have made him respect'd
among his Countrymen" – though he was inclined to blame Mai himself,
rather than his London associates.[19] Forster was pessimistic about Mai's

[18] Douglas Oliver, *Return to Tahiti: Bligh's Second Breadfruit Voyage* (Honolulu: University of Hawaii
Press, 1988), 227.
[19] *Journals of Captain Cook*, III, 1073, 1386.

chances of improving his social status. He foresaw that Mai would quickly return "to his first insignificance; whereas, had he been taught a trade, his knowledge would always have been real riches to him, and paved his road to honour and opulence among his countrymen."[20] He lamented that Mai had gained neither useful knowledge nor skills, and concluded that the nature of his education was clearly indicated in the paraphernalia with which he was equipped when he left England in 1776, which was made up of "an infinite variety of dresses, ornaments, and other trifles, which are daily invented in order to supply our artificial wants."[21]

In 1789, Hester Thrale Piozzi received news of Mai's death, and heard reports of the part his possessions played in fighting between the islanders of Raiatea and Huahine. Writing to a friend, she recalled that "poor Omai . . . was no small favourite of mine," and added, more sardonically: "Two Islands quarreling for the Possession of a German Organ and Puppet Show – Omai's best and most valuable Effects as I remember – would make an Excellent Subject for a mock Heroic Poem."[22] Her sentimental recollection of Mai, whom she had entertained in London, rapidly hardens into disdain, as he and the islanders in general become infected with the littleness and triviality of the European toys she believes they value so highly. The possessions with which Mai returned to the South Pacific, most of which seem to have been chosen for him and not by him,[23] included the things Piozzi and Forster mention – a barrel organ and a collection of miniature figures (of soldiers, animals, coaches, and so forth) which it was imagined he could use in his attempts to describe European life. In addition Mai was endowed with an assortment of fireworks; portraits of the king and queen and, perhaps, of Cook; an illustrated Bible; a jack-in-a-box; handkerchiefs printed with the map of England and Wales; two drums; and a suit of armor. Joseph Banks presented him with an electrical machine. As if to confirm him in, or at least remind him of, European ways of life he was provided with cooking and eating utensils, iron tools, and a few bits of furniture, as well as with linen clothes for himself and for gifts – and he had other trading goods. He was also endowed with some livestock and poultry, and seeds for a garden. Before Cook's ships departed he also acquired a compass, globes, sea charts,

[20] Forster, *Voyage*, II, 765.   [21] Ibid., I, II.

[22] Hester Thrale Piozzi to Samuel Lysons, July 8, 1789, in Edward A. Bloom and Lillian D. Bloom, eds., *The Piozzi Letters: Correspondence of Hester Lynch Piozzi, 1784–1821 (formerly Mrs. Thrale)* (6 vols., Newark: University of Delaware Press, 1989), I, 298. Thrale seems to have heard a version of the report from the *Lady Penrhyn*. McCormick, *Omai*, 267.

[23] The astronomer William Bayly commented on Mai's outfitting for his return that "Omi being a man of pleasure neglected to inspect into his own Affairs but left it entirely to other people." Those other people, Bayly thought, "used him exceeding ill." *Journals of Captain Cook*, II, 193 n2.

and maps, as well as some guns, powder, and shot. When a site had been selected, the ships' carpenters built Mai a European-style house designed "to contain his valuables, which would by no means have been secure in one of his own country."[24]

The assortment of objects with which Mai was endowed on his return is freighted with the significances his English hosts had attributed to his visit. As Nigel Leask has pointed out, the collection of figures suggests that "Mai's credit" as a narrator of European life "is made to depend upon a miniaturized, feminized, and domesticated simulacrum of civility."[25] My discussion suggests that Mai's dolls and trinkets may demonstrate how the progress of advanced civilizations is involved in frivolous utility and inconvenience. But Mai also acquired tools which he may have understood as more functional, such as the armaments and iron tools, as well as equipment associated with Cook's role as the emissary of imperial expansion. Anna Seward's *Elegy on Captain Cook* (1780), for example, celebrated the navigator's attempts to encourage the cultivation of European crops and animals on the islands he visited as conclusive evidence of the disinterested humanity of his mission.[26] It was hoped that these goods would enrich the diet of the islanders, establish a resource for European ships, and, in some locations at least, provide a means of testing the feasibility of colonial settlement.

Leask argues compellingly that Mai's collection of miniaturized figures "travesty the conventional eighteenth-century aesthetics of the sublime and beautiful. If Abyssinian savagery is metonymically represented in Georgian London by the gigantism of Bruce, then metropolitan society concomitantly presents itself on the savage periphery in the inverse form of the miniature."[27] The association of the miniature with the civilized is important to Adam Smith's discussion of the aesthetics of utility. Smith writes that wealth and greatness, and their trappings, are no more useful or convenient than toys or ingenious gadgets – "There is no real difference between them," he claims, "except that the conveniencies of the one are somewhat

[24] William Ellis, *An Authentic Narrative of a Voyage performed by Captain Cook and Captain Clerke, in his majesty's ships Resolution and Discovery* (2 vols., London: Robinson, 1782), I, 147. See McCormick, *Omai*, 180, 255.
[25] Leask, *Curiosity*, 62.
[26] See Anna Seward, *An Elegy on Captain Cook, To which is added, An Ode on the Sun* (2nd edn, London: J. Dodsley, 1780), p. 9: "To these the Hero leads his living store, / And pours new wonders on th'uncultur'd shore; / The silky fleece, fair fruit, and golden grain;/ And future herds and harvests bless the plain." Seward refers specifically to New Zealand. For further discussion of the elegy, see my *Small Change: Women, Learning, Patriotism, 1750–1810* (Chicago University Press, 2000), 253, 257–8.
[27] Leask, *Curiosity*, 62.

more observable than those of the other." He concludes that "To one who
was to live alone in a desolate island it might be a matter of doubt, perhaps, whether a palace, or a collection of such small conveniencies as are
commonly contained in a tweezer-case, would contribute most to his happiness and enjoyment." Mai's island is, I suppose, desolate in the absence of
other appurtenances of European civilization, or of spectators who might
be suitably impressed by a palace. Smith argues that ingenious contrivances
of frivolous utility, which are represented on a large scale by the palaces and
retinues of the great, and in small scale by the contents of tweezer-cases,
are worthwhile not as an end in themselves but because their contrivance
indicates the complex organization and ingenuity of the economy that
has produced them, and its allure works to animate "some degree of public
spirit." More practically, they seduce the rich into unnecessary expenditure,
which is the means by which the "invisible hand" distributes the "necessaries
of life" in the approximately egalitarian fashion he regards as promoting
the "interest of the society" and "the multiplication of the species."[28]

Mai's possessions, then, in their curious assortment of the functional or
useful and the frivolous or ornamental, demonstrate the ambivalence with
which English metropolitan society conceived of its own modernity. On
the one hand, iron tools and ship's instruments, animals and crops look
like the equipment of proto-colonial settlement. They seem to address the
practical concerns of professional men such as Forster and Samwell, who
understood technological advance as necessary to progressive civilization,
and perhaps they might also help to appease the ire of metropolitan critics
of the luxury and inutility of the voyages. The "editor" of the satirical poem
Omiah's Farewell (1776), to provide one more example of the currency of
this complaint, remarked that "OMIAH is now returning to his native isle,
fraught by royal order with squibs, crackers, and a various assortment of
fireworks, to show to the wild untutored Indian the great superiority of
an enlightened Christian prince."[29] The satirist points to what is clearly
and repeatedly implied in accounts of Mai – the sense that the failure
to return him improved with either some religious instruction or some
useful knowledge both belittles him and reveals inadequacies in British
culture, shortcomings that might hinder British imperial ambition. The
seeds and animals to which Cook, as well as Anna Seward, attached so much
importance might at least indicate an aspiration towards improvement,
towards furthering the spread of European notions of cultivation. Forster,

[28] Smith, *Theory of Moral Sentiments*, iv.i.8, 181–2; 10, 184; ii, 186.
[29] *Omiah's Farewell; Inscribed to the Ladies of London* (London: Kearsley, 1776), Preface, iv.

for example, emphasized the importance of the cattle and sheep, believing that their presence might "hereafter be conducive, by many intermediate causes, to the improvement of [the islanders'] intellectual faculties."[30]

That more practical and technological notion of progress, however, was not one that Mai's goods could do more than gesture towards. Cook's colonial gardens and Noah's ark-like collection of farm animals everywhere showed a worrying tendency to wither away and disappear. Mai himself, Cook thought, had no more than a fund of stories to his credit. In conversation with James Boswell, Cook commented wryly that he did not believe Mai's travels would improve his status, as he may have hoped: Cook "said that for some time after Omai's return home he would be a man of great consequence, as having so many wonders to tell. That he would not foresee that when he had told all he had to tell, he would sink into his former state." Cook concluded that he "would take care to leave the coast before Omai had time to be dissatisfied at home."[31] Mai's finery and toys, along with the manners which Forster saw as the "ornaments of civilized society," perhaps took a more thorough possession of him. Forster noted, in terms reminiscent of Smith's argument, that Mai did receive a kind of aesthetic education:

He was not able to form a general comprehensive view of our whole civilized system, and to abstract from thence what appeared most strikingly useful and applicable to the improvement of his country. His senses were charmed by beauty, symmetry, harmony, and magnificence; they called aloud for gratification, and he was accustomed to obey their voice.

Mai appreciates the ornamental achievements of metropolitan civilization, but Forster suggests that he responds to that spectacle appetitively, because "His judgement was in its infant state" and did not equip him to form general or abstract ideas. His collection of possessions – Forster itemizes "a portable organ, an electrical machine, a coat of mail, and suit of armour" – appeals to his "childish inclinations," his aesthetic appetite, but he is unable to deduce from them the sublime complexity of the social economy that has produced them.[32] In Smith's argument, of course, this failure of judgmental agency is all to the good; it is the beneficial imposition of nature, he argues, that leads the rich to pursue the "gratification of their own vain and insatiable desires" for goods which, when viewed in an "abstract

[30] Forster, *Voyage*, I, 12.
[31] Charles Ryskamp and Frederick A. Pottle, eds., *Boswell: The Ominous Years, 1774–1776* (Melbourne: Heinemann, 1963), London, April 2, 1776, 310–11.
[32] Forster, *Voyage*, I. 11.

and philosophical light," must "always appear in the highest degree con-temptible and trifling."[33]

What is problematic about reading Mai's acquisitions in Smith's terms, however, may be the extent to which they do take possession of him, and make him the exemplar of Anglicized civility, "more of the fine Gentleman than anything else"; they make him, like Smith's deluded wealthy, the more or less unwitting agent of a Eurocentric conception of providential nature. On his return to the islands in the *Bounty*, Bligh heard that Mai's acqui-sitions had briefly increased his consequence, but that he had not "gained any possessions or . . . higher rank than we left him in."[34] Mai's things, however, retained their prestige longer than their owner. The missionary William Ellis reported nearly half a century later that: "The spot where Mai's house stood is still called Beritani, or Britain, by the inhabitants of Huahine," and parts of Mai's armor were displayed on a house built on the spot. Ellis added that "A few of the trinkets, such as a jack-in-a-box . . . were preserved with care by one of the principal chiefs, who . . . considered them great curiosities, and exhibited them, as a mark of his condescension, to particular favourites."[35] Most accounts of Mai's return suggest that he was largely ignored or even unrecognized, until, as Cook noted, "knowl-idge of his riches" had been spread, but his possessions seemed to have been imbued with lasting value as tokens of the exotic.[36] The suit of armor had been given to Mai by the Earl of Sandwich, who had had it made for him by the artificers of the Tower of London.[37] Clothed in this final gesture of generosity, Mai seems briefly to be possessed by his things – to become British, like the spot where Ellis later saw the armor hanging (fig. 7) In "Omiah: an Ode" (published in 1784), a note explained that "Omiah has been presented with a rich suit of armour, to enable him to conquer Otaheite. He is to hold it by charter from the Crown, and has promised to acknowledge the right of taxation, and the supremacy of the British par-liament."[38] The satirist represents Mai in his armor as the agent of British imperialism, capable of compensating Britain for the humiliations of the American war.

---

[33] Smith, *Theory of Moral Sentiments*, IV.I.10, 184; 9, 183.   [34] Oliver, *Return*, 228.

[35] William Ellis, *Polynesian Researches* (1829), quoted in McCormick, *Omai*, 293.

[36] *Journals of Cook*, III, 193. The Europeans only seem to see the degree of interest and sentiment which they had clearly expected to be widespread in the reunion of Mai with his sister. See Cook's account, III, 192–3, 213, and Samwell's journal, III, 1052–3. On value created by association, see Nicholas Thomas, *Entangled Objects: Exchange, Material Culture, and Colonialism in the Pacific* (Cambridge, MA: Harvard University Press, 1991), ch. 3.

[37] See McCormick, *Omai*, 180.

[38] [?John Townshend], "Omiah: an Ode," in *The New Foundling Hospital for Wit* (6 vols., London, 1784), II, 132–6, quoted in McCormick, *Omai*, 186.

Figure 7 Royce after Dodd, "Omai's Public Entry on his first landing at Otaheite." Print from [John Rickman], *Journal of Captain Cook's Last Voyage*, opposite 136.

It is hard to see Mai, however, as the Smithian agent of commercial colonialism in the sense that Bernard Smith has argued is appropriate for Cook.
Where Cook can be understood as the representative of a distinctively modern form of imperialism exercised through transaction and negotiation, Mai
in his armor is a more ambiguous figure. For many British commentators,
the American war offered salutary confirmation of the need for a newly
modern version of imperialism. The Britishness Mai in his armor represents is as anachronistic as the Van Dyke dress that had both ennobled and
infantilized him in Reynolds's sketch. In the unauthorized *Journal* of John
Rickman, the only text in which Mai's return seems to make much of a
splash, he is represented (in an anecdote that may well be apocryphal) in a
parodic impersonation of British imperial identity. Rickman writes of the
astonishment of the islanders when Cook and Mai ride out on horseback:

> Omai, to excite their admiration the more, was dressed cap-a-pee in a suit of
> armour . . . and was mounted and caparisoned with his sword and pike, like St.
> George going to kill the dragon, whom he exactly represented; only that Omai
> had pistols in his holsters, of which the poor saint knew not the use. Omai,
> however, made good use of his arms, and when the crowd became clamorous, and
> troublesome, he every now and then pulled out a pistol and fired it among them,
> which never failed to send them scampering away.[39]

A central feature of Cook's characterization as a distinctively modern
hero was the notion of his humanity, manifested notably in his reputed
reluctance to use firearms: "Not a gun . . . was ever wantonly or unnecessarily
fired *by his order*."[40] If Mai was in some sense the emissary of British
civilization on his return to the South Pacific, freighted with tokens of the
ingenuity and sophistication of its economy, he was not simply the agent
of Smith's providential nature, which by its benevolent "deception . . .
rouses and keeps in continual motion the industry of mankind."[41] Mai's
Anglicization may confirm the global scope of British imperial ambition,
but he also indicates the limitations on the cultural aspiration that desires
to see admiration for the organizing principles, the beauty and symmetry
of the social economy, reflected from distant places. Rickman's anecdote
suggests that Mai is burdened with implications of European civilization
as advanced in its taste for ornament but anachronistic in its predelication

---

[39] [John Rickman], *Journal of Captain Cook's Last Voyage to the Pacific Ocean, on Discovery; performed
in the years 1776, 1777, 1778, 1779* (London: Newbery, 1781), 133–4.
[40] *Gentleman's Magazine*, review of *A Voyage towards the South Pole*, 1777. See also Bernard Smith,
"Cook's Posthumous Reputation," in Smith, *Imagining the Pacific: In the Wake of the Cook Voyages*
(New Haven, CT: Yale University Press, 1992), 227.
[41] Smith, *Theory of Moral Sentiments*, IV.I.10, 183.

for conquest – both forms of civilization discordant with notions of Cook's role as the agent of commercial modernity.

Ferguson's account of the state of commercial culture in which excellence becomes "a mere pageant" indicated the instability of the value of possessions and people in modern society. The extent to which the islanders' position is volatile is most clearly indicated in an incident reported in Prince Hoare's *Memoirs of Granville Sharpe* (1820) – an incident which must have taken place some years after Mai's return to the South Pacific. Hoare writes that "a native of Otaheiti had been enticed, by the offer of presents . . . on board an English vessel, kidnapped, and brought to England. Being an expert swimmer and diver, his skill had been very profitably employed during the voyage, in the capture of seals." When he arrived in England, the captain refused to pay him, and the merchants owning the ship told the Tahitian's representative that "they would spend 500l. in repelling any application of the kind, rather than pay the Otaheitean a farthing." The use of Sharpe's name, however, obliges the merchants to accept arbitration, and in the end they have to allow the Tahitian "the pay which had been solicited . . . which was that of an ordinary seaman."[42] The merchants attempt to exploit the Tahitian sailor's exotic status to deny him the wages and rights of an English seaman. In a similar sense, perhaps Mai may seem emptied of value, a mere curiosity (of the kind disparaged by Ferguson) rather than a Smithian contrivance of frivolous utility, when he is considered in the context of a discourse on modernity that emphasizes professional ambitions achieved through technological progress, or when accounts of Mai's gentility are juxtaposed with representations of Cook's achievements.

There has of course been much discussion in the past decade or so about the extent to which Cook participates in the guilt of colonial exploitation, and I do not intend to revisit that debate here.[43] Instead I want briefly to consider the extent to which Cook, as, in Bernard Smith's words, "a new kind of hero for a new time," is himself subject to evaluation within the terms of the commercial discourses that structured accounts of Mai in England.[44] When James Boswell met Cook in London in 1776, he

---

[42] Prince Hoare, *Memoirs of Granville Sharpe, Esq. Composed from his own Manuscripts, and other authentic documents in the possession of his family and of the African Institution* (London: Colburn, 1820), 249.

[43] See Gananath Obeyesekere, *The Apotheosis of Captain Cook: European Mythmaking in the Pacific*, with a new afterword (Princeton University Press, 1997), and Marshall Sahlins, *How "Natives" Think: About Captain Cook, For Example* (Chicago University Press, 1995).

[44] Bernard Smith, "Cook's Posthumous Reputation," in his *Imagining the Pacific: In the Wake of the Cook Voyages* (New Haven: Yale University Press, 1992), 231.

commented in the privacy of his journal that "It was curious to see Cook, a grave steady man, and his wife, a decent plump Englishwoman, and think that he was preparing to sail round the world." What is curious about Cook – and the mention of his wife reinforces this impression – is his domestic ordinariness, and the absence of any sign of the glamor or color that was usually imagined to accrue to the traveler. Boswell thinks that Cook has an "uncommon attention to veracity," and he produces an analogy for this virtue which emphasizes that he sees in Cook the exactness – even the petty-mindedness – of a small shopkeeper. Boswell writes, with characteristic self-congratulation: "My metaphor was that he [Cook] had a balance in his mind for truth as nice as the scales for weighing a guinea." Boswell is of course enthralled by the idea of circumnavigation, and fascinated by what Cook can tell him about his experiences, but like Fanny Burney perhaps, his comments on meeting Cook suggest that he finds him disappointingly lacking in social polish or ornamental flair. Though Cook talks to him, and is, he writes, "obliging and communicative," stimulating and feeding his interest in the voyages, he seems to lack the skills of polite conversation which were so important to the sociability of polite men and educated women in the metropolis.[45] Around the time of his death, Cook's wife was busy stitching him a waistcoat of tapa, bark-cloth from the South Pacific, to wear on his attendance at court, but the stiff white fabric would no doubt have contributed to the propriety of his dress uniform, and not lent him the exotic appeal of Mai, dressed in Manchester velvet and lace ruffles for his appearance in courtly society.[46]

After his death, of course, Cook's very ordinariness, the notion that he is nothing more exceptional than a self-educated Yorkshireman, becomes enormously important to his eulogists. So, for example, Andrew Kippis's *Life of Cook* (1788) followed many earlier accounts in emphasizing the professionalism of Cook's virtues – the sense that what he had was a double helping of the virtues every man keen to make his own way in the world should possess. In the opening paragraphs of his character of Cook, Kippis lists his genius, application, knowledge, perseverance, amiable virtues, and finally, simplicity of manners. Cook's genius is not about the sorts of qualities of intuition or comprehensive grasp that the term usually implies in this period – it is something more practical, and, I think, less gentlemanly. Kippis begins his account of Cook's genius rather defensively:

[45] *Boswell: The Ominous Years*, London, April 2, 1776, 309, 308.
[46] On Mai's attention to dress, see McCormick, *Omai*, 115, 125.

It cannot, I think, be denied, that genius belonged to Captain Cook in an eminent degree. By genius I do not here understand imagination merely, or that power of culling the flowers of fancy which poetry delights in; but an inventive mind; a mind full of resources; and which, by its own native vigour, can suggest noble objects of pursuit, and the most effectual methods of attaining them.[47]

The opposition of Cook's skills to what seem more impractical and feminine forms of genius works to elevate practical qualities of resourcefulness and so forth which perhaps might not otherwise so readily be accepted as the hallmarks of genius.

Cook's dedication is demonstrated rather crudely in the fact that his private life largely escapes representation. He is always portrayed in his uniform. Kippis comments, in the Preface to Cook's life, that:

The private incidents concerning him, though collected with the utmost diligence, can never compare, either in number or importance, with his public transactions. His public transactions are the things that mark the man, that display his mind and character; and, therefore, they are the grand objects to which the attention of his biographer must be directed.[48]

It is as though Cook hardly had a private life, hardly ever took off that uniform of office. John Webber's portrait of Cook is perhaps most reminiscent of the idea of Cook the practical and professional Yorkshireman (fig. 8). He stands against a suitable background of waves and rocks, wearing his uniform. In the full-length version of the picture (now in the National Art Gallery in Wellington), Cook holds his hat and a telescope, as if to confirm his dedication to his profession, whereas in this three-quarter-length version his hand is unoccupied, and, with its long fingers and apparently careful manicure, rather elegant. An observer commented on Webber's portrait in 1826 that Cook appeared "raw boned . . . and capable of enduring the greatest fatigue," and the comment links together the expression of tight-lipped determination, which suggests his professional attributes of perseverance and fortitude, and his gaunt and weather-beaten complexion.[49] It is, I think, unusual for portraits of naval officers to suggest that their complexions have been marked by their profession – the two other major portraits of Cook from these years, by Nathaniel Dance and William Hodges (fig. 9), endow him with an unlikely pallor which emphasizes

[47] Andrew Kippis, *The Life of Captain James Cook* (London: Nicol, 1788), ch. 7, 482.
[48] Kippis, *Cook*, Preface, ix.
[49] Letter from Molesworth Phillips to William Brockenden, April 5, 1826, quoted in Rudiger Joppien and Bernard Smith, *The Art of Captain Cook's Voyages, Vol. III: Catalogue, The Voyage of the Resolution and Discovery, 1776–1780* (New Haven: Yale University Press, 1988), 648.

Figure 8 John Webber, *Captain James Cook, RN*, 1782. Oil on canvas, 114.0 × 91.0 cm. Purchased by the Commonwealth Government with the generous assistance of Robert Oatley and John Schaeffer, 2000. Photography by David Reid.

his raw-bonedness – perhaps because a more weathered appearance has the associations so feared and remarked on by Sir Walter Elliot, in *Persuasion*, who needs to be reassured that Admiral Croft is "quite the gentleman in all his notions and behaviour" although he is "a little weather-beaten." Sir Walter, of course, closely associates the "deplorable looking"

Capt. James Cook
of the Endeavour.

Figure 9   William Hodges, *Captain James Cook*, ?1775 (National Maritime
Museum, London).

complexions of naval officers with his disgust for the naval profession as
the "means of bringing persons of obscure birth into undue distinction,
and raising men to honours which their fathers and grandfathers never
dreamt of."[50]

---

[50] Jane Austen, *Persuasion*, introduction Forrest Reid (London: Oxford University Press, 1930),
22–3, 20.

Bernard Smith has written of the "realism" of William Hodges's portrait of Cook (probably painted soon after the second voyage, at around the same time as Dance's). But this is not the same kind of realism as is shown in Webber's portrait. Hodges's image removes Cook's head and gleaming linen from any informing context but that of his dimly suggested uniformed torso. This dramatic representation emphasizes the alertness of Cook's expression, as though this painting, like Hodges's portrait of Mai, caught a fleeting expression. But here this animation, as Cook seems almost to strain out of the canvas, suggests that his professional dedication to his mission hardly allows him to sit still, or to be gazed at steadily. It is this image that provides the basis for one of John Flaxman's Wedgwood plaques (fig. 10), where the streaming hair, large eyes, and intent expression suggest the extent to which Cook's posthumous image begins more and more recognizably to bear the impress of the idea of his heroic genius. Nathaniel Dance's society portrait (fig. 11), in contrast, shows Cook sitting, bewigged, indoors. Cook looks across and out of the frame to the right, as though interrupted in his study of the chart before him, where his finger marks his place, and he looks studious, meditative, even polite, rather than the man of action he appears in both Webber's and Hodges's portraits. The image is not confidently informal, in the manner of, say, Reynolds's portrait of the young Joseph Banks in his study, with the signs of his interest in global travel around him. Cook is here unambiguously professional in his dress, his attentiveness, and perhaps also in the nature of his gaze. In the Webber portrait, his look is commanding, but the context, the sea, the rocks, even the weather, make that appropriate. In Dance's portrait, he is an authoritative figure, but it is less directly an authority over the viewer – more, perhaps, that sense of a specialized professional skill, involved in the mastery of charts and ships.

Cook himself, of course, insisted that he was a "plain man" with little formal education, and the notion of him as a self-made man is important to the idea of his heroic Britishness. His plainness is represented as though it were the antidote to the ornamental refinement and luxury of London life. So for example, the *St. James's Chronicle* commented admiringly that: "Capt. Cook's rising, from being the Son of a Day-Labourer, to the distinguished Rank he held in the British Navy, is a Proof what superiour Abilities can do, when they have a proper Field to display themselves in."[51] The *Westminster Magazine*, in an extended essay on the "Melancholy Catastrophe of Captain Cook's Death," hints that his origins were necessary to his success. The

[51] *St. James's Chronicle; or, British Evening-Post*, for January 27–29, 1780.

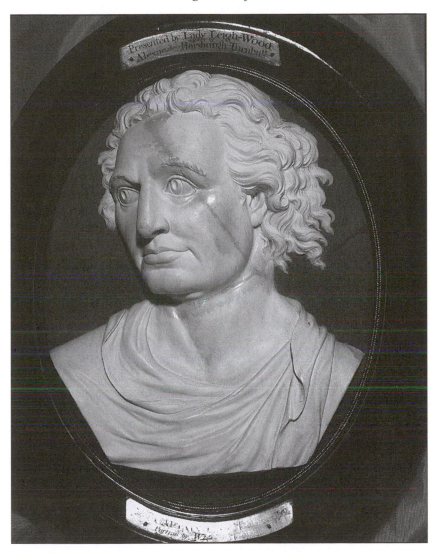

Figure 10 Wedgwood plaque bearing portrait of Cook, by John Flaxman after William Hodges (Turnbull Library, Wellington, NZ).

eulogist writes that: "no man seemed so well formed for enterprizes such as he was engaged in. He was fond of the pursuit, and sacrificed every consideration to them. He owed his rise entirely to his merit; and retained the modesty of his early state after he had risen beyond the expectations of his friends, and equal to his own." Voyages into unexplored territory

Figure 11 Nathaniel Dance, *James Cook* (National Maritime Museum, London).

Figure 12   John Hamilton Mortimer, *Group Portrait representing Captain Cook, Sir Joseph Banks, and others, c.* 1777 (National Library of Australia, Canberra).

through ice sheets and across the divisions of British society seem to draw on similar reserves of character. Sophie von La Roche recorded in her diary that during the "general mourning" for Cook's death "someone expressed the view that [Cook] had fulfilled his mission, and it was time for him to die. I would not have stirred a finger to save him." Frances Burney replied that this was "'a very sublime way of considering Cook's death'" – a response La Roche found "delicious."[52] For Burney and her well-educated circle, Cook is consumed, sublimed, by his professional dedication; he is a man so heroically purposive that even his death seems a small sacrifice to provide the narrative of his mission with a fitting closure.

At moments such as this, Cook's career can seem as much an ornament to advanced civilization as Mai's cosmopolitan gentility. John Hamilton Mortimer's *Group Portrait* (fig. 12), probably painted in 1771, after the first circumnavigation, shows Cook between his patrons, Lord Sandwich on the right, and Sir Joseph Banks on the left. This is perhaps the "proper Field"

---

[52] *Westminster Magazine*, January 1780, 7; *Sophie in London, 1786: Being the Diary of Sophie von la Roche*, intro. and trans. by Clare Williams (London: Jonathan Cape, 1933), 277.

spoken of in the *St. James's Chronicle*. Cook gestures towards the sea, where he will again display his superior abilities. His central position makes him the focus for the attention of the other four, and the image seems ambivalently poised between the suggestion that they admire his heroic endeavors, that he commands at least their interest, and the possibility that Sandwich and Banks display him as their protégé, with the relaxed confidence, almost negligence, of the massively propertied. Cook, like Mai, may be seen as a sign of the grandeur of men more powerful than himself, the ornament of their prosperous civilization and metropolitan polish. Cook may look like a more modern, or at least more Romantic figure than Mai, in his professional dedication, his purposiveness, his perceived capacity for toleration, and a sort of humanitarian cultural relativism. In contrast to Cook, the notions of British civilization and imperial identity that are associated with Mai may have looked anachronistic – too dependent on ornament and display, on aristocratic inutility. The two men are marginalized and disadvantaged/exploited by metropolitan society in what are evidently very different ways – by, for example, racial or regional difference, social status, linguistic competence, and elegance of manner. But they are both also, in their differences, central to the discursive contradictions about use and ornament, technological progress and civility, in which metropolitan society conceives of its own modernity.

CHAPTER 16

Thinking back: gender misrecognition and Polynesian subversions aboard the Cook voyages

Kathleen Wilson

Between 1768 and 1780, Captain James Cook and his crews embarked upon a set of voyages of discovery that would transform the face of the world. The achievements of the voyages, of course, have been celebrated and critiqued by an array of anthropologists, historical ethnographers, historians, art historians, literary critics, and scholars of subaltern and performance studies, illuminating both indigenous and British Enlightenment cultures and ecologies.[1] This chapter proposes to take a different tack, and address some of the confusions engendered by Cook's encounters with South Pacific peoples, focusing on the disruptions and silences produced by the arts and accounts of "discovery." The point of such an effort is not to try to "unmask" the veracity of British empirical observation or "speak" for

I would like to thank Jenny Mander of Cambridge University, and other participants of the 2001 symposium "Enlightened Masculinities" of the Feminism and Enlightenment project for valuable comments on this chapter.

[1] E.g., Christopher B. Balme, "Sexual Spectacles: Theatricality and the Performance of Sex in Early Encounters in the Pacific," *The Drama Review*, 44 (2000), 67–85; Greg Dening, *Mr. Bligh's Bad Language: Passion, Power and Theatre on the Bounty* (Cambridge University Press, 1992); Rod Edmond, *Representing the South Pacific: Colonial Discourse from Cook to Gauguin* (Cambridge University Press, 1997); John Gascoigne, *Joseph Banks and the English Enlightenment: Useful Knowledge and Polite Culture* (Cambridge University Press, 1994); Richard Grove, *Green Imperialism: Colonial Expansion, Tropical Island Edens and the Origins of Environmentalism, 1660–1860* (Cambridge University Press, 1995); David Mackay, *In the Wake of Cook: Exploration, Science and Empire* (New York: St. Martin's Press, 1985); Gananath Obeyesekere, *The Apotheosis of Captain Cook: European Mythmaking in the Pacific* (Princeton University Press, 1992); Roy Porter, "The Exotic as Erotic" in G. S. Rousseau and Roy Porter, eds., *Exoticism in the Enlightenment* Rousseau and Roy Porter (Manchester University Press, 1986), 117–44; Margaret Jolly and Martha Macintrye, eds., *Family and Gender in the South Pacific: Domestic Contradictions and the Colonial Impact* (Cambridge University Press, 1989); Leonore Manderson and Margaret Jolly, eds., *Sites of Desire: Economies of Pleasure: Sexualities in Asia and the Pacific* (University of Chicago Press, 1997); Bridget Orr, "'Southern Passions Mix with Northern Art': Miscegenation on the *Endeavour* Voyage," *Eighteenth Century Life*, 18 (1994), 212–31; Marshall Sahlins, *Islands of History* (University of Chicago Press, 1985); Marshall Sahlins, *How "Natives" Think: About Captain Cook, For Example* (University of Chicago Press, 1995); Nicholas Thomas, *In Oceania: Visions, Artifacts, Histories* (Durham: Duke University Press, 1997); Kathleen Wilson, *The Island Race: Englishness, Empire and Gender in the Eighteenth Century* (London: Routledge, 2003); and chapters 3 and 15 by Nussbaum and Guest, this volume.

eighteenth-century Polynesians by assigning them a western subjectivity irrelevant to their concerns. Rather, it is to recognize that the practices and epistemologies of Pacific peoples impressed themselves upon the explorers and the imperial archive in ways that altered both their substance and hence our ways of knowing them. For, despite the best intentions of men who believed themselves to be positioned at the cutting edge of History, Polynesian actors made their presence known in ways that could not and still cannot be assimilable within that history's narrative. I will focus in particular on the intriguing roles of gender misrecognition and the entanglements of desire evinced in some of the voyage journals and accounts, focusing on "conjunctures" rather than "cultures" *per se*,[2] and taking seriously the mutual confusions that abounded as Cook and his men attempted to use gender and sexual practice as guides to Pacific social systems, and the Pacific islanders themselves tried in turn to map their cosmogonies on to European bodies. Far from exhibiting some unilateral process of "othering" at work in the art of discovery, our exploration of gender misrecognition and Polynesian subversions highlights the intricate interplay of local modes of understanding on a global stage, and the dialogic nature of colonial encounter. The complex fields of identification at work in the crucible of first contact thus make visible the *unwriting* of History through the aporia of cultural translation.

WOMEN IN THE HISTORY OF MAN

Cook's mission of mapping and discovering the South Pacific took place in a period of growing political, intellectual, and cultural ferment in Britain, the global dimensions of which would become clear as the three voyages (1768–71, 1772–5, 1776–80) unfolded. War, conquest, imperial supremacy, and expeditions to "undiscovered" parts of the globe had created new responsibilities and anxieties for metropolitan and colonial peoples alike; these developments had also circulated new information about the diversity of humankind and the relative positions of Britons, Europeans, and indigenous peoples across the globe.[3] Ideas about natural and historical time were also changing, leading to the emergence of notions of "deep time" that

[2] This distinction is borrowed from James Clifford in his scintillating essay, "Taking Identity Politics Seriously: 'the Contradictory, Stony Ground . . .'" in Paul Gilroy, Lawrence Grossberg, and Angela McRobbre, eds., *Without Guarantees: In Honour of Stuart Hall* (London: Verso, 2000), 98. For conjunctural ethnography, see James Clifford, *The Predicament of Culture* (Cambridge, MA: Harvard University Press, 1998); and Kamala Visweswaran, *Fictions of Feminist Ethnography* (Minneapolis: University of Minnesota Press, 1994).
[3] For details, see Wilson, *Island Race*, ch. 2.

required the adjustment of humanity's cosmological, social, and biological location. As natural historians and philosophers came under greater pressure to found the study of human society upon a firm empirical base, travelers, colonizers, and explorers alike eagerly embraced the new national mission to describe and explain differences among the peoples of the world. The new history of humanity melded time and space to generalize and extend History to encompass the globe and reconceptualize relationships between parts of the world as temporal ones.[4] It also prompted competing theories about the ways in which different nations developed in relation to climate and "race," inventing ways to define "race" through migration and language, and novel opportunities to debate the status of gender and sexual difference as social or natural categories.[5] In particular, the unruliness of "talk," the effeminizing impact of empire on the national character and its spirit of inquiry and compassion, and both female sexual agency and male effeminacy were canvassed in public forums, and became issues which the cult of sensibility and Enlightenment progressivism ("the natural history of man") strove to explain. The latter concomitantly reconfigured ideas about empire, the position of women and their roles as signs and agents of social progress.[6] In this context, the voyages to the South Pacific provided an occasion not only to prove British altruism and expertise in the arts of discovery, but also to verify men's and women's "nature" and status through a widening comparative frame, constructed through first-hand, "eye-witness" observation.[7]

Cook's celebrated explorations were thus stridently gendered as well as intensely nationalistic. They were also powerfully imbued with a historicist mission to turn their work and its subjects into "History," providing the "facts" about new peoples that would help establish "permanent truths in the history of Man."[8] That the journals and logs of the senior and petty officers would be collected and used by the Admiralty for their "official" accounts of the voyages gave credibility to crew members' rather inflated sense of their own roles in turning the voyages into History. Twinning the sensibility of enlightened masculinity and non-aristocratic morality with

---

[4] See chapter 9 by Walter Johnson, this volume and Johannes Fabian, *Time and the Other: How Anthropology Makes its Objects* (New York: Columbia University Press, 1983).

[5] Grove, *Green Imperialism*, 230–5; Wilson, *Island Race*, 8–9.

[6] See chapters 2 and 15 by Gillian Russell and Harriet Guest, this volume; Wilson, *Island Race*, 18–27; Kathleen Wilson, "Empire, Gender and Modernity in the Eighteenth Century," in Philippa Levine, ed., *Gender and Empire* (Oxford University Press, 2004).

[7] Jonathan Lamb, *Preserving the Self in the South Seas 1680–1840* (University of Chicago, 2001).

[8] Samuel Stanhope Smith, *An Essay on the Causes of the Variety of Complexion and Figure in the Human Species* (Edinburgh, 1788), v–vi.

the benevolent and humanitarian goals of "discovery," the voyages sought to
bring indigenous peoples "within the pale of the offices of humanity . . . to
relieve the wants of their imperfect state of society," and so evince British
modernity and achievement.[9] These achievements were recorded in the
explorers' journals and relayed in voyage accounts to the British public in
a naturalist reportage that combined features of travelogue and empirical
description, even in its tales of the exotic and erotic.[10] The distinguished naturalists and artists on board (including Joseph Banks and Sydney Parkinson
on the first voyage, Johann Reinhold Forster, his son, George, and William
Hodges on the second, and John Webber on the third) as well as Cook and
his crew were well armed with Enlightenment social theory to gauge the
"stage" of material and civil progress of each new society encountered.

Central to this taxonomic effort was the assessment of the place of
women. "It is the practice of all uncivilized nations to deny their women the
common privileges of humans beings," George Forster noted. "The ideas
of finding happiness and comfort in the bosom of a companion only arise
with a higher degree of culture." Indeed, women, their physical and moral
attributes and social status, were more enthusiastically studied than in any
previous colonial encounter, and became vital, for example, to the Forsters'
influential distinction between the two "races" in the South Pacific.[11] Yet
the apparently successful incorporation of Pacific women into the "History
of Man" masked the confusion and chaos that these encounters had engendered, a good deal of which stemmed from the apparently insatiable desire
of the women in question for British officers and tars (which was more
troublesome from the men's theoretical perspective, apparently, than the
officers' and tars' desire for them).

Tahitian women, for example, had quickly become legendary for their
beauty and their supposed proclivities for "free love." The overtly erotic
dances and ceremonial disrobing performed by young Tahitian women, the
polygamous sexual antics among the *arioi*, the elite group of performers and
religious chiefs associated with the war god, Oro, and the more exogamous
sexual trysts of their non-elite sisters with British tars sparked fantasies in
English, as French, minds about the lack of guilt in the "state of nature."
Yet in the everyday interactions of "discovery," the Tahitian women's character generated debate among the voyagers and wreaked havoc with the

[9] Andrew Kippis, *The Life of Captain James Cook* (Basle, 1788), 371.
[10] Wilson, *Island Race*, 55–6.
[11] George Forster, *A voyage round the world during the Years 1772–1775* (2 vols., London, 1777), II, 324;
Harriet Guest, "Looking at Women," in Johann Reinhold Forster, *Observations Made on a Voyage
Round the World*, edited by Nicholas Thomas, Harriet Guest, and Michael Dettelbach (Honolulu:
University of Hawaii Press, 1996), xli–liv.

performance of appropriate masculinity by British and (in British eyes) Oceanic men alike. The gallant naturalist Joseph Banks, for example, revelled in the sexual alterity of Polynesian life to a degree that was taken to compromise his philosophical detachment. "In the Island of Otaheitie," he wrote in one account, echoing the rhapsodies of Bougainville, "Love is the Chief Occupation, the favourite, nay almost the Sole Luxury of the inhabitants."[12] His observations on the "civilities" and "politeness" of the women, who "sometimes by force seat[ed] themselves and us upon the mats" to pursue carnal pleasures, his amorous connection to "Oberea," the putative "queen" of Wallis's voyage, as well as his eagerness to act as "participant anthropologist" in local erotic rites, were gleefully lampooned by pundits in London as examples of the libertinage and depravity of aristocratic and savage sensibilities alike.[13] Banks's activities also raised hackles among some other officers aboard ship, not least for his exhibition of a marked disregard of masculine and bourgeois self-restraint as well as scientific curiosity.

In the event, Banks's judgments about Tahitians were not necessarily authoritative. Some observers defended Tahitian women's greater nonchalance towards matters of the flesh as a product of class (e.g., aristocratic luxury or lower-class depravity). The prosaic astronomer William Wales, of the second voyage, claimed that most married and unmarried women observed "proprieties" and that the women who offered themselves to the sailors were common whores. "A stranger who visits England might with equal justice draw the character of the Ladies there," Wales asserted, "from those which he might meet with on board the Ships in Plymouth Sound, at Spithead, or in the Thames; on the Point at Portsmouth, or in the Purlieus of Wapping."[14] Quaker and artist Sydney Parkinson disagreed, arguing that neither married nor unmarried women had "a very delicate sense of modesty: their husbands will allow you any liberty with their wives, except the last, which they do not approve" – yet he held the British to be as culpable for the (to him) disgraceful sexual traffic underway as the women. Characteristically Captain Cook was more measured in his assessments of the ladies, while also seeking to understand them within a global view of uniform human nature. He agreed that "Chastity indeed is but little Valued," but expressed horror at the *arioi* practice of infanticide, which allowed them to enjoy "free liberty in love without being troubled or disturbed by its consequences." On the second voyage, however, Cook

[12] Joseph Banks, "Thoughts on the Manners of the Women of Otaheite," MS 94, National Library of Australia.
[13] Joseph Banks, *Endeavour Journal 1769–70*, edited by J. C. Beaglehole (2 vols., Sydney: Angus and Robertson, 1962), I, 254; Porter, "The Exotic as Erotic," 118; Orr, "'Southern Passions,'" 212–31.
[14] *The Journals of Captain Cook*, edited by J. C. Beaglehole (3 vols., Cambridge University Press, 1957–65), II, 797.

defended Tahitian women against the charges of free love, and even argued that lower-class women had "learned" morality since the last visit – "on the whole I think the women in general were less free with their favours now than formerly" – although how they could have done so through contact with insatiable European crews remains obscure.[15]

Of course, the alleged "libertinage" of the native, mixed-race, or enslaved woman was a well-entrenched trope of British colonization and exploration narratives, elaborated on by fur traders, settlers, planters, merchants, and missionaries in the New World.[16] Yet under the weight of the voyages' imperative to close observation and comparison, and in the face of local societies still intact enough to translate novelty in their own terms, the yard-stick of Enlightenment gender roles could not cope with the complexities of Polynesian sexual and social practices. British tars were certainly delighted that the favors of Tahitian beauties could be won by bits of ribbon or mirror. But what appeared to them to be the "libertinism" of Polynesian women was, in the women's eyes, a traffic in men that allowed them to exploit the arrival of boatloads of strangers for their own advantage.

For Polynesians had their own ethnography and histories of travel, ones that were intertwined with a cosmogony linking sexual intercourse with access to divine power and social advancement.[17] Women's offering them-selves to British sailors may have been influenced by their beliefs that as foreigners they had close links to this sacred power and the offspring sired by them would give the women access to supernatural benefits in the form of ancestral *mana* (supernatural power). As Polynesian historians and anthro-pologists have argued, sex for Polynesians "was everything: rank, power, wealth, land and the security of all these," and sexual acts were conceived of as engaging men and women in a common opposition to the divine, allowing women in particular to "attract and transform the divine genera-tive forces."[18] Hence the women involved seemed determined at all costs to

[15] Sydney Parkinson, *Journal of a Voyage to the South Seas in His Majesty's Ship the Endeavour* (London, 1773), 25; *Journals of Captain Cook*, I, 127–8; II, 236–7.

[16] Wilson, "Gender, Empire and Modernity"; Gunlög Fur, "'Some Women are Wiser than Some Men': Gender and Native American History," in Nancy Shoemaker, ed., *Clearing a Path: Theorizing the Past in Native American Studies* (London: Routledge, 1996), 75–101. See also Kathleen Wilson, "The Female Rake: Gender, Libertinism and Enlightenment," in Lisa O'Connell and Peter Cryle, eds., *Libertinism and Enlightenment* (Basingstoke: Palgrave, 2003).

[17] The historical-ethnographic analysis in this chapter is much indebted to Douglas Oliver, *Ancient Tahitian Society* (3 vols., Honolulu: University of Hawaii Press, 1974), esp. Vol. II.

[18] Sahlins, *Islands of History*, 26, 7–8; Caroline Ralston, "Polyandry, 'Pollution,' 'Prostitution': The Problems of Eurocentrism and Androcentrism in Polynesian Studies," in Barbara Coine and E. A. Grosz, eds., *Crossing Boundaries: Feminisms and the Critique of Knowledge* (Sydney: Allen and Unwin, 1988), 71–80.

seize the opportunity offered them by the arrival of shiploads of strangers. This was often executed against the will of their objects, the British tars. "[We] found all the Women of these Island but little influenced by interested motives in their intercourse with us, as they would almost use violence to force you into their Embrace regardless whether we gave them any thing or not," Welsh surgeon's mate David Samwell complained at one point.[19]

As Polynesian women mapped their culture on to the European male body, they made that body the object in the process of their own spiritual and political aggrandizement. Alternately, when this illusion had waned, women would then offer themselves in return for "curiosities," displaying an avidity for ethnographic investigation themselves. Significantly, a large part of Cook's authority as commander rested upon his refusal to participate in this traffic as object or subject. His romantic disinterest and sexual self-control, however, elicited contempt from the women themselves. Hence at Tonga in June 1774 when Cook declined a beautiful young girl offered by her mother for his "personal use," he was roundly abused: "I understood very little of what she said, but her actions were expressive enough and shew'd that her words were to this effect, Sneering in my face and saying, what sort of a man are you thus to refuse the embraces of so fine a young Woman."[20]

The perception of a predatory sexual appetite of the women and the corresponding lack (so it was thought) of male authority over them troubled the voyagers exceedingly. They accordingly sought to exert their own masculine power and prowess through on-the-spot modification of "universal laws" that presupposed a normative European morality. John Marra, gunner's mate on the *Resolution*'s second voyage, theorized based on his experience that Society Islanders were "an effeminate race, intoxicated with pleasure, and enfeebled by indulgence."[21] Cook himself ventured a universal law on female chastity when, on the third voyage, contrary to expectations, the women of Van Diemen's Land (Tasmania) refused the tars' advances: "I believe it has generally been found amongst uncivilized people that where the Women are easy of access, the Men are the first who offer them to strangers, and where this is not the case they are not easily come at, neither large presents nor privacy will induce them to violate the laws of chastity or custom."[22] And J. R. Forster, who argued in his influential *Observations*

---

[19] *Journals of Captain Cook*, III, 1085.   [20] Ibid., II, 444.
[21] [John Marra], *Journal of the Resolution's Voyage in 1772, 1773, 1774 and 1775 on Discovery in the Southern Hemisphere* (London, 1775), 54.
[22] *Journals of Captain Cook*, III, 56.

Made During a Voyage Round the World (1778) that Polynesian women's good treatment by their men and quick sensibilities made them embodiments of their societies' progress towards civilization, still saw fit to upbraid the women in his journal for both their lack of chastity and their refusal to engage straightforwardly in sexual commerce: "the [Tahitian] women coquet in the most impudent manner, and shew uncommon fondness for Foreigners, but are all Jilts and coax the Foreigners out of anything they can get: and will not comply to sleep with them, unless . . . the bribe very great and tempting," he recorded.[23] The journal accounts thus make visible the power of the women's gaze to destabilize that of the explorers by turning the seamen into the objects of Polynesian categories of difference.

This power of the women is masked in the published voyage accounts, and papered over further in the representations of excessive Polynesian sexuality in the metropole, as Gillian Russell's chapter in this volume demonstrates. This textual disempowerment had concrete material consequences. The demonstration of allegedly "degenerated" gender roles among Polynesian and Aboriginal women (and, as we shall see, the varieties of "effeminacy" exhibited by their men) not only animated future political judgments about colonization, but also fired up British missionaries, who eschewed Enlightenment niceties to condemn the "heathen" practices and "depraved" sensibilities of South Pacific peoples as a whole. As much as property, means of subsistence, and "stage" of civilization, then, women's "nature" had a politics that reverberated across the networks of nation and empire, becoming a source of contestation and inspiration even in the antipodes of the world. Equally remarkable is the unassimilable nature of female sexual agency within the narratives of contact provided by the voyagers. Female "libertinism," embodied by the indigenous woman (or, indeed, as Russell's chapter shows, the British society hostess), shocked by demonstrating that women's "nature" and English superiority were neither natural nor inevitable, dissolving the premises of Enlightenment social theory in ways that required its continuous rewriting. Polynesian women thus marked a boundary – national, geographic, and moral – that could not be translated into "universal" human nature, except through the capricious languages of primitiveness or depravity. In other words, as theories of sexual and national difference foundered on the rocks of women's sexual agency, Polynesian women's "characters" – indeed, all women's characters? – spilled over into the realm of transgression and illegibility in a femininity that was doomed to be always estranged from itself. In this sense, "universal"

---

[23] Johann Reinhold Forster, *The Resolution Journal*, ed. Michael Hoare (London, 1982), II, 356–7.

theories of gender, as "universal" theories of capital, turned out to be "an empty place holder whose unstable outlines become barely visible only when a proxy, a particular, usurps its position."[24] But significantly, it is through these languages of depravity and licentiousness that indigenous women and working-class British women would continue to be identified into the nineteenth century.

MANLY EFFEMINACY

Male sexuality was another area where misrecognition confounded the voyagers' encounters with Pacific islanders. Let's listen to Wales talk about his attempts to put to rest among his own men the fear that the "natives" were "sodomites." Recording the details of his exploration of the island of Tana (Vanuatu) in the New Hebrides – one of the islands of the western Pacific that was universally regarded by Cook and his crew to be lagging far behind the Tahitians in civilization and physical beauty – Wales reported that some of his men had been followed into the bushes by ni-Vanuatu males "for a purpose I need not mention," and then remarked,

> there are People who . . . are not capable of defending the Whims they Adopt otherwise than by *It is so – I know it* . . . and some of this Cast have asserted, and I make no doubt *written down* . . . that most of the People we have lately been among are Sodomites, or Canibals, or both . . . [yet] no person had been attempted who had not either a softness in his features, or whose employment it was to Carry bundles of one kind or other which is the Office of their own Women.

Here Wales, like Cook a bluff and self-made Yorkshireman, tries to use his well-trained powers of observation to combat the prejudices of his crew and chalk up the miscues of the Tannese to gender confusion.[25] The visual and corporeal cues upon which European order depended were insufficient, it seems, in antipodean encounters, where British tars projected their own fears of sodomitical desire on to the ni-Vanuatu, and the ni-Vanuatu mapped their own culture on the European male body. From the ni-Vanuatu perspective, in a culture where women did most (though certainly not all) the carrying, and were in George Forster's view obliged "to perform all sorts of laborious, and humiliating operations," European men who did women's work looked like women or could be used as women. Equally possible is that the ni-Vanuatu could not conceive that shiploads of men could appear

[24] Dipesh Chakrabarty, *Provincializing Europe: Postcolonial Thought and Historical Difference* (Princeton University Press, 2000), 71.
[25] *Journals of Captain Cook*, II, 858–9, 790, 819.

without women in tow to do their carrying for them. Significantly, Wales himself put the burden of proof of masculinity back on the British tars themselves, admitting that the "softness" of features of some contributed to their misrecognition by the natives. Here he reflects a widely held view in Britain that "the prevalency of this passion [for sodomy] has for its object effeminate delicate beings only."[26]

Perhaps, as Gananath Obeyesekere has argued about Pacific cannibalism, the British sailors' suspicions about sodomy, arising after several months' incarceration in the cramped and homosocial holds of two sloops, revealed more about the practices aboard ship than they would like to think. Alternately, to follow this line of inquiry may be to treat these texts to what Lee Edelman has called, following Foucault, a "hermeneutics of suspicion," through which any sexual practice and all forms of homosociality become doubled, permeable, and suspect, and homosexuality is called into being through the forensic investigation of "subtexts."[27] Yet I would contend that a (non-homophobic) hermeneutics of suspicion may be precisely what is needed in order to illuminate what is at issue in these accounts: the dense sites of signification that nationalized bodies were made to bear, the failure (from the enlightened explorers' perspective) of native bodies to speak for themselves, and the murkiness created when cultures of identity circulate between nations at the point of contact. From this perspective, Wales's entry speaks to an array of issues surrounding sodomy and masculinity, both in English culture and in the arts of discovery, when for a variety of historical reasons the homophobic hermeneutics of suspicion that entangled the ship was projected on to indigenous societies.

For British seamen's prejudices seem to have been founded on the *terra firma* of metropolitan antipathy to "effeminates" that was a marked feature of the social and political landscape in the 1770s. Within England, sodomy was increasingly identified with aristocratic debauchery and excess or, still worse, with the perception of a depraved and degenerate character. Randolph Trumbach's recent argument that sodomy was becoming the touchstone of a gender revolution that legislated heterosexuality as the norm receives solid empirical support by the evidence of a rise in the expression of English hostility to sodomy in the last quarter of the eighteenth century, a hostility that exceeded perhaps anywhere else in Europe. In this period,

---

[26] *The Phoenix of Sodom or the Vere Street Coterie* (London, 1813), 2.
[27] Gananath Obeyesekere, "'British Cannibals': Contemplation of an Event in the Death and Resurrection of James Cook, Explorer," in Kwame Anthony Appiah and Henry Louis Gates, Jr., eds., *Identities* (University of Chicago Press, 1995), 7–31; Lee Edelman, "Homographesis," *Yale Journal of Criticism*, 3 (1993), 192.

bi- or homosexual men were banished to the continent by their families, and the numbers of pardons for the capital crime of sodomy steadily diminished. There was also an upsurge in formal charges of sodomy that began in the 1770s and reached a peak in the early 1800s, reflecting a backlash in England over non-procreative forms of sex in general.[28]

At the same time, such "effeminacy" in British society, which was seen to "pervert those appetites which nature has bestowed for the most beneficial purposes," was coming under scientific scrutiny. Social theorists like Lord Kames, William Robertson, and John Millar were at pains to explain same-sex desire as a feature of the degeneracy that is produced by luxury and excess in advanced societies, when the "free indulgence of appetites" is unrestrained, and the passions debased; yet they also hinted at its existence among "primitive" cultures, where emotional languor and lack of sensibility could fail to spark "that passion which was destined to perpetuate life, to be the bond of social union, and the source of tenderness and joy."[29] The problematics of "effeminacy" – which I would describe as the attribution of a damaged or failed gender to certain kinds of men, which may or may not be evinced in sodomitical desire – rested on the status of gender difference in this period as innate or acquired and on the dynamic relations existing between sexual practice and gender in late eighteenth-century British culture.[30] Yet the perception of effeminate desires or practices among indigenous peoples of the Pacific clearly mobilized the fears of difference and social exile involved with the signification of sodomy in England, as British tars expressed a terror over losing proper gender through the intimation of inappropriate desire.

Obviously, the exploration of foreign territories and bodies invoked the concomitant fear of being explored. In such scenarios – and there are many such scenes of gender confusion in the journals of the voyages, working across many social terrains – gender, sexual practice, and "national" difference seemed easily confused, underlining the degree to which the *familiarity* of bodies was the foundation for more complex and elaborate forms of classification and distinction. What is much less remarked upon is the circulation of subjectivity in such scenarios: as in these examples, who is the explorer and who the explored? Polynesians certainly had their own

---

[28] Randolph Trumbach, *Sex and the Gender Revolution, Vol. I: Heterosexuality and the Third Gender in Enlightenment London* (University of Chicago Press, 1998); Wilson, *Island Race*, 190–1 and references there.

[29] Henry Home, Lord Kames, *Sketches of the History of Man* (London, 1778), I, 400–1; II, 90–1; John Millar, *The Origin of the Distinction of Ranks* (Edinburgh, 1806), 100–5, 180, 191.

[30] See Wilson, *Island Race*, 18–27.

doubts about the virility of their visitors, finding the homosociality of the explorers' sloop suspect and derisive, in some cases even undertaking investigations to discover if they were "whole men," and raising questions about their inclinations and civility that the British themselves could never quite satisfactorily answer.[31]

Wales's journal entry invites us further into this tangled circuitry of colonial identification, alterity, exchange, and transformation. He goes on to elaborate his theory about the gender confusion that gave rise to the unfortunate misapprehension that the ni-Vanuatu were sodomites, while also making clear that the purpose he "need not mention" was universally recognized, and *could* be signed without difficulty in the gestural economy of encounter:

The Man who carried Mr. Forster's Plant Bag had, I was told, been two or three times attemp[t]ed, and he happening to go into the Bushes on some occasion or other whilst we were set down drinking our Cocoa-nuts etc, I pointed it out to the Natives who sat round us, with a sort of sly look and *significant action* at the same time, on which two of them Jump'd up and were following him with great glee; but some of our Party bursting out into a laugh, those who were by . . . called out *Erramange! Erramange!* (its a Man! Its a Man!) on which the others returned, very much abashed on the Occasion.

The "sly look and *significant action*" were both conveyed through gestural signs common in encounters in which neither party spoke the other's language; yet the acceptance of gestural language as a reliable indicator of sexual intention is, and was, clearly problematical. The Forsters would also hypothesize, entirely on the basis of such gestural signs, that the ni-Vanuatu were also eaters of human flesh. Wales, however, initially refused to believe that Maori were "cannibals" despite mounting "evidence" (the pantomime of cannibalism put on by the Maori) and the conviction to the contrary of all the rest of the company. He protested "how far we are liable to be misled by Signs, report and prejudice."[32] In the passage above, however, Wales indicates both that gestural sign (of sodomy? or heterosexual intercourse? it is unclear which sign was being made, or indeed if they were different) could convey the truth both to and of the ni-Vanuatu, and that the suspicious traffic flowed both ways. What should we make of this exchange?

European prejudices were both inverted and confirmed in this social performance. As previously noted, while sodomy and same-sex desire were by no means seen as unitary in the last quarter of the eighteenth century,

[31] See, e.g., James Cook and James King, *A Voyage to the Pacific Ocean*, 2nd edn (3 vols., London, 1785), III, 26; *Journals of Captain Cook*, III, 815–20; W. D. Ellis, *An authentic narrative of a voyage performed by Captain Cook* (London, 1782), II, 153.
[32] *Journals of Captain Cook*, II, 859–60, 791; Forster, *Resolution Journal*, v, 595.

both were, to varying degrees, coming to be attached to the same object of suspicion: the "effeminate" man. In Britain, this (usually elite-identified) individual was the product of spending too much time around women, or, as Millar theorized, of societies where women had too much civil or political power; in either case, he was beginning to be thought to be the most likely to harbor same-sex desires. There was an increasing, although not invariable, convergence, in other words, between gender and sexual practice, and a demand for men that the outward performance of gender be matched by inner desire. Hence the great surprise and alarm among the British public at the sodomy prosecution and subsequent exile of the manly Isaac Bickerstaffe, playwright and collaborator of Garrick.[33] In the encounter above, however, same-sex or sodomitical desire is feared as a function of primitive, rather than advanced and corrupted, sensibilities, which would require, according to late eighteenth-century stadial models of social development, that it had been there all along, a part of humanity in its "original" as in its "advanced" state (a view which anticipated missionaries" condemnation of sodomy as a "heathenish" practice at all levels). That the ni-Vanuatu were in a "primitive" state was not in doubt, although the Forsters theorized that their nation may have degenerated from the happiness of the Tahitians due to their less advantageous climate. And certainly gestural sign was associated by some with cultural primitiveness. The case had been made very eloquently by Rousseau, who argued that "if the only needs we ever experience were physical, we should most likely never have been able to speak; we would fully express our meanings by the language of gestures alone." On the other hand, on the basis of evidence culled from the voyages of Bougainville and Cook, as well as European communities of the deaf, some Enlightenment thinkers had elevated gestural sign to the level of a philosophical artifact, as a "natural" and possibly even universal language.[34] From that perspective, sign language did seem to provide in first contact a theatrical, if provisional, "mode of exchange, a physical and symbolic space inscribed with meaning," as Paul Carter has argued of contact performances in general.[35] Yet what that meaning was to the different parties remains elusive. In other words, the indeterminacy of both sign and

---

[33] Philip Carter, *Men and the Emergence of Polite Society in Britain 1660–1800* (Basingstoke: Macmillan, 2001); Michèle Cohen, *Fashioning Masculinity* (London: Routledge, 1998); Millar, *Origin*, 52–5; Laurence Senelick, "Mollies or Men of Mode? Sodomy and the Eighteenth-Century London Stage," *Journal of the History of Sexuality*, 1 (1974–6), 33–67.

[34] For this, see Nicholas Mirzoeff, *Silent Poetry: Deafness, Sign and Visual Culture in Modern France* (Princeton University Press, 1995), 30–5; quotation from Rousseau's *Essays on the Origins of Language* (1749) is on 53.

[35] Paul Carter, "Making Contact: History and Performance," in Carter, *Living in a New Country: History, Travelling and Language* (London: Faber, 1992), 163.

sodomy are glossed in Wales's account of the encounter: in the state of
nature being enacted for the British in western Polynesia through a gestural
economy, even the most stalwart empiricist was led to believe the "unnatural crime" was not only recognized but could be made intelligible through
a sort of kinesthetic lingua franca, the wink and the nod. Communication
is achieved as meaning is deferred, and sodomy becomes the place were
civilized and savage meet – a predilection of those with too much luxury and too much contact with women (as the British had long believed
of Islamic nations),[36] as well as, apparently, those who neither spent time
with nor appreciated women. Clearly, the enlightened explorers identified
themselves with neither camp.

On the other hand, just as there was some ritual cannibalism practiced
in certain South Pacific societies, so there were people who engaged in
sodomy. The expectations of sexual exchange that the British fostered did
not necessarily translate into the "natural" sex roles ordained by European
culture. Indeed, multiple genders and a dissociation between sexual practice and identity seemed to have been marked features of pre-Christian
Polynesian societies. The *mahu* of Tahiti and the Marquesas, for example,
were young boys who were deliberately brought up to dress and behave
as women and as grown men openly practiced transvestism, fellatio, and,
perhaps, sodomy. Within the gender complimentarity of eastern Polynesian culture, the *mahu* were seen possibly as a third gender, or as women;
men having sexual relations with them did not think of themselves as
"sodomites," nor did *mahu* have sex with each other.[37] The *mahu* may have
been "discovered" by the British on the second voyage as they prepared
for final departure in 1774, although the record on this is, not surprisingly,
murky; Forster senior may have been alluding to them when he decried that
"appetite for sensual pleasure" accompanying opulence in a society, which,
"if no restraint is laid on its gratification, it grows stronger and stronger,
so as at last to extinguish all the notions of propriety and decency."[38] Ten
years later, Captain Bligh (himself suspected of being "a bit peculiar" by
his own men) would express in lurid tones his revulsion at this example
of Tahitian effeminacy, although, significantly, he was also forced to admit

[36] For which, see Nabil Matar, *Turks, Moors and Englishmen, Vol. I: The Age of Discovery* (New York: Columbia University Press, 1999).
[37] See Douglas L. Oliver, *Oceania: The Native Cultures of Australia and the Pacific Islands* (Honolulu: University of Hawaii Press, 1989), 635–8; and Oliver, *Ancient Tahitian Society*, ii, 370; Niel Gunson, "Sacred Women Chiefs and Female Headmen in Polynesian History," *Journal of Pacific History*, 22 (1987), 58–9; Ben. R. Finney, "Notes on Bond-Friendship in Tahiti," *Journal of Polynesian Society*, 73 (1964), 434.
[38] Forster, *Observations*, 254.

that "those connected with [the *mahu*] have their beastly pleasures gratified between his thighs, but are no farther sodomites as they all positively deny the crime."[39] But Bligh, and the missionaries who followed, rather missed the point. The social acceptance of the *mahu* in eastern Polynesian societies may have actually expressed the associations of women's reproductive functions with the divine – and hence the identification of the feminine with positive, rather than negative, hierarchies and characteristics.[40]

The Hawaiian *āikane* was indeed less hidden from the History made on the Cook voyages than the *mahu*, and so they will complete this reading of gender misrecognition and narrative failure on the Cook voyages. In Hawaii the *āikane* were a distinctive social and cultural presence: young male warriors who served as intermediaries, agents, and male sexual companions to the chiefs of the islands.[41] Unlike the *mahu*, they otherwise fulfilled typical male roles, including having wives and children. The British were openly fascinated by them. The journals of several of the voyagers record many examples of chiefs or *āikane* expressing interest in British officers and crew, offering hogs in exchange for the younger and better-looking men. To take one example: Lieutenant James King, handsome and respected young officer aboard the *Resolution*, had recorded in his journal that the Hawaiian people "will fall very short of the Society and Friendly Isles in that very good test of Civilization, the rank and consequence of Women" for not only were the women forced to eat separately but they were also "depriv'd of the natural affections of their Husbands . . . [since] the foulest polutions disgrace the Men." King perhaps had reason to be worried: he was repeatedly mistaken by Hawaiians not only as Cook's son but also as his *āikane*. Yet his later rather phlegmatic report that one Hawaiian chief had negotiated with Cook "to leave me behind; I had proposals by our friends to elope, and they promised to hide me in the hills till the Ships were gone, and to make me a great man" attempted to make light of the concern, expressed elsewhere by himself and some of the other men, at the effort to make him an object in an "unnatural" and "foul" sexual exchange.[42] Here, English heterosexual masculinity is produced by the identification

[39] William Bligh, *The Log of the Bounty* (2 vols., London: Golden Cockerel Press, 1935), I, 25, 16–17.
[40] See, e.g., Ralston, "Polyandry, 'Pollution,' 'Prostitution'," 71–80; J. Linnekin, *Sacred Queens and Women of Consequence: Rank, Gender and Colonialism in the Hawaiian Islands* (Ann Arbor: University of Michigan Press, 1990).
[41] Robert Morris, "*Aikane*: Accounts of Same-Sex Relationships in the Journals of Captain Cook's Third Voyage," *Journal of Homosexuality*, 19 (1990), 21–54; Morris, "Same-Sex Friendships in Hawaiian Lore: Constructing the Canon," in Stephen O. Murray, ed., *Oceanic Homosexualities* (New York: 1992), 71–103. See also Lee Wallace, "Too Darn Hot: Sexual Contact in the Sandwich Islands on Cook's Third Voyage," *Eighteenth Century Life*, 18 (1994), 232–42.
[42] *Journals of Captain Cook*, III, 624, 518–19.

of the *āikane* as sodomites; but the intimation of same-sex desire is also used as an instrument of exploration, as European men used their own perceived desirability to indigenous men to acquire advantages in the exchanges underway.

Indeed, it is clear in a number of other cases – not least through the abundant descriptions of the genital symbolism of eastern Polynesia (which the British compared to "the Priapus of the Romans"), the "frequent Enquires" made about the *āikane*, the bond-friendships made between the officers and chiefs (which involved "kissing" or nose-rubbing), and the apparent ease with which King recorded the effort to traffic in male bodies – that the homoerotic aspects of native culture were not rejected by some of the explorers, and could even provide a kind of entrée into local life.[43] King himself may have used his own physical attractiveness (described by Beaglehole as "too small-bodied, too well-bred, too genteel, for a young man who . . . may have considered himself a tar") to "conciliate" the islanders and "gain their esteem."[44] The politics of identity within Britain may also partially illuminate those at work in these encounters. As Bickerstaffe's case eloquently proved, even by the last quarter of the century sexual identity was not solely determined by object choice, nor was gender an automatic outcome of sexual practice, and the efforts to make them meld (through reformation of manners campaigns, executions for sodomy, and other aspects of the "gender revolution") were not invariably successful. Moreover, in the South Pacific the imperatives of British masculinity and British discovery collided, as the voyagers were called upon both to maintain a manly sensitivity to local customs and to eschew effeminizing desires. For the seaman, oceans away from the soothing commonplaces and coercive social pressures of "home," homoeroticism or the expression of same-sex desire may have offered a "liminal" space, as Victor Turner has defined it, "a realm of pure possibility whence novel configurations of ideas and relations may arise," that allowed him to cross over to a multiply-determined "other side." Tattooing constituted another such act and symbol of transgressiveness, through which the sailor expressed his identification with Oceanic mores and gained the islanders' acceptance. Significantly, tattoos were also associated in British accounts with Oceanic sexual excess.[45] As Peter Haywood,

---

[43] Ibid., III, 1185.
[44] Beaglehole in ibid., III, lxxviii; Wallace also makes this point in "Too Darn Hot," 236.
[45] For liminality, see Victor Turner, *The Forest of Symbols* (Ithaca: Cornell University Press, 1967), 94–7 and *Dramas, Fields and Metaphors* (Ithaca: Cornell University Press, 1974), 274. In a description of Omai, the tattoos on his hands were interpreted as Tahitian signs of marriage: "Omiah . . . has been honoured with eight or ten sets of these marks, having already had as many wives." *Annual Register,* 17 (1774), 61.

mutineer of the infamous *Bounty*, explained: "I was tattooed, not to gratify my own desire, but theirs; for it was my constant endeavour to acquiesce in any little custom which I thought agreeable to them . . . provided I gained by it their friendship and esteem."[46] The intimation of same-sex desire may have similarly eased some of the anxiety generated through the arts of discovery by allowing the stranger to cross over into the native culture – and perhaps even to become a different kind of national and sexual subject. At the very least, given that within the terms of eighteenth-century social science, desire was not extinguished but inflamed by restraint, the homophobia of the ship could produce its own rebellion.[47] Fields of identification, then, sexual and national, clashed and circulated between the two cultures at their points of meeting, and their nature or outcomes were neither predictable nor codifiable. Rather, the attempts to bring unfamiliar bodies and unconventional practices into the time of History resulted in narratives that were only partially legible, and in explorers whose own identities and desires were catapulted into play.

A DIFFERENT MAP OF MANKIND

The traffic in men transformed the enlightened explorers into the objects of Polynesian knowledge, who thereby read their own culture on the European male body. But this exchange is of much broader historical significance. The "crime that can never be mentioned" but was everywhere suspected points to the circuitry of identity, alterity, exchange, and transformation that was both charged and recuperated by the systems of observation and empirical recording. Who is the object and who the subject of these exchanges? Who is ethnographer and who the "primitive"? The fragments through which the narrative of "discovery" emerged highlight the epistemic violence visited through the multiple acts of cultural translation. There is no "whole" in these accounts or perspectives, only fragments which suggest "knowledge forms that are not tied to the will that produces the state," and all of which "challenge, not only the idea of wholeness, but the very idea of the fragment itself."[48] The attempted imposition of British "order," by the explorers or their historians, can only temporarily divert attention from what Michael

---

[46] Quoted in Sir John Barrow, *A Description of Pitcairn's Island and Its Inhabitants with an Authentic Account of the Mutiny* (New York: 1845), 131.

[47] As Millar wrote, one of "the great expedients of nature" was to convert a "simple desire or appetite . . . into a violent passion" by restraint or prohibition: Millar, *Origin*, 58, 61.

[48] Dipesh Chakrabarty, *Habitations of Modernity* (University of Chicago Press, 2002), 34–5.

Taussig has called in another context the "unstable interplay of truth and illusion."[49]

Cook and his men aimed to discover and record empirical facts about an unknown world, and their cultural as well as topographical mappings changed the world in the process. The psychic impact of these processes on the colonizers and their forms of knowledge has received, perhaps, too little direct attention. Fantasy conditioned empirical observation, and vice versa. The empirical "facts" of territorial and sexual conquest clearly summoned up the fantasy of being taken, as well as taking; and as desire, identification, and dis-identification worked to naturalize conquest and allay its anxieties, the unnatural nature of the act of conquest comes back to haunt in the figure of the sodomite – the absent presence (or present absence) on all the voyages. Perhaps these examples suggest that through the arts of discovery the emergence of the modern sexual regime was indeed being felt and fabricated across the world. But it is also clear that suspect practices could not necessarily produce and certainly could not prove the essentialized identities that such a regime required. The multiple images of Oceanic and British bodies reveal the fictive nature and irresolvable tensions within those categories of difference invented in the crucible of first contact. The same accounts that inaugurate the labor of colonial discourse in the South Pacific thus raise the central question: who was looking at whom? What was seen in the act of looking and who was the discoverer? Looking at natives looking back at them, could the scientific explorers of Cook's voyages be so sure they were not looking at themselves? From this perspective, gender misrecognition and Polynesian subversions marked the *unwriting* of nationality and gender into History, and the indeterminacies of sexual practices – in the time of the great Captain Cook, as well as in our own.

[49] Michael Taussig, *Shamanism, Colonialism and the Wild Man: A Story in Terror and Healing* (University of Chicago Press, 1987), 121.

Further reading

I EMPIRE AT HOME: DIFFERENCE, REPRESENTATION, EXPERIENCE

Aravamudan, Srinivas, *Tropicopolitans: Colonialism and Agency, 1688–1804* (Durham: Duke University Press, 1999).

Armitage, David, *The Ideological Origins of the British Empire* (Cambridge University Press, 2000).

Bar-Yosef, Eitan, *Images of the Holy Land in English Culture 1799–1917* (Oxford University Press, forthcoming).

Bhabha, Homi, *The Location of Culture* (New York: Routledge, 1994).

Brewer, John, *The Sinews of Power: War, Money and the English State, 1688–1783* (London: Hutchinson, 1989).

Brown, Laura, *Ends of Empire: Women and Identity in Early Eighteenth-Century Literature* (Ithaca: Cornell University Press, 1993).

Fables of Modernity (Ithaca: Cornell University Press, 2001).

Chakrabarty, Dipesh, *Provincializing Europe: Postcolonial Thought and Historical Difference* (Princeton University Press, 2000).

Habitations of Modernity (University of Chicago Press, 2002).

Clastres, Pierre, *The Archaeology of Violence* [1980], trans. Jeanine Herman (New York: Semiotext(e), 1994).

Clifford, James, *The Predicament of Culture* (Cambridge, MA: Harvard University Press, 1998).

Cohn, Bernard, *Colonialism and its Forms of Knowledge: The British in India* (Princeton University Press, 1996).

Corrigan, Phillip, and Derek Sayer, *The Great Arch: State-Making and Cultural Revolution* (Oxford: Basil Blackwell, 1985).

Dirks, Nicholas, *Colonialism and Culture* (Ann Arbor: University of Michigan Press, 1992).

Dolan, Brian, *Exploring European Frontiers: British Travelers in the Age of Enlightenment* (New York: St. Martin's Press, 2000).

Dresser, Madge, *Slavery Obscured: The Social History of the Slave Trade in an English Provincial Port* (London: Continuum, 2001).

Elsner, Jas, and Joan-Pau Rubiés, eds., *Voyages and Visions: Towards a Cultural History of Travel* (London: Reaktion Books, 1999).

Fabian, Johannes, *Time and the Other: How Anthropology Makes its Objects* (New York: Columbia University Press, 1983).

Fisher, Michael, *The First Indian Author in English: Dean Mahomet in India, Ireland and England* (Oxford University Press, 2000).

　Counterflows to Colonialism: Indians in Britain, c. 1600–1857 (London: Permanent Black, 2003).

Fryer, Peter, *Staying Power: The History of Black People in Britain* (London: Pluto Press, 1994).

Gikandi, Simon, *Maps of Englishness: Writing Identity in the Culture of Colonialism* (New York: Columbia University Press, 1996).

Gould, Elijah, *The Persistence of Empire* (Chapel Hill: University of North Carolina Press, 2000).

Hall, Catherine, ed., *Cultures of Empire* (Manchester University Press, 2000).

　Civilizing Subjects: Metropole and Colony in the English Imagination 1830–1867 (London: Polity, 2002).

Hall, Stuart, "When was the 'Post-colonial'? Thinking at the Limit," in Iain Chambers and Gidia Curti, eds., *The Post-colonial Question: Common Skies, Divided Horizons* (London: Routledge, 1996), 242–60.

Hawley, John C., and Erick D. Anger, eds., *Christian Encounters with the Other* (New York University Press, 1998).

Hendricks, Margo, and Patricia Parker, eds., *Women, "Race" and Writing in Early Modern Europe* (London: Routledge, 1994).

Hindraker, Eric, "The 'Four Indian Kings' and the Imaginative Construction of the British Empire," *William and Mary Quarterly*, 3rd ser., 53 (1996), 487–526.

Holt, Thomas, "Marking: Race, Race-Making and the Writing of History," *American Historical Review* (1995), 1–20.

Hsia, Adrian, ed., *The Vision of China in the English Literature of the Seventeenth and Eighteenth Centuries* (Hong Kong: Chinese University Press, 1998).

Jones, Colin, and Dror Wahrman, eds., *The Age of Cultural Revolutions* (Berkeley and Los Angeles: University of California Press, 2001).

Joseph, Betty, *The Patriarchive: Gender, History and Colonial Narratives, 1720–1840* (University of Chicago Press, 2003).

Leask, Nigel, *British Romantic Writers and the East: Anxieties of Empire* (Cambridge University Press, 1992).

　Curiosity and the Aesthetics of Travel Writing, 1770–1840 (Oxford University Press, 2002).

Marshall, Peter, "Britain and the World in the Eighteenth Century: IV, the Turning outwards of Britain," *Transactions of the Royal Historical Society*, 6th ser., 11 (2001), 1–15.

Marshall, Peter, and Gywn Williams, *The Great Map of Mankind: British Perceptions of the World in the Age of Enlightenment* (London: Macmillan, 1982).

Midgley, Clare, *Women Against Slavery: The British Campaigns* (London: Routledge, 1994).

Nussbaum, Felicity A., *Torrid Zones: Maternity, Sexuality and Empire in Eighteenth Century English Narrative* (Baltimore: The Johns Hopkins University Press, 1995).

ed., *The Global Eighteenth Century* (Baltimore: The Johns Hopkins University Press, 2003).

Obeyesekere, Gananath, *The Apotheosis of Captain Cook* (Princeton University Press, 1992).

Ogborn, Miles, *Spaces of Modernity: London's Geographies 1680–1780* (New York: Guildford Press, 1998).

Pocock, J. G. A., *Barbarism and Religion*, (2 vols. Cambridge University Press, 1999–2000).

Prakash, Gyan, "Subaltern Studies as a Form of Postcolonial Criticism," *AHR*, 99 (1994), 1475–90.

ed., *After Colonialism: Imperial Histories and Postcolonial Displacements* (Princeton University Press, 1995).

Pratt, Mary, *Imperial Eyes: Travel Writing and Transculturation* (London: Routledge, 1992).

Ragussis, Michael, *Figures of Conversion: "The Jewish Question" and English National Identity* (Durham: Duke University Press, 1995).

Richardson, Alan, and Sonia Hofkosh, *Romanticism, Race and Imperial Culture 1780–1834* (Bloomington: Indiana University Press, 1996).

Rogers, Nicholas, *Whigs and Cities* (Oxford University Press, 1989).

Russell, Gillian, *The Theatres of War: Performance, Politics and Society, 1793–1815* (Oxford University Press, 1995).

Said, Edward, *Culture and Imperialism* (London: Chatto and Windus, 1993).

Sakai, Naoki, *Translation and Subjectivity* (Minneapolis: University of Minnesota Press, 1997).

Shapin, Stephen, *A Social History of Truth* (University of Chicago Press, 1994).

Sharpe, Jenny, *Allegories of Empire* (Minneapolis: University of Minnesota Press, 1993).

Spaas, Lieve, and Brian Stimpson, eds., *Robinson Crusoe: Myths and Metamorphoses* (New York: St. Martin's Press, 1996).

Stone, Lawrence, ed., *An Imperial State at War: Britain from 1689 to 1875* (London: Routledge, 1994).

Sussman, Charlotte, *Consuming Anxieties: Consumer Protest, Gender and British Slavery 1713–1833* (Stanford University Press, 2000).

Taylor, Stephen, Richard Connors, and Clyve Jones, eds., *Hanoverian Britain and Empire* (Woodbridge: Boydell Press, 1998).

Teltscher, Kate, *India Inscribed: European and British Writing on India 1600–1800* (Oxford University Press, 1995).

Thomas, Nicholas, *Colonialism's Culture* (Durham: Duke University Press, 1994).

Tobin, Beth Fowkes, *Picturing Imperial Power: Colonial Subjects in British Painting* (Durham: Duke University Press, 1999).

Tournier, Michel, *Friday*, trans. Norman Denny (Baltimore: The Johns Hopkins University Press, 1997).

Visram, Roz, *Asians in Britain: 400 Years of History* (London: Pluto Press, 2002).

Walvin, James, *Fruits of Empire: Exotic Produce and British Taste, 1600–1800* (New York University Press, 1997).

Wheeler, Roxann, *The Complexion of Race: Categories of Difference in Eighteenth-Century British Culture* (Philadelphia: University of Pennsylvania Press, 2000).

Wilson, Kathleen, "The Good, the Bad and the Impotent: Imperialism and the Politics of Identity in Georgian Britain," in Ann Bermingham and John Brewer, eds., *The Consumption of Culture: Image, Object, Text* (London: Routledge, 1995).

The Sense of the People: Politics, Culture and Imperialism in England, 1715–1785 (Cambridge University Press, 1995).

Young, Robert, *White Mythologies: History Writing and the West* (London: Routledge, 1990).

II PROMISED LANDS: IMPERIAL ASPIRATIONS AND PRACTICE

Bayly, C. A., *Imperial Meridian* (London: Longman, 1989).

Empire and Information: Intelligence Gathering and Social Communication in India 1780–1870 (Cambridge University Press, 1996).

"The First Age of Global Imperialism, 1760–1830," *Journal of Imperial and Commonwealth History*, 26 (1998), 28–48.

Benton, Lauren A., *Law and Colonial Cultures: Legal Regimes in World History 1499–1900* (Cambridge University Press, 2002).

Blaut, J. M., *The Colonizer's Model of the World: Geographical Diffusionism and Eurocentric History* (New York: Guildford Press, 1993).

Bowen, H. V., *Elites, Enterprise, and the Making of the British Overseas Empire, 1688–1775* (Basingstoke and New York: Macmillan and St. Martin's Press, 1996).

Canny, Nicholas, ed,. *The Oxford History of the British Empire, Vol I: The Origins of Empire* (Oxford University Press, 1998).

Chatterjee, Partha, *The Nation and its Fragments* (Princeton University Press, 1993).

Colley, Linda, *Britons: Forging the Nation, 1707–1837* (New Haven: Yale University Press, 1992).

Cooper, Frederick, and Ann Laura Stoler, eds., *Tensions of Empire: Colonial Subjects in a Bourgeois World* (Ann Arbor: University of Michigan Press, 1998).

Dirks, Nicholas, *Castes of Mind: Colonialism and the Making of Modern India* (Princeton University Press, 2001).

Drayton, Richard, *Nature's Government: Science, Imperial Britain, and the "Improvement" of the World* (New Haven: Yale University Press, 2000).

Edney, Matthew, *Mapping an Empire: The Geographical Construction of British India, 1765–1843* (University of Chicago Press, 1997).

Gascoigne, John, *Joseph Banks and the English Enlightenment: Useful Knowledge and Polite Culture* (Cambridge University Press, 1994).

Science in the Service of Empire: Joseph Banks, the British State and the Uses of Science in the Age of Revolution (Cambridge University Press, 1998).

Grove, Richard, *Green Imperialism: Colonial Expansion, Tropical Island Edens and the Origins of Environmentalism, 1660–1860* (Cambridge University Press, 1995).

Guha, Ranajit, *Dominance without Hegemony: History and Power in Colonial India* (Cambridge, MA: Harvard University Press, 1997).

Guha, Ranajit, and Gayatri Spivak, eds., *Selected Subaltern Studies* (New York: Oxford University Press, 1988).

Harrison, Mark, *Climates and Constitutions* (Delhi: Oxford University Press, 1999).

Kosselleck, Reinhart, *Futures Past: On the Semantics of Historical Time*, trans. Keith Gribe (Cambridge, MA: MIT Press, 1985).

Livingstone, David N., and Charles W. J. Withers, eds., *Geography and Enlightenment* (University of Chicago Press, 1999).

Lowe, Lisa, *Critical Terrains: French and British Orientalisms* (Ithaca: Cornell University Press, 1991).

McCalman, Iain, "New Jerusalems: Prophecy, Dissent and Radical Culture in England 1786–1830", in Knud Haakonssen, ed., *Enlightenment and Religion: Rational Dissent in Eighteenth Century Britain* (Cambridge University Press, 1996), 312–35.

Mani, Lata, *Contentious Traditions: The Debate on Sati in Colonial India* (Berkeley and Los Angeles: University of California Press, 1998).

Marshall, Peter, *Imperial Britain* (London: University of London, 1994).

ed., *The Oxford History of the British Empire, Vol. II: The Eighteenth Century* (Oxford University Press, 1998).

Mehta, Uday Singh, *Liberalism and Empire: A Study in Nineteenth-Century British Liberal Thought* (University of Chicago Press, 1999).

Miller, David Philip, and Peter Hanns Reill, eds., *Visions of Empire: Voyages, Botany and Representations of Nature* (Cambridge University Press, 1996).

Mudimbe, V. Y., *The Invention of Africa: Gnosis, Philosophy and the Order of Knowledge* (Indianapolis: Indiana University Press, 1988).

Parthasarathi, Prasannan, *The Transition to a Colonial Economy: Weavers, Merchants and Kings in South India, 1720–1800* (Cambridge University Press, 2001).

Pocock, J. G. A., *The Ancient Constitution and the Feudal Law: A Study of English Historical Thought in the Seventeenth Century* (Cambridge University Press, 1990).

Raj, Kapil, "Colonial Encounters and the Forging of New Knowledge and National Identities: Great Britain and India, 1760–1850," *Osiris*, 15 (2001), 119–34.

Said, Edward, *Orientalism: Western Conceptions of the Orient* (New York: Vintage Books, 1978).

Sen, Sudipta, *Distant Sovereignty: National Imperialism and the Origins of British India* (London: Routledge, 2002).

Empire of Free Trade: The East India Company and the Making of the Colonial Marketplace (Philadelphia: University of Pennsylvania Press, 1998).

III TIME, IDENTITY, AND ATLANTIC INTERCULTURE

Armitage, David, and Michael Braddick, eds., *The British Atlantic World* (Basingstoke: Palgrave, 2002).

Bailyn, Bernard, *The Peopling of British North America: An Introduction* (New York: Knopf, 1986).

Bailyn, Bernard, and Philip Morgan, eds., *Strangers within the Realm: The Cultural Margins of the First British Empire* (Chapel Hill: University of North Carolina Press, 1991).

Beckles, Hilary McD., *Natural Rebels: A Social History of Enslaved Black Women in Barbados* (New Brunswick: Rutgers University Press, 1989).

  Centering Women: Gender Discourses in Caribbean Slave Society (Kingston: Ian Randle, 1999).

Benítez-Rojo, Antonio, *The Repeating Island* (Durham: Duke University Press, 1996).

Berlin, Ira, *Many Thousands Gone: The First Two Centuries of Slavery in North America* (Cambridge, MA: Harvard University Press, 1998).

Bernhard, Virginia, *Slaves and Slaveholders in Bermuda, 1616–1782* (Columbia: University of Missouri Press, 1999).

Blackburn, Robin, *The Making of New World Slavery* (London: Verso, 1998).

  The Overthrow of New World Slavery (London: Verso, 1998).

Breen, T. H., "An 'Empire of Goods': The Anglicization of Colonial America, 1690–1776," *Journal of British Studies*, 25 (1986), 467–99.

  "The Baubles of Britain: The American and Consumer Revolutions of the Eighteenth Century," *Past & Present*, 119 (1988), 73–104.

Brown, Chris, "Empire without Slaves: British Concepts of Emancipation in the Age of the American Revolution," *William and Mary Quarterly*, 3rd ser., 56 (1999), 273–306.

Brown, Kathleen, *Good Wives, Nasty Wenches, and Anxious Patriarchs: Gender, Race and Power in Colonial Virginia* (Chapel Hill: University of North Carolina Press, 1996).

Bush, Barbara, *Slave Women in Caribbean Society* (London: 1990).

Canny, Nicholas, and Anthony Pagder, eds., *Colonial Identity in the Atlantic World, 1500–1800* (Princeton University Press, 1987).

  Kingdom and Colony: Ireland in the Atlantic World 1560–1800 (Baltimore: The Johns Hopkins University Press, 1988).

  Making Ireland British, 1580–1650 (Oxford University Press, 2001).

Costa, Emilia Viotti da, *Crowns of Glory, Tears of Blood: The Demerara Slave Rebellion of 1823* (Oxford University Press, 1994).

Craton, Michael, *Empire, Enslavement and Freedom in the Caribbean* (Kingston: Ian Randle, 1997).

Creighton Margaret S., and Lisa Norling, eds., *Iron Men, Wooden Women: Gender and Seafaring in the Atlantic World, 1700–1920* (Baltimore: The Johns Hopkins University Press, 1996).

Curtain, Philip, *The Rise and Fall of the Plantation Complex: Essays in Atlantic History* (Cambridge University Press, 1990).

Daniels, Christine, and Michael V. Kennedy, eds., *Negotiated Empires: Centers and Peripheries in the Americas 1500–1820* (London: Routledge, 2002).

Daunton, Martin, and Rick Halpern, eds., *Empire and Others: British Encounters with Indigenous Peoples, 1600–1850* (London: UCL Press, 1999).

Docker, John, *1492: The Poetics of Diaspora* (London: Continuum, 2002).

Dunn, Richard S., *Sugar and Slaves: The Rise of the Planter Class in the English West Indies, 1624–1713* (Chapel Hill: University of North Carolina Press, 2000).

Eltis, David, *The Rise of African Slavery in the Americas* (Cambridge University Press, 2000).

ed., *Free and Coerced Migration: Global Perspectives* (Stanford University Press, 2002).

Gallay, Alan, *The Indian Slave Trade: The Rise of the English Empire in the American South, 1670–1717* (New Haven: Yale University Press, 2002).

Games, Alison, *Migration and the Origins of the English Atlantic World* (Cambridge, MA: Harvard University Press, 1999).

Giles, Paul, *Transatlantic Insurrections: British Culture and the Formation of American Literature 1730–1860* (Philadelphia: University of Pennsylvania Press, 2001).

Gilroy, Paul, *The Black Atlantic: Modernity and Double Consciousness* (Cambridge, MA: Harvard University Press, 1992).

Greene, Jack P., *Negotiated Authorities: Essays in Colonial, Political and Constitutional History* (Charlottesville: University of Virginia Press, 1994).

Hall, Stuart, "Cultural Identity and Diaspora," in Nicholas Mirzoeff, ed., *Diaspora and Visual Culture: Representing Africans and Jews* (London: Routledge, 2000), 21–34.

Hancock, David, *Citizens of the World: London Merchants and the Integration of the British Atlantic Community, 1735–1785* (Cambridge University Press, 1995).

"Commerce and Conversation in the Eighteenth-Century Atlantic: The Invention of Madeira Wine," *Journal of Interdisciplinary History*, 29 (1998), 197–219.

Harding, Nicholas B., "North African Piracy, the Hanoverian Carrying Trade, and the British State, 1728–1828," *Historical Journal*, 43 (2000), 25–47.

Hulme, Peter, *Colonial Encounters: Europe and the Native Caribbean, 1492–1797* (London: Methuen, 1986).

Isaac, Rhys, *The Transformation of Virginia 1740–1790* (Chapel Hill: University of North Carolina Press, 1999).

James, C. L. R., *The Black Jacobins: Toussaint L'Ouverture and the San Domingo Revolution* (London: Virgin Press, 1938).

Johnson, Walter, *Soul by Soul: Life Inside the Antebellum Slave Market* (Harvard University Press, 1999).

Jordan, Winthrop D., *White over Black: American Attitudes Towards the Negro, 1550–1820* (Chapel Hill: University of North Carolina Press, 2001).

Kale, Madhavi, *Fragments of Empire: Capital, Slavery and Indian Indentured Labor Migration in the British Caribbean* (Philadelphia: University of Pennsylvania Press, 1999).

Kidd, Colin, *British Identities before Nationalism: Ethnicity and Nationhood in the Atlantic World, 1600–1800* (Cambridge University Press, 1999).

Kupperman, Karen, *Indians and English: Facing Off in Early America* (Ithaca: Cornell University Press, 2000).

ed., *America in European Consciousness, 1493–1750* (Chapel Hill: University of North Carolina Press, 1995).

Landers, Jane, *Black Society in Spanish Florida* (Urbana: University of Illinois Press, 1999).

Landsman, Ned, "Migration and Settlement," in Daniel Vickers, ed., *A Companion to Colonial America* (Oxford: Blackwell, 2003), 76–98.

ed., *Nation and Province in the First British Empire: Scotland and the Americas, 1600–1800* (Lewisburg: Bucknell University Press, 2001).

Law, Robin, *The Slave Coast of West Africa 1550–1750: The Impact of the Atlantic Slave Trade on an African Society* (Oxford: Claredon Press, 1991).

Linebaugh, Peter, and Marcus Rediker, *The Many-Headed Hydra: The Hidden History of the Revolutionary Atlantic* (Boston: Beacon, 2000).

Lovejoy, Paul, ed., *Identity in the Shadow of Slavery* (London: Continuum, 2000).

Morgan, Philip D., *Slave Counterpoint: Black Culture in the Eighteenth-Century Chesapeake and Lowcountry* (Chapel Hill: University of North Carolina Press, 1998).

Ortiz, Fernando, *Cuban Counterpoint*, ed. Fernando Coronil (Durham: Duke University Press, 1994).

Plane, Ann Marie, *Colonial Intimacies: Indian Marriage in Early New England* (Ithaca: Cornell University Press, 2000).

Pocock, J. G. A., "British History: A Plea for a New Subject," *Journal of Modern History*, 47 (1975), 601–21.

Roach, Joseph, *Cities of the Dead: Circum-Atlantic Performance* (New York: Columbia University Press, 1996).

Scott, Julius, "Criss-Crossing Empire: Ships, Sailors and Resistance in the Lesser Antilles in the Eighteenth Century," in E. Pacquette and S. Engerman, eds., *The Lesser Antilles in the Age of European Expansion* (Gainesville: University of Florida, 1996), 156–82.

Shepherd, Verene, Bridget Brereton, and Barbara Bailey, eds., *Engendering History: Caribbean Women in Historical Perspective* (Kingston: Ian Randle, 1995).

Shields, David S., *Civil Tongues and Polite Letters in British America* (Chapel Hill: University of North Carolina Press, 1997).

Thornton, John, *Africa and Africans in the Making of the Atlantic World* (Cambridge University Press, 1998).

Tomlins, Christopher L., and Bruce H. Mann, eds., *The Many Legalities of Early America* (Chapel Hill: University of North Carolina Press, 2001).

Waldstreicher, David, "Reading the Runaways: Self-Fashioning, Print Culture and Confidence in Slavery in the Eighteenth-Century Mid-Atlantic World," *William and Mary Quarterly*, 3rd ser., 56 (1999), 243–72.

Whelan, Kevin, *The Tree of Liberty: Radicalism, Catholicism and the Construction of Irish Identity* (Notre Dame: University of Notre Dame Press, 1996).

Williams, Eric, *Capitalism and Slavery* (London: Andre Deutsch, 1964).

IV ENGLISHNESS, GENDER, AND THE ARTS OF DISCOVERY

Bannerji, Himani, "Politics and the Writing of History," in Ruth Roach Pierson and Nupur Chaudhuri, eds., *Nation, Empire, Colony: Historicizing Gender and Race* (Bloomington: Indiana University Press, 1998), 275–300.

Burton, Antoinette, "Thinking Beyond the Boundaries: Empire, Feminism and the Domains of History," *Social History*, 26 (2001), 60–71.

Chatterjee, Indrani, "Colouring Subalternity: Slaves, Concubines and Social Orphans in Early Colonial India," *Subaltern Studies* X (New Delhi: Oxford University Press, 1999), 49–97.

Gender, Slavery and the Law in Colonial India (Oxford University Press, 1999).

Coleman, Deidre, ed., *Maiden Voyages and Infant Colonies: Two Women's Travel Narratives of the 1790s* (Leicester University Press, 1999).

Colley, Linda, *Captives: Britain and the World, 1600–1850* (London: Jonathan Cape, 2002).

Collingham, Elizabeth, *Imperial Bodies: The Physical Experience of the Raj c. 1800–1947* (London: Polity Press, 2001).

Creed, Barbara, and Jeanette Hoorn, eds., *Body Trade: Captivity, Cannibalism and Colonialism in the Pacific* (Annadale, Australia: Pluto Press, 2001).

Dalrymple, William, *White Mughals: Love and Betrayal in Eighteenth Century India* (London: HarperCollins, 2002).

Damousi, Joy, *Depraved and Disorderly: Female Convicts, Sexuality and Gender in Colonial Australia* (Cambridge University Press, 1997).

Dening, Greg, *Mr. Bligh's Bad Language: Passion, Power and Theatre on the Bounty* (Cambridge University Press, 1992).

Ghosh, Durba, *Colonial Companions: Sexual Transgressions, Racial Mixing and Gendered Order in Early Colonial India, 1760–1840* (forthcoming).

Guest, Harriet, "The Great Distinction: Figures of the Exotic in the Work of William Hodges," in Isobel Armstrong, ed., *New Feminist Discourses: Critical Essays on Theories and Texts* (London, 1992), 320–42.

"Curiously Marked: Tattooing, Masculinity and Nationality in Eighteenth-Century British Perceptions of the South Pacific," in John Barrell, ed., *Painting and the Politics of Culture: New Essays in British Art, 1700–1850* (Oxford University Press, 1998), 101–34.

"Looking at Women," in J. R. Forster, *Observations made on a Voyage Round the World*, eds. Nicholas Thomas, Harriet Guest, and Michael Dettenbach (Honolulu: University of Hawaii Press, 1999), xli–liv.

Hendricks, Margo, and Patricia Parker, eds., *Women, "Race," and Writing in the Early Modern Period* (London: Routledge, 1994).

Jolly, Margaret, and Martha Macintrye, eds., *Family and Gender in the South Pacific: Domestic Contradictions and the Colonial Impact* (Cambridge University Press, 1989).

Lamb, Jonathan, *Preserving the Self in the South Seas 1680–1840* (University of Chicago Press, 2001).

ed., *The South Pacific in the Eighteenth Century*, special issue of *Eighteenth Century Life*, 18 (1994).

Manderson, Leonore, and Margaret Jolly, eds., *Sites of Desire: Economies of Pleasure: Sexualities in Asia and the Pacific* (University of Chicago Press, 1997).

Midgley, Clare, ed., *Gender and Imperialism* (London: Routledge, 1998).

Matar, Nabil, *Turks, Moors and Englishmen in the Age of Discovery* (New York: Columbia University Press, 1999).

Melman, Billie, *Women's Orients: English Women and the Middle East, 1718–1918* (Ann Arbor: University of Michigan Press, 1992).

Metcalf, Thomas R., *Ideologies of the Raj* (Cambridge University Press, 1995).

Morgan, Jennifer L., "'Some Could Suckle over Their Shoulder': Male Travelers, Female Bodies, and the Gendering of Racial Ideology 1500–1700," *William and Mary Quarterly*, 3rd ser., 54 (1997), 167–92.

Ross, Robert, "Oppression, Sexuality and Slavery at the Cape of Good Hope," *Historical Reflections*, 6 (1979), 421–33.

Sahlins, Marshall, *Islands of History* (University of Chicago Press, 1985).

How "Natives" Think: About Captain Cook, For Example (University of Chicago Press, 1995).

Schwartz, Stuart, ed, *Implicit Understandings: Observing, Reporting and Reflecting on the Encounters between Europeans and Other Peoples in the Early Modern Era* (Cambridge University Press, 1994).

Sinha, Mrinalini, "Britain and the Empire: Toward a New Agenda for Imperial History," *Radical History Review*, 72 (1998), 163–73.

Smith, Merrill D., eds., *Sex and Sexuality in Early America* (New York University Press, 1998).

Spivak, Gayatri Chakravorty, "The Rani of Sirmur: An Essay in Reading the Archives," *History and Theory*, 38 (1985), 247–72.

"Can the Subaltern Speak?" in Cary Nelson and Lawrence Grossberg, eds., *Marxism and the Interpretation of Culture* (Urbana: University of Illinois Press, 1988), 271–313.

A Critique of Postcolonial Reason (Cambridge, MA: Harvard University Press, 1999).

Stoler, Ann Laura, *Carnal Knowledge and Imperial Power: Race and the Intimate in Colonial Rule* (Berkeley and Los Angeles: University of California Press, 2002).

Strobel, Margaret, *European Women and the Second British Empire* (Bloomington: Indiana University Press, 1991).

Sturma, Michael, *South Sea Maidens: Western Fantasy and Sexual Politics in the South Pacific* (London: Greenwood Press, 2001).

Thomas, Nicholas, *In Oceania: Visions, Artifacts, Histories* (Durham: Duke University Press, 1997).

Turley, Hans, *Rum, Sodomy and the Lash: Piracy, Sexuality, and Masculine Identity* (New York University Press, 1999).

Vaughan, Megan, "Slavery and Colonial Identity in Eighteenth-Century Mauritius," *Transactions of the Royal Historical Society*, 6th ser., 10 (2000), 189–215.

Wilson, Kathleen, *The Island Race: Englishness, Empire and Gender in the Eighteenth Century* (London: Routledge, 2003).

"Empire, Gender and Modernity in the Eighteenth Century," in Philippa Levine, ed., *Gender and Empire* (Oxford University Press, 2004).

Index